D1172117

Woodrow Wilson

Woodrow Wilson

KENDRICK A. CLEMENTS
ERIC A. CHEEZUM
University of South Carolina

CQ PRESS

A Division of Congressional Quarterly Inc.
Washington, D.C.

CQ Press
1255 22nd Street, N.W., Suite 400
Washington, D.C. 20037

(202) 729-1900; toll-free, 1-866-4CQ-PRESS (1-866-427-7737)

www.cqpress.com

Grateful acknowledgment is made to Princeton University Press for use of
material from *The Papers of Woodrow Wilson,* 69 vols. (1966–1994), edited
by Arthur S. Link and others. Copyright © various years by Princeton
University Press. Reprinted by permission of Princeton University Press,
Princeton, N.J.

Cover illustration by Talia Greenberg
Design by Karen Doody
Composition by Auburn Associates, Inc., Baltimore, Md.
Editorial development by the Moschovitis Group, Inc., New York, N.Y.

Printed and bound in the United States of America

07 06 05 04 03   5 4 3 2 1

Library of Congress Cataloging-in-Publication Data

Clements, Kendrick A.
  Woodrow Wilson / Kendrick A. Clements, Eric A. Cheezum.
    p. cm. — (American presidents reference series)
Includes bibliographical references and index.
  ISBN 1-56802-765-6
  1. Wilson, Woodrow, 1856-1924. 2. Presidents—United
States—Biography. 3. United States—Politics and
government—1913-1921. 4. United States—Politics and
government—1913-1921—Sources. I. Cheezum, Eric A. II. Title. III.
Series.
  E767.C625 2003
  973.91′3′092—dc21

                                                          2003014551

Contents

Preface

When he was still actively teaching, Woodrow Wilson wrote, "I like to read *biography*. It is the only way to read history." In compiling what we hope is a convenient and useful reference work on America's twenty-eighth president, we have followed that advice, focusing on the man as the heart and soul of policy, highlighting his many successes (some badly neglected), and explaining some of his most notorious failures. Wilson has left behind a wealth of papers—expertly edited and compiled by Arthur S. Link and his fellow editors—that give scholars direct access to the emotions, strategies, and intentions that animated his decisions.

The Wilson depicted through the writings in this volume is a complex and at times contradictory man. Sometimes he was kind and forgiving; other times he was vain and unpredictable. Occasionally, despite his great intelligence, he made foolish mistakes and covered them with bluster or appeals to high principles. Wilson was both an orator and a backroom negotiator, a master of Realpolitik and a man of high ideals. The flexibility provided by these contradictions formed the foundation of one of the most successful presidential administrations in United States history, but Wilson's conflicting qualities also help to explain his ultimate downfall.

Biographers have long struggled with the contradictions of Wilson's personality and character. Many have perceived him as a visionary activist limited by self-destructive personality faults. In our generation, his ambivalence on the subject of race, for instance, has tainted and obscured Wilson's legislative successes and his obvious skill at administration. His self-defeating behavior during the debate over the ratification of the Treaty of Versailles has overshadowed his effort to reform the international order.

In our interpretation of Wilson's leadership we have emphasized the qualities that made him successful, while at the same time reassessing the nature of Wilsonian activism. In domestic affairs, Wilson's reputation suggests he was an advocate of big government. In fact, Wilson demanded that government be "responsible," capable of expanding to meet the needs of progressive reform but also self-consciously limited enough to step out of the way and let individuals conduct their own affairs. He picked and chose reforms with a view to liberating the private sector rather than imposing heavy federal controls that could never be responsible but would always be inefficient and cloying to personal initiative. In foreign policy, Wilson gradually learned that the international world was too fragile for anyone—American or otherwise—to dictate from a "bully pulpit" and that military force could only be a last resort when diplomacy failed. The objective of every armed intervention under the Wilson administration was to promote American values more than American interests. Both at home and abroad, he spent his presidency attempting to solve the problems of the present within the ideological framework of the past.

This volume charts Wilson's extraordinary life and career, from birth in Staunton, Virginia, to death at 2340 S Street, Washington, D.C. The reader will find entwined with his biography analyses of the goals of Wilson's politics and scholarship, descriptions of his substantial success in accomplishing most of them, and discussions of the growing pains that attended the development of the modern presidency and the industrial state, the management and fighting of World War I, and the end of U.S. isolationism. In the section on Wilson's years after the White House and his continuing legacy, we suggest why Wilson's "responsible" progressivism remains relevant today despite its seeming repudiation at the end of his life. A collection of documents at the end of each chapter illustrates important moments in Wilson's life and presidency in the words of the actors themselves, while bibliographic essays guide researchers to further resources. In addition, a reference section at the end of the book contains full publishing information on works cited as sources within this text.

In looking for inspiration from the past to speak to modern-day problems, we follow in Wilson's footsteps. We hope this biography demonstrates why Woodrow Wilson remains one of the most important American presidents.

We would like to thank Aaron Haberman and Harriett Hurt for their suggestions about parts of the text, Eleanora von Dehsen for her thoughtful and considerate editorial guidance, Kerry Kern for her copy editing skills, and Belinda Josey for shepherding us through the final stages of this project. Finally, we also wish to express our appreciation to John Milton Cooper, Arthur S. Link, and Dora Mitchell for encouraging our interest in Wilson at crucial moments.

Kendrick A. Clements
Eric A. Cheezum
Columbia, South Carolina

President Wilson meets with his cabinet, 1913.

Introduction

Woodrow Wilson became president of the United States at the height of the Progressive reform movement. He quickly demonstrated exceptional skill in securing congressional approval for his proposals, and within a year and a half had won passage of tariff reduction, banking and currency reform, and antitrust legislation—fulfilling all his 1912 campaign promises. His success in getting Congress to adopt his program so quickly was remarkable, the more so given his relative lack of political experience when he became president and the absence of a national crisis to make the legislators compliant. Many of the achievements of his administration, including the federal income tax, the Federal Reserve System, the Federal Trade Commission, and woman suffrage, continue to have a major influence on national life. Although his initial objectives were largely achieved by the end of 1914, his vision of the proper role of government in the United States continued to expand, and in 1916, on the eve of his second national campaign, he threw his support behind new reforms, including the banning of products produced by child labor from interstate commerce, a Federal Land Bank for farmers, the first federal revenue-sharing experiment in the Good Roads Act of 1916, and a promise of independence to the Philippines.

In a modern industrial nation, Wilson argued, the federal government must expand its responsibilities to deal with national problems, but the ultimate goal of that expansion was to increase economic freedom and opportunity for individuals. Government, in short, must be responsive to the wishes and needs of the people. While this might require the enlargement of government's activities, at the same time leaders must always be mindful of their obligation to control the growth and nature of federal power so as not to threaten the individual freedom they were seeking to expand. Ensuring that government was both *responsible* and *limited* was one of Wilson's central objectives and an important contribution to the theory of the American government.

In international affairs, Wilson faced the beginning of the three great revolutions of the twentieth century—in China, Mexico, and Russia. These upheavals challenged the world domination of the British, French, Austro-Hungarian, Russian, and Ottoman empires. Wilson believed that change could not be halted, as the European powers wanted, and attempted to encourage economic and social reform, and the growth of democracy, in the revolutionary states. He had little success in leading revolutionaries into paths of peaceful change, and his well-intentioned efforts to assist them were sometimes misinterpreted, producing conflict rather than cooperation, as happened in China and Mexico. Nevertheless, Wilson was the first Western leader to speak out against imperialism, and his voice inspired the anticolonial movement that would change the world later in the twentieth century.

Like his immediate predecessors—William McKinley (1897–1901), Theodore Roosevelt (1901–1909), and William H. Taft (1909–1913)—Wilson believed that America's economic might should translate into world power, but he was not always sure what the nature of that power should be or how to wield it. In the Dominican Republic and Haiti, Wilson's benevolent intentions led to unfortunate military occupations; in Mexico, limited military interventions almost caused war; and, in Asia, attempts to assist China poisoned relations with Japan. World War I transformed the United States into the world's greatest creditor and thrust American economic and military power to the center of the world stage, whether America was ready for the responsibility or not. Learning as he went, Wilson did his best to define the role the nation would play on that stage in responsible and generous terms, while at the same time protecting American national interests. Believing that stability and orderly change served the interests of other nations as well as the United States, Wilson made those the central objectives of American foreign policy—and they have remained so ever since.

World War I, beginning in August 1914, was the greatest challenge of Wilson's presidency. Keenly aware that Americans saw the war as distant from their concerns and worried about the loyalty of millions of recent immigrants, Wilson declared American neutrality. Before long, however, cultural ties to Britain, economic links to the British and French, and the German use of submarine warfare eroded his ability to remain neutral. As he studied the situation in Europe, the president became convinced that there was a unique opportunity for the United States to lead in the creation of a new international order—a League of Nations—that would replace the failed balance of power system and imperialism with an organization that would maintain peace through collective action. In April 1917 Wilson asked Congress to declare war on Germany.

The United States was ill-prepared for war, and the administration's efforts to mobilize economic and military resources led to mistakes and controversy. Despite problems, however, one million American troops arrived in France in time to blunt the last German offensive and contribute significantly to the Allied victory. By the end of the war, the United States had become not only a major military power but also the economic backbone of the Allied effort.

In November 1918 Germany agreed to end the war on the understanding that the final peace would be based on the "Fourteen Points" Wilson had laid out in January 1918. He believed a treaty based on these terms would eliminate the problems that had caused the war, establish a peace that would be fair to all the belligerents, and create a League of Nations to prevent future wars. America's principal allies, Britain, France, Italy, and Japan, did not fully share the president's ideas about peace. They meant to punish and weaken Germany and to redeem their own costs by taking money and territory from the defeated enemy. Although Wilson went to the Paris peace conference to defend his program personally, he was only partly successful in bending the Allies to his wishes. He secured his League of Nations, but on many other issues he had to make costly compromises, ending up with an imperfect treaty that embittered the Germans and disappointed many of his American supporters.

In the Senate, a significant minority had serious objections to various aspects of the treaty and pledged to amend or defeat it by denying the president the two-thirds support needed for approval. After failing to win over undecided senators during the summer of 1919, Wilson took his case to the people in a speaking trip through the West. He hoped an aroused public would demand the Senate approve the treaty, but just as he was concluding his trip, he fell ill. A few days later he suffered a debilitating stroke and was unable to lead the pro-treaty forces during the final, crucial days before the Senate vote on November 19, 1919. Since there was a question of whether Americans were willing to reduce America's freedom to act in the world by accepting the obligations of collective security in the League, Wilson's illness may have made no difference to the outcome when the Senate voted on the treaty, but many people then and since believed a healthy president might have been able to change the outcome. Living out his last months in the White House as an invalid, Wilson saw his greatest dream shattered.

The image of Wilson as a failure that was created by the defeat of the Treaty of Versailles is wrong. Even though the United States did not join the League of Nations, the idea of collective security that Wilson had proposed remained alive in America, to be resurrected in the United Nations during World War II. Other ideals he set out in the Fourteen Points—including anti-imperialism, disarmament, national self-determination, the removal of trade barriers among nations, and the promotion of democracy—remain at the heart of American foreign policy into the twenty-first century.

Likewise, Wilson's legacy still endures in U.S. domestic policy. His methods of leading Congress have been copied by his successors, and most Americans have come to think of the executive as the dominant branch of the federal government as a result of his focus on presidential leadership. His substantive achievements, including the income tax, the Federal Reserve System, the Federal Trade Commission, the Farm Loan Bank, and the county agricultural agent system, remain important parts of the federal government's services to Americans. The methods of mobilization invented by the Wilson administration during World War I served as models for parts of Franklin Roosevelt's New Deal and for wartime organization during World War II. Small wonder that historians who understand that the defeat of the Treaty of Versailles was only one part of his record have consistently ranked Wilson among the top five or six American presidents.

BIBLIOGRAPHIC ESSAY

A good place to begin any study of Wilson and his times is with the two bibliographies that focus specifically on the topic. The more extensive of the two is John M. Mulder, Ernest M. White, and Ethel S. White, comp., *Woodrow Wilson: A Bibliography* (Westport, Conn.: Greenwood, 1997). The other is Peter H. Buckingham, comp., *Woodrow Wilson: A Bibliography of His Times and Presidency* (Wilmington, Del.: Scholarly Resources, 1990).

Basic sources for Wilson and his administration are available in both manuscript and published forms. Wilson's personal papers are at the Library of Congress, but there is also a published sixty-nine-volume collection edited by Arthur S. Link and others, *The Papers of Woodrow Wilson* (Princeton: Princeton University Press, 1966–1994). The published volumes include not only documents written by Wilson, but also those addressed to him, as well as diary entries, letters, and documents—both public and private—written by other people that are helpful to a full understanding of his life and times. For the convenience of readers who may wish to pursue further research, documents in the second part of this book are cited to the published *Papers* rather than to the manuscript collections from which they came originally. Volumes 13, 26, 39, 52, and 69 from the collection are indexes that make finding specific information relatively easy. Papers, memoirs, and other records from people in the Wilson administration are also plentiful, both in published and unpublished forms. (See the bibliographic essay following Chapter 5 for some of these.)

The first major biography of Wilson was by Ray Stannard Baker, *Woodrow Wilson: Life and Letters,* 8 vols. (Garden City, N.Y.: Doubleday, Page & Co., 1927–1939). Because it was based in part on interviews with Wilson, as well as on his papers, this remains a helpful source. Arthur S. Link began a new multivolume biography just after World War II, but unfortunately he was able to carry the story only to April 1917 before his death. For the period prior to 1917, the standard biography remains Arthur S. Link, *Wilson,* 5 vols. (Princeton: Princeton University Press, 1947–1965). Other modern studies include John Morton Blum, *Woodrow Wilson and the Politics of Morality* (Boston: Little, Brown, 1956); Arthur Walworth, *Woodrow Wilson,* 2 vols. (New York: Norton, 1978), which won the Pulitzer Prize; Kendrick A. Clements, *Woodrow Wilson: World Statesman* (Boston: Twayne, 1987); August Heckscher, *Woodrow Wilson* (New York: Scribner's, 1991), which is particularly sensitive on Wilson as a person; and Kendrick A. Clements, *The Presidency of Woodrow Wilson* (Lawrence: University Press of Kansas, 1992).

Wilson poses on the front porch with his wife, Ellen Louise Axson Wilson, and their three daughters, Jessie, Eleanor, and Margaret, 1912.

CHAPTER ONE

From Pastor's Son to Nobel Laureate

Biographical Sketch

W oodrow Wilson's father, Joseph Ruggles Wilson, met his mother, Jessie Woodrow, in Steubenville, Ohio, in 1847. She was a student at the women's academy there. A graduate of Jefferson College in Pennsylvania who had also studied at the Princeton Theological Seminary, Joseph Wilson was teaching at the boys' academy in the town. They were married in June 1849, and two weeks later he was ordained as a Presbyterian minister. He did not immediately begin preaching but instead spent several years teaching rhetoric, chemistry, and natural science at colleges in the Midwest and Virginia.

CHILDHOOD, 1856–1873

While Joseph and Jessie Wilson were at Hampden-Sydney College in Virginia, two daughters, Marion and Annie, were born in 1851 and 1853. Two years later, in 1855, Wilson accepted a pastorate in Staunton, Virginia. There, near midnight on the night of December 28–29, 1856, his first son, Thomas Woodrow Wilson, was born. A fourth child, Joseph Ruggles Wilson Jr., was born in 1867 in Augusta, Georgia.

Ambitious and energetic, Joseph Wilson accepted a call in 1857 to a larger and wealthier congregation in Augusta and was installed as minister there in January 1858. Tommy, as the family called him, was two when they moved to Augusta, where he spent most of his childhood. He later said that his first memory was of standing at the family's gate in 1860 and hearing that Lincoln's election meant there would be war.

The war divided the Wilson family. While Joseph's two older brothers joined the Union Army, he stayed in the South. He preached that the Bible justified slavery, helped to organize the southern Presbyterian church that split off from the northern church in 1861, spent a summer in the Confederate Army in South Carolina, and, after the battle of Chickamauga in 1863, briefly turned his churchyard into an army camp and the church into a hospital for wounded Confederate soldiers. Young Tommy was shielded by the family from unpleasant scenes of the war and later remembered little specific about it, but as biographer August Heckscher argues, "a sense of the war's encroaching chaos remained with him in later life, less in the form of conscious memories than of impulses to create unity and stability in the world around him" (Heckscher 1991, 13).

Tommy was a shy child, prone to dreaming, who built for himself a fantasy world in which he undertook adventures around the world as a British admiral or general (see Document 1.1). "I lived a dream life (almost too exclusively, perhaps) when I was a lad," he remembered later, "and even now my thought goes back for refreshment to those days when all the world seemed to me a place of heroic adventure, in which one's heart must keep its own counsel" (Link and others 1977, 23:240). He did not learn the alphabet until he was nine and did not really learn to read until he was eleven or twelve. Biographers have suggested various explanations for this delay, including the effects of the war on education in the South and psychological conflict with his father. The more recent consensus is that he probably suffered from at least a mild form of dyslexia, which would also help to account for his early interest in learning shorthand, his eager adoption of the typewriter (both devices used by dyslexics to deal with their problems), and his difficulties in learning foreign languages.

Wilson's family did not push him to leave the nest. His two older sisters pampered him, and his mother was protective and a little snobbish about the social limitations of Augusta. His father, a man of definite ideas and strong personality, welcomed the opportunity to become his son's first and most important teacher. When not with his parents or his sisters, Tommy played with cousins who lived nearby and helped to organize a baseball team among local boys, but he was in no more hurry to break away from the family than they were to have him go. "I suppose that nothing is more painful in the recollections of some of us," he said later, "than the efforts that were made to make us like grown-up people" (quoted in Heckscher 1991, 14).

In 1870, when Tommy was thirteen, the family moved to Columbia, South Carolina, where Joseph Ruggles Wilson joined the faculty at the Columbia Theological Seminary. Jessie's brother, James Woodrow, also taught there, and he and Joseph became closer than Joseph was with his own brothers, alienated by the Civil War. In part, Woodrow Wilson's later decision to drop his first name was a gesture of admiration for Uncle James, whose moral and intellectual integrity was much admired in the family.

The Wilsons liked Columbia, which was rapidly rebuilding after its destruction by fire in 1865, and built a comfortable house near the seminary to become their permanent home. Tommy joined another baseball team and attended school in a converted barn across the street from his house. His main influence remained his father, who frequently read aloud to the family from British books and magazines and encouraged the boy to write his impressions of things he read or saw. If Tommy wrote carelessly, Joseph could be caustic in his criticism, but he blended censure with love, and, in an age where education usually meant rote memorization, he encouraged his son to value original thought and analysis (see Document 1.2). "The penalty for cramming one's mind with other men's thoughts is to have no thoughts of one's own," was the way Wilson remembered the lesson (Link and others 1967, 3:144). Years later, when he was president of Princeton, he applied his father's principle, changing the college's teaching method from "recitations" of memorized lessons to discussions of issues among small groups of students led by young instructors.

Religion was an important part of life in the Wilson home, with daily Bible readings and occasional mealtime discussions of religious questions. Tommy frequently accompanied his father to the seminary, where he visited classes and made friends with some of the students, who were only a few years older than he. One of them, Francis J. Brooke, organized informal prayer meetings and during them Wilson had a strong religious experience. In July 1873 he became a member of Columbia's First Presbyterian Church, where his father sometimes preached. His faith, which he believed required Christians to struggle against evil in themselves and others and to emphasize service more than personal salvation, was a foundation for every action and decision throughout his life (see Document 1.3).

The Wilsons' cultural sophistication distinguished them somewhat from most of their southern neighbors and perhaps weakened Woodrow's ties to the region. Although in later years he liked to say that the South was "the only place in the country, the only place in the world, where nothing has to be explained to me" (quoted in Link 1947, 3), in reality he became a southern-born northerner, just as his father became a northern-born southerner. After he left the South in 1875 to attend Princeton University, he returned for only brief periods. By 1912, when he ran for president, his southern accent was gone, and whatever he might say, he no longer saw the world only through southern eyes.

College Years, 1873–1879

In September 1873 Wilson, though only sixteen, left Columbia to attend Davidson College in North Carolina. He did well academically, but for a still-immature boy, leaving home was difficult, and during the year he suffered a series of illnesses, probably at least partly psychosomatic. It did not help that while he was away his father resigned his professorship over a dispute about whether the seminary students would be required to attend Sunday services on the campus. Soon after Wilson completed his freshman year at Davidson, the family moved from Columbia to Wilmington, North Carolina, where Joseph Wilson became pastor of the First Presbyterian Church, a well-paid position that nevertheless seemed to him a step down from the seminary in Columbia. The combination of Tommy's homesickness and the family's tribulations led him to decide not to return to Davidson in the fall. During 1874–1875 he lived and studied at home.

The Wilsons' home in Wilmington was not as comfortable as the one they had left in Columbia. Joseph was unhappy with his new position, sometimes fleeing on solo holidays to northern resorts, and Jessie began to develop a series of vague "complaints" that made her a semi-invalid prior to her death in 1888. Tommy had no friends in the new city. While his mother assured him he would make some, he seems instead to have spent much of his free time at the city's wharves, sketching ships and drifting again into seafaring fantasies (see Document 1.4). Wilmington, he said a few years later, was "an exceedingly dingy, uninteresting town with no natural attraction but its splendid river" (Link and others 1967, 2:571). In the autumn of 1875 he found it much easier leaving for Princeton than going to Davidson had been two years previously.

Princeton, where Wilson entered as a freshman, did not challenge him intellectually. Although its president, James McCosh, elected in 1868, was trying to raise standards, Wilson found most of his professors undemanding and his classes dull. Bored, he began to read on his own, focusing on the British history, political theory, and literature that his father loved and forming an idealized image of Britain's Parliament as an institution where policy grew out of intellectual debates (see Document 1.5). He supplemented his self-education by discussions with equally idealistic classmates, practiced defending his ideas in debate clubs, and honed his arguments in editorials for the college newspaper, *The Princetonian*, of which he became editor. The college's emphasis on religion had long pushed its students toward the ministry, but in the more secular atmosphere of Wilson's era, a career in public service was equally attractive. There were frequent and intense discussions, particularly within Wilson's circle of friends, of how Christian ideals could be implemented in public life.

Wilson lived an insulated and privileged life at Princeton, largely detached from the changes then sweeping the nation. The summer of 1876, between his freshman and sophomore years, was marked by the massacre of Custer's forces at Little Big Horn and the first demonstration of the telephone at the Centennial exposition at Philadelphia, but Wilson did not see the future of the nation in either the West or industry. When Wilson visited the exposition in September 1876, he was unimpressed by the exhibits of arts, science, and technology. Only several years later did it occur to him that the Philadelphia displays had been "a fit symbol and assurance of the settled peace and prosperity which were in store for the country in the future" (Wilson 1893, 236). Likewise, Wilson avoided the subject of the Reconstruction of his own South that came to an end that year, even though he would subsequently characterize the period as "an extraordinary carnival of public crime . . . under the forms of law" (Wilson 1893, 223).

The one public event of 1876 that really captured Wilson's interest was the presidential election. The corruption of the Grant administration was jarringly at odds with his own vision of a pure British system, fueled by intellectual debate and dedicated to the national interest. He predicted, pessimistically, that without substantial reform, "the American

Republic will . . . never celebrate another Centennial" (Link and others 1966, 1:143). When the election produced a near-tie and was followed by months of controversy before the Republican, Rutherford B. Hayes, emerged as a tarnished winner, Wilson lost faith in American politics, at least for the time being. In 1879 he published his first article, "Cabinet Government in the United States," which proposed replacing the divided branches of the American government with a parliamentary system like that of his ideal, Britain (see Document 1.6).

During the next several years Wilson built on and extended his 1879 argument. What America needed, he thought, was not only better national leadership but also a better way for the people to hold leaders responsible for their actions, and he did not see how that could be done within the existing system. In his first book, *Congressional Government,* published in 1885, he declared that instead of being a leader, the president had been reduced to "*mere* administration, mere obedience of directions from the masters of policy, the Standing Committees" of Congress (see Document 1.7). Except for his veto, the president "might, not inconveniently, be a permanent officer; the first official of a carefully-graded and impartially regulated civil service system. . . ." (Wilson 1885, 254).

Believing that Congress, then the dominant branch of the federal government, was controlled by politicians who cared more about local interests than national issues, Wilson saw a parliamentary system as a means of restoring energy and direction to the government. At the same time, he thought such a system might offer him a personal opportunity to use the public speaking skills he had been honing since his childhood. "I've fallen fairly in love with speechmaking," he said, arguing that a skilled orator "can gain a hearing when others might find difficulty in doing so, and can, by an effort, change a vote while others fail to command their hearers' sympathies" (Link and others 1967, 2:10). In his imagination, Prime Minister Wilson stood before an enthralled Congress, winning its members to the support of his policies through the drama and logic of his argument. After he graduated from Princeton, he decided, he would go to law school to prepare himself for a political career.

LAW AND GRADUATE SCHOOL, 1879–1886

Reality did not conform to Wilson's fantasy. In the autumn of 1879 he enrolled in the University of Virginia law school, where he soon discovered that legal study involved a great deal of drudgery. To a Princeton classmate he wrote that he was "struggling, hopefully but not with . . . *over*-much courage, through its intricacies, and am swallowing the vast amount of its technicalities with as good a grace and as straight a face as an offended palate will allow" (Link and others 1966, 1:591). After his first year and a half he dropped out of law school and returned home to complete the last semester of his studies on his own, as had been common a half-century earlier. In October 1882 Wilson passed the Georgia bar examination with distinction and set up practice in Atlanta with another University of Virginia student, Edward I. Renick.

The Wilson-Renick partnership was pleasant, but client-less. Wilson spent his time reading history and politics and was forced to borrow from his father to pay his expenses. After six months in Atlanta he was convinced that entering the law had been a mistake. He wrote: "The profession I chose was politics; the profession I entered was the law. I entered the one because I thought it would lead to the other" (Link and others 1967, 2:500). By the spring of 1883 he had decided the goal was not worth its cost. When his father agreed to pay his tuition and expenses for the graduate program in history and political science at the Johns Hopkins University in Baltimore, Wilson happily abandoned Atlanta and the legal profession (see Document 1.8). "The philosophical *study* of the law—which must be a pleasure to any thoughtful man—is a very different matter from its scheming and haggling practice," he told a friend (Link and others 1967, 2:351).

One of Wilson's few legal commissions took him to Rome, Georgia, in April 1883. There he met Ellen Axson, the daughter of a Presbyterian minister. Then twenty-three, Ellen was a talented artist, whose "sunny, loving heart and . . . quick, earnest, thoughtful mind" immediately attracted Woodrow (Link and others 1967, 3:86). They soon fell in love, but Ellen resisted his desire to be married at once because she was the homemaker for her widowed father and three siblings and because she wanted to explore a career as an artist before settling down. Wilson reluctantly accepted her plan to study for a year at the Art Students' League in New York but continued to importune her. Finally, she relented, and on June 24, 1885, they were married in her grandfather's church in Savannah (see Document 1.9).

Wilson pursued his studies at Johns Hopkins with an ardor equal to that with which he wooed Ellen, although he lamented that an academic career would never enable him to "participate actively in public affairs" and would force him to content himself "with becoming an *outside* force in politics . . . through literary and non-partisan agencies" (Link and others 1967, 2:501). The professors gave him great freedom to pursue his interest in the philosophy and structure of politics, praising his analysis of Congress's operation as "better than anything in that line that has been done heretofore" (Link and others 1967, 3:172). Within a little more than a year he completed his study of Congress, and in 1885 it was published as a book, *Congressional Government*. A year later, in 1886, Johns Hopkins bent its rules to accept the book as completing the requirements for his Ph.D. He remains the only American president to hold a doctorate.

ACADEMIC LIFE AND FAMILY, 1886–1902

While awaiting the university's decision about his degree, Wilson accepted a teaching position at Bryn Mawr, a women's college in Pennsylvania not far from Baltimore. In September 1885 the newlywed Wilsons arrived there to begin their life together. The school was new, the salary small, but although Wilson declared that he "would a *great* deal rather teach *men* anywhere, and especially in the South, than girls at Bryn Mawr or anywhere else," he felt at home in the academic world (Link and others 1967, 3:517–518). In April 1886 the Wilsons' first child, Margaret Woodrow Wilson, was born, and a little over a year later, in August 1887, a second daughter, Jessie Woodrow Wilson, arrived.

By that time Wilson, feeling the pinch of his small salary, was actively seeking a new position. In the spring of 1888 he accepted a professorship of history and political economy at Wesleyan University in Connecticut. The Wesleyan position carried a higher salary and offered Wilson the opportunity to teach men at an established university. Perhaps more important than the gender of the students, however, was the fact that Wesleyan gave Wilson a light course load and permitted him to experiment with teaching methods other than the textbook and recitation system that he had found stultifying at Princeton and Bryn Mawr. The college also encouraged its faculty to pursue their own research, and in 1889 Wilson published his second book, *The State*, a comparative study of European governments based on extensive reading in German and French sources (see Document 1.10). In October of that same year the Wilsons' third daughter, Eleanor Randolph Wilson, was born. Wilson had hoped the third child would be a son, but Nell, as she was called, soon became his favorite.

The State established Wilson as an important scholar and gave him confidence he had finally found the right career. "Since I have been here," he told Ellen in 1889, "a distinct *feeling* of maturity—or rather of maturing—has come over me. . . . I need no longer hesitate . . . to assert myself and my opinions in the presence of . . . 'my elders' " (Link and others 1969, 6:139). Indeed, his "elders" were listening with growing respect to his opinions on a variety of topics. In recognition of his pioneering work on governmental administration, Johns Hopkins offered him a visiting lectureship on the subject (see Document 1.11), and Professor Albert Bushnell Hart of Harvard invited him to write a history of the Civil War and Reconstruction for a distinguished series of which Hart was the editor. The book, *Division and Reunion, 1829–1889*, published in 1893, was based on careful research and offered a relatively unbiased interpretation of a still sensitive subject. In 1890, crowning this period of scholarly achievement, Princeton offered Wilson an opportunity to return to his alma mater as professor of jurisprudence and political economy. At the age of thirty-three he became the college's most highly paid and, within a short time, most popular professor.

Great though Wilson's satisfaction was with his academic success, he had not given up his hope of wider influence (see Document 1.12). Fearing that he had been "shut off from my heart's *first*—primary—ambition and purpose, which was, to take an active, if possible a leading, part in public life, and stake out for myself, if I had the ability, a statesman's career," he decided to aim his next books at a wider popular audience (Link and others 1970, 8:220). The principal fruit of this decision was the publication, in 1902, of a history of the United States. The nation's past, he wrote, "has taught us how to become strong, and will teach us, if we heed its moral, how to become wise, also, and single-minded" (Link and others 1971, 10:222). *A History of the American People* was enormously successful, appearing first as a series of articles in *Harper's Magazine* and then published in a lavishly illustrated five-volume edition that became a best seller.

Publication of *A History of the American People* brought invitations, which Wilson relished, to speak to a variety of audiences on issues having to do with politics. For a number of years he had been so focused on his academic work that he had not paid close attention to national events. Now he realized that the country's situation was changing. The rise of "modern industrial organization," he wrote in *The State*, "distorted competition" and permitted "the rich and the strong to combine against the poor and the weak" (Link and others 1969, 6:304). It seemed to him that because corporations had become national, only the federal government could regulate them, but when he wrote the book he did not see how that might be done, given the dominance of the federal system by a leaderless Congress. The Spanish-American War in 1898 suggested a solution to him (see Document 1.13). "The plunge into international politics and into the administration of distant dependencies" as a result of the war, he wrote in a preface to the 1900 edition of *Congressional Government*, had given the president "greatly increased power and opportunity for constructive statesmanship" (Wilson 1885 [1900 ed.], xi–xii). Perhaps that new initiative might be applied to domestic as well as foreign problems.

Less than a year after the 1900 edition of *Congressional Government* was published, Theodore Roosevelt succeeded the assassinated William McKinley, and the modern era of the presidency began. Seven years later, in a series of lectures at Columbia University, Wilson declared that the chief executive was no longer a mere administrator and might even dominate the federal government. The president, he proclaimed, is "the political leader of the nation, or has it in his choice to be. The nation as a whole has chosen him, and is conscious that it has no other political spokesman. . . . Let him once win the admiration and confidence of the country, and no other single force can withstand him. . . . He is the representative of no constituency, but of the whole people. . . . If he rightly interpret the national thought and boldly insist upon it, he is irresistible. . . ." (Wilson 1908, 68). The publication of these lectures was at once a private manifesto and evidence that Wilson had returned to serious analysis of the contemporary political scene (see Document 1.14). His smoldering political ambition was again aflame.

Seeing no immediate way to fulfill his ambition, Wilson threw himself fully into his work at Princeton. In 1896, when the college was about to celebrate its sesquicentennial, Wilson was invited to make the main speech at the festivities. In "Princeton in the Nation's Service," he called on the university to educate its students as Wilson had educated himself, with a mixture of religion and the liberal arts that he believed would equip and motivate them to become moral and political leaders, regardless of their professions. The praise for his speech from all elements of the university community marked him as a faculty leader and the logical successor to President Francis L. Patton, who retired a few years later. On June 9, 1902, Princeton's board of trustees unanimously elected Wilson the thirteenth president of the university.

PRESIDENT OF PRINCETON, 1902–1910

Wilson became president of Princeton at a moment of change and uncertainty in American higher education. In the nineteenth century colleges and universities emphasized the classics, mathematics, and theology. By 1900 there was widespread agreement that the old curriculum was inadequate to prepare students for life in an urban, industrial nation, but there was no consensus on what changes were needed. Some reformers proposed to allow students to choose any courses they wanted; others suggested emphasizing practical subjects that would prepare students for careers. Wilson saw merit in these proposals but believed that Princeton's role should be to train its graduates as generalists who would be qualified "to see how the interests of all the people are linked together" (Link and others 1977, 23:88).

In a report to the board of trustees in October 1902 Wilson recommended the introduction of new subjects to the university's curriculum and the establishment of a British-style tutorial system, under which lectures and recitations would be replaced or supplemented by meetings of students in small groups with young "preceptors" hired to encourage discussion of books and ideas. He also proposed the creation, "at the very heart" of the campus, of a new graduate college whose intellectual activity could stimulate the whole academic community (Link and others 1972, 14:223) (see Document 1.15). The trustees were startled but agreed to raise the money needed to implement Wilson's proposals.

Meanwhile, Wilson's personal life was in turmoil. His father, a widower since Jessie's death in 1888, came to live with the Wilsons in Princeton and soon became a demanding invalid. By the time he died on January 21, 1903, Ellen confessed that her nerves were stretched to the breaking point. Soon after the funeral, Ellen's brother, Stockton Axson, a popular professor of English literature at Princeton, suffered the first of a series of mental breakdowns, and the Wilsons' middle daughter,

Jessie, contracted a serious illness. In June 1904 Woodrow's right hand suddenly became partially paralyzed. He dismissed it as "writer's cramp," but it persisted for months and must have worried him. That autumn he developed an intestinal hernia and had to have an operation to correct it, which was followed by phlebitis in one of his legs that kept him confined to bed until February 1905. Scarcely had he recovered from that when their youngest daughter Nell had to be operated on for tubercular neck glands. While she was recovering, Ellen's younger brother, Eddie, tragically drowned, along with his wife and baby. Ellen, who had borne the burden of all these disasters, went into a deep depression, hardly speaking for weeks. Alarmed about her condition, Wilson arranged for her to spend the summer at an artists' colony at Lyme, Connecticut, where she resumed her painting and recovered some but not all of her equanimity.

Bad as all this was, there was worse to come. During the spring of 1906 Wilson delivered twenty-one speeches to alumni and other groups to build support for his next round of planned reforms at the college. On the morning of May 28, he awoke blind in one eye. During what Ellen described as "a dreadful week" of medical tests and uncertainty, Wilson was so tense and nervous that he had to move to a friend's house to avoid the noise and bustle of the president's house on the eve of graduation.

First reports were encouraging—merely a burst blood vessel in the eye as a result of "overstrain" that could be corrected by rest (Link and others 1973, 16:423). At the urging of the trustees, the Wilsons planned a vacation in the Lake Country of England. Then, not long before they were to leave, came a second, less encouraging medical report. The problem, Ellen now understood, was hardening of the arteries and high blood pressure, a "dying by inches, and incurable," as she put it (Link and others 1973, 16:430). Although the family had a wonderful summer in England, and Wilson returned to Princeton with his vision largely restored and his general health improved, the specter of his illness was never far behind him.

In the autumn of 1906 Wilson decided to propose a new round of reforms for the university. The preceptorial system was working well, but most students were still more interested in their social lives than intellectual pursuits. The problem, Wilson believed, was the distraction provided by the private, selective eating clubs in which students lived and socialized. At the trustees' meeting in December 1906 he proposed to replace the clubs with residential quadrangles where students and selected faculty members would live together and discuss academic issues in "a sort of family life, not merely as neighbors in the dormitories but also as comrades at meals and in many daily activities" (Link and others 1974, 17:185–186).

Although startled by the proposal, the trustees agreed in June 1907 to go forward with the plan (see Document 1.16). Neither they nor Wilson anticipated the hostile reaction the announcement provoked from alumni, who remembered eating club experiences as highlights of their Princeton years. The summer of 1907 was marked by what Ellen called "quadrangling." In October, with alumni donations falling sharply, the trustees rescinded their support of the plan (Saunders 1985, 182).

Fortunately for Wilson, by the time the quadrangle controversy came to a head, new opportunities were opening for him. George Brinton McClellan Harvey, the publisher of *Harper's Weekly* and a conservative Democrat who was eager to find someone to challenge two-time presidential nominee William Jennings Bryan for leadership of the Democratic Party, believed that Wilson was a moderate who might have broad popular appeal. In February 1906 Harvey invited Wilson to a dinner at the Lotos Club in New York. There he praised the Princeton president as "a man who combines the activities of the present with the sober influences of the past" and suggested that Wilson would be an ideal presidential candidate (see Document 1.17).

Wilson did not at first take Harvey's suggestion seriously, but further stresses, both at Princeton and in his personal life, gradually changed his mind. Already contending with the quadrangle dispute in the spring of 1907, Wilson's plans for the university were frustrated still more by a conflict with the dean of the graduate school, Andrew West, who wanted to build a graduate college not in the center of the campus as Wilson had recommended in 1902, but "near the campus and yet sufficiently retired to ensure the residential separation of the graduate from the undergraduate students" (Link and others 1974, 17:143). Convinced that such a separation would undermine the intellectual community he was trying to build at Princeton, Wilson in May 1907 told the trustees, in effect, that they must decide whether he or West would control the future direction of the university.

The struggles over the quadrangle plan and the graduate college were extremely stressful for Wilson. In November 1907 he suffered what he referred to as "an attack of Neuritis" but which may have been a mild stroke that left his right arm partially paralyzed for several weeks (Link and others 1974, 17:549). Taken in context with the eye episode of the previous year, this new health problem was particularly alarming, and Wilson quickly accepted his doctors' advice to take a vacation. The previous year Wilson had wintered in Bermuda; in January 1908 he returned there to convalesce, leaving Ellen in Princeton to deal with family and college matters.

During his previous visit to Bermuda Wilson was introduced to Mary Allen Hulbert Peck, a charming woman in her mid-forties who was separated from her husband and ran a salon in Bermuda that drew luminaries, including Mark Twain. She and Wilson quickly became close friends. Whether there was more than friendship is impossible to determine, but Ellen certainly suspected something and warned her husband against the appearance of impropriety. She was right; even without any evidence, rumors of a Wilson-Peck affair circulated during the 1916 presidential election.

The years between 1906 and 1910 were in some ways the nadir of Wilson's life. Although to outward appearances he had achieved great success, with a fulfilling career and a happy family, in fact his plans for Princeton had been blocked, his family had experienced a series of traumatic crises, and he himself had undergone two frightening and mysterious illnesses. His relationship with Mary Peck, whether intimate or not, was an affirmation of his vitality and attractiveness to a desirable woman at a moment when his personal and professional future was uncertain. It is likely it helped him to get through a difficult period, and Ellen's wise recognition that Mary posed no real threat to her marriage minimized damage. Despite Mary Peck, the Wilsons remained devoted to each other until Ellen's death in August 1914.

In 1910 Wilson's battles over the graduate college issue reached a final crisis. Prior to that year an open break between Wilson and Dean West was avoided because there was not enough money to build a graduate college anywhere. In May 1910, however, Dean West announced he had secured a $2 million bequest, enough to build the college where he wanted it. "We have beaten the living, but we cannot fight the dead," Wilson told his wife gloomily, but even as he contemplated resigning the Princeton presidency, his old admirer George Harvey reappeared with a new and attractive opportunity.

GOVERNOR OF NEW JERSEY, 1910–1912

By 1910 Wilson's battles with Dean West over the graduate college, and with the alumni over the quadrangle plan, made it difficult for him to continue as president of Princeton, but the quadrangle controversy had won him a national reputation as a progressive. He saw the plan as a way of improving undergraduate education, but reporters seized on the idea that it would do away with the elitist eating clubs and proclaimed him a democratic crusader. This provided the opportunity publisher Harvey had been seeking, and with the support of New Jersey's Democratic bosses, Harvey engineered Wilson's nomination as the Democratic candidate for governor and skillfully managed his successful campaign (see Chapter 2).

It was one thing to win the election with the support of the party bosses, and quite another to achieve reform against the opposition of the political machines. The reality of the situation was made clear to Wilson soon after the election when James Smith, a party boss and former United States senator, indicated his desire to be returned to the Senate by the state legislature (until the ratification of the Seventeenth Amendment to the Constitution in 1913, senators were elected by state legislatures, not by the people). Although personally grateful to Smith, Wilson realized that if the bosses controlled the Senate election, they would control his whole administration. With some embarrassment, he told George Harvey that although he had "a very high opinion of Senator Smith . . . his election would be intolerable to the very people who elected me and gave us a majority in the legislature" (Link and others 1976, 22:46).

Acting with remarkable audacity, Wilson called on Robert Davis, Democratic boss of Hudson County, to ask for his support against Smith. Davis replied that, although he had no personal stake in the matter, he had already promised Smith his support. He proposed that if Wilson would stay out of the senatorial battle, "we'll support your whole legislative program." The offer must have been attractive, but Wilson did not hesitate. "If you beat me in this first fight," he responded, "how do I know you won't be able to beat me in everything?" (quoted in Hirst 1965, 130). Wilson's realism won Davis's respect, and he told the governor-elect that, although he would keep his promise to Smith, he would not enforce discipline on his supporters. Over the next several weeks a number of them, sensing a change in the state's power structure, quietly defected to Wilson's side.

In addition to seeking to breach the solidarity of the bosses, Wilson met personally with nearly every member of the incoming legislature. Early in December he told Smith privately that he felt confident of victory, but the boss refused to believe this neophyte could beat him. Wilson then took the issue to the people, delivering a series of speeches around the state in an unprecedented attempt to arouse popular pressure on the legislature. When the legislature took its first vote on January 24, 1911, Smith received only ten of fifty votes, and the next day he released the last of his supporters. "I feel that I should no longer stay the consummation of the Executive's purposes," he observed dryly (quoted in Link 1947, 234).

Wilson's victory in the senatorial fight established him as a dominant force in the legislature. "I look forward with genuine pleasure," he told the legislators on January 17, 1911, "to the prospect of being your comrade" in "the journey of duty" as the legislature took up his reform proposals (quoted in Link 1947, 234). Those proposals were largely the work of George Record, a longtime reformer whose support during the 1910 election had been crucial to Wilson's success. Although Record had no official position, Wilson asked him to draft bills providing for the nomination of candidates by public primaries rather than party conventions and regulating campaign contributions and election practices. The two bills, handed to the governor by Record within ten days, became the administration's first legislative priorities.

The direct primary bill, sponsored by Assemblyman Elmer H. Geran, one of Wilson's former students, was a frontal challenge to the power of the political machines, and they fought it fiercely. Wilson assumed direct control of the fight for the measure. On two occasions he met personally with Democratic legislators to answer questions and build support for the bill, and he reached out to Republicans by offering to accept amendments that did not subvert its basic principles. The point, he said, was to get "as good a bill as can be got," not "to talk it to death," and to "waive all minor objections" (Link and others 1976, 22:471–472). He even invited James Nugent, one of the bosses, to his office and asked him to support the bill. Nugent was so flabbergasted at this effrontery that he accused Wilson of using patronage to line up support for the measure. Outraged at the suggestion that he would stoop to using the methods of the machines, Wilson threw Nugent out of his office, and the news of the boss's humiliation swept through the capitol. A few days later the bill sailed through both houses of the legislature.

The day after the passage of the Geran bill, the legislature passed the second of Record's proposals, a corrupt practices act that set strict disclosure standards for private campaign contributions, banned corporate contributions, and outlawed corrupt election practices. A few days later the legislature also endorsed the Egan bill, which created a public utilities commission with power to set rates and standards of service for railroad, trolley, power, telephone, sewer, gas, and other public utility companies.

A fourth reform measure, the Edge bill to create a fund subsidized by employers to provide compensation for workers injured on the job, had been initiated by Wilson's Republican predecessor and was pending before the legislature when he took office. Wilson's principal contribution to its passage in early April was to persuade the state's labor unions that the bill was the best that could be hoped for at the time and that the establishment of any workmen's compensation system would be to their benefit in the long run.

Important as was Wilson's role in the passage of some of these reform measures, the role of George Record and the example of the Edge Act demonstrate that he was by no means the only leader of reform in New Jersey. The tide of reform sentiment was running strongly in both parties, and even without Wilson's influence reforms would almost certainly have been passed. Indeed, several measures, including a wages and hours law for women and children, a factory inspection law, laws regulating food storage and inspection, public school reforms, and other reform measures, passed without the governor taking a significant role in the legislative process. Wilson's dramatic fights against the bosses were important because they gave reform additional momentum, but he rode as much as led the progressive movement in New Jersey.

Nevertheless, across the country Wilson was credited with the burst of reform activity that transformed New Jersey, almost overnight, from one of the most corrupt to one of the most progressive states in the nation. On the strength of his success, in the spring of 1911 Wilson began to be discussed nationally as a presidential candidate. Even as the legislature was finishing up the last of its work, his friends were beginning to set up a national campaign organization, and he was planning speaking trips across the country (see Chapter 2).

Like other governors in a similar situation, Wilson found that it was not easy to lead his state while running for president. James Nugent, who had been humiliated by Wilson during the fight over the Geran bill, proclaimed his determination to have revenge, publicly describing the governor as "an ingrate and a liar" (Link and others 1977, 23:235n.1). In October Wilson learned that the Democratic machines intended to instruct their supporters to sit out the elections for the legislature in November in the hope that the election of Republican majorities would damage the governor's presidential ambitions. He declared that the bosses' action would "cause a very serious reaction even among machine politicians . . . because it is obviously a bad game to deprive your own party of power in order to accomplish a personal revenge," but the damage was done (Link and others 1977, 23:546–547). When Republicans won control of both houses of the legislature, a *New York Times* reporter summed up Wilson's dilemma: "Whether Gov. Wilson's name will go before the Democratic National Convention for the Presidential nomination will depend in a measure on what progress he makes with the Republican Legislature. . . ." (Link and others 1977, 23:629).

Wilson understood the situation and did his best. On January 9, 1912, he made a low-key speech to the legislature, urging bipartisanship and proposing to build on the previous session's successes in the relatively uncontroversial area of administrative reform. Avoiding specific recommendations, he urged legislators to make state government more "efficient, responsible, and economical" by reorganizing the "utterly confusing" tangle of boards and commissions that overlapped and duplicated each other, and he proposed reforms of the legal and taxation systems to make them fairer to all citizens (Link and others 1977, 24:23, 20).

Perhaps if Wilson had not been running for president and had been able to work closely with the legislature, as he had the year before, he might have had some success with his new agenda. In practice, although he was out of the state only two days while the legislature was in session, he provided no leadership. He offered no specific bills, lobbied very little for pending reforms, and never met even with Democratic legislators. His most active role was in vetoing bills he considered partisan and reactionary. The previous year he had vetoed almost no bills; in 1912 he vetoed fifty-seven, almost 10 percent of the total. He did his best to blame the situation on the Republicans, but the stalemate in New Jersey politics in the spring of 1912 contributed to erosion of support for Wilson's presidential candidacy. By the eve of the national

Democratic convention, he was in trouble, both at home and with the national party.

Except for the temporary damage done to his presidential aspirations, Wilson's problems in New Jersey in 1912 were relatively minor. Most of what he and other reformers had been seeking was accomplished during the 1911 session. In 1912 his enemies, both Democratic and Republican, seized the opportunity presented by his presidential candidacy to embarrass him, but by that time he was already moving beyond their reach. Although historians Alexander and Juliette George may be correct in arguing that Wilson's lack of success during his second year as governor represented a repetition of the self-defeating behavior that had marked his last years at Princeton, Republican control of the legislature and Wilson's frequent absences from the state as he campaigned for the presidency provide an equally persuasive explanation of the unproductiveness of the 1912 legislative session. As he moved toward Washington, Wilson had every reason to be confident in his ability to manage the national political system as effectively as he had that in New Jersey.

WILSON'S FIRST TERM, 1912–1916

After a colorful campaign that pitted Wilson against the Republican incumbent, William Howard Taft, and Progressive Party candidate Theodore Roosevelt, Wilson entered the presidency in March 1913 with Democratic majorities in both houses of Congress but only 42 percent of the popular vote. Nevertheless, he immediately summoned Congress to a special session to secure action on his promise of a "New Freedom."

Working closely with congressional leaders, Wilson secured the passage of his first priority, a reduction in the tariff, by the beginning of October, and his second goal, a major reform of the banking and currency system, just before Christmas. A third major reform, the modernization of the federal antitrust law and creation of a Federal Trade Commission, was completed in the autumn of 1914. Two years after he was first elected, Wilson had achieved all the reforms he had promised during his campaign.

Although Wilson had told a friend before his inauguration that it would be "an irony of fate" if he had to focus on foreign problems because all his training and experience had been in domestic issues, the president nevertheless pursued a vigorous foreign policy. Within days of his inauguration Wilson announced that the United States would recognize the new, republican government of China and would discourage

American bankers' participation in an international loan project developed during the Taft administration because Wilson believed such foreign loans impaired Chinese independence. He also announced that his administration would deny recognition to Latin American regimes that seized power illegally.

Wilson's Latin American statement referred particularly to Mexico, where a military coup had recently overthrown a democratic government. For the remainder of his term Wilson struggled to find a policy for dealing with Mexico that would encourage the restoration of democracy but minimize American intervention. Elsewhere in the Caribbean basin, most notably in Haiti and the Dominican Republic, he found similar challenges. His goal, in Asia and Latin America, was the promotion of democracy, constitutional government, and economic development within a framework of self-determination, but turning the objective into specific policies often proved difficult.

In the summer of 1914 the assassination in Sarajevo of the heir to the Austro-Hungarian throne precipitated the beginning of World War I. Wilson never doubted that the correct policy for the United States was neutrality, but emotional and economic ties to the warring nations plus the introduction by the Germans of a new weapon—the submarine—made neutrality increasingly difficult.

While Wilson struggled with the challenges posed by the war, his personal life was also in turmoil. Ellen Wilson had been feeling weak and tired ever since the summer of 1913, but she attributed it to fatigue as the result of planning for two of their daughters' weddings: Jessie's to Francis Sayre on November 25, 1913, and Nell's to Secretary of the Treasury William Gibbs McAdoo on May 7, 1914, both at the White House. Shortly after Nell's wedding Ellen collapsed completely. The president's physician, Dr. Cary T. Grayson, diagnosed her illness as Bright's disease, an incurable form of cancer. Throughout the summer of 1914 she was bedridden, with the president often at her side holding her hand. That was where he was when she died on August 6.

For two weeks after Ellen's death Wilson was "nearly paralyzed" with grief and depression (Link 1965, 463). So close to the surface were his emotions that he dared not even speak of her to family and friends, for fear he would break down. He threw himself into work to keep going, but although the problems were urgent, he was not at his best in addressing them. Always dependent upon the support of the women in his life,

Wilson found Ellen's death hard to bear, and the fact that two of his daughters, including Nell, his favorite, were away with their new husbands left him doubly lonely. The autumn and winter of 1914–1915 were cheerless times in the White House.

Then, in March 1915, Wilson's cousin introduced him to a friend, Edith Bolling Galt. Wilson and Galt, a wealthy widow, were immediately attracted to each other (see Document 1.18). After a brief and secret courtship, the couple announced their engagement on October 6, 1915, and were married on December 18. Although some people were scandalized by the speed of the president's remarriage after Ellen's death, family and friends were delighted that he was back on an even keel emotionally.

In the autumn of 1914, following Ellen's death and the completion of his original legislative program, Wilson told a number of people that he had no desire to run for reelection, but his new relationship with Edith restored his emotional health, and during 1915 he began to think about politics again. The time was opportune. Theodore Roosevelt was telling his friends that he did not want to run again as a Progressive, and that left his followers the choice of returning to a Republican Party dominated by conservatives or turning to the Democrats. Wilson, who had become increasingly convinced that there were more things the federal government ought to be doing, saw in the situation an opportunity to turn the Democratic Party into a broad-based reform coalition. In the spring of 1916 he endorsed new social legislation that enabled him to claim during the 1916 campaign that the Democrats had not only enacted their own reform program but most of the Progressive Party's program as well.

At the same time, having deferred a crisis with Germany over the submarine sinking of the *Lusitania* in May 1915, and then having extorted from the Germans a series of promises not to use submarines to attack passenger vessels, Wilson could also claim in 1916 that he had maintained peace with honor. In November a substantial number of former Progressives joined with Democrats to give Wilson a greater mandate than he had in 1912.

WILSON'S SECOND ADMINISTRATION, 1916–1920

War dominated Wilson's second term. Despite his efforts to maintain peace and to mediate the conflict, a German decision to launch unrestricted submarine warfare in early 1917 led to an American declaration of war in April 1917. Mobilization of an ill-prepared nation and planning for peace after the war now became major concerns.

As a result of the enormous capacity of the American economy, the country managed to patch together an army of nearly four million and transport more than one million soldiers to France, where they arrived in the summer of 1918 just in time to stop and push back the German advance. The economy stuttered and wheezed but poured out money, food, weapons, fuel, and supplies to support domestic consumption as well as the military and the European Allies.

On January 18, 1918, Wilson laid out his vision of the postwar settlement in his "Fourteen Points" speech to a joint session of Congress. From the American point of view, its most important proposal was that the United States abandon its traditional isolationism and join a postwar League of Nations whose members would collectively maintain the world's peace. To ensure that the peace actually approximated his plan, Wilson decided he would go personally to the peace conference in Paris. No previous president had ever left the Western Hemisphere, and no other president has ever been gone from the country for as long as Wilson would be—more than six months.

The president received a hero's welcome on his arrival in Europe, but the Allied leaders did not share the popular enthusiasm for him. They wanted to squeeze everything they could get out of the Germans, and they saw Wilson's Fourteen Points as an obstacle to their aims. In long sessions of hard bargaining, Wilson got his League of Nations as part of the Treaty of Versailles but was forced to compromise on many other issues. He hoped that Americans would agree with him that even if the treaty was imperfect, the League of Nations provided a mechanism for correcting injustices and mistakes.

Back in the United States, Wilson presented the treaty to the Senate in July 1919 and then had to watch while critics attacked virtually every aspect of it. In September the president decided to take the issue to the country with a speaking trip throughout the West. Traveling more than 10,000 miles by train in less than thirty days and delivering more than thirty major speeches without amplification, he hoped to arouse a great wave of public support for the League of Nations that would compel the Senate to approve the treaty.

Wilson's family and friends opposed his making the trip. For more than six months he had been engaged in difficult and stressful negotiations for twelve or fifteen hours a day in Europe, and he looked and felt exhausted.

Moreover, he had recently been seriously ill—once in April in Paris, when he had what doctors diagnosed as influenza, and again in July, when he had an attack of what his personal physician, Dr. Grayson, announced was dysentery. On the trip he began to suffer from terrible headaches and asthma so severe he could not sleep lying down. Modern physicians see his symptoms as indicative of congestive heart failure resulting from years of untreated high blood pressure.

On September 25, following a speech in Colorado, Wilson collapsed and had to be rushed back to Washington, where he suffered a massive stroke on October 2, 1919. The stroke, serious in itself, left him paralyzed on one side and was followed by infection and kidney failure. For weeks he did not leave his bed and saw no one but physicians and family. He could not act as president, but his wife, convinced that he would die if he did not have his duty to sustain him, refused even to consider having him resign. Grayson abetted her deception by announcing that the president's illness was not serious and that he was recovering rapidly. When rumors of Wilson's condition circulated in the Senate, Grayson and Edith arranged a carefully staged interview in which a small delegation of senators were brought into the sickroom and carefully seated on the president's nonparalyzed side, while he repeated a few well-worn jokes. They departed, falsely reassured.

In reality, even as Wilson crept back from the brink of death, he remained physically an invalid and mentally debilitated, although his doctors did not understand the full seriousness of his emotional and mental problems. The government continued to carry out its basic functions, but urgent issues of foreign and domestic policy drifted without guidance from the White House. In November 1919, with word coming from Wilson's sickroom that the president opposed any amendments to the treaty, the Senate defeated it. Four months later, in March 1920, when a second vote was scheduled, Wilson still refused any compromise, and once again the pact was rejected. Imprisoned by his illness, the president did not even meet his cabinet until April, yet he fantasized about running for a third term in what he called "a great and solemn referendum" on the treaty.

RETIREMENT

Wiser heads prevailed, and the 1920 Democratic convention nominated James M. Cox and Franklin Roosevelt for president and vice president on a platform that urged the approval of the Treaty of Versailles. In

November the Republican ticket of Warren Harding and Calvin Coolidge buried Cox and Roosevelt, with more than sixteen million votes to the Democrats' nine million. Wilson was too ill and frail to attend the public ceremonies of his successor's inauguration and slipped away quietly to the Wilsons' new home on S Street in Washington (see Chapter 6).

Despite the Senate's rejection of the treaty and the seemingly decisive public repudiation of the Democrats in the election, Wilson remained convinced that the American people would eventually vindicate his policy. At the S Street house he saw a few visitors, old friends mostly, and worked when he could on "The Document," a draft political platform for 1924. He also managed to dictate a few paragraphs, later published in *The Atlantic,* about the danger of international revolution that he believed was being exacerbated by American isolationism and reactionary policies. On Armistice Day 1923 he struggled through a brief speech that was broadcast on a nationwide radio network.

Even more than most former presidents, Woodrow Wilson ceased to influence events after he left office. He was awarded the Nobel Peace Prize in 1920; world leaders—or more often, former leaders—paid courtesy calls at S Street; and small groups of veterans often came to see their former president's house, but real power had moved elsewhere. As Wilson's health began to decline seriously at the end of January 1924, a crowd of a few hundred gathered across the street from his house, and newspapers reported on his condition. His death on February 3, 1924, rated headlines around the world, but there was not the slightest possibility that it would lead the Republican administration to change its policy. Not until another twenty years had passed would a majority of Americans become convinced that the rejection of the League of Nations had been a mistake and embrace the "second chance" offered by the United Nations.

BIBLIOGRAPHIC ESSAY

The best books on Wilson's early years are John M. Mulder, *Woodrow Wilson: The Years of Preparation* (Princeton: Princeton University Press, 1978); Niels Aage Thorsen, *The Political Thought of Woodrow Wilson, 1875–1910* (Princeton: Princeton University Press, 1988); and Daniel D. Stid, *The President as Statesman: Woodrow Wilson and the Constitution* (Lawrence: University Press of Kansas, 1998). The volumes of Arthur S. Link's multivolume biography of Wilson cited in this chapter are *Wilson: The Road to the White House* (Princeton: Princeton University Press, 1947), and

Wilson: The New Freedom (Princeton: Princeton University Press, 1965). See also the collection of Link's essays, *The Higher Realism of Woodrow Wilson and Other Essays* (Nashville: Vanderbilt University Press, 1971). An early account by a New Jersey supporter remains useful: James Kerney, *The Political Education of Woodrow Wilson* (New York: Century, 1926).

Alexander L. George and Juliette L. George, in *Woodrow Wilson and Colonel House: A Personality Study* (New York: John Day, 1956), argue that Wilson was programmed for failure by conflicts with his domineering father, an interpretation that has been strongly challenged but not entirely refuted by Arthur S. Link, John Mulder, and others. Laurence R. Veysey's article, "The Academic Mind of Woodrow Wilson," *Mississippi Valley Historical Review* 49 (March 1963): 613–634, provides a judicious assessment of Wilson's leadership at Princeton. Also useful is Craig Hardin, *Woodrow Wilson at Princeton* (Norman: University of Oklahoma Press, 1960). Wilson's brother-in-law, Stockton Axson, wrote down his impressions of Wilson's personality and career at various times, and that memoir, long used by biographers, is now available in print. It is Stockton Axson, *"Brother Woodrow": A Memoir of Woodrow Wilson*, ed. by Arthur S. Link and others (Princeton: Princeton University Press, 1993). For information on Wilson's influential first wife, see the excellent biography by Frances Wright Saunders, *Ellen Axson Wilson: First Lady Between Two Worlds* (Chapel Hill: University of North Carolina Press, 1985).

Wilson was himself a prolific author. His books include *Congressional Government: A Study in American Politics* (Boston: Houghton Mifflin, 1885); *The State: Elements of Historical and Practical Politics; A Sketch of Institutional History and Administration* (Boston: D.C. Heath, 1889); *Division and Reunion, 1829–1889* (New York: Longmans, Green, 1893); *A History of the American People*, 5 vols. (New York: Harper, 1902); and *Constitutional Government in the United States* (New York: Columbia University Press, 1908). Among his many articles are "Cabinet Government in the United States," *International Review* 7 (August 1879): 146–163, and "The Study of Administration," *Political Science Quarterly* 2 (July 1887): 197–222.

Primary sources for Wilson's governorship of New Jersey are limited, but David W. Hirst, *Woodrow Wilson, Reform Governor: A Documentary Narrative* (Princeton: Van Nostrand, 1965) provides a collection of relevant documents linked by thoughtful editorial comments.

See the sources discussed in the bibliographic essay following the Introduction for additional information.

Document 1.1   An Imaginary Order

As a child, Wilson often dreamed he was a British admiral or general. He was sixteen in 1873 when he drafted this imaginary order. It opens a window into the elaborate fantasy life of his youth.

(To the officers & men of) Her Majesty's Royal Rifle Brigade, Stationed at York, Yorkshire Co., England. To Colonel James Atwood.

You are hereby commanded to be at these headquarters with your whole brigade, 1,000 men, on the 10th of September next, with tents and campaigning outfit.

(Signed) Thomas W. Wilson, Lieutenant-General, Duke of Eagleton, Commander-in-cheif [sic] Royal Lance Guards & Royal Rifle Brigade.

Source: Arthur S. Link and others, eds., *The Papers of Woodrow Wilson, 1856–1880* (Princeton: Princeton University Press, 1966), 1:25.

Document 1.2   Letter from Joseph Ruggles Wilson to Wilson, March 27, 1877

Some biographers have seen the relationship between Wilson and his father as loving; others regard it as strained and competitive. This letter is characteristic of their surviving correspondence.

Your letters always give me great pleasure. The style in which they are written has been much improved within a year or less. The intelligence they convey is uniformily [sic] gratifying. And, all things considered, they are as long as necessity demands: although I often wish they were longer. Your cheerfulness is most gratifying to us all. There is no better gift than this, and none more deserving of cultivation. One of the principal uses of our wonderfully humane religion is to promote buoyancy of disposition, by freeing the soul from that which is alone worthy of the name, *Burden:* the sense of sin. I trust that your good spirits, darling boy, are due in great part to an easy conscience—to the smile of God. I am sure that you will rate at its true value the estimation into which you are rapidly growing among your fellow-students. Your dear mother and I rejoice in the evidences which go to show that your manly character and your superior talents are appreciated. But be not "puffed up." Let the esteem you have won be only as a stimulant to fresh exertion—regard it not as a final crown but only as an encouragement toward royalty in goodness and learning. You have so far justified our expectations—but not more than justified them—for we knew what you could do. And we as well know that what you have achieved is nothing to what you can accomplish. Modest energy spurred by Christian principle may properly lay claim to every rightful honor. . . .

Source: Arthur S. Link and others, eds., *The Papers of Woodrow Wilson, 1856–1880* (Princeton: Princeton University Press, 1966), 1:254–255.

Document 1.3   Wilson on Religion

In this brief excerpt from a speech at the seventieth anniversary of the founding of the Pittsburgh YMCA on October 24, 1914, Wilson declared his conviction that religion is less about personal salvation than service to others.

. . . I wonder if we attach sufficient importance to Christianity as a mere instrumentality in the life of mankind. For one, I am not fond of thinking of Christianity as the means of saving individual souls. I have always been very impatient of processes and institutions which said that their purpose was to put every man in the way of developing his character. My advice is: Don't think about your character. If you will think about what you ought to do for other people, your character will take care of itself. Character is a by-product, and any man who devotes himself to its cultivation in his own case will become a selfish prig. The only way your powers can become great is by exerting them outside the circle of your own narrow, special, selfish interests. And that is the lesson of Christianity. Christ came into the world to save others, not to save himself; and no man is a true Christian who does not think constantly of how he can lift his brother, how he can assist his friend, how he can enlighten mankind, how he can make virtue the rule of conduct in the circle in which he lives. . . .

Source: Arthur S. Link and others, eds., *The Papers of Woodrow Wilson, September 6–December 31, 1914* (Princeton: Princeton University Press, 1979), 31:221.

Document 1.4   Letter from Jesse Wilson to Wilson, May 20, 1874
Shortly before this letter was written, Wilson's father, Joseph Ruggles Wilson, had resigned his position at the Columbia Theological Seminary and accepted a call from the First Presbyterian Church in Wilmington, N.C. Evidently Wilson, who had found it difficult being away from home at Davidson College during 1873–1874, was anxious about the family's move. This letter reveals the close bond between mother and son.

My darling Boy,   Columbia, S. C., May 20th 1874

I am so anxious about that cold of yours. How did you take it? Surely you have not laid aside your winter-clothing? Another danger is in sitting without fire these cool nights. Do be careful, my dear boy, for my sake. You seem depressed—but that is because you are not well. You need not imagine that you are not a favorite. Everybody here likes and admires you. I could not begin to tell you the kind and flattering things that are said about you, by everybody that knows you. Yes, you will have no lack of friends in Wilmington—of the warmest sort. There seem to be an unusual number of young people about your age there—and of a superior kind— and they are prepared to take an unusual interest in you particularly. Why my darling, nobody could *help* loving you, if they were to try!

Source: Arthur S. Link and others, eds., *The Papers of Woodrow Wilson, 1856–1880* (Princeton: Princeton University Press, 1966), 1:50.

Document 1.5   Life at Princeton
Wilson kept a shorthand diary during his freshman year at Princeton. This excerpt provides a vignette of his daily life.

[June] 10th Saturday. Read a little oratory this morning analyzing some sentences containing figures of different sorts. Very interesting work. Played the Lit boys at noon five innings and beat them by a score of 8 to 7. We would have beaten them much worse if we had all our players—we had two men with us that did play on the nine and that were not as good as the regular men. I pitched. Tried to read this afternoon but owing to the hot weather was too sleepy to do much of it. . . .

Spent most of the evening in reading Macaulay's History of England 13th chapter and have consequently been most highly entertained. No modern writer can compare with Macaulay as a historian in my opinion. I read very slowly but enjoy immensely as I go along. I sometimes wish that I could read a little faster but I do not know that it would be an advantage. . . .

Macaulay had such a clear conception of everything that he describes in his History and such mastery of language in which he expressed his thoughts that he presents all the events of history before one's eyes in the most vivid and yet concise way. . . .

Source: Arthur S. Link and others, eds., *The Papers of Woodrow Wilson, 1856–1880* (Princeton: Princeton University Press, 1966), 1:137.

Document 1.6   Excerpt, "Cabinet Government in the United States," 1879

As a college student Wilson lost faith in American politics and proposed replacing the American presidential system with a parliamentary system modeled on that of his ideal, Britain. This excerpt is from Wilson's first published article, "Cabinet Government in the United States," which appeared in the International Review *in August 1879.*

. . . We are thus again brought into the presence of the cardinal fact of this discussion,—that *debate* is the essential function of a popular representative body. In the severe, distinct, and sharp enunciation of underlying principles, the unsparing examination and telling criticism of opposite positions, the careful, painstaking unravelling of all the issues involved, which are incident to the free discussion of questions of public policy, we see the best, the only effective, means of educating public opinion. . . .

There is no one in Congress to speak for the nation. Congress is a conglomeration of inharmonious elements; a collection of men representing each his neighborhood, each his local interest; an alarmingly large proportion of its legislation is "special"; all of it is at best only a limping compromise between the conflicting interests of the innumerable localities represented. There is no guiding or harmonizing power. Are the people in favor of a particular policy, what means have they of forcing it upon the sovereign legislature at Washington? None but the most imperfect. If they return representatives who favor it (and this is the most they can do) these represen-

tatives being under no directing power will find a mutual agreement impracticable among so many, and will finally settle upon some policy which sat-
isfies nobody, removes no difficulty, and makes little definite or valuable provision for the future. They must, indeed, be content with whatever measure
the appropriate committee chances to introduce. Responsible ministries, on
the other hand, form the policy of their parties; the strength of their party
is at their command; the course of legislation turns upon the acceptance
or rejection by the houses of definite and consistent plans upon which they
determine. In forming its judgment of their policy, the nation knows
whereof it is judging and, with biennial Congresses, it may soon decide
whether any given policy shall stand or fall. The question would then no
longer be, What representatives shall we choose to represent our chances in
this haphazard game of legislation? But, What plans of national administration shall we sanction? Would not party programmes mean something
then? Could they be constructed only to deceive and bewilder?

But, above and beyond all this, a responsible Cabinet constitutes a link
between the executive and legislative departments of the Government
which experience declares in the clearest tones to be absolutely necessary
in a well-regulated, well-proportioned body politic. None can so well judge
of the perfections or imperfections of a law as those who have to administer it. Look, for example, at the important matter of taxation. The only
legitimate object of taxation is the support of Government; and who can
so well determine the requisite revenue as those who conduct the Government? Who can so well choose feasible means of taxation, available
sources of revenue, as those who have to meet the practical difficulties of
tax-collection? And what surer guarantee against exorbitant estimates and
unwise taxation, than the necessity of full explanation and defence before
the whole House? The same principles, of course, apply to all legislation
upon matters connected with any of the Executive departments. . . .

Source: Arthur S. Link and others, eds., *The Papers of Woodrow Wilson, 1856–1880*
(Princeton: Princeton University Press, 1966), 1:500–503.

Document 1.7   Critique of Congress, 1881

*In this circa May 1, 1881, essay, Wilson laid out his objections to the way Con-
gress then worked and proposed replacing the American system with a parliamentary system modeled on that of Britain. Four years later he would write*

an extended critique of Congress in his first book, Congressional Government: A Study in American Politics.

. . . No one can understand the workings of Congress who does not comprehend the functions of its Standing Committees. . . .

The language of the Constitution did all that language could to prevent any one of the departments from gaining supremacy over the others, but facts were more absolute than constitutional provisions. Holding as it did all the substantial powers of government, the Congress was in reality the regnant department. No practicable distribution of authority between the several branches could have prevented the law-making body from dominating. The Legislature soon realized its own supremacy and soon provided means for exercising effective control over the administration of national affairs. Adopting the usual division of executive departments, the House set in authority over the Treasury a standing Committee of Ways and Means and a standing Committee on Appropriations; over the department of State a similar Committee on Foreign Affairs; over the Interior department like Committees on Indian Affairs, on Commerce, and on Patents; over the War Office and the Navy bureau a Military and a Naval Committee respectively; over the Post Office, a Committee on Post Offices and Post Routes; and over the department of Justice a Committee on the Judiciary. In the Senate a similar distribution of labor was made. . . .

Legislation originates in the Committee rooms. There all the deliberating that means anything is done. The speeches made on the floor of the House are addressed to constituencies. Indeed, if not intended for the ears of constituents, they might as well not be spoken: they are never heard amidst the disorderly noises which assail the ears of all who enter the vast Hall of the House. . . .

This plan of legislating by means of committees, though its results are not always the best, and though it does not always operate equitably, is a very natural arrangement, and one which is apparently demanded by the necessities of the case. . . . Either the House must consent to remain in all the helplessness of a mass-meeting, or it must have these Committees, or it must put itself under the guidance of a Cabinet, as the British Parliament has done, make that Cabinet its standing executive committee and grant it the prerogative of initiative in legislation. The first of course no sane men could think of doing; to do the last would be to violate that sacred theory of Montesquieu's, as it was understood on this side of the sea, by uniting the legislative and executive departments in the persons of the Cabinet ministers. These Secretaries would both lead the House and rule the executive—would rule the executive because they led the House. So the Committees must be chosen.

True the Committee scheme was not a perfect one. The Speaker of the House must appoint the committees, and thus, instead of being simply the presiding officer chosen because of his impartiality and his knowledge of parliamentary law, must be a party leader selected because of his partiality and knowledge of party management. Then, too, these committees must deliberate away from the eye of the public, in the unapproachable privacy of separate rooms, and the door must thus be left open for corruption to steal in upon committee-men. . . .

This thing of Congress delegating its deliberative duties to Committees of its members does seem to defeat some of the most important purposes of its Constitution—seems, for instance, to preclude such exhaustive public debate of its measures as is necessary to the enlightenment of the country and to the incorrupt and deliberate performance of its principal functions—but what better arrangement could be made? Were it not for that theory concerning the separation of the departments, the officers of the Cabinet might be introduced to fulfil [*sic*] the essential offices of the Standing Committees in directing legislation. They would constitute an executive committee of the Houses and a connecting link between the Legislature and the Executive such as would greatly facilitate the operations of government. They could never force Congress beyond its wishes, and they would always be able to acquaint it with the needs of the departments. They would be in a position intelligently to direct legislation without having the power to misdirect it. They would have every means of information without any means of undue concealment. They would have it at heart to protect the Executive against encroachments and would be equally interested in preserving the prerogatives of the Legislature. Instead of being witnesses to inform committees, they would be witnesses to inform and counsellors [sic] to guide Congress. Frauds could no longer hide in the records of the departments and corruption could no longer tempt. Who would be worth corrupting except these Secretaries who would daily have to account for themselves and their policy in the trying hours of keen, eager, and searching, public debate? . . .

Source: Arthur S. Link and others, eds., *The Papers of Woodrow Wilson, 1881–1884* (Princeton: Princeton University Press, 1967), 2:55–60.

Document 1.8   Two of Wilsons' Views on His Career

In this April 14, 1883 letter of application to the graduate program in history and political science at the Johns Hopkins University in Baltimore, Wilson accurately describes his intellectual interests but understates his ambition, which is more accurately depicted in an October 30, 1883, letter to Ellen Axson, printed as the second document here.

. . . My record since my graduation from Princeton in 1879 has of course been a very brief one. Much of the time which has elapsed since that date I have devoted to the study of the law, though I have always found time to continue with more or less thoroughness my reading of English history and to pursue what has, ever since the first years of my college course, been my favorite exercise, the study of political science. Not having had the advantage of access to any complete or considerable library my reading in these branches has been necessarily confined to such books as are in my own very limited collection; but of some topics I have been able to obtain a very tolerable knowledge. Following inclination rather than any definite system, I have acquired a thorough knowledge of the English constitution, for instance; and I have gathered from such sources as were accessible a tolerably complete acquaintance with the constitutional history of the United States, as well as with the present actual operation of the federal system. My study of constitutional history, especially of the constitutional history of England, has of course been greatly facilitated by my contemporaneous study of the law, a study to which I was introduced by the distinguished Professor John B. Minor of the University of Virginia and which I pursued for a year and some months under his admirable guidance.

My object in seeking appointment to a fellowship is to prepare myself for a professorship. Even my own limited observation has shown me that the study of history, of political economy, and of political science is sadly neglected in the colleges of the South, and it is a knowledge of this fact and of the new importance which has now come to be attached to these branches,—coupled with a conviction that I can accomplish the most useful results by entering a profession which is entirely in keeping with my most pronounced tastes and by continuing investigations which are unmistakably in the direction of my natural bent, which prompt this application. I have been enough of a student of these branches to have clearly ascertained my decided predilection for them, and I can, therefore, without presumption claim to possess that unfaltering fondness for this special department of study and that serious ambition to devote my best energies to perfecting myself in it which are declared by your regulations to be the chief qualifications required of candidates for fellowships. . . .

. . . I left college on the wrong tack. I had then, as I have still, a very earnest political creed and very pronounced political ambitions. . . . The profession I chose was politics; the profession I entered was the law. I entered the one because I thought it would lead to the other. It was once the sure road; and Congress is still full of lawyers. But this is the time of leisured classes—or, at least, that time is very near at hand—and the time of crowded professions. . . .

A man who has to earn a livlihood [*sic*] cannot nowadays turn aside from his trade for intervals of office-holding and political activity. . . . The law is more than ever before a jealous mistress. Whoever thinks, as I thought, that he can practice law successfully and study history and politics at the same time is wofully [*sic*] mistaken. If he is to make a living at the bar he must be a lawyer *and nothing else*. . . .

A professorship was the only feasible place for me, the only place that would afford leisure for reading and for original work, the only strictly literary berth with an income attached. . . . Indeed I knew very well that a man without independent fortune must in any event content himself with becoming an outside force in politics, and I was well enough satisfied with the prospect of having whatever influence I might be able to exercise make itself felt through literary and non-partisan agencies: for my predilections, ever since I had any that were definite have always turned very strongly towards a literary life, not-withstanding my decided taste for oratory, which is supposed to be the peculiar province of public men. . . .

Source: Arthur S. Link and others, eds., *The Papers of Woodrow Wilson, 1881–1884* (Princeton University Press, 1967), 2:338–339, 499–502.

Document 1.9   Letter from Wilson to Ellen Axson, September 18, 1883

Ellen Axson and Woodrow Wilson met in Rome, Georgia, in April 1883. Their relations remained formal until, during a chance meeting in Asheville, North Carolina, on September 14, 1883, he impetuously confessed his love for her and she agreed to marry him. This letter to her, the first after their engagement, marks the beginning of a thirty-one-year love affair that was only cut short by her death in August 1914.

My own darling,

. . . I wonder if you are longing for me as I am longing for you? Why, my darling, I can't tell you how completely I am yours in my every thought. I did not know myself how much I loved you until I found out that you love me; and I did not realize how happy I had been made by that sweet discovery until I was fairly away from you and on my journey. That scene at the hotel—the formal, embarrassed, almost stiff, declaration in the public hall-way, the sweet hesitating acceptance, the constraint of surroundings, and the hateful publicity—the whole scene forms a very curious memory, as well as a very dear one, dos'nt [*sic*] it? Were ever the advances of a lover met as mine were-by sweet, self-sacrificial doubt, by persuasions of his lady-love that maybe she was not worthy of him and could not make him happy? If you could know my heart as I know it, you would have very few doubts and fears as to the future, my pet. No love like mine can be a mistaken love, when it is returned by love like yours; and I am sure you would be supremely content if I could find language in which to tell you how happy I am. Before I left you on Sabbath [Sept. 16] I did not realize what had happened. But what could be sweeter that [*sic*] my feelings when I was alone in the driving, noisy train, and had time to think? Why I thought that my heart would grow too big for its tenement. The deep sense of joy and peace that came over me was like the stealing delight of soft distant music—no it was'nt [*sic*]. It was not like anything but itself, not like anything I ever imagined—But, why should I go on so? All that I can say is summed up in the simple truth that I love you with all my heart. Do you know that you did not say that you love me—did not say it in so many words? And now I am longing to hear you say those words.

I can't help smiling at your idea that you are homely. My humble opinion is that yours is the sweetest face in the world, and everybody that has ever seen you agrees in thinking it lovely both in form and in expression. I can't allow you to entertain that extremely original idea of yours any longer, but must ask you to come into the orthodox creed. You are not of that respectable class of plain women with whom we are all called upon to sympathize. . . .

Source: Arthur S. Link and others, eds., *The Papers of Woodrow Wilson, 1881–1884* (Princeton: Princeton University Press, 1967), 2:427–428.

Document 1.10   Letter from Wilson to Daniel Collamore Heath, March 30, 1886

In this letter to the publisher, Daniel Collamore Heath, Wilson outlined his ideas for a textbook on comparative government for high school students. Although by the time The State *was published in 1889, it was aimed at a more mature audience, Wilson's comparative approach was original. As the first textbook of its kind,* The State *was used for a generation by students all over the world.*

. . . My plan will be to tell the story of government first and let the lessons in duty follow as natural, inevitable conclusions. I shall expend the very best efforts of my reason and my imagination in striving to show how the government we have was born and brought up, what its family connections were and are, what its experiences have been—everything that promises to arrest the boy['']s attention. I shall seek every illustration possible from the things that come within a boy's own life, and shall depend on my success in getting him thoroughly interested in the thing, government, for my later success in arousing his interest in the idea, government.

To come down to concrete particulars, these are the topics with which I shall begin:

The system of govt. under which we live—a rapid, but vivid, outline of its character.

It took a long history to build up this structure: what was the character of that history, and how has it made our character and our politics different from those of other peoples?

The Germans and their institutions as seen by Caesar and Tacitus, as telling what we might have been had we been born soon enough!—what the Romans thought of the German institutions, and the success of the Germans against the Romans. How some boys in a school in Maryland developed institutions just like those of the Germans.

How the political life of these men, our ancestors, changed in Gaul and Britain.

The sort of Govt. that England came at length to have.

The sort she had when our forefathers came to this country, and the sort they wanted to establish in the New World.

The establishment and growth of the colonies—the towns in New England, the broad counties in Va., etc. . . .

Source: Arthur S. Link and others, eds., *The Papers of Woodrow Wilson, 1885–1888* (Princeton: Princeton University Press, 1968), 5:150.

Document 1.11   Excerpt, "The Study of Administration," 1887

Wilson's article, "The Study of Administration," from which this excerpt is taken, was published in the Political Science Quarterly *in July 1887. In the article, which initiated the academic study of administration in America, he urged the study of foreign administrative practices in order to make American governments more efficient.*

. . . The science of administration is the latest fruit of that study of the science of politics which was begun some twenty-two hundred years ago. It is a birth of our own century, almost of our own generation. . . .

[A]t the same time that the functions of government are every day becoming more complex and difficult, they are also vastly multiplying in number. Administration is everywhere putting its hands to new undertakings. . . . [E]ven if our government is not to follow the lead of the governments of Europe in buying or building both telegraph and railroad lines, no one can doubt that in some way it must make itself master of masterful corporations. . . . Such things must be studied in order to be well done. . . . Seeing every day new things which the state ought to do, the next thing is to see clearly how it ought to do them. . . .

When we study the administrative systems of France and Germany, knowing that we are not in search of political principles, we need not care a peppercorn for the constitutional or political reasons which Frenchmen or Germans give for their practices when explaining them to us. If I see a murderous fellow sharpening a knife cleverly, I can borrow his way of sharpening the knife without borrowing his probable intention to commit murder with it; and so, if I see a monarchist dyed in the wool managing a public bureau well, I can learn his business methods without changing one of my republican spots. He may serve his king; I will continue to serve the people; but I should like to serve my sovereign as well as he serves his. . . .

Source: Arthur S. Link and others, eds., *The Papers of Woodrow Wilson, 1885–1888* (Princeton: Princeton University Press, 1968), 5:360, 362–363, 379.

Document 1.12   Excerpt, "Democracy"

Wilson's lecture, "Democracy," from which the following passage is taken, was given repeatedly during the 1890s. It outlines his conception of leadership in a democracy.

. . . What we really mean when we say that the people govern is that they freely consent to be governed, on condition that *a certain part* of them *do* the governing,—that part which shall, by one process or another, be selected out of the mass and elevated to places of rule:—and *that is the best democratic government* in which the processes of this selection are best: where *self-*selection for leadership and influence is most encouraged: virtue provoked to exhibit itself and excite emulation; strength and originality heartened to display themselves and compete for the best prizes; knowledge invited to speak and approve itself useful: where the texts of patriotism read after the manner of that noble sentence of Milton's: "I cannot praise a fugitive and cloistered virtue, unexercised and unbreathed, that never sallies out and seeks her adversary, but slinks out of the race, where that immortal garland is to be run for not without dust and heat." A self-instructed, self-mastered, self-elevated man, *like Lincoln,* is no more a man of the people than Washington was. He has *come out* from the people; has separated himself from the indistinguishable mass of unknown men by reason of excellency and knowledge; has *raised himself above* the common level of others and constituted himself a master-spirit among men, holding credentials of rulership which they can never show unless they *likewise strive* as he strove.

That this is a much higher conception, and a much nobler, than the other, I need not claim. The people do indeed govern. They govern just in proportion as they produce the stuff out of which governors and kings are made; just so far as they show the discrimination to choose such when they are made manifest. The advantage of democracy over aristocracy and monarchy is not an advantage of structure, of nice adjustments of balance and successful regulations of force: in these points aristocracies and monarchies have often proved superior to democracy. *They* have a quickness and certainty of resolution and movement which democracy can hardly hope to acquire. Democracy's advantage, rather, is its variety and symmetry of development, its fulness of opportunity and richness of material. In it, not a few men of privileged blood only, but all men of original force are quickened to make the most of themselves. . . .

Source: Arthur S. Link and others, eds., *The Papers of Woodrow Wilson, 1890–1892* (Princeton: Princeton University Press, 1969), 7:357.

Document 1.13   Memorandum, "What Ought We To Do?" circa August 1, 1898

In this unpublished memorandum, Wilson declared his belief in the purity of American motives in the Spanish-American War and applauded the new world role thrust on the United States by the war's outcome.

. . . We did not enter upon a war of conquest. We had neither dreamed of nor desired victories at the ends of the earth and the spoils of war had not entered in our calculations. It was for us a war begun without calculations, upon an impulse of humane indignation and pity,—because we saw at our very doors a government unmindful of justice or of mercy, contemptuous in its every practice of the principles we professed to live for, oppressive and yet not efficient or fit to rule, spoiling men and thwarting the very bounties of nature in fair islands which it had pillaged and not used. Its character seemed of a sudden revealed to us, by an act of assassination. . . .

It may be that we were a trifle too hasty in some of the things that followed. No doubt it would have been handsomer to hold to a somewhat more deliberate pace in negotiation; as if we really expected it to change the whole course of affairs; and certainly it would have been more prudent to muster, drill, and equip an army before plunging into war. But very likely history will judge us leniently in these details, if it find us sincere in purpose and just in the motives that led us to take up arms. . . . [Spain] cannot have been surprised by what followed; and even our manners in the business were as good as need be when rough work is to be done.

Whatever our judgments or scruples in these matters, the thing is done; cannot be undone; and our future must spring out of it. The processes of our modem life are swift: we cannot stay them by regrets. Only those nations shall approve themselves masterful and fit to act either for themselves or others in such a time which show themselves capable of thinking on the run and amidst the whirl of events. If a nation have the habit of thought, that habit will tell then, and show itself a sort of instinct of steadiness and wisdom. It is for such moments a nation gets itself in training while peace holds and the elements of its life are at rest. . . . The scenes, the stage itself upon which we act, are changed. We have left the continent which has hitherto been our only field of action and have gone out upon the seas, where the nations are rivals and we cannot live or act apart. . . .

Source: Arthur S. Link and others, eds., *The Papers of Woodrow Wilson, 1896–1898* (Princeton: Princeton University Press, 1971), 10:574–575.

Document 1.14   Excerpt, *Constitutional Government in the United States*, 1908

By 1908, when Constitutional Government in the United States *was published, Wilson had become less convinced that a parliamentary form of government would be best for the United States. He argued in this series of lectures that the president could be an effective leader within the American system.*

. . . What is it that a nominating convention wants in the man it is to present to the country for its suffrages? A man who will be and who will seem to the country in some sort an embodiment of the character and purpose it wishes its government to have, — a man who understands his own day and the needs of the country, and who has the personality and the initiative to enforce his views both upon the people and upon Congress. . . . What the country will demand of the candidate will be, not that he be an astute politician, skilled and practised in affairs, but that he be a man such as it can trust, in character, in intention, in knowledge of its needs, in perception of the best means by which those needs may be met, in capacity to prevail by reason of his own weight and integrity. Sometimes the country believes in a party, but more often it believes in a man; and conventions have often shown the instinct to perceive which it is that the country needs in a particular presidential year, a mere representative partisan, a military hero, or some one who will genuinely speak for the country itself, whatever be his training and antecedents. It is in this sense that the President has the role of party leader thrust upon him by the very method by which he is chosen.

As legal executive, his constitutional aspect, the President cannot be thought of alone. He cannot execute laws. Their actual daily execution must be taken care of by the several executive departments and by the now innumerable body of federal officials throughout the country. In respect of the strictly executive duties of his office the President may be said to administer the presidency in conjunction with the members of his cabinet, like the chairman of a commission. He is even of necessity much less active in the actual carrying out of the law than are his colleagues and advisers. It is therefore becoming more and more true, as the business of the government becomes more and more complex and extended, that the President is becoming more and more a political and less and less an executive officer. His executive powers are in commission, while his political powers more and more centre and accumulate upon him and are in their very nature personal and inalienable.

Only the larger sort of executive questions are brought to him. Departments which run with easy routine and whose transactions bring few questions of general policy to the surface may proceed with their business for months and even years together without demanding his attention; and no department is in any sense under his direct charge. Cabinet meetings do not discuss detail: they are concerned only with the larger matters of policy or expediency which important business is constantly disclosing. There are no more hours in the President's day than in another man's. If he is indeed the executive, he must act almost entirely by delegation, and is in the hands of his colleagues. He is likely to be praised if things go well, and blamed if they go wrong; but his only real control is of the persons to whom he deputes the performance of executive duties. . . .

He cannot escape being the leader of his party except by incapacity and lack of personal force, because he is at once the choice of the party and of the nation. He is the party nominee, and the only party nominee for whom the whole nation votes. Members of the House and Senate are representatives of localities, are voted for only by sections of voters, or by local bodies of electors like the members of the state legislatures. There is no national party choice except that of President. . . .

[H]e is also the political leader of the nation, or has it in his choice to be. The nation as a whole has chosen him, and is conscious that it has no other political spokesman. His is the only national voice in affairs. Let him once win the admiration and confidence of the country, and no other single force can withstand him, no combination of forces will easily overpower him. His position takes the imagination of the country. He is the representative of no constituency, but of the whole people. When he speaks in his true character, he speaks for no special interest. If he rightly interpret the national thought and boldly insist upon it, he is irresistible; and the country never feels the zest of action so much as when its President is of such insight and calibre. Its instinct is for unified action, and it craves a single leader. It is for this reason that it will often prefer to choose a man rather than a party. A President whom it trusts can not only lead it, but form it to his own views. . . .

The political powers of the President are not quite so obvious in their scope and character when we consider his relations with Congress as when we consider his relations to his party and to the nation. . . . Leadership in government naturally belongs to its executive officers, who are daily in contact with practical conditions and exigencies and whose reputations alike for good judgment and for fidelity are at stake much more than are those of the members of the legislative body at every turn of the law's application. The law-making part of the government ought certainly to be very hospitable to the suggestions of the planning and acting part of it. Those Presidents who have felt themselves bound to adhere to the strict literary theory of the Constitution have scrupulously refrained from attempting to determine either the subjects or the character of legislation, except so far as they were obliged to decide for themselves, after Congress had acted, whether they should acquiesce in it or not. And yet the Constitution explicitly authorizes the President to recommend to Congress "such measures as he shall deem necessary and expedient," and it is not necessary to the integrity of even the literary theory of the Constitution to insist that such recommendations should be merely perfunctory. . . . The Constitution bids him speak, and times of stress and change must more and more thrust upon him the attitude of originator of policies.

His is the vital place of action in the system, whether he accept it as such or not, and the office is the measure of the man,—of his wisdom as well as of his force. His veto abundantly equips him to stay the hand of Congress when he will. It is seldom possible to pass a measure over his veto, and no President has hesitated to use the veto when his own judgment of the public good was seriously at issue with that of the houses. . . .

One of the greatest of the President's powers I have not yet spoken of at all: his control, which is very absolute, of the foreign relations of the nation. The initiative in foreign affairs, which the President possesses without any restriction whatever, is virtually the power to control them absolutely. The President cannot conclude a treaty with a foreign power without the consent of the Senate, but he may guide every step of diplomacy, and to guide diplomacy is to determine what treaties must be made, if the faith and prestige of the government are to be maintained. He need disclose no step of negotiation until it is complete, and when in any critical matter it is completed the government is virtually committed. Whatever its disinclination, the Senate may feel itself committed also. . . .

The President can never again be the mere domestic figure he has been throughout so large a part of our history. The nation has risen to the first rank in power and resources. The other nations of the world look askance upon her, half in envy, half in fear, and wonder with a deep anxiety what she will do with her vast strength. . . .

Source: Woodrow Wilson, *Constitutional Government in the United States* (New York: Columbia University Press, 1908), 65, 67–68, 72–73, 76–79.

Document 1.15   Report to the Princeton Board of Trustees, October 21, 1902

Elected to the presidency of Princeton in June 1902, Wilson delivered his first major report to the Board of Trustees in October. In it he proposed to restructure the curriculum, radically change teaching methods, hire a number of young faculty members to teach by tutorial methods, and build a number of new buildings, including a graduate college. The breathtaking bill for all of this would be more than $12 million.

I feel that the most serviceable way in which I can begin my administration is to render to you a somewhat detailed account of the position and needs of the University.

It is only candid to say that its position is, in many respects, critical, and that its needs are great and numerous; but it is reassuring to know that the critical situation has arisen, not out of any essential unsoundness or out of any demoralization that has touched the spirit of the place, but only out of its imperfect development and its insufficient resources. I never knew a body of men who, taken as a whole, were more worthy of trust and confidence than the Faculty of this University. They have the real spirit of devotion and of unselfish service; they are seriously and intelligently interested in the welfare and improvement of the University; and they are ready to advance its interests in any way that may afford them a hope of realizing their ideals. It is no small part of our strength that they hold for the most part the same ideals and seem one and all to have taken on the wholesome spirit of the place. The institution is in all its personnel and action sound and vigorous. . . .

I believe that some part of the strain of routine work we are now under can be removed by a thorough-going readjustment. The University has had a remarkable growth in the last thirty years, but it has been a growth which has resulted, I dare say, from the necessity of the case, in a miscellaneous enlargement rather than in a systematic develop[m]ent. It has consisted in a multiplication of courses which have in large part remained uncoordinated. The order of studies, their sequence, their relation to one another, their grouping, their respective values: all these things need immediate reconsideration. The Faculty is inclined to take these questions up with zeal and in the best spirit, and I believe that before the end of the year we shall have thrown the whole schedule of studies into the new and better scheme. . . .

But what we need more than mere reorganization is in many things a radical change of method. The method of the drill subjects which can be taught by the recitation of small groups of men in a class-room is sufficiently ascertained and fixed; and the laboratories need little reconsideration of method. Give them but apparatus and space enough and they are made efficient. But there are whole groups of subjects in which our methods of instruction need to be fundamentally altered, and these are the subjects which the majority of men in the upper years of study pursue: philosophy, the great modern literatures, history, politics, jurisprudence, economics,—the studies which, outside the field of the sciences, contain the thought of the modern world. We have tried to teach these by lectures and have failed. They are essentially reading subjects. They cannot be learned from the mouth of any one man or out of the pages of any one book. Their students must be reading and thinking men.

Lectures in such subjects are useful,—useful in proportion as the lecturer is stimulating or able to impart by example the zest and the method of exact enquiry. Lectures in such subjects, it seems to me, ought to be of two kinds, and of two kinds only: those which exhibit the whole broad field of the subject and draw the student to all its outlooks and lines of suggestion, putting him under the stimulation of seeing all its broad significance and of realizing all the interesting questions which lie involved in it, and those which illustrate for the student the exact, intensive way in which a scholar should thoroughly canvass some one question or phase of a subject and illustrate the intimate methods of research. For the rest, university men should be made to get up subjects, not lectures, for examination,—and get them up for themselves. The examinations should not be on the contents of a course of lectures or on any single discussion of a subject, but on the subject itself as a whole, as it may be got up out of a library of books. If our Juniors and Seniors idle their time away and get little or no stimulation and culture out of the closing years of their course, it is because there is nothing for them to do but to listen to lectures. They read only if they please. The evil will be remedied only when they are made to read and cover great subjects by their own efforts, under the stimulation of lectures.

The way to do this is to make use, in a modified form, of the English tutorial system. Under that system men are examined, not on particular courses of lectures (they may attend the lectures of distinguished lecturers or not, as they please) nor on particular books, but upon subjects which they are expected to get up for themselves, and upon which they are tested by outside examiners. Tutors superintend and assist their reading, show them the best books in which to get at the subjects assigned, act as their coaches and advisors in their preparation for the general tests which await them. . . .

On the side of university growth our first and most obvious need is a Graduate College. Professor West has made us familiar with the plans for such a college which he has conceived. Those plans seem to me in every way admirable and worthy of adoption. To carry them out would unquestionably give us a place of unique distinction among American universities. He has conceived the idea of a Graduate College of residence: a great quadrangle in which our graduate students should be housed like a household with their own commons and their own rooms of conference, under a master whose residence should stand at a corner of the quadrangle in the midst of them. This is not merely a pleasing fancy of an English college placed in the midst of our campus to ornament it. In conceiving this little community of scholars set up at the heart of Princeton, Professor West has got at the real gist of the matter, the real means by which a group of graduate students are most apt to stimulate and set the pace for the whole University. . . .

I append a table of the estimate cost of these additions, necessary to create a real university in Princeton:

Graduate School,	$3,000,000
School of Jurisprudence,	2,400,000
Electrical School,	750,000
Museum of Natural History,	$6,650,000

This total, added to the total sum needed to make our work sound and honest as it stands, makes a grand total . . . of $12,502,832. . . .

Source: Arthur S. Link and others, eds., *The Papers of Woodrow Wilson, 1902–1903* (Princeton: Princeton University Press, 1972), 14:150, 152–154, 157–160.

Document 1.16   Report to the Princeton Board of Trustees, June 10, 1907

In December 1906 Wilson proposed to the Princeton trustees a plan to require all undergraduates to live in "quadrangles." The proposal, which would have wiped out the university's fraternity-like eating clubs, aroused an angry outburst from alumni but helped to establish Wilson's national reputation as a democratic reformer. In this report to the trustees he explained his reasons for the proposal.

I am very glad indeed to have an opportunity to explain a plan which, though certainly radical in character, can easily be so misunderstood as to seem much more radical than it is. It is a scheme I have long had in mind as a necessary means of giving Princeton not only social but also academic coordination and of making her new methods of study a vital part of her undergraduate life.

The plan in its briefest form is this: to draw the undergraduates together into residential quads. in which they shall eat as well as lodge together, and in which they shall, under the presidency of a resident member of the Faculty, regulate their own corporate life by some simple method of self-government. For this purpose it would be necessary to place all future dormitories in such relation to those already erected as to form close geographical units, and to erect in connection with each group a building which shall contain a dining room, kitchen and serving rooms, a handsome common room for social purposes, and rooms for the member of the Faculty who shall preside in the quad. Every undergraduate would be required actually to live in his quad.—that is, to take his meals there as well as lodge there; and the residents of each quad. would be made up as nearly as might be of equal numbers of Seniors, Juniors, Sophomores, and Freshmen: because it is clear to every one that the life of the University can be best regulated and developed only when the under-classmen are in constant association with upper-classmen upon such terms as to be formed and guided by them. The self-government of each group would naturally be vested in the Seniors, or in the Seniors and Juniors, who were members of the quad.

The objects of this arrangement would be (1) to place unmarried members of the Faculty in residence in the quads. in order to bring them into close, habitual, natural association with the undergraduates and so intimately tie the intellectual and social life of the place into one another; (2) to associate the four classes in a genuinely organic manner and make of the University a real social body, to the exclusion of cliques and separate class social organizations; (3) to give the University the kind of common consciousness which apparently comes from the closer sorts of social contact, to be had only outside the classroom, and most easily to be got about a common table, and in the contacts of a common life.

This plan directly affects the upper-class clubs because, under it, it would be necessary to keep the most influential and efficient Seniors and Juniors in residence in the quads. for their government and direction. It would be clearly out of the question to let them eat elsewhere and find their chief interests elsewhere, leaving the quads. to Freshmen and Sophomores and a minority of upperclassmen who would be too few to play any true part of influence or control. The adoption of the plan would obviously make it necessary that the clubs should allow themselves to be absorbed into the University, by the natural process of becoming themselves residential quads., and by so retaining their historical identity at the same time that they showed their devotion to the University by an act of supreme self-sacrifice. I cannot imagine a service to the University which would bring more distinction, more éclat throughout the entire university world, or which would give to our present clubs a position of greater interest and importance in the history of academic life in America. . . .

Source: Arthur S. Link and others, eds., *The Papers of Woodrow Wilson, 1907–1908* (Princeton: Princeton University Press, 1974), 17:204–205.

Document 1.17   Speech, George Brinton McClellan Harvey, February 3, 1906

In February 1906, in a speech before an invited group of influential men, publisher George Brinton McClellan Harvey suggested that Woodrow Wilson, then president of Princeton University, would make an excellent presidential candidate. He calls Wilson a statesman who can appeal to reformers of the present while retaining the conservative values of the past.

. . . Woodrow Wilson was born in an atmosphere surcharged with true statesmanship. The fates directed his steps in other paths, but the effect of that association with the traditions of his fathers remains. That he is preeminent as a lucid interpreter of history we all know. But he is more than that. One who reads under-standingly the record of his country as set down by him cannot fail to be impressed with the belief that he is by instinct a statesman. The complete grasp of fundamentals, the seemingly unconscious application of primary truths to changing conditions, the breadth of thought and reason manifested on the pages of his books, constitute as clear evidence of sagacity, worthy of the best and noblest of Virginia's traditions, as was that truly eloquent appeal which last year he addressed to his brethren of the South, to rise manfully from the ashes of prejudice and lethargy and come back into their own.

It is that type of man that we shall soon, if indeed we do not already, need in public life. Nobody would think of criticizing the general reformation of the human race now going on by executive decree. But progress in that direction is making so rapidly that the great work itself is sure soon to be accomplished, of course to the complete satisfaction of all concerned.

When that time shall be reached, the country will need at least a short breathing-spell for what the physicians term a period of perfect rest. That day, not now so far distant, will call for a man who combines the activities of the present with the sober influences of the past. If one could be found who should unite in his personality, in addition to these qualities, the instinct of true statesmanship, as the effect of early environment and the no less valuable capacity of practical application as the result of subsequent endeavors in another field, the ideal would be at hand. Such a man it is my firm belief, and I venture earnestly to insist, is to be found in Woodrow Wilson of Virginia and New Jersey.

As one of a considerable number of Democrats who have become tired of voting Republican tickets, it is with a sense almost of rapture that I contemplate even the remotest possibility of casting a ballot for the president of Princeton University to become President of the United States. . . .

Source: Arthur S. Link and others, eds., *The Papers of Woodrow Wilson, 1905–1907* (Princeton: Princeton University Press, 1973), 16:300.

Document 1.18   Letter from Edith Bolling Galt to Annie Bolling, March 23, 1915

In this letter, from Edith Bolling Galt to her sister-in-law, Annie Bolling, the woman who would become Wilson's second wife describes her first evening with the president. This firsthand account differs from several published versions of their meeting.

. . . I am just home from the White House where I spent the evening and dined informally with the President.

He is perfectly charming and one of the easiest and most delightful hosts I have ever known.

You know Miss Bones [Wilson's cousin, who was acting as his hostess in the months after Ellen's death] and I have gotten to be great friends & we walk together 3 or 4 times a week, and last Thursday I had her come to lunch with me. And Dr. Grayson [Cary T. Grayson, Wilson's personal physician] invited himself to come too.

It seems at breakfast a day or so afterwards something was said about it, and the President said Why don't you ask her here sometime say Tuesday, but not to lunch, for I always have to leave, but ask her for dinner when I can spend the evening. They sent the big car for me, & I picked up Dr. Grayson, and there were no other guests, but Col. Brown from Atlanta, who was staying there. I sat by the Pres. right, & Dr. Grayson next to me, and we had the most delightful dinner, right after which we went up in the Oval Room where, before a big wood fire we had coffee and all sorts of interesting conversation. Dr. G. had to go to see Mr. McAdoo, and Col. Brown was going on the 9 ock [*sic*] train so Miss Bones & I had the Pres. to ourselves and he was full of interesting stories and a fund of information, and finally, at Miss B's request, read us three English poems, and as a reader he is unequalled. . . .

Source: Arthur S. Link and others, eds., *The Papers of Woodrow Wilson, January 1–April 16, 1915* (Princeton: Princeton University Press, 1980), 32:423.

President Wilson and his second wife, Edith Bolling Galt Wilson, at his inauguration, 1917.

CHAPTER TWO

Campaigns and Elections

A s a young scholar Woodrow Wilson theorized about turning the United States into a parliamentary democracy. Thirty years later, when he ran for the governorship of New Jersey, he was so innocent about the realities of political life that he planned to pay his campaign expenses out of his pocket change. Yet by 1916 he had become a sophisticated professional who, while juggling complex international crises, within less than a year built a new political coalition to pass an advanced reform program and win himself a solid reelection. Then, even more rapidly than he had climbed to the pinnacle of political success, Wilson slid to the bottom. In 1918, following an ill-advised call by the president for the voters to elect a Democratic majority to Congress, the Republicans regained control of both houses in time to defeat the Treaty of Versailles. A year later, in October 1919, a massive stroke left Wilson an invalid and undermined his political judgment as well as his physical ability to govern. The master politician of 1916 had, less than three years later, become weak and ineffective.

New Jersey Gubernatorial Election of 1910

By 1910 Wilson's plans to restructure student living arrangements at Princeton and to build a new graduate college in the middle of the campus were stalemated, and his prospects as president of the university were shrinking. Accordingly, he was delighted when publisher George Brinton McClellan Harvey approached him with a plan for a political career. Harvey, the conservative publisher of *Harper's Weekly*, deplored the liberalism of William Jennings Bryan and was seeking an attractive conservative to challenge Bryan for control of the Democratic Party. Perhaps, Harvey suggested, it might be possible for Wilson to be elected governor of New Jersey as a stepping stone to the White House.

Wilson entered the gubernatorial race at a time when New Jersey politics were changing. For many years political machines had dominated the state, turning out reliable majorities for corrupt politicians in return for payments from businesses that were awarded lucrative contracts. So loose were New Jersey's business laws that many national companies incorporated there, earning for the state the nickname "mother of trusts." But as the national progressive movement built momentum, reformers chipped away at the power of the machines. In 1890 a little noticed reform measure, the Werts Law, slipped through the legislature. It gradually transferred control over elections from the parties to the state government. As a result, rank-and-file party members became less important in organizing and conducting elections, and the political machines lost touch with their members. In addition, in 1908 the state legislature passed a law that allowed county and local governments to adopt a civil service system, thus reducing the ability of political machines to reward their supporters and cutting the political influence of government workers. As a result of these changes, the intense identification of voters with their parties that had produced large voter turnouts in the late nineteenth century diminished, and the grip of machine politicians weakened. The ability of candidates to reach the public through newspapers and advertising became more important than the influence of the bosses, and because the national political parties could provide the money for such publicity, their power increased.

By 1910 New Jersey's major Democratic bosses—James Smith Jr. of Newark and Robert Davis of Jersey City—were growing desperate as their influence weakened. As the Trenton *True American* newspaper suggested with tongue in cheek, a short-term salvation might be to find "a Democrat of high character" who would attract middle- and upper-class voters but who was politically inexperienced and thus might be controlled by the bosses after the election (quoted in Reynolds 1988, 138). Harvey, a shrewd journalist, understood this situation and saw in it an opportunity to begin pushing Wilson forward as a conservative competitor to William Jennings Bryan in the national Democratic Party.

Harvey won the bosses' support for Wilson, while assuring the potential candidate that the nomination would be delivered with no conditions attached. Wilson responded that under those circumstances he would consider it his "duty" to give it "very serious consideration" (Link and others 1975, 20:147). Later that summer he assured a friend that, because the nomination came "unsought, unanimously, and without pledges to anybody about anything," he felt obliged to accept it (Link and others 1975, 20:577). The bosses, who had assumed he could be manipulated easily, were about to discover that he was less naive than he seemed.

When reports of the plan to nominate Wilson began to leak out during the summer of 1910, reformers who had hoped for an opportunity to clean up the party were outraged. Few of them knew the Princeton president, and those who did were unimpressed by his record at the college. They demanded that he speak out on the issue of reform, but Wilson, on the advice of Harvey, spent most of the summer with his family at Lyme, Connecticut, saying nothing about politics and quietly writing the party platform on which he would run. On September 9, less than a week before the Democratic convention was to meet, Harvey assured him that "all reports are good. There will be only one ballot" (Link and others 1976, 21:88).

As Harvey had predicted, Wilson was nominated on the first ballot. The bosses had paid little attention when Wilson told them privately that he would accept the nomination only if it came without promises or conditions, but they were concerned when he said the same thing in his acceptance speech. Reformers, who had expected nothing, were correspondingly delighted and even more pleased when he went on to affirm in specific terms his support for the reforms promised in the party platform and to assure the delegates that, if elected, he would fight for "reorganization and economy in administration, the equality of taxation and the control of corporations" (see Document 2.1).

Wilson assumed he would be elected as easily as he had been nominated. He promised to speak in each county before the election but remained in seclusion during most of the summer, avoiding reporters and issuing no political statements, even after the Republicans nominated Vivian M. Lewis, a moderate reformer with long experience. Wilson told friends that there was no reason to raise campaign funds. He would pay his expenses out of his own pocket.

Ever the realist, Harvey quickly squelched that idea and began raising money, eventually collecting about $119,000. He also insisted that Wilson expand his campaign schedule. Once convinced of the necessity of an active campaign, Wilson proved a strong candidate, studying the issues carefully and delivering a series of increasingly specific and effective speeches. He also demonstrated an eye for political theater. When his opponent declared that he would be a "constitutional governor," meaning that he would not interfere improperly with the legislature, Wilson shot back that he meant to be an "unconstitutional governor" who would force the legislators to obey the wishes of the people. He was only an "amateur politician," he bragged, and as such he was free—unlike his Republican opponent whom he accused of subservience to reactionary interests—to represent the people's needs vigorously (Link and others 1976, 21:229–231). His statement ignored the way he had gotten the Democratic nomination and unfairly slandered Lewis, but it was good politics.

Even more important was an exchange between Wilson and the best-known Republican reformer in New Jersey, George Lawrence Record. Although he had never held office, Record had been an intellectual power behind every reform effort in the state since the 1890s. Early in October Record invited Wilson to debate the issues. Wilson declined to debate with a private citizen, but against the recommendation of his advisers he agreed to answer in writing any questions Record might propound. On October 17 Record sent a letter containing nineteen specific questions, which he challenged Wilson to answer with a simple "yes" or "no."

A week later Wilson responded. To the astonishment of observers, he committed himself unequivocally to every major reform Record mentioned and even went further to volunteer a denunciation of the bosses who had arranged his nomination (see Document 2.2). Although there was nothing really new in Wilson's letter, his explicit acceptance of positions endorsed by the leading Republican reformer cut the ground out from under his opponent's feet. "Damn Record," said Republican leaders privately, "the campaign's over." Wilson's supporters, who had initially opposed his answering Record, were jubilant (quoted in Hirst 1965, 106).

During the final two weeks of the campaign Wilson shifted into high gear, delivering seventeen speeches. He reiterated his specific promises, but the essence of his appeal to the voters was to trust his leadership. The theory of executive responsibility that he had been evolving for several years could now be put to the test, and he welcomed the opportunity. "Government is personal, gentlemen, the responsibilities of government are personal," he told an audience in Passaic. "You cannot put it on the government of New Jersey that it has not yielded the things you want; you have to put it on the men who have conducted the government of New Jersey" (Link and others 1976, 21:501).

New Jersey voters apparently liked Wilson's willingness to embrace the responsibility of leadership, and on election day they gave him a substantial majority: 233,682 to 184,626. He won 54 percent of the vote and carried fifteen of the state's twenty-one counties. In addition, the Democrats won four of the seven open state senate seats and forty-two of the sixty seats in the assembly. In the recent past, only one other gubernatorial candidate, a Republican, had run equally strongly in this normally Republican state. The bosses, it appeared, had seriously underestimated the naive college professor's political talents.

PRESIDENTIAL ELECTION OF 1912

Wilson's 1912 presidential campaign had its beginnings in a conversation that he had with George Harvey in 1910 when the publisher was urging him to run for governor of New Jersey. The governorship, Wilson told a friend confidentially, was "the mere preliminary of a plan to nominate me in 1912 for the presidency" (Link and others 1975, 20:543). By 1911 the first stage of the plan was successful. Now recognized nationally for his reform record, Wilson emerged as a strong candidate for the 1912 Democratic presidential nomination (for Wilson's governorship, see Chapter 1).

Although Harvey, the original Wilson booster, began to distance himself in 1911 when the governor endorsed progressive reforms, his place was taken by new supporters who were drawn to Wilson because of his southern background. The core of this support was from the Southern Society of New York, particularly William F. McCombs of Arkansas, Walter F. McCorkle of Virginia, and Walter Hines Page, North Carolinian editor of *World's Work* magazine. In February 1911 they were joined by

Vance Criswell McCormick, a Harrisburg, Pennsylvania, publisher and reform leader. At a meeting with Wilson in March members of the group agreed to set up a publicity office in New York, to begin creating a national organization, and to arrange a speaking trip through the West for the potential candidate. They hired Frank Parker Stockbridge, a reporter, to arrange invitations, publicity, and accommodations, and McCombs, McCorkle, and Page personally contributed $3,000 to finance the trip.

Shortly after Wilson left for a mid-March speech in Atlanta, Ellen Wilson learned that William Jennings Bryan was coming to Princeton. Bryan still commanded the loyalty of millions of people in the South and West and could be a powerful ally or enemy for Wilson, so Ellen urged her husband to return at once and meet the Nebraskan. He did so, and the two men sounded each other out over dinner. Bryan was concerned about Wilson's wealthy supporters and somewhat doubtful about the seriousness of his commitment to reform; Wilson had long regarded Bryan as a dangerous radical. As they talked, however, they found they liked each other, and possible differences seemed less important. No commitments had been made, but both men understood that an alliance might be possible. Three weeks later Wilson made the courtship public, declaring in a speech in Newark that "Mr. Bryan has shown that stout heart which in spite of the long years of repeated disappointments has always followed the star of hope, and it is because he has cried America awake that some other men have been able to translate into action the doctrines that he has so diligently preached" (Link and others 1976, 22:536).

Along with his meetings with Bryan, Wilson strengthened his Southern base, speaking to the Southern Commercial Congress at Atlanta and to influential Virginians in Norfolk. Wherever he went, he made political contacts and enjoyed the praise of men who sensed an opportunity for the post–Civil War "New South" to achieve national power. Wilson was concerned that he was more "radical" than these Southern supporters, but he underestimated the strength of the reform movement in the South (Link and others 1976, 22:598). Following the Populist movement of the 1890s a "political convulsion" had swept Southern politics, resulting largely from the rise of a new, urban middle class that regarded traditional social problems as soluble through government action (Link 1947, 316). Gradually, Wilson realized that although suspicion of the federal government still lingered in the region, the South's new leaders shared his belief that national problems required national solutions.

In May 1911 *World's Work* issued a Wilson edition, with the governor's picture on the cover and articles and editorials praising his accomplishments in New Jersey. Other newspapers and magazines also published laudatory articles, and with this free publicity behind him Wilson set out on his first campaign trip to the West. Although these early speeches have been characterized by a biographer as "meaningless, trite, or a mixture of sentimental and religious optimism, unfounded in historical experience" (Link 1947, 326), Wilson nevertheless generated popular excitement and support. He managed to convey enthusiasm for reform without alienating conservatives and thus united the disparate elements of the Democratic Party in a way that Bryan had not been able to do.

Near the end of the trip, Wilson met in Washington with Democratic congressional leaders, complimenting them lavishly on their recent work for tariff reduction and building personal ties that would pay off handsomely later. Meetings with two potential rivals, Speaker of the House James Beauchamp ("Champ") Clark of Missouri and Rep. Oscar W. Underwood of Alabama, were somewhat less successful. Privately, Wilson made it clear that he did not consider either man presidential timber.

From a practical standpoint, Wilson's most important meetings in Washington were with his closest supporters—Page, McCombs, McCorkle, McCormick, Stockbridge, and Joseph Tumulty, a New Jersey attorney who since 1910 had been his private secretary and assistant. They were eager to use the momentum that had been generated by the trip out West to launch a national campaign organization, but Wilson was hesitant. It was important, he argued, for a reform candidate not to create the impression of having a traditional political organization. He preferred to start slowly, letting Stockbridge handle publicity for the time being and otherwise letting "the movement in my favor" seem to "take care of itself" (Link and others 1977, 23:135). On this basis Stockbridge set up a small office in New York City, from which he mailed out copies of speeches, photographs, and other publicity material. Later that summer, William Gibbs McAdoo, a Georgia-born lawyer who had made a fortune leading the project to construct a tunnel under the Hudson River, joined the growing organization. Although he had no official title, McAdoo was vital to Wilson because of his organizational skills and ties to prominent businessmen in New York.

In keeping with his desire for a low-key campaign, Wilson accepted few of the many invitations to speak that he received in the summer of 1911. He did, however, agree to speak to the Pennsylvania Federation of Democratic Clubs at Harrisburg on June 15. Pennsylvania was important not only because it had a large number of delegates to the national party convention, but also because Wilson might tip the balance in a close struggle between progressives and conservatives in the state. In the Harrisburg speech he for the first time put aside platitudes to denounce what he labeled "the money monopoly." "The large money resources of this country," he declared, "are not at the command of those who do not submit to the direction and domination of small groups of capitalists." The big bankers, he charged, forced capital into the projects they controlled in order to "chill and check and destroy genuine economic freedom." It must be the "earnest determination" of the next administration to restore equal access to money for everyone (Link and others 1977, 23:158–159). Although Wilson later worried that he had perhaps been rash in speaking so strongly, the reaction in Pennsylvania and across the country was overwhelmingly favorable. In July both wings of the Pennsylvania party joined to endorse Wilson, giving him his first large bloc of delegates to the Democratic convention.

In Pennsylvania Wilson began to define the issues that would become his "New Freedom" campaign program, and at the same time his supporters worked to create an organization to win him the nomination. In the summer of 1911 McAdoo joined on an informal basis, and in October William McCombs, one of Wilson's former students with a Harvard law degree and a successful New York law practice, was named campaign manager. McCombs seemed particularly well suited to raising the money needed for the campaign, but by December he had brought in only $35,000. Instead, he devoted himself to forging ties with existing Democratic organizations across the country—exactly the approach that Wilson had previously said that he wanted to avoid.

Although McCombs was fiercely loyal, which made Wilson reluctant to fire him, his commitment to working through the regular machinery of the Democratic Party, coupled with his extreme jealousy and insistence on control, led Wilson to look elsewhere for political advice. Gradually, two overlapping and sometimes conflicting organizations emerged: one, dominated by McCombs, worked with regular Democratic political organizations across the country; the other, informally run by McAdoo and a new recruit, Edward M. House of Texas, handled fund raising and policy. The system caused problems but worked because McAdoo and House proved adept at keeping McCombs quiet if not happy.

Wilson first met House on November 24, 1911, at House's apartment in New York. Independently wealthy and in somewhat frail health, House had no interest in office himself but had a reputation for good political advice. House had managed several successful gubernatorial campaigns in his home state in the late 1890s and early 1900s. The first of those, arranged for James S. Hogg in 1892, resulted in House receiving an appointment to Hogg's staff, the honorary title of "colonel," and the role of *eminence gris* in Texas gubernatorial politics. When House moved to New York in 1910 to look for wider political frontiers, he kept his title, reputation, and ambition, but now sought to fulfill his burning desire to make someone president who would bring to fruition the progressive reforms that he spelled out in his anonymously published novel, *Philip Dru, Administrator* (House 1912). Wilson and House liked each other immediately, and House concluded that the reform governor from New Jersey could become his Philip Dru. By early 1912 the Texan had secured a place alongside McAdoo in Wilson's inner circle of advisers.

In the spring of 1912 Wilson's rivals for the Democratic nomination thought they had found a way to destroy Wilson's standing with progressives by publishing a 1907 letter he had written critical of William Jennings Bryan. Reflecting a conservatism he no longer felt, the letter to Adrian F. Joline, president of a midwestern railroad and a Princeton trustee, had expressed a wish "that we could do something at once dignified and effective to knock Mr. Bryan once for all into a cocked hat" (Link and others 1974, 17:124). Wilson's friends were horrified by the publication of the letter, but fortunately Bryan brushed it off as an attempt by reactionaries to split the progressives. When the two men shared a platform at the annual Jackson Day dinner in Raleigh on January 8, 1912, Wilson seized the opportunity to make a gracious speech paying tribute to the man America knew as "The Great Commoner," and his importance in winning national support for reform. Bryan responded that he cared more for principles than for office and promised to support anyone who bore the standard of those principles for the party. Although ambiguous, his remarks indicated that at least he was keeping an open mind about Wilson.

The passing of the Joline letter cloud did not bring Wilson into the sunlight, however. In November 1911 House Speaker Clark launched a bid for the Democratic nomination and, with the support of friends in Congress, focused on the states, mostly in the West, that selected convention delegates through public primaries. As a reform candidate, Wilson could not evade that challenge. Clark carried five of the eight states involved, including the large delegations from California and Massachusetts. The outcome exacerbated tensions among Wilson's supporters, with McCombs attributing it to the failure to build ties to the regular party organizations and others blaming McCombs himself for failing to raise enough money and antagonizing potential donors. Some suspected that other candidates were ganging up to stop Wilson.

By May 1912 Wilson's campaign was faltering. It was low on money, the candidate had fallen briefly ill, and Col. House was exploring the possibility of shifting his support to Bryan instead of Wilson. Wilson's organization, like the party as a whole, seemed to be disintegrating in the face of probable success. Conflict in the Republican Party between William Howard Taft and Theodore Roosevelt indicated that this would be the Democrats' best chance to capture the White House for many years, but the squabbling Democrats appeared determined to throw away their opportunity by choosing a weak or unknown candidate.

The peril was obvious as soon as the convention met on June 20. The Arrangements Committee, entrusted with picking a temporary chairman, was unable to decide between a conservative and a progressive. They tried to compromise by proposing New Yorker Alton Parker, the 1904 Democratic presidential candidate, a conservative but seemingly innocuous choice. Bryan denounced Parker as a tool of Wall Street and wired the front-runners, Clark and Wilson, demanding they join him in opposing Parker. The telegram divided Wilson's supporters. McCombs drafted a straddling response, but Ellen Wilson and Tumulty urged him to join Bryan. His reply, which began, "You are quite right," proved to be a master stroke, for Clark was evasive (Link and others 1977, 24:493). With Bryan still on the sidelines, Wilson now appeared to be the only true progressive in the race, but Clark still had many committed delegates, and there were other problems for Wilson as well. Two conservative candidates, Rep. Oscar W. Underwood of Alabama and Gov. Judson Harmon of Ohio, were unlikely to win the nomination but might influence the outcome by throwing their support to another candidate, while political machines in New York, Illinois, and Indiana controlled sizable blocks of votes that were available to the highest bidder.

On the first ballot, taken just after midnight on the morning of Friday, June 30, Clark had 440 votes to Wilson's 324, well short of the two-thirds needed for victory. Later that day, after an adjournment, the balloting resumed, and on the tenth ballot New York switched from Harmon to Clark. Here, it seemed, was the payoff for Clark's refusal to endorse Bryan's denunciation of the New York machine. Almost everyone expected a stampede to Clark, but it never came. North Carolina, next in the alphabet, affirmed its support for Wilson, and Ohio stuck to Harmon. When Oklahoma was called, one of its delegates asked that the delegation be polled individually, to see whether they wanted to shift from Wilson to Clark, but Wilson's Oklahoma manager, "Alfalfa Bill" Murray, bellowed out that his state would never join New York's Tammany Hall (the corrupt Democratic machine) in supporting Clark. Wilson supporters throughout the hall erupted in a demonstration, and when voting resumed, Clark had secured a majority but not the two-thirds necessary to win.

While this drama was playing out on the convention floor, McCombs and other Wilson managers were quietly making a deal with the Underwood forces. Knowing that Underwood had no interest in the vice presidency, they did not offer that. Instead they promised that if Wilson withdrew, he would deliver his votes to Underwood, provided the Underwood people prevented any defections from their side. This deal did not guarantee either Wilson or Underwood the nomination, but it created a bloc to stop Clark.

At home in Princeton, Wilson was discouraged by reports from the convention. He had always believed that the nomination should be decided by a simple majority, and Clark now had that. McCombs, always mercurial, reported by telephone that things were going badly. It is unclear whether McCombs suggested that Wilson consider withdrawing or if Wilson originated the idea, but in any case Wilson sent McCombs a telegram authorizing withdrawal. Fortunately for Wilson, by the time he received the telegram, McCombs's mood had changed, and the telegram stayed in his pocket.

On the fourteenth ballot Bryan arose dramatically to announce that although Nebraska was pledged to Clark, he could not vote for anyone who received the votes of the machine-controlled New York delegation, so he would switch his vote to Wilson. Contrary to popular belief, the announcement had little effect, and the convention adjourned on Saturday night, July 1, after the twenty-sixth ballot, on which Clark received 463.5 votes, Wilson 407.5, and Underwood 112.5.

During the Sunday adjournment Bryan may have maneuvered to capture the nomination for himself. Certainly the leaders of the machines in New York, Indiana, and Illinois were working to find an alternative to Clark and Wilson, but it was evident when balloting resumed on Monday that no great shift had taken place. Sensing that Clark's support had peaked, McCombs approached the Indiana delegation with an offer of a deal: the vice presidency for their support. On the twenty-eighth ballot Indiana announced its shift to Wilson, beginning a slow but steady erosion of Clark's strength. On the forty-second ballot the Illinois bosses, seeing momentum building, also switched to Wilson. It was now clear that he would win, and on the forty-sixth ballot Underwood released his supporters and confirmed the nomination. Indiana's switch, rather than Bryan's, seems to have been the decisive moment in the voting.

Wilson hated McCombs' backroom bargaining but felt he had no choice but to accept Indiana's Thomas R. Marshall as his vice-presidential candidate. The manager's skill had been vital to Wilson's victory, but on top of earlier tensions, McCombs' advice about withdrawal and his secret deal-making destroyed Wilson's confidence in him. The candidate agreed to have McCombs named as chairman of the Democratic National Committee, but he made it clear that McAdoo would actually run the campaign.

Wilson's nomination seemed to bring the Democrats something they had never had before—a reform leader with both rural and urban appeal. For all his importance in popularizing issues such as the income tax, the direct election of senators, woman suffrage, tariff reduction, the reform of banking laws, and regulation of big business, Bryan had never won the trust of most voters in the big urban-industrial states. As a result, during the Bryan era most urban reformers preferred Theodore Roosevelt to Bryan, but by 1912 Roosevelt could no longer command the support of a united Republican Party. During the administration of his successor, William Howard Taft, conservatives gained control of the party, leaving Republican progressives angry and frustrated. In 1910, when Roosevelt returned from a hunting trip to Africa, smoldering differences burst into open flame. Taft openly supported conservatives in the fall congressional elections, while Roosevelt called for strong, new federal laws and regulations to make "the executive power" the "steward of the public welfare" (Hagedorn 1925, 19:27). When Taft's organization dominated the

Republican convention and renominated the incumbent, Roosevelt and his followers walked out and held a separate convention in Chicago that August. There they created the "Bull Moose" Progressive Party and nominated Roosevelt. A seemingly united Democratic Party thus faced the bitterly divided Republicans.

The Democrats still faced some internal strife. Relations between Wilson and Clark were chilly, and the role played by the Indiana and Illinois machines in securing Wilson's nomination worried reformers. Organizational problems and personal conflicts between McCombs and others threatened to disrupt the campaign. Money was also a problem initially. Wilson righteously declared that the campaign would return all contributions over $1,000, thereby forcing party leaders to spend enormous amounts of time trying to solicit thousands of smaller donations, but after a few weeks the $1,000 limit was quietly dropped. McCombs was gently pushed aside as principal fund raiser, and a new finance committee eventually raised more than $1 million, almost half of which came from only 155 contributors. When the campaign ended, the coffers actually contained a surplus of $25,000. On the whole, once the nomination was settled, the Democrats' problems, compared to those of their opponents, were minor.

On August 7, the day after Roosevelt electrified his followers at the Progressive Party convention in Chicago, Wilson delivered his acceptance speech in New Jersey. Where Roosevelt proclaimed his determination to "stand at Armageddon, and . . . battle for the Lord" (Schlesinger and Israel 1971, 3:2226), Wilson delivered a careful, reasoned speech that bored his listeners but read well in the next day's papers (see Document 2.3). In many ways, the difference in approach reflected in the two speeches, rather than substantive disagreement about issues, was what the campaign would come to be about. Although the two men disagreed on some issues—Roosevelt favored protectionism while Wilson wanted tariff reduction, and Roosevelt preferred to regulate big business while Wilson hoped to restore competition—their real difference was over the general role of the federal government. As he had said in 1910, Roosevelt believed the federal government should be a "steward" for the American people, acting vigorously wherever necessary to safeguard the rights and interests of all citizens. Wilson, by contrast, preferred to minimize the federal role, using Washington's power only when essential to establish and maintain individual opportunity and free economic competition.

The election was also about personality. With the incumbent Taft effectively sidelined by mid-August, Wilson and Roosevelt faced each other head to head. Even with a united party behind him, Wilson realized he was in for a tough fight. Roosevelt was "a real, vivid person," he told a friend, whom the American people had "seen and shouted themselves hoarse over and voted for, millions strong," while Wilson described himself as "a vague, conjectural personality, more made up of opinions and academic prepossessions than of human traits and red corpuscles" (Link and others 1978, 25:56) (see Document 2.4).

Despite Wilson's fear that Roosevelt's colorful personality would be an insurmountable advantage, the voters seemed unexcited about either man. Regular Republicans, convinced that the Roosevelt storm would soon blow itself out, leaving them in charge of the party machinery, made little effort to get out the vote. The virtual certainty of a Wilson victory, plus the apathy of Republican leaders, seem to account for the fact that the election produced the lowest percentage of turnout by eligible voters between 1836 and 1920. On election day only about 150,000 more voters appeared than had cast ballots in the 1908 election, and much of that increase was attributable to the fact that the Socialist Party more than doubled its vote between 1908 and 1912. Although Wilson won the election handily with 6,294,326 popular votes to Roosevelt's 4,120,207 and Taft's 3,486,343, and with 435 electoral votes to 88 for Roosevelt and 8 for Taft, he actually received 100,000 fewer popular votes than Bryan in 1908. Nationally, Wilson won only 41.8 percent of the popular vote (see Document 2.5).

Despite Wilson's overwhelming victory in the electoral college and the fact that the Democrats won 291 of the 435 seats in the House of Representatives and 51 of 96 seats in the Senate, the triumph meant less than it seemed. Wilson won more than 50 percent of the popular vote in only the eleven states of the old Confederacy. Outside the South, his largest support came from the rural area that stretched from the upper Midwest into the Southwest where Bryan was strongest. In short, Wilson was unable to expand the Democratic base much beyond what Bryan had built, he certainly did not attract enough urban voters to establish the Democrats as the majority party, and he did not win the clear mandate upon which his theory of presidential leadership was premised. Under those circumstances, Wilson's legislative achievements over the next several years seem all the more remarkable.

CONGRESSIONAL ELECTIONS OF 1914

By the autumn of 1914 Wilson's 1912 campaign promises of tariff reduction, banking and currency reform, and antitrust legislation had all been fulfilled. "The reconstructive legislation which for the past two decades the opinions of the country has demanded . . . has now been enacted," he declared in October (Link and others 1979, 31:187–188). The completion of his program and the death of his wife in August left the president with little interest in that year's congressional elections (see Document 2.6).

Without leadership or a new program, the Democrats held on to control of both Houses of Congress, but their House majority was reduced from seventy-three to twenty-five, and the Republicans captured or retained governorships in several key states. The losses fitted into a common pattern for midterm elections, but they were a warning that Wilson needed to take the initiative if he hoped to win reelection in 1916. If it was true, as Joseph Tumulty heard, that Roosevelt was advising his followers "to use their own inclinations as to future party affiliations" (quoted in Sarasohn 1989, 174) it seemed probable that most of them would return to the Republicans. Tumulty and other Democratic progressives therefore urged the president to develop a new program that might attract Roosevelt's followers and maintain the momentum of reform.

In the days after the midterm election the question was whether Wilson was able or willing to make the effort. Distracted and depressed, he dismissed the new ideas being pushed by reformers, such as bills to ban child labor or to create special credit facilities for farmers, as "class legislation" that would favor a few Americans at the expense of all. Instead he focused on the dangers to American interests posed by events in revolutionary Mexico and the European war. His first duty—and perhaps the only thing for which he had energy—was to protect the United States from the perils of a threatening world situation.

PRESIDENTIAL ELECTION OF 1916

By 1916 Wilson had recovered his zest for politics, but the reunited Republican Party and criticism of the administration's policy toward Germany made the election close. Not until two days after the election was it clear that Wilson had carried California and won reelection.

Wilson's goal prior to the election was to turn the Democrats into the majority party by attracting Republican progressives who had supported Theodore Roosevelt in 1912 and were unwilling to return to the Republican Party as Roosevelt advised. Signaling his acceptance of many of the ideas Roosevelt had espoused in 1912, Wilson nominated the progressive lawyer Louis Brandeis to the Supreme Court, urged the creation of a Federal Tariff Commission, endorsed woman suffrage, and supported a new farm credit system, a federal road construction act, a law prohibiting child labor, a federal workman's compensation act, and an eight-hour workday for railroad employees. Many of these measures had been included in Roosevelt's 1912 Progressive Party platform, but the particular benefits extended to farmers and rural areas of the country also made them appealing to Democrats.

In foreign policy, Wilson emphasized the Democrats' success in avoiding war with Germany or Mexico but also reached out to moderate Republicans by proposing a modest program to enlarge the army and navy. German Americans and extreme isolationists were unhappy with any preparedness program, but since the Republicans were more bellicose, there was really nowhere else for them to go.

By the time the Democratic convention met on June 14 in St. Louis, the measures Wilson had succeeded in gaining from Congress, or were pending, had relieved progressives' fears about militarism and offered reforms attractive to labor, farmers, social workers, women, and many other groups. Wilson had succeeded in gently maneuvering William McCombs into resigning as chairman of the Democratic National Committee and secured the naming of Vance McCormick as his successor. In a convention hall draped with red, white, and blue bunting, the delegates shouted themselves hoarse for "Americanism," renominated Wilson, and coined the famous slogan, "He kept us out of war."

The party's platform not only took credit for all the reforms recently adopted but, in a glance to the future, reiterated a theme Wilson had addressed first in a speech to the League to Enforce Peace on May 27, a promise that the United States would "become a partner in any feasible association of nations" formed to protect the right of national self-determination, respect for the integrity of all nations, and the maintenance of the peace (Link and others 1981, 37:116). As Wilson biographer Arthur Link pointed out, the platform was historic because it "put the Democratic party, for the first time, squarely behind a policy of internationalism in the conduct of foreign affairs, and the bold use of federal power to achieve economic progress and social justice at home" (see Document 2.7). Whereas just a few months earlier pundits were generally predicting that a reunited Republican Party would sweep Wilson out of office, by the time the campaign began, the president had found ways to appeal to practically every progressive-minded person and group in the country.

The Republicans, meeting in Chicago, made only a half-hearted effort to reach out to Roosevelt's followers. Their platform endorsed moderate protectionism, moderate reforms, and moderate preparedness. When Sen. Albert Fall of New Mexico nominated Roosevelt, there was an outburst of enthusiasm from the galleries, but the former president had little support among the delegates. The Progressives, who were meeting at their own convention on the other side of Chicago, were equally dubious about the Republicans. Committees from the two conventions met to seek common ground, but there seemed to be none, despite pressure from Roosevelt to reunite the party. In the end, the Progressives nominated Roosevelt, but when he refused the nomination, most of them rejoined the Republicans and supported the party's nominee, Charles Evans Hughes. A minority endorsed Wilson.

Hughes, then a recently resigned associate justice of the United States Supreme Court, had been a successful governor of New York, where his reforms paralleled Wilson's in New Jersey. Named to the Court by President Taft in 1910, he was popular among his colleagues for his wit and legal knowledge, but on the campaign trail his speeches sounded more like legal briefs than political rhetoric, and listeners often suspected he would rather be in the courtroom than on the platform. Roosevelt derided him as "a bearded iceberg" (Schlesinger and Israel 1971, 2255). During the campaign Hughes energetically kissed babies and shook hands, gradually warming his frosty image, but he never found an effective campaign theme. An inept campaign organization compounded his problems, particularly in the pivotal state of California.

Wilson, on the other hand, played up the advantages of incumbency, staying close to Washington to sign bills and manage foreign relations. From time to time he gave a "front porch speech" from his summer home in New Jersey, but he left most of the arduous campaigning to other Democrats, including William Jennings Bryan, who loyally spoke throughout the West. The support of labor and farm organizations was also an asset, although the campaign was sometimes short of money because of defections of businessmen after Wilson signed the Adamson Act (September 3, 1916), which imposed an eight-hour workday on the railroads. Yet for all Wilson's strengths and Hughes's weaknesses, the outcome hinged on one thing: Wilson's success in attracting enough of Roosevelt's former supporters to counter the Republicans' twenty-year advantage as the majority party. Unless he could do that, he would lose the election and certainly would fail to change the long-term balance of the parties.

By the evening of election day, November 7, Wilson had 251 electoral votes to Hughes's 247, but there were still 33 outstanding—13 from California, 12 from Minnesota, 3 from North Dakota, and 5 from New Mexico. Not until November 9 was it clear that New Mexico, North Dakota, and, finally, California, had gone for Wilson, giving him 277 electoral votes to Hughes's 254. The popular vote was much less close. Wilson had 9,126,063 (or 49.2 percent of the vote) and Hughes had 8,547,039. Perhaps most gratifying of all, Wilson had received 2,831,737 more votes than in 1912. Once again his main strength was in the South, where he won everything except West Virginia, and in the trans-Mississippi West, which he swept except for Iowa, Minnesota, Oregon, and South Dakota (see Document 2.8).

In the weeks just after the election it seemed as if Wilson's hope of reconstructing the Democratic Party as a majority coalition with a basic commitment to reform might be within reach. The twin themes of progressivism and peace had attracted farmers, labor, reformers (even Socialists and others on the left wing of the reform movement), women (where they could vote), and members of various ethnic groups.

CONGRESSIONAL ELECTIONS OF 1918

The administration's conduct of the war, and the nature of the peace that might follow it, dominated the congressional elections of 1918. Wilson's 1916 campaign slogan, "He kept us out of war," had expressed a hope more than a promise. When the German government announced early in 1917 that they would use submarines to sink any ship, neutral or belligerent, on its way to the British Isles, the United States was under attack. On April 2, 1917, the president asked Congress to declare war.

Because the country was almost completely unprepared for war, the following months saw a mad scramble to mobilize industry, create and equip an army and navy, and get soldiers to France. Blunders, delays, and missteps were complicated by the worst winter in years in 1917–1918. The Republicans loudly proclaimed their support for the war and lambasted Wilson's management of it at every turn, repeatedly demanding creation of a special civilian board to take over control of mobilization from the president. By the autumn of 1918 Wilson was furious at what he saw as Republican sabotage of the war effort and resolute that the Republicans would have no voice in determining peace terms as the war approached its end. On October 18 the president showed a few close advisers the draft of a statement blasting the Republicans for their lack of support and urging the voters to elect a Democratic majority in the approaching congressional elections. On October 24 the statement, softened only a little in response to his advisers' concerns, appeared in the newspapers (see Document 2.9).

The statement's charge that the Republicans had "unquestionably been pro-war, but they have been anti-administration," and the warning that election of Republican majorities in either branch of Congress would "be interpreted on the other side of the water as a repudiation of my leadership" were direct challenges to the Republicans (Link and others 1985, 51:381–382). Republicans welcomed the fight, redoubled their campaign efforts, and on election day turned a Democratic majority of eleven in the Senate into a Republican majority of two and a Democratic majority of six in the House into a Republican majority of fifty.

Historians have debated exactly how much Wilson's appeal to the voters affected the outcome. Such reversals are common in midterm elections, particularly in a president's second term, and in this case there were reasons other than the president's statement for the shift. Among other things, western farmers were unhappy with the controlled price of wheat, and some of Wilson's liberal supporters were embittered by the administration's wartime infringements of civil rights. Quite possibly the outcome of the elections would have been little or no different without Wilson's statement.

On the other hand, the president's injection of the peace negotiations into partisan politics had serious effects in the future. Everyone knew there were differences between Wilson and the leaders of the Republican Party about what America should be trying to accomplish at Paris, but no one had defined those questions as tests of party loyalty. Now, on the eve of his departure for the Paris peace conference, Wilson identified his peace proposals with the Democratic Party and asked the country for a vote of confidence in the *party's* program. When his appeal was rejected, the battle lines were drawn. A partisan challenge had been added to the issues intrinsic in a complex postwar settlement. From that standpoint, Wilson had made a serious mistake.

PRESIDENTIAL ELECTION OF 1920

By the time politicians began to prepare for the 1920 presidential election, the war and the peace conference were over, and the United States Senate had rejected the Treaty of Versailles and American membership in the League of Nations not once, but twice. Wilson had tried to save the treaty with a dramatic speaking trip through the western United States, but he had collapsed near the end of the trip and soon after suffered a major stroke that left him paralyzed and bedridden for months. Isolated by his illness and shielded by his wife and physician from most political news, the president stubbornly refused to compromise with critics of the treaty.

From his sickbed, Wilson fantasized about running for a third term following the Senate's second rejection of the treaty on March 19, 1920 (see Document 2.10). His physician, Dr. Cary Grayson, and Tumulty were appalled by this idea, but they were silenced by Edith Wilson, who insisted that a series of bulletins describing her husband's wonderful recovery be issued to the press. It was only after the president met with the cabinet for the first time on April 13 that it became obvious that the farce could not go on. When Secretary of State Bainbridge Colby loyally tried to secure Wilson's nomination at the Democratic convention in San Francisco, Dr. Grayson contacted party leaders and begged them not to allow this humiliation. Governor James M. Cox and former Assistant Secretary of the Navy Franklin D. Roosevelt eventually became the party's nominees. The Democratic platform endorsed American membership in the League of Nations, and Cox and Roosevelt paid dutiful calls at the White House, but Wilson took no part in the campaign, and the election turned more on domestic issues than foreign policy. Nevertheless, sick and detached from reality, the president cherished the belief that he would be vindicated by the voters. Informed by his aides that the Republicans seemed certain to win, he was unbelieving, and when the Republican landslide was announced, he was unmoved. "I have not lost faith in the American people," he told his brother-in-law. "They have merely been temporarily deceived. They will realize their error in a little while" (Axson 1993, 199).

By November 1920 Wilson had recovered little from his stroke of October 1919, and nowhere was his decline more obvious than in his political skills. His ability to understand a complex political situation, to plan a strategy for dealing with it, and to negotiate and bargain to get what he wanted, which had been so evident during the first year of his presidency and reached an apogee in 1916, had vanished four years later—as dead as the Treaty of Versailles.

In 1916 Wilson's success in adding some of Theodore Roosevelt's Progressive Party supporters to the existing Democratic core created a possibility that he could turn the Democrats into what historian David Sarasohn describes as a "party of reform" and supplant the Republicans as the normal choice of a majority of voters. But the 1916 coalition proved more fragile than Wilson expected. The war undermined Democratic support in many ethnic communities, and the growing cultural conservatism of the rural South and West alienated many of the urban voters whose support Wilson had sought. Yet although religious fundamentalism, Prohibition, the revived Ku Klux Klan, anti-Catholicism, and xenophobia were disruptive to the coalition of 1916, neither these forces nor the war were sufficient to reduce the party completely to its pre-1910 impotence. Throughout the 1920s the Democrats did reasonably well, except in presidential elections, winning governorships and substantial minorities in Congress, sometimes from areas that had been solidly Republican before 1916. Wilson was in no condition in 1920 to build on the foundations he had laid four years previously, but Franklin Roosevelt would benefit during the 1930s from Wilson's work in expanding the Democrats' appeal.

BIBLIOGRAPHIC ESSAY

Valuable background on conditions in New Jersey prior to Wilson's governorship may be found in Ransom E. Noble, *New Jersey Progressivism before Wilson* (Princeton: Princeton University Press, 1947), and John F. Reynolds, *Testing Democracy: Electoral Behavior and Progressive Reform in New Jersey, 1880–1920* (Chapel Hill: University of North Carolina Press, 1988). For the election, see David Hirst's *Woodrow Wilson, Reform Governor,* and Arthur Link's *Road to the White House,* both described in Chapter 1.

The three-way contest of 1912 has drawn considerable attention from historians. The most common interpretation is that the split in the Republican Party enabled Wilson to win. This argument has been made effectively in Francis L. Broderick, *Progressivism at Risk: Electing a President in 1912* (Westport, Conn.: Greenwood, 1989), but David Sarasohn, in a provocative book, *The Party of Reform: Democrats in the Progressive Era* (Jackson: University of Mississippi Press, 1989), contends that if Theodore Roosevelt had not run in 1912, Wilson would have attracted the progressives from both parties and won more decisively. The interactions between these two long-time rivals during the election and throughout their careers are explored in John Milton Cooper, *The Warrior and the Priest: Woodrow Wilson and Theodore Roosevelt* (Cambridge, Mass.: Belknap Press, 1983). The Southern roots of Wilson's candidacy are described in Dewey Grantham, *Southern Progressivism: The Reconciliation of Progress and Tradition* (Knoxville: University of Tennessee Press, 1983), and William A. Link, *The Paradox of Southern Progressivism, 1880–1930* (Chapel Hill: University of North Carolina Press, 1992). Theodore Roosevelt's speeches during the campaign can be found in Hermann Hagedorn, ed., *The Works of Theodore Roosevelt,* memorial ed., 24 vols. (New York: Scribner's, 1923–1926). Also helpful for understanding this election are essays by David Burner and George E. Mowry in Arthur M. Schlesinger and Fred L. Israel, eds., *History of American Presidential Elections, 1789–1968,* vol. 3 (New York: Chelsea House, 1971). For the organizational problems plaguing the Wilson campaign, see Ralph M. Goldman, *The National Party Chairmen and Committees: Factionalism at the Top* (Armonk, N.Y.: Sharpe, 1990).

The 1916 contest deserves more attention than it has received, but see S. D. Lovell, *The Presidential Election of 1916* (Carbondale: Southern Illinois University Press, 1980), and the essay by Arthur S. Link and William M. Leary Jr., "Election of 1916," in Schlesinger and Israel, eds., *History of American Presidential Elections,* vol. 3, as well as Arthur S. Link, *Wilson: Confusions and Crises, 1915–1916* (Princeton: Princeton University Press, 1964). A brief account that suggests what might be done with this subject can be found in John A. Thompson, *Woodrow Wilson* (London and New York: Longman, 2002). Valuable for an analysis of the problems Wilson faced in trying to turn the Democrats into the majority party is the noted study by Walter Dean Burnham, *Critical Elections and the Mainspring of American Politics* (New York: Norton, 1966).

The standard account of the circumstances surrounding the 1918 election is Seward W. Livermore, *Politics Is Adjourned: Woodrow Wilson and the War Congress, 1916–1918* (Middletown, Conn.: Wesleyan University Press, 1966), while Kurt Wimer has discussed Wilson's fantasies about a third term in 1920 in "Woodrow Wilson and a Third Nomination," *Pennsylvania History* 29 (April 1962): 193–211. Stockton Axson's memoir, *"Brother Woodrow,"* cited in Chapter 1, provides interesting insight into Wilson's mind at this crucial juncture. A more general study of the 1920 election is Wesley M. Bagby, *The Road to Normalcy: The Presidential Campaign and Election of 1920* (Baltimore: Johns Hopkins University Press, 1962).

The works discussed in the bibliographic note following the Introduction should also be consulted for further information.

Document 2.1 Acceptance Speech, Gubernatorial Nomination, September 15, 1910
With the help of the state's political bosses, Wilson was nominated for governor on the first ballot at the New Jersey Democratic convention. Yet, in his acceptance speech he stressed that he had made promises to no one and pledged himself "only to the service of the people."

You have conferred upon me a very great honor. I accept the nomination you have tendered me with the deepest gratification that you should have thought me worthy to lead the Democrats of New Jersey in this stirring time of opportunity.

Even more than the great honor of your nomination I feel the deep responsibility it imposes upon me. For responsibility is proportioned to opportunity.

As you know, I did not seek this nomination. It has come to me absolutely unsolicited. With the consequence that I shall enter upon the duties of the office of Governor, if elected, with absolutely no pledge of any kind to prevent me from serving the people of the State with singleness of purpose. Not only have no pledges of any kind been given, but none have been proposed or desired.

In accepting the nomination, therefore, I am pledging myself only to the service of the people and the party which intends to advance their interests. I cannot but regard the circumstances as marking the beginning of a new and more ideal era in our politics. Certainly they enhance very greatly the honor you have conferred upon me and enlarge the opportunities in equal degree. . . .

Your [platform] deserves and will win [the voters'] confidence. But we shall keep their confidence only by performance, by achievement and by proving our capacity to conduct the administration and reform the legislation of the State in the spirit of our declarations not only, but also with the sagacity and firmness of practical men who not only purpose, but do what is sensible and effective. . . .

I take the three great questions before us to be reorganization and economy in administration, the equalization of taxation and the control of corporations. There are other very important questions that confront us as they confront all the other States of the Union in this day of re-adjustment; the question of the proper liability of employers, for example, the question of corrupt practices in elections, the question of conservation, but the three I have named dominate all the rest. . . .

We shall not act either justly or wisely if we attack established interests as public enemies. . . . It is easy to condemn wrong and to fulminate against wrong-doers in effective rhetorical phrases; but that does not bring either reform or ease of mind. Reform will come only when we have done some careful thinking as to exactly what the things are that are being done in contravention of the public interest and as to the most simple, direct and effective way of getting at the men who do them. . . . There must be implacable determination to see the right done, but strong purpose, which does not flinch because some must suffer, is perfectly compatible with fairness and justice and a clear view of the actual facts. . . .

Our system of taxation is as ill-digested, as piecemeal and as haphazardous as our system of administration. It cannot be changed suddenly or too radically, but many changes should be inaugurated and the whole system by degrees reconsidered and altered, so as to fit modern economical conditions more equitably. . . . The question of the control of corporations is a very difficult one, upon which no man can speak with confidence; but some things are plain. It is plain, as far as New Jersey is concerned that we must have a Public Service Commission with the amplest powers to oversee and regulate the administration of public service corporations throughout the State. . . .

It is the States, not the Federal authorities, that create corporations. The regulation of corporations is the duty of the State much more directly than it is the duty of the government of the United States. It is my strong hope that New Jersey may lead the way in reform; by scrutinizing very carefully the enterprises she consents to incorporate. . . . This can be done and done effectually. I covet for New Jersey the honor of doing it. . . .

Source: Arthur S. Link and others, eds. *The Papers of Woodrow Wilson, 1910* (Princeton: Princeton University Press, 1976), 21:91–94.

Document 2.2   Response to George Lawrence Record, October 24, 1910

George Lawrence Record, a well-known reformer in New Jersey, challenged Wilson to take a clear position on a series of issues. Over the objections of his advisers, Wilson agreed to answer Record's questions in writing. His forthright answers won him many supporters from both parties.

In order to reply as clearly as possible to your questions, I will quote them and append the answers.

1. "That the public utilities commission should have full power to fix just and reasonable rates to be charged by all public service corporations. Do you favor this?" Yes.

2. "That the physical property of each public utility corporation which is devoted to a public use should be valued by the State. Do you favor this?" Yes.

3. "That such physical valuation should be taken as the assessment upon which such corporations shall pay local taxes. Do you favor this?" Yes.

4. "That such valuation should be used as a basis for fixing rates to be charged by these corporations and that such rates should be so limited as to allow them to earn not exceeding six per cent. upon this valuation. Do you favor this?" No. I think that such valuation should form a very important part of the basis upon which rates should be fixed, but not the whole basis. All the financial, physical, and economic circumstances of the business should be taken into consideration. The percentage of profit allowed should be determined by the commission after full inquiry, and not by statute.

5. "That the present primary law should be extended to the selection of candidates for party nominations for governor, congressmen, and delegates to national conventions. Do you favor this?" Yes, though I should wish a better primary law than the present.

6. "That United States Senators should be elected by popular vote. Do you favor this?" Yes. . . .

9. "That primary and election officers should be appointed by some impartial agency, like a court. Do you favor this?" Yes.

10. "There should be a drastic corrupt practices act, forbidding all political expenditures except for the objects named in the act, with drastic penalties for the violation of the act; prohibiting the employment of more than two workers or watchers at the polls on primary or election day representing any one party, or group of candidates; prohibiting the hiring of vehicles for transporting voters; limiting the amount to be expended by candidates; prohibiting political contributions by corporations. Do you favor this?["] Yes.

11. "That every industry employing workmen shall be compelled to bear the expense of all injuries to employees which happen in the industry without wilful [sic] negligence of such employees. Do you favor this?["] Yes. . . .

14. "Do you admit that the boss system exists as I have described it? If so, how do you propose to abolish it?" Of course I admit it. Its existence is notorious. I have made it my business for many years to observe and understand that system, and I hate it as thoroughly as I understand it. You are quite right in saying that the system is bi-partisan; that it constitutes "the most dangerous condition in the public life of our State and nation today"; and that it has virtually, for the time being, "destroyed representative government and in its place set up a government of privilege." I would propose to abolish it by the above reforms, by the election to office of men who will refuse to submit to it and bend all their energies to break it up, and by pitiless publicity. . . .

16. "I join you in condemning the Republican [bosses]. I have been fighting them for years and shall continue to fight them. Will you join me in denouncing the Democratic [bosses], as parties to the same political system? If not, why not?" Certainly! I will join you or any one else in denouncing and fighting any and every one, of either party, who attempts such outrages against the government and public morality. . . .

18. "Is there any organized movement in the Democratic party in this State which corresponds to the Progressive Republican movement of which you have favorably spoken?" I understand the present platform and the present principal nominations of the Democratic party in this State to be such an organized movement. It will be more fully organized if those nominees are elected. This is, as I interpret it, the spirit of the whole remarkable Democratic revival which we are witnessing not only in New Jersey but in many other States.

Before I pass to the next question, will you not permit me to frame one which you have not asked but which I am sure lies implied in those I have just answered? You wish to know what my relations would be with the Democrats whose power and influence you fear, should I be elected Governor, particularly in such important matters as appointments and the signing of bills, and I am very glad to tell you. If elected, I shall not, either in the matter of appointments to office or assent to legislation, or in shaping any part of the policy of my administration, submit to the dictation of any person or persons, special interest, or organization. I will always welcome advice and suggestions from any citizen, whether boss, leader, organization man or plain citizen, and I shall constantly seek the advice of influential and disinterested men, representative of their communities and disconnected from political "organizations" entirely; but all suggestions and all advice will be considered on their merits, and no additional weight will be given to any man's advice or suggestion because of his exercising or supposing that he exercises some sort of political influence or control. I should deem myself forever disgraced should I in even the slightest degree cooperate in any such system or any such transactions as you describe in your characterization of the "boss" system. I regard myself as pledged to the regeneration of the Democratic party which I have forecast above. . . .

Allow me to thank you for this opportunity to express with the greatest possible definiteness my convictions upon the issues of the present campaign, and also for your very kind expressions of confidence and regard, which I highly appreciate.

Source: Arthur S. Link and others, eds., *The Papers of Woodrow Wilson, 1910* (Princeton: Princeton University Press, 1976), 21:406–409, 411.

Document 2.3   Acceptance Speech, Democratic National Convention, August 7, 1912

After forty-six ballots, Wilson became the Democrats' 1912 presidential candidate. He formally accepted the Democratic nomination in a speech that promised a wide range of progressive reforms and a government that would not be the pawn of private interests.

I accept the nomination with a deep sense of its unusual significance and of the great honor done me, and also with a very profound sense of my responsibility to the party and to the Nation. . . .

We stand in the presence of an awakened Nation, impatient of partisan make-believe. . . . The Nation has awakened to a sense of neglected ideals and neglected duties; to a consciousness that the rank and file of her people find life very hard to sustain, that her young men find opportunity embarrassed, and that her older men find business difficult to renew and maintain because of circumstances of privilege and private advantage which have interlaced their subtle threads throughout almost every part of the framework of our present law. . . .

There are two great things to do. One is to set up this rule of justice and of right in such matters as the tariff, the regulation of the trusts, and the prevention of monopoly, the adaptation of our banking and currency laws to the various uses to which our people must put them, the treatment of those who do the daily labor in our factories and mines and throughout all our great industrial and commercial undertakings. . . . The other, the additional duty, is the great task of protecting our people and our resources and of keeping open to the whole people the doors of opportunity through which they must, generation by generation, pass if they are to make conquest of their fortunes in health, in freedom, in peace, and in contentment. . . .

I am not one of those who think that competition can be established by law against the drift of a world-wide economic tendency; neither am I one of those who believe that business done upon a great scale by a single organization—call it corporation, or what you will—is necessarily dangerous to the liberties, even the economic liberties, of a great people like our own, full of intelligence and of indomitable energy. I am not afraid of anything that is normal. I dare say we shall never return to the old order of individual competition, and that the organization of business upon a great scale of cooperation is, up to a certain point, itself normal and inevitable.

Power in the hands of great business men does not make me appre-
hensive, unless it springs out of advantages which they have not created for
themselves. Big business is not dangerous because it is big, but because
its bigness is an unwholesome inflation created by privileges and exemptions which it ought not to enjoy. While competition can not be created
by statutory enactment, it can in large measure be revived by changing the
laws and forbidding the practices that killed it, and by enacting laws that
will give it heart and occasion again. We can arrest and prevent monopoly. It has assumed new shapes and adopted new processes in our time, but
these are now being disclosed and can be dealt with.

The general terms of the present Federal antitrust law, forbidding "combinations in restraint of trade," have apparently proved ineffectual. . . . It
will be necessary to supplement the present law with such laws, both civil
and criminal, as will effectually punish and prevent [monopolies], adding
such other laws as may be necessary to provide suitable and adequate judicial processes, whether civil or criminal, to disclose them and follow them
to final verdict and judgment. They must be specifically and directly met
by law as they develop.

But the problem and the difficulty are much greater than that. There
are not merely great trusts and combinations which are to be controlled
and deprived of their power to create monopolies and destroy rivals; there
is something bigger still than they are and more subtle, more evasive, more
difficult to deal with. There are vast confederacies (as I may perhaps call
them for the sake of convenience) of banks, railways, express companies,
insurance companies, manufacturing corporations, mining corporations,
power and development companies, and all the rest of the circle, bound
together by the fact that the ownership of their stock and the members of
their boards of directors are controlled and determined by comparatively
small and closely interrelated groups of persons who, by their informal confederacy, may control, if they please and when they will, both credit and
enterprise. There is nothing illegal about these confederacies, so far as I
can perceive. They have come about very naturally, generally without plan
or deliberation, rather because there was so much money to be invested,
and it was in the hands, at great financial centers, of men acquainted with
one another and intimately associated in business, than because any one
had conceived and was carrying out a plan of general control; but they
are none the less potent a force in our economic and financial system on
that account. They are part of our problem. Their very existence gives rise

to the suspicion of a "money trust," a concentration of the control of credit which may at any time become infinitely dangerous to free enterprise. If such a concentration and control does not actually exist it is evident that it can easily be set up and used at will. Laws must be devised which will prevent this, if laws can be worked out by fair and free counsel that will accomplish that result without destroying or seriously embarrassing any sound or legitimate business undertaking or necessary and wholesome arrangement. . . .

A presidential campaign may easily degenerate into a mere personal contest and so lose its real dignity and significance. There is no indispensable man. The Government will not collapse and go to pieces if any one of the gentlemen who are seeking to be entrusted with its guidance should be left at home. But men are instruments. We are as important as the cause we represent, and in order to be important must really represent a cause. What is our cause? . . . We represent the desire to set up an unentangled government, a government that can not be used for private purposes, either in the field of business or in the field of politics; a government that will not tolerate the use of the organization of a great party to serve the personal aims and ambitions of any individual, and that will not permit legislation to be employed to further any private interest. It is a great conception, but I am free to serve it, as you also are. I could not have accepted a nomination which left me bound to any man or group of men. No man can be just who is not free; and no man who has to show favors ought to undertake the solemn responsibility of government in any rank or post whatever, least of all in the supreme post of President of the United States.

Source: Arthur S. Schlesinger Jr. and Fred L. Israel, eds., *History of Presidential Elections, 1789–1968* (New York: Chelsea House, 1971), 3:2227–2236.

Document 2.4   Excerpt, Speech, October 7, 1912

As these excerpts from a speech in Denver demonstrate, Wilson could deliver an old-fashioned stump speech as well as an intellectual analysis of policy. In it he denounces government controlled by business interests.

. . . At present the Government of the United States is not free. It is dominated by those men who have set up an economic control in this country. For monopolies in this country do not stand single and separate. They stand united in their force to resist all change. And this united force is all but too great for the government itself. Therefore, ladies and gentlemen, you have to choose on the fifth of November next what the future development of the United States is going to be. . . .

You will observe that this is our problem. All the world knows that this is our problem. First of all to change the tariff laws of the United States so that no special privilege will find cover underneath it at any point. Neither the regular Republicans nor the irregular Republicans [that is, the Progressive Party supporting Theodore Roosevelt] propose any fundamental change whatever in the tariff. All the world knows that springing out of the tariff question is the great question of the trusts, which is the question of established monopoly. And the only proposal with regard to that comes from the third party, which proposes to make monopoly permanent and legal and to regulate it in our interest. To regulate it in our interest? If you say no, you haven't read the platform itself. The platform states that their object is to accept the existing conditions and set up a commission which shall have, without too much restriction of law, the right of constructive regulation, that is to say, discretionary regulation, over the exercise of these monopolistic powers. . . . Therefore, we have in this third party not even a proposal to change the existing partnership between big business and the Government of the United States. . . .

I challenge [the monopolies] to come into a fair field . . . to beat independent competitors. They cannot do it. But they are going to have to try. I am not of that hopeful disposition to believe that we can teach the trusts to be pitiful and good and righteous. And knowing as I do, and as every thoughtful man in the United States knows, that these men have been masters of the government, I am not hopeful of making the government masters of them. . . .

This is not a campaign against individuals. It is a crusade against powers that have governed us, that have limited our development, that have determined our lives, that have set us in a straitjacket to do as they please. This is a second struggle for emancipation. . . .

I have the honor to represent, for the time being, the principles and the purposes and the impulses of what I believe to be a majority of the American people. But I want to say to you with perfect sincerity that some other man could do it just as well, provided he had this passion, this passion for the right settlement of the question whether we are to be dominated by economic monopoly or not. . . .

Suppose we depended upon these gentlemen who have the trusts in their control for the future development of the United States? Are nations, I ask you, developed from the top? Every nation is like a great tree. It may display a beautiful foliage. It may produce excellent fruit upon its branches, but its strength lies down in the dark, hidden, and fertile soil. And the future masters of America, if we are true to America, are coming from the unknown quarters. If this is a true democracy, no man can predict where the leaders of America are coming from. I suspect that it is harder for a leader to be born in a palace than to be born in a cabin. I suspect that it is harder for men at the top to understand the ardors, the hopes, the terrors of America than for men at the bottom. I suspect that men in the ranks who are struggling for a mere foothold, who are fearful lest their health should give way and their children should starve, know more of what America has to do than any other men in the country. . . .

And so my appeal is the old appeal—as old as the history of human liberty. When I look at this great flag of ours, I seem to see in it alternate strips of parchment and of blood. On the parchment are inscribed the ancient sentences of our great Bill of Rights, and the blood is the blood that has been spilled to give those sentences validity. And into the blue heaven in the corner has swung star after star, the symbol of a great commonwealth —the star of Colorado along with the star of ancient Virginia. And these stars will shine there with undiminished luster only so long as we remember the liberties of men and see to it that it is never again necessary to shed a single tear or a single drop of blood in their vindication.

Source: Arthur S. Link and others, eds., *The Papers of Woodrow Wilson, 1912* (Princeton: Princeton University Press, 1978), 25:369–377.

Document 2.5   1912 Presidential Election

As this table makes clear, Wilson won majorities only in the eleven states of the former Confederacy and carried other states largely because of the split between Taft and Roosevelt.

1912 Presidential Election

STATE	TOTAL VOTE	WOODROW WILSON (Democratic) Votes	%	THEODORE ROOSEVELT (Progressive) Votes	%	WILLIAM H. TAFT (Republican) Votes	%	EUGENE V. DEBS (Socialist) Votes	%	OTHER VOTES	%	PLURALITY	
Alabama	117,959	82,438	69.9	22,680	19.2	9,807	8.3	3,029	2.6	5	0.0	59,758	D
Arizona	23,687	10,324	43.6	6,949	29.3	2,986	12.6	3,163	13.4	265	1.1	3,375	D
Arkansas	125,104	68,814	55.0	21,644	17.3	25,585	20.5	8,153	6.5	908	0.7	43,229	D
California	677,877	283,436	41.8	283,610	41.8	3,847	0.6	79,201	11.7	27,783	4.1	174	PR
Colorado	265,954	113,912	42.8	71,752	27.0	58,386	22.0	16,366	6.2	5,538	2.1	42,160	D
Connecticut	190,404	74,561	39.2	34,129	17.9	68,324	35.9	10,056	5.3	3,334	1.8	6,237	D
Delaware	48,690	22,631	46.5	8,886	18.3	15,997	32.9	556	1.1	620	1.3	6,634	D
Florida[a]	51,911	36,417	70.2	4,555	8.8	4,279	8.2	4,806	9.3	1,854	3.6	31,862	D
Georgia	121,470	93,087	76.6	21,985	18.1	5,191	4.3	1,058	0.9	149	0.1	71,102	D
Idaho	105,754	33,921	32.1	25,527	24.1	32,810	31.0	11,960	11.3	1,536	1.5	1,111	D
Illinois	1,146,173	405,048	35.3	386,478	33.7	253,593	22.1	81,278	7.1	19,776	1.7	18,570	D
Indiana	654,474	281,890	43.1	162,007	24.8	151,267	23.1	36,931	5.6	22,379	3.4	119,883	D
Iowa	492,353	185,322	37.6	161,819	32.9	119,805	24.3	16,967	3.4	8,440	1.7	23,503	D
Kansas	365,560	143,663	39.3	120,210	32.9	74,845	20.5	26,779	7.3	63	0.0	23,453	D
Kentucky[b]	453,707	219,585	48.4	102,766	22.7	115,520	25.5	11,647	2.6	4,189	0.9	104,065	D
Louisiana	79,248	60,871	76.8	9,283	11.7	3,833	4.8	5,261	6.6	—	0.0	51,588	D
Maine	129,641	51,113	39.4	48,495	37.4	26,545	20.5	2,541	2.0	947	0.7	2,618	D
Maryland	231,981	112,674	48.6	57,789	24.9	54,956	23.7	3,996	1.7	2,566	1.1	54,885	D
Massachusetts	488,056	173,408	35.5	142,228	29.1	155,948	32.0	12,616	2.6	3,856	0.8	17,460	D
Michigan	547,971	150,201	27.4	213,243	38.9	151,434	27.6	23,060	4.2	10,033	1.8	61,809	PR
Minnesota	334,219	106,426	31.8	125,856	37.7	64,334	19.2	27,505	8.2	10,098	3.0	19,430	PR
Mississippi	64,483	57,324	88.9	3,549	5.5	1,560	2.4	2,050	3.2	—	0.0	53,775	D
Missouri	698,566	330,746	47.3	124,375	17.8	207,821	29.7	28,466	4.1	7,158	1.0	122,925	D
Montana	80,256	28,129	35.0	22,709	28.3	18,575	23.1	10,811	13.5	32	0.0	5,420	D
Nebraska	249,483	109,008	43.7	72,681	29.1	54,226	21.7	10,185	4.1	3,383	1.4	36,327	D
Nevada	20,115	7,986	39.7	5,620	27.9	3,196	15.9	3,313	16.5	—	0.0	2,366	D

(Table continues)

1912 Presidential Election (continued)

STATE	TOTAL VOTE	WOODROW WILSON (Democratic) Votes	%	THEODORE ROOSEVELT (Progressive) Votes	%	WILLIAM H. TAFT (Republican) Votes	%	EUGENE V. DEBS (Socialist) Votes	%	OTHER VOTES	%	PLURALITY	
New Hampshire	87,961	34,724	39.5	17,794	20.2	32,927	37.4	1,981	2.3	535	0.6	1,797	D
New Jersey	433,663	178,638	41.2	145,679	33.6	89,066	20.5	15,948	3.7	4,332	1.0	32,959	D
New Mexico	48,807	20,437	41.9	8,347	17.1	17,164	35.2	2,859	5.9	—	0.0	3,273	D
New York	1,588,315	655,573	41.3	390,093	24.6	455,487	28.7	63,434	4.0	23,728	1.5	200,086	D
North Carolina	243,776	144,407	59.2	69,135	28.4	29,129	11.9	987	0.4	118	0.0	75,272	D
North Dakota	86,474	29,549	34.2	25,726	29.7	22,990	26.6	6,966	8.1	1,243	1.4	3,823	D
Ohio	1,037,114	424,834	41.0	229,807	22.2	278,168	26.8	90,164	8.7	14,141	1.4	146,666	D
Oklahoma	253,694	119,143	47.0	—	0.0	90,726	35.8	41,630	16.4	2,195	0.9	28,417	D
Oregon	137,040	47,064	34.3	37,600	27.4	34,673	25.3	13,343	9.7	4,360	3.2	9,464	D
Pennsylvania	1,217,736	395,637	32.5	444,894	36.5	273,360	22.4	83,614	6.9	20,231	1.7	49,257	PR
Rhode Island	77,894	30,412	39.0	16,878	21.7	27,703	35.6	2,049	2.6	852	1.1	2,709	D
South Carolina	50,403	48,355	95.9	1,293	2.6	536	1.1	164	0.3	55	0.1	47,062	D
South Dakota	116,327	48,942	42.1	58,811	50.6		0.0	4,664	4.0	3,910	3.4	9,869	PR
Tennessee	251,933	133,021	52.8	54,041	21.5	60,475	24.0	3,564	1.4	832	0.3	72,546	D
Texas	300,961	218,921	72.7	26,715	8.9	28,310	9.4	24,884	8.3	2,131	0.7	190,611	D
Utah	112,272	36,576	32.6	24,174	21.5	42,013	37.4	8,999	8.0	510	0.5	5,437	R
Vermont	62,804	15,350	24.4	22,129	35.2	23,303	37.1	928	1.5	1,094	1.7	1,174	R
Virginia	136,975	90,332	65.9	21,776	15.9	23,288	17.0	820	0.6	759	0.6	67,044	D
Washington	322,799	86,840	26.9	113,698	35.2	70,445	21.8	40,134	12.4	11,682	3.6	26,858	PR
West Virginia	268,728	113,097	42.1	79,112	29.4	56,754	21.1	15,248	5.7	4,517	1.7	33,985	D
Wisconsin	399,975	164,230	41.1	62,448	15.6	130,596	32.7	33,476	8.4	9,225	2.3	33,634	D
Wyoming	42,283	15,310	36.2	9,232	21.8	14,560	34.4	2,760	6.5	421	1.0	750	D
Totals	15,043,029	6,294,326	41.8	4,120,207	27.4	3,486,343	23.2	900,370	6.0	241,783	1.6	2,174,119	D

Source: Presidential Elections, 1789–2000 (Washington, D.C.: CQ Press, 2002), 134.

[a] Figures from Svend Petersen, A Statistical History of the American Presidential Elections (Westport, Conn.: Greenwood Press, 1981); Edgar E. Robinson, The Presidential Vote 1896–1932 (Stanford, Calif.: Stanford University Press, 1934).

Document 2.6   Letter from Wilson to Powell Evans, October 20, 1914; Letter from Wilson to Mary Allen Hulbert, November 4, 1914; House Diary, November 4, 1914

By the autumn of 1914 Wilson was saying publicly that his legislative program was essentially complete, as he did in this letter to Powell Evans, a Philadelphia Republican businessman who had supported him in 1912. But, in private, he admitted that he was depressed after the death of his wife, Ellen, in August and declared that he had lost his interest in politics, as he said in the letter to Mary Allen Hulbert. At the same time, his description in a conversation with Edward House (recorded in House's diary, November 4, 1914) of the recent congressional elections as a repudiation of his administration implied that he was not as detached from politics as he believed.

LETTER TO POWELL EVANS

. . . The situation is just this: the reconstructive legislation which for the last two decades the opinion of the country has demanded and which political parties have vied with each other in promising in one form or another has now been enacted. That programme is practically completed. Until the present European war is over and normal conditions have been restored it will not be possible to determine how readily or how completely the business of the country has adjusted itself to the new conditions. When that is clear instrumentalities already created will be ready and in operation which will show just where the laws are working in harmony with the facts and where they are not.

Meanwhile, and for a long time to come, legislative questions will be questions of progress, of suiting means to new ends, of facilitating business and using to the utmost the resources of the country in the vast development of our business and our enterprise, which, I think, has but just begun. . . .

LETTER TO MARY ALLEN HULBERT

. . . My own individual life has gone utterly to pieces. I do not care a fig for anything that affects me. I could laugh aloud to see the papers, and those for whom they write, assuming every day that a second term in 1916 is in my thoughts and that I want it! If they only knew my supreme indifference to that and to everything else that affects me personally, they would devote their foolish and futile brains to some other topic that they do not understand! . . .

HOUSE'S DIARY ENTRY

. . . He spoke of the result of the recent elections, and was distressed because it seemed hardly worth while to work as hard as he had worked during the past two years and to have it so stantly [scantily] appreciated. I tried to console him by stating that he was not running and they were voting for others and not for him. He replied "People are not so stupid not to know that to vote against a democratic ticket is to vote indirectly against me. . . ."

Source: Arthur S. Link and others, eds., *The Papers of Woodrow Wilson, September 6–December 31, 1914* (Princeton: Princeton University Press, 1979), 31:187–188, 265, 280.

Document 2.7   Excerpts, 1916 Democratic Party National Platform

Wilson's major biographer, Arthur S. Link, described the 1916 Democratic Party national platform (of which Wilson was the principal author) as "one of the most significant documents in the history of modern American democracy" because it "put the Democratic party, for the first time, squarely behind a policy of internationalism in the conduct of foreign affairs, and the bold use of federal power to achieve economic progress and social justice at home" (Schlesinger and Israel 1971, 2253).

I. RECORD OF ACHIEVEMENT

. . . We found our country hampered by special privilege, a vicious tariff, obsolete banking laws and an inelastic currency. Our foreign affairs were dominated by commercial interests for their selfish ends. The Republican Party, despite repeated pledges, was impotent to correct abuses which it had fostered. Under our Administration, under a leadership which has never faltered, these abuses have been corrected, and our people have been freed therefrom.

Our archaic banking and currency system, prolific of panic and disaster under Republican administrations,—long the refuge of the money trust,—

has been supplanted by the Federal Reserve Act, a true democracy of credit under government control, already proved a financial bulwark in a world crisis, mobilizing our resources, placing abundant credit at the disposal of legitimate industry and making a currency panic impossible.

We have created a Federal Trade Commission to accommodate perplexing questions arising under the anti-trust laws so that monopoly may be strangled at its birth and legitimate industry encouraged. Fair competition in business is now assured.

We have effected an adjustment of the tariff, adequate for revenue under peace conditions, and fair to the consumer and to the producer. We have adjusted the burdens of taxation so that swollen incomes bear their equitable share. Our revenues have been sufficient in times of world stress, and will largely exceed the expenditures for the current fiscal year.

We have lifted human labor from the category of commodities and have secured to the workingman the right of voluntary association for his protection and welfare. . . .

V. PREPAREDNESS

Along with the proof of our character as a Nation must go the proof of our power to play the part that legitimately belongs to us. The people of the United States love peace. They respect the rights and covet the friendship of all other nations. They desire neither any additional territory nor any advantage which cannot be peacefully gained by their skill, their industry, or their enterprise; but they insist upon having absolute freedom of National life and policy, and feel that they owe it to themselves and to the role of spirited independence which it is their sole ambition to play that they should render themselves secure against the hazard of interference from any quarter, and should be able to protect their rights upon the seas or in any part of the world. We therefore favor the maintenance of an army fully adequate to the requirements of order, of safety, and of the protection of the nation's rights, the fullest development of modern methods of seacoast defense and the maintenance of an adequate reserve of citizens trained to arms and prepared to safeguard the people and territory of the United States against any danger of hostile action which may unexpectedly arise; and a fixed policy for the continuous development of a navy, worthy to support the great naval traditions of the United States and fully equal to the international tasks which this Nation hopes and expects to take a part in performing. . . .

VI. INTERNATIONAL RELATION[S]

The Democratic administration has throughout the present war scrupulously and successfully held to the old paths of neutrality and to the peaceful pursuit of the legitimate objects of our National life which statesmen of all parties and creeds have prescribed for themselves in America since the beginning of our history. But the circumstances of the last two years have revealed necessities of international action which no former generation can have foreseen. We hold that it is the duty of the United States to use its power, not only to make itself safe at home, but also to make secure its just interests throughout the world, and, both for this end and in the interest of humanity, to assist the world in securing settled peace and justice. We believe that every people has the right to choose the sovereignty under which it shall live; that the small states of the world have a right to enjoy from other nations the same respect for their sovereignty and for their territorial integrity that great and powerful nations expect and insist upon; and that the world has a right to be free from every disturbance of its peace that has its origin in aggression or disregard of the rights of people and nations; and we believe that the time has come when it is the duty of the United States to join the other nations of the world in any feasible association that will effectively serve those principles, to maintain inviolate the complete security of the highway of the seas for the common and unhindered use of all nations. . . .

VIII. MEXICO

. . . The want of a stable, responsible government in Mexico, capable of repressing and punishing marauders and bandit bands, who have not only taken the lives and seized and destroyed the property of American citizens in that country, but have insolently invaded our soil, made war upon and murdered our people thereon, has rendered it necessary temporarily to occupy, by our armed forces, a portion of the territory of that friendly state. Until, by the restoration of law and order therein, a repetition of such incursions is improbable, the necessity for their remaining will continue. Intervention, implying as it does, military subjugation, is revolting to the people of the United States, notwithstanding the provocation to that course has been great and should be resorted to, if at all, only as a last recourse. The stubborn resistance of the President and his advisers to every demand and suggestion to enter upon it, is creditable alike to them and to the people in whose name he speaks. . . .

XI. THE ADMINISTRATION AND THE FARMER

We favor the vigorous prosecution of investigations and plans to render agriculture more profitable and country life more healthful, comfortable and attractive, and we believe that this should be a dominant aim of the nation as well as of the States. With all its recent improvement, farming still lags behind other occupations in development as a business, and the advantages of an advancing civilization have not accrued to rural communities in a fair proportion. Much has been accomplished in this field under the present administration, far more than under any previous administration. In the Federal Reserve Act of the last Congress, and the Rural Credits Act of the present Congress, the machinery has been created which will make credit available to the farmer constantly and readily, placing him at last upon a footing of equality with the merchant and the manufacturer in securing the capital necessary to carry on his enterprises. . . . Both Houses have passed a good-roads measure, which will be of far reaching benefit to all agricultural communities. Above all, the most extraordinary and significant progress has been made, under the direction of the Department of Agriculture, in extending and perfecting practical farm demonstration work which is so rapidly substituting scientific for empirical farming. . . .

XIII. GOVERNMENT EMPLOYMENT

We hold that the life, health and strength of the men, women and children of the Nation are its greatest asset and that in the conservation of these the Federal Government, wherever it acts as the employer of labor, should both on its own account and as an example, put into effect the following principles of just employment:

1. A living wage for all employees.
2. A working day not to exceed eight hours, with one day of rest in seven.
3. The adoption of safety appliances and the establishment of thoroughly sanitary conditions of labor.
4. Adequate compensation for industrial accidents.
5. The standards of the "Uniform Child Labor Law," wherever minors are employed.
6. Such provisions for decency, comfort and health in the employment of women as should be accorded the mothers of the race.

7. An equitable retirement law providing for the retirement of super-annuated and disabled employees of the civil service, to the end that a higher standard of efficiency may be maintained.

We believe also that the adoption of similar principles should be urged and applied in the legislation of the States with regard to labor within their borders and that through every possible agency the life and health of the people of the nation should be conserved. . . .

XX. WOMAN SUFFRAGE

We recommend the extension of the franchise to the women of the country by the States upon the same terms as to men.

XXVIII. CONCLUSION

This is a critical hour in the history of America, a critical hour in the history of the world. Upon the record above set forth, which shows great constructive achievement in following out a consistent policy for our domestic and internal development; upon the record of the Democratic administration, which has maintained the honor, the dignity and the interests of the United States, and, at the same time, retained the respect and friendship of all the nations of the world; and upon the great policies for the future strengthening of the life of our country, the enlargement of our National vision and the ennobling of our international relations, as set forth above, we appeal with confidence to the voters of the country.

Source: Arthur S. Schlesinger Jr. and Fred L. Israel, eds., *History of American Presidential Elections, 1789–1868* (N.Y.: Chelsea House, 1971), 3:2271–2281.

Document 2.8   1916 Presidential Election
Wilson again carried the South and added to it most of the West to win a clear victory in both the popular and electoral college votes in 1916.

1916 Presidential Election

STATE	TOTAL VOTE	WOODROW WILSON (Democratic) Votes	%	CHARLES E. HUGHES (Republican) Votes	%	ALLAN L. BENSON (Socialist) Votes	%	J. FRANK HANLY (Prohibition) Votes	%	OTHER VOTES	%	PLURALITY	
Alabama[a]	131,142	99,409	75.6	28,809	21.9	1,925	1.5	999	0.8	—	0.0	70,600	D
Arizona	58,019	33,170	57.2	20,522	35.4	3,174	5.5	1,153	2.0	—	0.0	12,648	D
Arkansas[b]	168,348	112,186	66.6	47,148	28.0	6,999	4.2	2,015	1.2	—	0.0	65,038	D
California	999,250	465,936	46.6	462,516	46.3	42,898	4.3	27,713	2.8	187	0.0	3,420	D
Colorado[b]	294,375	178,816	60.5	102,308	34.8	10,049	3.4	2,793	0.9	409	0.1	76,508	D
Connecticut	213,874	99,786	46.7	106,514	49.8	5,179	2.4	1,789	0.8	606	0.3	6,728	R
Delaware	51,810	24,753	47.8	26,011	50.2	480	0.9	566	1.1	—	0.0	1,258	R
Florida	80,734	55,984	69.3	14,611	18.1	5,353	6.6	4,786	5.9	—	0.0	41,373	D
Georgia[c]	158,690	125,845	79.3	11,225	7.1	967	0.6	—	0.0	20,653	12.9	105,192	D
Idaho	134,615	70,054	52.0	55,368	41.1	8,066	6.0	1,127	0.8	—	0.0	14,686	D
Illinois	2,192,707	950,229	43.3	1,152,549	52.6	61,394	2.8	26,047	1.2	2,488	0.1	202,320	R
Indiana	718,853	334,063	46.5	341,005	47.4	21,860	3.0	16,368	2.3	5,557	0.8	6,942	R
Iowa	518,738	221,699	42.7	280,439	54.1	10,976	2.1	3,371	0.6	2,253	0.4	58,740	R
Kansas	629,813	314,588	49.9	277,658	44.1	24,685	3.9	12,882	2.0	—	0.0	36,930	D
Kentucky	520,078	269,990	51.9	241,854	46.5	4,734	0.9	3,039	0.6	461	0.1	28,136	D
Louisiana	92,974	79,875	85.9	6,466	7.0	284	0.3	—	0.0	6,349	6.8	73,409	D
Maine	136,314	64,033	47.0	69,508	51.0	2,177	1.6	596	0.4	—	0.0	5,475	R
Maryland	262,039	138,359	52.8	117,347	44.8	2,674	1.0	2,903	1.1	756	0.3	21,012	D
Massachusetts	531,822	247,885	46.6	268,784	50.5	11,058	2.1	2,993	0.6	1,102	0.2	20,899	R
Michigan	646,873	283,993	43.9	337,952	52.2	16,012	2.5	8,085	1.2	831	0.1	53,959	R
Minnesota	387,367	179,155	46.2	179,544	46.3	20,117	5.2	7,793	2.0	758	0.2	389	R
Mississippi	86,679	80,422	92.8	4,253	4.9	1,484	1.7	—	0.0	520	0.6	76,169	D
Missouri	786,773	398,032	50.6	369,339	46.9	14,612	1.9	3,887	0.5	903	0.1	28,693	D
Montana	178,009	101,104	56.8	66,933	37.6	9,634	5.4	—	0.0	338	0.2	34,171	D
Nebraska	287,315	158,827	55.3	117,771	41.0	7,141	2.5	2,952	1.0	624	0.2	41,056	D
Nevada	33,314	17,776	53.4	12,127	36.4	3,065	9.2	346	1.0	—	0.0	5,649	D

(Table continues)

1916 Presidential Election (continued)

STATE	TOTAL VOTE	WOODROW WILSON (Democratic) Votes	%	CHARLES E. HUGHES (Republican) Votes	%	ALLAN L. BENSON (Socialist) Votes	%	J. FRANK HANLY (Prohibition) Votes	%	OTHER VOTES	%	PLURALITY	
New Hampshire	89,127	43,781	49.1	43,725	49.1	1,318	1.5	303	0.3	—	0.0	56	D
New Jersey	494,442	211,018	42.7	268,982	54.4	10,405	2.1	3,182	0.6	855	0.2	57,964	R
New Mexico	66,879	33,693	50.4	31,097	46.5	1,977	3.0	112	0.2	—	0.0	2,596	D
New York	1,706,305	759,426	44.5	879,238	51.5	45,944	2.7	19,031	1.1	2,666	0.2	119,812	R
North Carolina	289,837	168,383	58.1	120,890	41.7	509	0.2	55	0.0	—	0.0	47,493	D
North Dakota	115,390	55,206	47.8	53,471	46.3	5,716	5.0	997	0.9	—	0.0	1,735	D
Ohio	1,165,091	604,161	51.9	514,753	44.2	38,092	3.3	8,085	0.7	—	0.0	89,408	D
Oklahoma	292,327	148,123	50.7	97,233	33.3	45,091	15.4	1,646	0.6	234	0.1	50,890	D
Oregon	261,650	120,087	45.9	126,813	48.5	9,711	3.7	4,729	1.8	310	0.1	6,726	R
Pennsylvania	1,297,189	521,784	40.2	703,823	54.3	42,638	3.3	28,525	2.2	419	0.0	182,039	R
Rhode Island	87,816	40,394	46.0	44,858	51.1	1,914	2.2	470	0.5	180	0.2	4,464	R
South Carolina	63,950	61,845	96.7	1,550	2.4	135	0.2	—	0.0	420	0.7	60,295	D
South Dakota	128,942	59,191	45.9	64,217	49.8	3,760	2.9	1,774	1.4	—	0.0	5,026	R
Tennessee	272,190	153,280	56.3	116,223	42.7	2,542	0.9	145	0.1	—	0.0	37,057	D
Texas[d]	372,467	286,514	76.9	64,999	17.5	18,969	5.1	1,985	0.5	—	0.0	221,515	D
Utah	143,145	84,145	58.8	54,137	37.8	4,460	3.1	149	0.1	254	0.2	30,008	D
Vermont	64,475	22,708	35.2	40,250	62.4	798	1.2	709	1.1	10	0.0	17,542	R
Virginia[a]	153,993	102,825	66.8	49,358	32.1	1,060	0.7	683	0.4	67	0.0	53,467	D
Washington	380,994	183,388	48.1	167,208	43.9	22,800	6.0	6,868	1.8	730	0.2	16,180	D
West Virginia	289,671	140,403	48.5	143,124	49.4	6,144	2.1	—	0.0	—	0.0	2,721	R
Wisconsin	447,134	191,363	42.8	220,822	49.4	27,631	6.2	7,318	1.6	—	0.0	29,459	R
Wyoming	51,906	28,376	54.7	21,698	41.8	1,459	2.8	373	0.7	—	0.0	6,678	D
Totals	18,535,445	9,126,063	49.2	8,547,039	46.1	590,110	3.2	221,293	1.2	50,940	0.3	579,024	D

Source: *Presidential Elections, 1789–2000* (Washington, D.C.: CQ Press, 2002), 135.

a Figures from Svend Petersen, *A Statistical History of the American Presidential Elections* (Westport, Conn.: Greenwood Press, 1981); Edgar E. Robinson, *The Presidential Vote 1896–1932* (Stanford, Calif.: Stanford University Press, 1934).

b Figures from Petersen, *A Statistical History*.

c Figures from Petersen, *A Statistical History*. Plurality of 105,192 votes is calculated on the basis of 20,653 votes cast for the Progressive Party.

d Figures from Petersen, *A Statistical History*, *Texas Almanac*.

Document 2.9 Appeal to Voters, October 25, 1918

Wilson issued this appeal to the voters to elect Democrats to Congress. Commonly regarded as a mistake, the appeal reflected Wilson's frustrations at what he saw as Republican obstruction of the administration's mobilization program and his belief that the upcoming peace conference in Europe offered him an opportunity to create a new international system that would be effective only if the United States participated. He feared, correctly, that the Republicans in the Senate would not support his efforts.

My Fellow Countrymen: The Congressional elections are at hand. They occur in the most critical period our country has ever faced or is likely to face in our time. If you have approved of my leadership and wish me to continue to be your unembarrassed spokesman in affairs at home and abroad, I earnestly beg that you will express yourselves unmistakably to that effect by returning a Democratic majority to both the Senate and the House of Representatives. . . .

I have no thought of suggesting that any political party is paramount in matters of patriotism. I feel too keenly the sacrifices which have been made in this war by all our citizens, irrespective of party affiliations, to harbour such an idea. I mean only that the difficulties and delicacies of our present task are of a sort that makes it imperatively necessary that the nation should give its undivided support to the government under a unified leadership, and that a Republican Congress would divide the leadership.

The leaders of the minority in the present Congress have unquestionably been pro-war, but they have been anti-administration. At almost every turn, since we entered the war, they have sought to take the choice of policy and the conduct of the war out of my hands and put it under the control of instrumentalities of their own choosing. This is no time either for divided counsel or for divided leadership. Unity of command is as necessary now in civil action as it is upon the field of battle. If the control of the House and Senate should be taken away from the party now in power, an opposing majority could assume control of legislation and oblige all action to be taken amidst contest and obstruction.

The return of a Republican majority to either House of the Congress would, moreover certainly be interpreted on the other side of the water as a repudiation of my leadership. Spokesmen of the Republican party are urging you to elect a Republican Congress in order to back up and support the President, but even if they should in this way impose upon some credulous voters on this side of the water, they would impose on no one on the other side. It is well understood there as well as here that the Republican leaders desire not so much to support the President as to control him. The peoples of the allied countries with whom we are associated against Germany are quite familiar with the significance of elections. They would find it very difficult to believe that the voters of the United States had chosen to support their President by electing to the Congress a majority controlled by those who are not in fact in sympathy with the attitude and action of the Administration.

I need not tell you, my fellow countrymen, that I am asking your support not for my own sake or for the sake of a political party, but for the sake of the nation itself, in order that its inward unity of purpose may be evident to all the world. In ordinary times I would not feel at liberty to make such an appeal to you. In ordinary times divided counsels can be endured without permanent hurt to the country. But these are not ordinary times. If in these critical days it is your wish to sustain me with undivided minds, I beg that you will say so in a way which it will not be possible to misunderstand either here at home or among our associates on the other side of the sea. I submit my difficulties and my hopes to you.

Source: Arthur S. Link and others, eds., *The Papers of Woodrow Wilson, September 14–November 8, 1918* (Princeton: Princeton University Press, 1985), 51:381–382.

Document 2.10   Memorandum, March 25, 1920

Almost six months after his stroke of October 2, 1919, Wilson remained a complete invalid, largely incapable of conducting the business of the presidency. He nevertheless contemplated making a third run for the White House, which Dr. Grayson believed "would kill him." On March 23, 1920, Joseph Tumulty wrote to Edith Wilson urging the president to issue a statement that he would not be a candidate, but as Grayson quoted the president in a memorandum on March 25, the advice fell on deaf ears.

"Tumulty has sent me a letter asking that I come out and say that I would not run again for the Presidency. I do not see anything to be gained at this time by doing so except to turn the leadership of the Democratic Party over to William Jennings Bryan. In my opinion this would be a pretty state

of affairs for the country and for the world at this stage of world conditions. I feel that it would be presumptuous and in bad taste for me to come
out and decline something that has not been offered to me. No group of
men has given me any assurance that it wanted me to be a candidate for
renomination. In fact, everyone seems to be opposed to my running. And
I think it would be entirely out of place for me to say now that I would not
run. With things in such a turmoil in the United States and throughout
the world as they are today, the Democratic Convention in San Francisco
may get into a hopeless tie-up, and it may, by the time of the Convention,
become imperative that the League of Nations and the Peace Treaty be
made the dominant issue. The Convention may come to a dead-lock as
to candidates, and there may be practically a universal demand for the selection of some one to lead them out of the wilderness. The members of the
Convention may feel that I am the logical one to lead—perhaps the only
one to champion this cause. In such circumstances I would feel obliged
to accept the nomination even if I thought it would cost me my life. I have
given my vitality, and almost my life, for the League of Nations, and I
would rather lead a fight for the League of Nations and lose both my reputation and my life than to shirk a duty of this kind if it is absolutely necessary for me to make the fight and if there is no one else to do it. . . ."

Source: Arthur S. Link and others, eds., *The Papers of Woodrow Wilson, February
28–July 31, 1920* (Princeton: Princeton University Press, 1991), 65:123.

President Wilson signs legislation September 2, 1916, intended to discourage the use of child labor. The Supreme Court struck down the law in 1918.

CHAPTER THREE

Administration Policies

D uring the 1912 presidential campaign Woodrow Wilson identified three priorities for his administration: tariff reduction, banking and currency reform, and a new antitrust law. Together, these three made up what he called the "New Freedom." Its central theme was that government should act to curtail the power of the great corporations that, Wilson had argued as early as 1889, "distorted competition" and permitted "the rich and strong to combine against the poor and the weak." Government had a duty, he asserted, to make "competition equal" and to protect society against "permanent injury and deterioration" (Wilson 1889, 659, 664). But while Wilson knew in general what he wanted his administration to accomplish, specific policies were subject to the evolution of his thought and the pushing and hauling of politics.

By the autumn of 1914 Wilson's initial New Freedom program was complete. During the next two years, he moved beyond his first, relatively limited conception of the proper federal role to support new programs for farmers and workers that he had previously viewed as special interest legislation. As he began his campaign for reelection in 1916 he endorsed laws for the protection of the interests of farmers, railroad workers, merchant seamen, and others. He was slow to endorse federal action in other areas, however, resisting pressure to support woman suffrage and Prohibition. These social reforms, he argued, were the proper concern of the states, not the federal government.

Wilson's ideas about foreign policy, less specific when he took office, also evolved with experience. In Latin America, Asia, and especially in World War I, the United States faced unprecedented challenges to its ideals and interests. Wilson tried to develop policies that would serve America's practical interests but would at the same time also advance democracy, strengthen peace, and encourage orderly change. Increasingly, he came to believe that those objects could best be promoted through collective action with other nations, a view that clashed with traditional American isolationism.

THE NEW FREEDOM: FIRST PHASE

Woodrow Wilson thought that the goal of reform must be to create a condition in which personal opportunity and responsibility were the norm. Once that was done, he believed, government's role could be limited to guarding against the distortion or corruption of that order. An old friend, David Benton Jones, stated the argument succinctly in a letter to Wilson in July 1912. The government, wrote Jones, "must establish and maintain *competitive conditions* in the industrial field. It cannot compel competition, but it can prevent a corporation from monopolizing the raw materials of production and it can and must prevent agreements and practices which limit or restrain trade in the distribution of its products. If it does this it is certain that in time competition or the danger of competition will be a powerful regulator of prices" (Link and others 1977, 24:549). In short, the object of reform was to achieve a free market in which Wilson believed the natural effects of competition would make the system substantially self regulating.

Although Wilson regarded free competition as desirable, he did not think that situation was completely attainable in the modern world, nor did he believe that the market alone could protect all the interests of society. The growth of big business, he said in his 1912 speech accepting the Democratic presidential nomination, was part of "a world-wide economic tendency," and he doubted that it was possible to "return to the old order of individual competition." Government's role in "the regulation of trusts and the prevention of monopoly" must be permanent. Beyond assuring a competitive marketplace, he added, government must also protect the health and safety of industrial workers. Laws regulating workplace safety, he contended, were not measures to benefit a single

class but were "taken in the interest of the whole people, whose partnership and right action we are trying to establish and make real and
practical" (Link and others 1978, 25:5, 11, 14).

Wilson thus assigned to government a central and substantial role in
the management of the economy. It was "the end of government *to
accomplish the objects of organized society,*" he had written in 1889, and
this primary obligation to be responsible to the wishes of the people took
precedence over the desirable objective of limiting the size and scope of
government activities (Wilson 1889, 660). When he spoke of a program
of "conservative reform," as he did in 1904, he was alluding to this conception of a *limited* but *responsible* government, and where responsibility clashed with limitation, he gave the preference to responsibility (Link
and others 1973, 15:548). "We used to say . . . that the best government
was the government that did as little as possible," he observed in 1912.
"But we are coming now to realize that life is so complicated . . . that
the law has to step in and create the conditions . . . which will make it
tolerable for us to live" (Link and others 1978, 25:259–260).

Tariffs

Like many other Democrats of his era, Wilson believed that cutting the
tariff would weaken the trusts by opening the American market to low-
priced foreign products. In the more open marketplace thus created, he
thought, small American companies would also find new opportunities.
Cutting the tariff would encourage competition, while cheaper goods
benefited consumers. Tariff reduction, from this point of view, was a perfect example of conservative reform, and since it was a long-standing
objective of southern Democrats, it was politically appealing as well. Wilson therefore emphasized the tariff in his acceptance speech and made
it the first priority for the New Freedom (see Document 3.1).

The timing of Wilson's attack on the tariff was excellent. Although
both wings of the Republican Party still supported protectionism, progressives in that party argued that tariff rates should be based on the
advice of an expert commission who would develop a "scientific" tariff
reflecting real economic needs, rather than the usual trading of favors
among legislators. The dispute contributed to the split in the Republican Party that helped Wilson win in 1912, and it created the possibility that his administration might attract bipartisan support for tariff
reform.

Although political leaders were not yet aware of the fact, big business was losing interest in the protective tariff as American corporations focused increasingly on world markets and investment opportunities. In the late nineteenth century, when the tariff was highest, American companies had been going through a period of savage competition and were desperate to keep foreign rivals from making the situation worse. By 1912, however, consolidation had reduced domestic competition, and the resulting corporate giants faced international competition with equanimity. Not only did they no longer fear foreign competitors, but the high American tariff gave other nations an excuse to maintain their own barriers to American products.

Shortly after his inauguration, Wilson called a special session of Congress to consider tariff reform. He assumed the proposal would be opposed strongly by the corporations. To dramatize the issue and weaken expected business hostility, the president broke with precedent, going personally to Capital Hill on April 8 to speak in support of what came to be known as the Underwood Tariff Bill. Subsequently, he campaigned vigorously for the bill and warned in a press conference against the influence of lobbyists. But, in fact, major corporations supported the measure and their officers testified in its favor. "I approve of the Underwood Bill," said a former president of United States Steel. Ogden Armour, president of one of the largest meat-packing companies, agreed, as did a representative of the Eastman Kodak Company, manufacturer of almost 90 percent of all cameras sold in the United States, and an officer of the Singer Company, America's largest manufacturer of sewing machines (quoted in Burdick 1968, 280). By contrast, a number of smaller manufacturers testified in favor of continued protection, arguing that it shielded them from devastating foreign competition, but their influence could not prevail against the combined influence of the president and the big corporations.

In the long run, the bill's real importance, and its most bitterly fought aspect, was not its reduction of duties, but the fact that it included, almost as an afterthought, a national income tax authorized under the provisions of the recently adopted Sixteenth Amendment to the Constitution. The new tax was intended to replace revenue that would be lost when the tariff was reduced, but progressives in the Senate quickly saw its potential as an instrument of social policy. Their proposal in August 1913 that the tax rate on incomes over $100,000 be increased from 3 to 10 percent aroused conservatives in both parties and threatened to defeat the bill. Wilson, on vacation in New Hampshire, conferred at long distance with Democratic leaders in the Senate, and together they engineered a compromise, setting the top rate at 7 rather than 10 percent. Secretary of State William Jennings Bryan publicly urged progressives to support the compromise, and conservatives were placated by the administration's rejection of an inheritance tax amendment. Having passed the House in May, the bill squeaked through the Senate on September 9 with a seven-vote majority.

Even though the Underwood Bill did not weaken great corporations and stimulate competition as much as Wilson anticipated, it nevertheless exemplified his belief that laws should be "made more for the beginners in every enterprise than for those who have achieved" (Link and others 1978, 25:197). Through the promotion of economic competition and the progressive taxation of incomes, the bill aspired to take special privileges away from the rich and powerful while providing new opportunities for ordinary citizens to get ahead. In the main, it aimed to achieve its ends less through governmental control of the economy than through the *removal* of artificial constraints and the creation of opportunities for competition. But Wilson was no free market doctrinaire. His endorsement of the income tax provision of the bill, and his willingness to see its maximum rate increased from 3 to 7 percent, suggested his acceptance of the permanent role of the federal government in the direction of the economy.

Banking and Currency

A similar absence of theoretical rigidity was evident in the administration's banking and currency policy, where the central issue was whether bankers or the government would control the system. When Wilson took office he believed that "the credit of this country must be opened upon equal terms . . . to everybody," and that what he called the New York "money monopoly" must be brought under control, but he had no specific plan in mind for achieving his goals (Link and others 1978, 27:33; 1977, 23:157). His statements did not address the question of whether the system would be publicly or privately directed.

During a banking panic in 1907 the defects of the existing banking system—lack of responsiveness to expansions and contractions of the economy, absence of national oversight, inability to mobilize reserves, difficulty in moving money from place to place, and the vulnerability of the whole structure to hysteria—led to the creation of a commission to study the problem, which was chaired by Sen. Nelson W. Aldrich, R-R.I. In 1911 the Aldrich Commission proposed the creation of a privately owned national bank, with fifteen branches across the country that would become "bankers' banks," dealing only with banks, not with the public. Ordinary banks would deposit a portion of their reserves, both in cash and in "commercial paper" (the promissory notes signed by businesses when they borrow from a bank), with the National Reserve Association, as Aldrich called his proposed organization. The whole reserve fund would be available to support member banks in times of crisis, and the association would also be authorized to issue a new paper currency, to be called national reserve notes. Since the currency would be based in part on commercial paper, the amount in circulation would expand and contract with expansions and contractions of the business cycle. The notes would be a privately issued currency, backed by the National Reserve Association, not the federal government.

The National Reserve proposal seemed likely to fix many of the problems that had led to the 1907 panic, but it was immediately attacked by small businessmen and bankers, as well as southern and western farmers, who saw it as perpetuating control of the nation's financial system by the big banks of New York. During the spring of 1913 Wilson worked with legislative leaders, particularly Rep. Carter Glass, D-Va., to develop an administration bill. Their first draft accepted the National Reserve Association idea in principle, but put the whole thing under close federal supervision. When the president asked his advisers for comments on the bill, Secretary of State William Jennings Bryan insisted that the federal government, not bankers, must control the system and back the currency. Treasury Secretary William Gibbs McAdoo and Wilson's informal adviser, Louis D. Brandeis, agreed. Business, said Brandeis, must be sure that "the Government will control the currency . . . and that whatever money is available, will be available for business generally, and not be subject to the control of a favored few" (Link and others 1978, 27: 520–521). These arguments, stressing equality of opportunity for all parts of the country and for small as well as big business, had a strong appeal for Wilson. On June 23, in a speech to a joint session of Congress, he argued that "the control of the system of banking and of issue which our new laws are to set up must be public, not private, must be vested in the Government itself, so that the banks may be the instruments, not the masters, of business and of individual enterprise and initiative" (Link and others 1978, 27:572–573) (see Document 3.2).

During the summer and autumn the Federal Reserve bill moved gradually through Congress. In the House, southern and western members of Congress attached an amendment making receipts for warehoused agricultural products as well as commercial paper part of the system's reserves, but even so, rural suspicion of the proposed system was so great that it took all of Bryan's influence to win passage of the bill. In the Senate, problems came mainly from conservatives, who preferred Wilson's original idea of a private system under federal supervision, but eventually the administration prevailed, and on December 23 Wilson signed the Federal Reserve Act into law.

Together, the tariff bill and the Federal Reserve Act completed the first phase of the New Freedom. As Wilson saw it, the tariff would give small businesses an opportunity to compete with great corporations, and the Federal Reserve System would provide them with the resources to do so. His goal in both cases was to open economic opportunity to everyone, but as he developed the specific measures to do so, he concluded that the federal government would have to play an expanded and permanent supervisory role. If government was to assure Americans equal economic opportunity, the size and scope of government would have to be less limited than he originally thought desirable.

THE NEW FREEDOM: SECOND PHASE

A second phase of the New Freedom, characterized by further expansion of federal authority, began with antitrust legislation. The problem of monopolies, or "trusts" as they were then called, had first been addressed by Congress in 1890 with the passage of the Sherman Antitrust Act, which declared illegal any "contract, combination . . . , or conspiracy, in restraint of trade" (Van Cise 1962, 7). Enforcement of the law required that the federal government sue suspected offenders in court, which was a slow, expensive, and uncertain process for both government and business. A further weakness of the law became evident in 1911 when the Supreme Court ruled in *Standard Oil Co. v. United States* that the Sherman Act applied only to unreasonable or excessive restraints of trade. The "rule of reason" left everyone confused about exactly what was or was not reasonable.

During the 1912 campaign Woodrow Wilson talked about the trusts in rather vague terms, arguing that if laws could be passed that would ban practices that contributed to the building and maintenance of monopolies, the natural forces of competition would create a healthy economy with opportunities for everyone. Roosevelt had proposed to achieve the same goal in a different way, by creating "a national industrial commission" with "complete power to regulate and control all the great industrial concerns engaged in interstate business," but Wilson dismissed that idea contemptuously (Hagedorn 1975, 19:388). "When once the government regulates the monopoly," he said, "then monopoly will have to see to it that it regulates the government" (Link and others 1978, 25:73); big business, in other words, would soon learn how to dominate a regulatory body.

The alternative—legally banning specific anti-competitive practices—sounded attractive but proved difficult. When Wilson asked Brandeis for advice, the lawyer pointed out that any list of forbidden actions would merely challenge the creativity of corporate attorneys. By the end of the 1912 campaign Wilson found himself reduced to promising vaguely that his administration would "take care of the little businessman and see that any unfair interference with the growth of his business shall be a criminal offense" (Link and others 1978, 25:427).

In his first annual message on December 2, 1913, Wilson proposed that instead of trying to rewrite the murky language of the Sherman Act, the 1890 statute should be left to "stand, unaltered, . . . with its debatable ground about it, but that we should as much as possible reduce the areas of that debatable ground by further and more explicit legislation" (Link and others 1979, 29:7). Drafting that legislation proved difficult, however, and by the time Wilson went before a joint session of Congress on January 20, 1914, to outline a specific proposal, his position had begun to change (see Document 3.3). While he called for "a further and more explicit legislative definition of the policy and meaning of the existing antitrust law," he also proposed the creation of an "interstate trade commission" that sounded very much like the "national industrial commission" that Theodore Roosevelt had proposed in 1912 (Link and others 1979, 29:156–157). Later that spring the two rather contradictory approaches to the trust question were embodied in two separate bills. The Clayton antitrust bill attempted to identify and ban specific anti-competitive practices, and an Interstate Trade Commission (later renamed Federal Trade Commission) bill proposed to set up a five-member appointed commission with discretionary power to identify, investigate, and prohibit unfair practices.

On October 15, 1914, Wilson signed the Clayton Act into law, but by that time he had entirely lost faith in that approach to the problem. The problems in specifying unfair practices, he admitted, had made the final bill "so weak you cannot tell it from water" (Link and others 1979, 31:122). He lauded the Federal Trade Commission bill, on the other hand, which he signed on September 26, as creating "elasticity without real indefiniteness, so that we may adjust our regulation to actual conditions, local as well as national" (Link and others 1979, 30:320). Once again, he had been forced to the conclusion that in order to be responsible to the interests of the people, the powers of the government could not be narrowly limited (see Document 3.4).

While the administration struggled with a redefinition of antitrust law, it also pursued a vigorous antitrust policy under the Sherman Act. Successive attorneys general James C. McReynolds (March 1913–August 1914) and Thomas W. Gregory (September 1914–March 1919) brought seventy-five antitrust suits in the federal courts and eventually won about 70 percent of them. During the war business leaders proposed a temporary suspension of enforcement to accelerate mobilization, but Wilson was reluctant to do so. In 1918, as the situation became more serious, he agreed to postpone some pending suits, but the Justice Department also began ten new ones against non-critical industries.

Antitrust policy underlines how Wilson's approach to government was changed by experience. As a presidential candidate he had argued that the ideal situation for the economy would be a system of impartial laws that would define practices and leave everyone, large and small, free to compete. The Clayton Act reflected that ideal, but the Federal Trade Commission and antitrust prosecutions represented the reality forced on him by circumstances. Many years earlier, during his study of governmental administration, Wilson had written that administrative actions were, in themselves, *"a source of Law,"* but the full implications of that insight did not strike him until he entered the White House and realized the limitations of law (Link and others 1969, 6:485). Not only was law, in this instance, a crude instrument for defining illegal practices, but the application and enforcement of law required discretion and created, in the process, rules and regulations that had the force of law. If the federal government was to take *any* role in regulating the economy, there seemed to be no escape from a substantial expansion of federal power. Once again, *responsible* government trumped *limited* government.

EXPANDING THE ROLE OF GOVERNMENT, 1914–1916

While Woodrow Wilson moved relatively easily from the objective of creating equal economic opportunity for everyone to recognition that doing so required constant intervention and supervision by government, he had more difficulty in supporting measures that seemed to him to benefit only specific groups within society (see Document 3.5). His evolution to acceptance of an expanded federal role in these areas was gradual and was certainly linked to his desire for reelection in 1916. Thus in 1914 he said that "no child labor law yet proposed has seemed to me constitutional," yet in 1916 he urged Congress to pass the Keating-Owen Child Labor bill, declaring that he supported it "with all my heart" (Link and others 1979, 29:170; Link and others 1981, 37:469).

In 1916 Wilson frankly embraced the idea of federal activism that had been implicit in much of his earlier policy, but his new program actually represented less a change of direction than a recommitment to action after a two-year hiatus during which he had been focused on private problems and foreign policy. If his rhetoric no longer reflected the ideal of individual competition in a free economy that had been dominant in 1912, the shift reflected both the evolution of his own thought and the practical necessity of appealing to Roosevelt's erstwhile supporters in the upcoming presidential election.

The president announced his return to the leadership of reform on January 28, 1916, by nominating Louis Brandeis, a lawyer and longtime union supporter, to be an associate justice of the United States Supreme Court. The nomination drew an immediate and unanimous chorus of approval from Jews, progressive politicians, and especially from organized labor. It took intense personal lobbying by the president to secure a favorable vote from the Senate (47–22) on June 1, and his willingness to make the fight cemented his relations with liberals. As one put it, the appointment was a symbol of "freedom from the trammels of race prejudice; freedom from subservience to the money power; freedom to think and to act and to speak as men ought to think and act and speak in a real democracy" (quoted in Link 1964, 362).

Having begun with the Brandeis nomination, Wilson quickly moved forward on other issues. On January 24 he informed the House majority leader, Claude Kitchin, that he wanted to create a non-partisan Federal Tariff Commission to advise on tariff policy. Wilson had been extremely cool to the idea of a commission when Roosevelt suggested it in 1912, and as late as August 1915 he had described it as Republican "nonsense" (quoted in Link 1964, 342). But in early January he changed his mind after receiving a letter from Sen. Robert L. Owen, D-Okla., who argued that a commission was "a matter of Party expediency" that "would conciliate two millions or three millions of progressive men [in the Republican Party] who would be glad to support the Democratic Party except for their obsession on the protective tariff principle" (Link and others 1980, 35:433, 434). He had changed his mind, Wilson said publicly, because the disruption of world trade resulting from the war necessitated a careful reexamination of American foreign trade policy. Congress authorized the commission as part of a revenue bill early in September.

A second issue upon which Wilson shifted position was the creation of a special farm credit system. The goal—finding some way to extend long-term credit to farmers—was one with which Wilson had always agreed, but when the issue came up in 1914 he threatened to veto any system that would be run and guaranteed by the federal government. "I have a very deep conviction," he had said then, "that it is unwise and unjustifiable to extend the credit of the Government to a single class of the community" (Link and others 1979, 30:24). In his third annual message to Congress in December 1915, however, Wilson hinted that he might be changing his mind on this matter also, although he was vague about what he would accept. Taking a chance on the president's attitude, Sen. Henry Hollis, D-N.H., and Rep. Asbury Francis Lever, D-S.C., drafted a bill to create a federal land bank system that would depend primarily upon private capital but would be backed by a federal guarantee. To their pleasure, Wilson not only approved the plan but threw the full weight of the administration behind it. The president signed the bill in a ceremony at the White House on July 17, justifying what he had previously described as special interest legislation, as a law intended to rectify the special *disadvantages* under which farmers had been suffering, and thus a measure to create equal opportunities for all (see Document 3.6).

Wilson made a similar argument in signing the Federal Aid Road Act on July 11 (creating a revenue-sharing arrangement with the states to build roads to give farmers equal access to markets), the Warehouse Act on August 11 (to enable farmers to store their crops in federal warehouses and use the stored crops as collateral), the Keating-Owen Child Labor Act on September 3 (to ban the interstate shipment of goods manufactured with child labor), the Adamson Act on September 2 (mandating an eight-hour day for railroad workers on safety grounds), and the Workmen's Compensation Act on September 7 (for federal employees). In addition, the Jones Act, passed by Congress on August 29 and strongly supported by the administration, formally promised independence to the Philippines and set up a new government designed to move in that direction.

Much of the Wilson administration's legislation strengthened the power of the federal government, but, true to his southern heritage, Wilson preferred to strengthen local government whenever he could achieve his aims that way. One important new program, begun in 1914 under the Smith-Lever Act, attempted to protect local rights while at the same time bringing the benefits of federal expertise to farmers. The Smith-Lever Act authorized the Department of Agriculture to hire agricultural agents to advise farmers in every county that wanted them and that would share part of the cost of the system. Although the program did not improve agricultural conditions as much as the administration originally hoped, it proved extremely popular. The cost- and power-sharing provisions of the Smith-Lever Act were carried even further in the 1916 federal highway construction act, which initiated the concept of revenue sharing, under which the federal government provided money but largely relinquished control over planning and construction to state governments.

"*Government,*" Wilson had written in 1889, "*does now whatever experience permits or the times demand*" and he followed that principle as president, but always somewhat uneasily (Wilson 1889, 651). During the second phase of the New Freedom, the demands of the times forced Wilson to enlarge his definition of proper governmental functions, even before the war compelled further increases in the government's role in American society. The president was never entirely comfortable with this expansion of federal power, however. While he supported the Federal Trade Commission Act, Wilson also backed the Smith-Lever Act, which attempted to achieve national goals through invigorated local governments. *Responsible* government, in short, did not necessarily mean the abandonment of *limited* government.

Wilson's conception of limited government did not usually include the old southern Democratic idea of state rights. Even in his early writings he was a strong nationalist, but as president he occasionally found it convenient to use the state rights argument when he did not want to have the federal government do something. Such was the case with Prohibition and, for several years, with woman suffrage.

Prohibition

"I don't drink, but I am not a prohibitionist," Woodrow Wilson told the group about to install him as governor of New Jersey in July 1910. "I believe that the question is outside of politics. I believe in home rule, and that the issue should be settled by local option in each community" (Link and others 1975, 20:565). Before the Civil War, temperance reformers had taken the same position, but when their hard-won laws were ruled unconstitutional in state courts, leading temperance groups like the Anti-Saloon League concluded that liquor was "a national sin, requiring a national solution" (Hamm 1995, 26). By the early twentieth century they were arguing for a constitutional amendment.

In 1913 members of the Anti-Saloon League proposed an amendment to prohibit nationally the "sale, manufacture for sale, and importation for sale of beverages containing alcohol" (quoted in Kyvig 1996, 221). Support for the measure grew gradually, however, and it was not until the declaration of war in April 1917 that victory finally seemed possible. Sale of alcohol was halted around military bases, and, owing to its importance in feeding troops, the use of precious grain in production of alcohol was forbidden. In the same session of Congress, the temperance amendment was revised to make illegal not just the sale, but all manufacturing and trafficking of alcoholic beverages. Prohibitionists were delighted, but Wilson remained unenthusiastic. The issue was a distraction from more important affairs and potentially explosive politically, but he could influence the outcome very little, given the processes of the Constitution. As he told his private secretary Joseph Tumulty in 1917, "I should like very much to keep out of the prohibition mix-up" (Link and others 1984, 45:275).

In December 1917 Congress passed the amendment and sent it to the states for ratification. It called for complete prohibition of alcohol "for beverage purposes," with enforcement power concurrent between the federal and state governments. Within a year and a half the thirty-six states needed to ratify the amendment had acted, and eventually all but Illinois, Indiana, and Rhode Island fell into line. When Wilson signed the amendment in March 1919, he told a friend "that the new law could cause some personal deprivation, but that, once the country became adjusted to it, that it would be of inestimable value. He believed that the masses of the people were behind it upon conviction" (Link and others 1986, 55:489).

Nevertheless, it is clear that Wilson disagreed with a national solution to what he considered a state or local, or even a personal, problem, and feared Prohibition's power to damage his 1916 coalition. His veto of 1919's Volstead Act, which made specific the general provisions of the eighteenth amendment by banning production and distribution of beverages containing over half a percent of alcohol—and thus essentially *all* alcohol—demonstrated his opposition (see Document 3.7). As he wrote in June 1920:

In the absence of a specific definition of what is [meant] by "intoxicating liquors" in the Eighteenth Amendment, the Volstead Act arbitrarily established the term to mean any beverage containing an excess of one-half of one per cent of alcohol. . . . The injustice and the absurdity of such a definition are obvious. Human experience is filled with incontrovertible evidence that beverages containing a much higher percentage of alcohol cannot by any distortion of fact be termed intoxicants. To frame a law upon such a false basis of fact is openly to invite mental resentment against it. (Link and others 1991, 65:454)

After the Volstead Act was passed over Wilson's veto on October 24, 1919, he remained opposed to it. In March 1923, as he pieced together a blueprint for the Democratic Party's approach to national and international politics known as "The Document," he included a suggestion from a friend, Frank Cobb, that the Volstead Act be repealed, "except in respect to foreign and interstate commerce," and its enforcement "be referred to the several states under the 'concurrent' power clause" (Link and others 1993, 68:304). He was delighted to discover that Supreme Court Justice Brandeis agreed that "the attainment of our American ideals is impossible, unless the States guard jealously this field of Governmental action, and perform zealously their appropriate duties" (Link and others 1993, 68:334). Although in other instances Wilson had little difficulty in asserting federal authority over issues, in this case he remained a defender of state rights.

Woman Suffrage

Like Prohibition, Woodrow Wilson initially described woman suffrage as a question for the states, not the national government. "Suffrage is not a national issue, so far. It is a local issue for each State to settle for itself," he told reporters in 1911 when questioned during a campaign stop in California, where the matter had come up for referendum (quoted in Lunardini and Knock 1980–1981, 657). When it became evident during the 1912 presidential campaign that suffrage had broad public support, Wilson grew more cautious. Accosted by a suffragette in Pittsburgh, he explained "that he had not fully considered it and must ask to be excused from making a positive answer." His questioner told him to "lay jokes aside and come to the point," but Wilson was not joking. "I spoke in all sincerity," he told her. "It is a big question and I am only about half way through it. My mind works somewhat slowly and on this subject I really have not come to any conclusion" (Link and others 1977, 24:315). With only nine western states allowing women to vote in 1912, Wilson could still evade the issue, but time was running out.

On March 3, 1913, the day before Wilson's inauguration, some 5,000 suffragists led by Alice Paul of the National American Woman Suffrage Association were attacked by spectators as they marched up Pennsylvania Avenue. The riot injured several marchers and resulted in a congressional investigation and the dismissal of Washington's police chief. It focused national attention on the suffrage issue, and in the spring and early summer of 1913 advocates gained three separate interviews with the president. Wilson proved resistant, however, claiming disingenuously in December 1913 that he could not support suffrage because the Democratic Party had not taken a stand on the issue (see Document 3.8).

By 1915 suffrage had gained so much momentum that it was no longer politically wise to oppose it, but Wilson continued to argue that it was a matter to be decided by the states, not the federal government. During 1915 and 1916 he publicly urged the granting of suffrage on a state-by-state basis, voted for it in an October 1915 New Jersey referendum, and in 1916 he saw to it that the national Democratic platform endorsed the idea (see Document 3.9). When Republican presidential candidate Charles Evans Hughes threw his party's support behind a national amendment, Wilson stood by his state rights position, commenting that, "If I should change my personal attitude now I should seem to the country like nothing better than an angler for votes" (Link and others 1981, 37:529).

Nevertheless, 1916 saw a gradual shift in Wilson's position on the suffrage issue. In keeping with his general transition toward national solutions for other problems that year, as well as with the consensus among members of his family and administration that the time was right, the president gradually softened his state rights approach. Moreover, he benefited from women's votes in suffrage states during the 1916 presidential election, and thereafter he was more receptive to the cause.

During the war years, Wilson took pains to include women in the war effort. Prominent woman suffragists were appointed to the Women's Committee of the Council of National Defense, and the president persuaded the House of Representatives to create a committee on Woman Suffrage, although he continued to oppose a constitutional amendment. Only after Alice Paul's Woman's Party spent the summer picketing in front of the White House did he become convinced that "the marvelous heroism and splendid loyalty of our women, and the services they have rendered the nation" during the war justified making suffrage a national priority (Link and others 1984, 46:81).

However belatedly and reluctantly Wilson came to support suffrage, once converted he became a vigorous advocate. When a suffrage amendment came before the House for consideration in January 1918, he endorsed the measure "as an act of right and justice" (quoted in Kyvig 1996, 233). The statement mollified southern and western Democrats, and the amendment passed 274–136. The Senate put up greater resistance. Throughout 1918 Wilson labored to win approval for the amendment, bombarding senators who were undecided or opposed with pleas for support. Despite Wilson's speech to the Senate on September 30 in support of the measure, the amendment fell short of the necessary two-thirds vote needed for passage (see Document 3.10).

In his December 1918 State of the Union address Wilson again recommended passage of the suffrage amendment. Women, he told Congress, had been instrumental in winning the war:

The least tribute we can pay them is to make them the equals of men in political rights as they have proved themselves their equals in every field of practical work they have entered, whether for themselves or for their country. These great days of completed achievement would be sadly marred were we to omit that act of justice. (Link and others 1986, 53:277)

Suffragists expected the amendment to pass in this new Congress, but asked Wilson to speak to several uncommitted senators to make sure of it. The president obliged with a vigorous letter-writing campaign. To the friend of one senator he wrote, "I am taking the liberty of writing this to ask if you would not be willing to exert what friendly influence you can . . . to induce him to vote for the suffrage amendment. I have this very much at heart, and would be delighted if you could help" (Link and others 1986, 53:287). In Paris in January 1919, Wilson was concerned enough about the status of its passage to ask Tumulty specifically, "Is there anything else that I can do that might help to bring about the passage of the Suffrage Amendment?" (Link and others 1986, 53:711). Over the next few days he cabled reluctant senators to urge their support of the measure.

When the amendment was defeated by only one vote—55–29—in February 1919, Wilson campaigned even harder for it, writing to wavering senators throughout the spring. He welcomed the opening of the 66th Congress on May 20, 1919, with a message arguing,

It seems to me that every consideration of justice and of public advantage calls for the immediate adoption of that amendment and its submission forthwith to the legislatures of the several states. Throughout all the world this long delayed extension of the suffrage is looked for; in the United States, longer, I believe, than anywhere else. (Link and others 1988, 59:296)

Congress finally agreed. On May 21 the House passed the amendment, 304–90; on June 4 the Senate approved it, 56–25. Wilson's elation was genuine when he cabled National American Woman Suffrage Association president Carrie Chapman Catt two days later to congratulate her on the victory: "I join with you and all friends of the suffrage cause in rejoicing over the adoption of the suffrage amendment by the Congress. Please accept and convey to your associates my warmest congratulations" (Link and others 1989, 60:247).

Over the next year and a half, Wilson was too preoccupied by the situation in Europe and his own health to concern himself with ratification, but suffragists called on him again in the summer of 1920. The Tennessee legislature had not called a special session to ratify the amendment, so Wilson was asked to demand this of the governor, Albert Houston Roberts, which he duly did. On August 18 Tennessee ratified, and the amendment was added to the Constitution.

It is difficult to know for certain whether Wilson's conversion to support of suffrage was the result of political expediency or genuine conviction, but it is noteworthy that once convinced, his scruples about state rights vanished. Here as elsewhere, he sometimes used a state rights argument as an excuse for inactivity in a matter where he disliked the course proposed, but it seems to have been a political expedient rather than a serious conviction about a real limitation of federal power.

Civil Rights and Liberties

Woodrow Wilson's endorsement of woman suffrage did not carry over to general support for civil rights. Despite receiving significant black support in the 1912 election, the Wilson administration increased segregation of the civil service even as it reduced the number of black federal workers. Socially, African Americans experienced upward mobility during World War I, but these gains were reversed when the United States demobilized, resulting in frustration, economic disruption, and ultimately rioting in 1919 and 1920. More broadly, the Wilson administration also violated civil rights by condoning persecution of radicals, critics of the economic system, and opponents of American involvement in the war, regardless of race.

Wilson demonstrated insensitivity to civil rights issues early in his administration. Although he promised African Americans fair treatment during the 1912 campaign, once in office the administration appointed whites to a number of high-visibility posts traditionally held by African Americans, including the legation in Haiti. The authority Wilson delegated to his cabinet members compounded the problem, allowing racists like Postmaster General Albert Burleson and Secretary of the Treasury William Gibbs McAdoo, to institute rigorous segregation in their departments. In the Washington office of the post office department, for instance, Burleson segregated service at public windows, downgraded all but one black worker to the dead letter office, and shielded the remaining worker behind screens so whites in the office would not have to look at him (see Document 3.11).

Other departments, most notably labor and agriculture, successfully resisted segregation. Assistant Secretary of Labor Louis Post was a founding member of the National Association for the Advancement of Colored People (NAACP) and actively opposed discrimination. During the war the Labor Department's southern offices recruited blacks as well as whites for defense jobs and even paid the workers' way to their new employment; indirectly, the practice helped to speed up the "Great Migration" of blacks from the South that began during the war. In the Agriculture Department black and white scientists routinely worked side by side throughout the Wilson years.

During the summer and fall of 1913 public meetings and protests in the black press forced Wilson to take notice of segregation policies in the administration, and at the end of the year he quietly passed the word to avoid further extensions of the practice. He did not, however, order a reversal of current practices.

Personally, Wilson was paternalistic toward African Americans, as was evident in an interview with William Monroe Trotter in November 1914. Trotter had come to the White House on behalf of the NAACP to protest the administration's segregation policies. The meeting did not go well, but Wilson's remarks accentuated its failure, seeming to suggest that African Americans should not press for equal rights. "Now, you may differ with me in judgment," the president told Trotter. "It is going to take generations to work this thing out. And mark these pages, it will come quickest if these questions aren't raised. It will come quickest if you men go about the work of your race, if you will go about and see that the race makes good and nobody can say that there is any kind of work that they can't do as well as anybody else" (Link and others 1979, 31:303). Wilson may have meant to be optimistic about the future, but his implication that immediate equality was impossible was deeply offensive to Trotter and those he represented (see Document 3.12).

More sensational was a story about the private screening at the White House of D. W. Griffith's film, *The Birth of a Nation,* which had been adapted from the book, *The Clansman,* by Thomas Dixon. Dixon, a former student of Wilson's, arranged to show the film to the president, his family, and some guests on February 18, 1915. Afterwards, Wilson supposedly expressed his admiration for the film, telling Dixon, "It is like writing history with lightning. And my only regret is that it is all so terribly true." In fact, the quotation first appeared in print after Wilson's death and its authenticity was challenged by one of the evening's guests who later said, "Wilson seemed lost in thought during the showing, and . . . he walked out of the room without saying a word when the movie was over" (Link and others 1980, 32:267). At the time, Wilson responded to criticism of the film and of its White House screening by issuing a statement: "The President was entirely unaware of the character of the play before it was presented and has at no time expressed his approbation of it. Its exhibition at the White House was a courtesy extended to an old acquaintance" (Link and others 1980, 33:86). But disclaimer or not, the screening was a public relations blunder that has provided an unfortunate shorthand definition of Wilson's racial outlook ever since.

World War I both improved and worsened the prospects of African Americans in Wilson's America. The curtailing of immigration that occurred when war broke out, and the 1917 draft, cut off the cheap labor that drove northern industry and created new opportunities for southern blacks. But the emigrants did not often find equality in the North, either. In East St. Louis in 1916 and 1917, for instance, white workers' resentment of black strikebreakers in the aluminum industry exploded into rioting, and nine whites and an unknown but significant number of African Americans were killed. Wilson ignored the situation, refusing both to grant interviews with black leaders and to intervene with federal force.

In 1919 Chicago, like East St. Louis, was torn apart by rioting. A fortnight of violence and destruction hit the city beginning July 27, with gangs of blacks and whites savagely attacking one another, and chunks of the city in flames. Twenty-three blacks and fifteen whites were killed, while hundreds more were injured and thousands were left homeless by fires. Similar riots exploded across the country that summer, in areas where black immigration had been most prevalent. Again, the federal government did nothing.

Riots were not the only problem African Americans faced. Between 1917 and 1919 lynchings nearly doubled, causing much concern among black leaders and provoking appeals to the White House. The National Association of Colored Women had already written Wilson in August 1916 to call his attention to the prevalence of lynching in the United

States. "This heinous crime," they declared, "is striking at the root of American civilization. We respectfully call upon you, our chief executive, to declare to this convention your position on this question" (Link and others 1982, 38:15). In Wilson's first public statement on the subject, he replied two days later that "he deplores most earnestly and deeply the violence you alluded to and believes with you that it is a serious menace to the whole structure and spirit of our civilization" (Link and others 1982, 38:24).

The situation did not improve during the next two years. On June 15, 1918, Booker T. Washington's successor at Tuskegee University, Robert R. Moton, urged Wilson to denounce lynching. Wilson told Moton on June 18 that "I have been seeking an opportunity to do what you suggest and if I do not find it soon, I will do it without an opportunity" (Link and others 1985, 48:346). Concerned about the treatment of African Americans in the military, Secretary of War Newton Baker added his voice to the protests in July, arguing that the increasing frequency and ferocity of lynching was causing "unrest among the negroes of the country." He advised the president to ask a governor, whose state had recently experienced a lynching, to vigorously "search out and prosecute the offenders" and thus make an indirect statement. The NAACP echoed the plea on July 25 (Link and others 1985, 48:476).

Wilson responded on July 26 with a speech that denounced lynching as unpatriotic. "There have been many lynchings," he said, "and every one of them has been a blow at the heart of ordered law and humane justice. . . . How shall we commend democracy to the acceptance of other peoples, if we disgrace our own by proving that it is, after all, no protection to the weak?" (Link and others 1985, 49:97, 98).

After leaving the White House, Wilson remained concerned about lynching but only in private. In a 1922 letter, he thanked a man in Manassas, Virginia, for rescuing a man about to be assaulted by a mob. "There is," the ex-president wrote, "it seems to me, no better way to advance the honour and preserve the civilization of the country we love than to absolutely prevent and discredit the barbarous practice of lynching" (Link and others 1993, 68:102). But the letter was never sent. The fact that Wilson, except when pushed to react to some particular atrocity, never expressed public outrage at lynching speaks more to his general insensitivity toward the matter than to outright bigotry. He concerned himself with civil rights issues only insofar as they intersected with reform efforts, and often, because Congress and his administration were filled with southern Democrats, he found himself trading black rights for reforms he thought more essential.

Wilson's administration was insensitive not only to black rights but to civil rights in general. During the war the president supported the adoption of laws authorizing censorship and the jailing of dissenters, culminating in 1919 with the beginning of a "Red Scare." The scare, which drew on fears that the new communist (Bolshevik) government in Russia would export revolution to the United States, brought excesses of repression. In April 1919 a series of bombs sent through the mail to public officials aroused alarm about American radicalism. Labor demonstrators in Boston and New York were attacked on May 1 by mobs hoping to quell the "Red" menace, and, when, a month later, coordinated explosions in eight cities killed two people and a bomb damaged Attorney General A. Mitchell Palmer's house, hysteria gripped the press and public.

In the face of such terrorism, the government began to crack down on suspected Communists. Palmer oversaw the creation of the General Intelligence Division, under J. Edgar Hoover, to pursue radicals. After congressional hearings in October 1919 criticized Palmer's failure to pursue Reds with more zeal, he initiated the so-called Palmer Raids on the Union of Russian Workers. The raids pushed the boundaries of legality, often occurring without warrants or involving break-ins, but under the Alien Act of 1918, Palmer was able to deport some 250 "alien radicals" with little public protest. In January 1920 government agents carried out raids in thirty-three cities that led to the arrest of more than 2,500 people. The hysteria lasted until spring 1920, and, like racial tensions, its legacy extended far into the twentieth century (see Document 3.13).

NEW FREEDOM FOREIGN POLICY

Woodrow Wilson did not study foreign policy during his academic years, nor did he discuss it much in the 1912 campaign. He was confident that the United States had the power to do what it wanted in the world, and he had faith in the altruism of his own motives, but he knew little about specific issues when he took office. Even more than its domestic policy, the administration's foreign policy evolved as experience modified easy assumptions, yet a core of principled commitment to the promotion of democracy and the peaceful resolution of disputes remained unchanged throughout Wilson's eight years in office.

East Asia

Wilson's convictions underlay changes in American policy in Asia that the president made soon after his inauguration. In China a revolutionary government had overthrown the Empress Dowager and now sought foreign recognition. State Department experts remaining from the Taft administration believed the new government was unstable and advised coordinating American policy with that of other powers with economic and strategic interests in the area, but Wilson rejected their advice. He suspected that Republicans in the State Department, like the foreigners in China, were more interested in investments than the welfare of the Chinese. On March 18, 1913, he announced that the United States would withdraw from an international consortium supported by the Taft administration to control international loans to China (see Document 3.14).

In Wilson's opinion, the consortium (made up of banks from the United States, Britain, Russia, Germany, France, and Japan) infringed China's "administrative independence," and he promised that the United States would act independently in assisting China to develop its resources (Link and others 1978, 27:193). A few days later he extended diplomatic recognition to the new Chinese government, declaring that "certain great powers" were withholding recognition only to extort concessions (Houston 1926, 1:49).

Taft's goal in securing American membership in the international loan consortium had been to restrain the sometimes predatory behavior of lenders from other nations. When American bankers withdrew, other members of the consortium were free to impose any conditions they pleased on Chinese borrowers. By the end of World War I Wilson realized that his initial policy had been naïve, and in 1918 the State Department arranged for American participation in a new international loan consortium for China.

Just as Wilson discovered that translating principle into policy in China was difficult, he found that dealing with Japan raised problems for which principle seemed to offer no guidance. Soon after he took office the California legislature began debating a bill to prevent Asian immigrants from owning land. Prejudice against Asians on the West Coast was an old story, but the Japanese were outraged at this new discrimination, and a brief war scare erupted (see Chapter 5).

Wilson sent Secretary of State William Jennings Bryan to California in a fruitless effort to stop the passage of the offensive legislation, and Bryan assured the Japanese that he would negotiate as long as necessary in pursuit of a settlement, but the Japanese refused to be placated with mere words. They wanted a treaty banning discrimination that, under the Constitution, would nullify the California law. Their request put the administration in an extremely difficult position. Although no one in Washington wanted war, the idea of using a treaty to block a state's action was an obvious attack on state rights, and, more broadly, the possibility that racial equality might be mandated by treaty was unacceptable.

Faced with this clash of principles, Wilson eventually decided that preserving peace with Japan was more important than protecting state rights, so early in 1914, after secret negotiations, the United States and Japan signed a treaty prohibiting future discrimination (but not affecting California's law). Realizing how controversial such a treaty would be, Wilson held off on submitting it to the Senate in the spring of 1914 while antitrust legislation was pending, and after the outbreak of World War I he shelved it entirely because of new controversies with Japan. The administration's willingness to consider a treaty that would have been explosive in the United States suggests a deep commitment to justice and the peaceful resolution of disputes, but, as it turned out, Wilson's even stronger commitment to supporting China against Japanese aggression poisoned relations between Tokyo and Washington for many years to come.

The Twenty-One Demands

World War I severely disrupted American relations with both China and Japan. In 1914, fearing that the war would extend into China, the State Department made several proposals to neutralize the western Pacific, but these went by the wayside when Japan invaded China's eastern seaboard. Citing its 1902 alliance with Britain and protesting that it would respect Chinese territory and neutrality, in late August Japan overran the German leasehold in Kiaochow (Jiaozhou), pledging to return it eventually to China. American diplomats in China had warned that Japan might simply find an excuse to invade; Kiaochow seemed to prove it. Acknowledging the lack of concrete American interests in China, the State

Department refused to act, explaining cynically that Chinese independence really was not worth involvement in international turmoil.

On January 18, 1915, the Japanese minister to Beijing followed up
the Kiaochow invasion by presenting China with twenty-one demands
that, if accepted, would have reduced China to a Japanese colony (see
Document 3.15). Washington, stunned by Japan's action, took almost
two months to react to the new situation. Wilson did not want to abandon China, but neither did he want to antagonize Japan for fear that its
anger would be taken out on China. Moreover, as relations with Germany grew tenser in the spring of 1915, Wilson could scarcely afford
another crisis.

On March 13 Wilson sent to Tokyo a note that awkwardly combined
protest and appeasement. It objected to demands that impinged upon
Chinese independence but went on to say that "the United States frankly
recognizes that territorial contiguity creates special relations between
Japan" and neighboring portions of China (Link and others 1980,
32:367n.1). The unfortunate "territorial contiguity" phrase convinced
the Japanese they had nothing to fear from the United States, and they
promptly reinstated all their demands—although now describing them
as only "requests." Realizing belatedly that the March 13 note had been
a mistake, Wilson told Bryan in April that "I am convinced we shall have
to try in every practicable way to defend China" and warned him, "We
shall have to be very chary hereafter about seeming to concede the rea-
sonableness of any of Japan's demands or requests" (Link and others
1980, 32:531).

More notes followed at the beginning of May, as Wilson attempted to
prevent any further damage. On May 5 the United States informed Japan
that few, if any, of the demands were acceptable, including those to which
they had earlier assented in March. At the same time, however, Japanese
diplomats put together an "ultimatum" that was presented to Beijing on
May 7. Designed largely to preserve Japanese prestige, the "ultimatum"
greatly softened the demands, thus ending the Sino-Japanese crisis, however imperfectly.

Wilson was unsatisfied. Still believing Japan intended to force acceptance of the demands, he dispatched a final note on May 11, warning
that the United States would not be party to any agreement that violated
the Open Door or American treaty rights in China. This caveat was useful because it provided a basis for American objections to any future

Japanese acts that might endanger American treaty rights in China. In addition, it helped to mitigate, but not negate, his prior tactical error of recognizing Japan's "special interests." Tokyo was outraged by the note and watched for an opportunity to renew its claims in China. When the United States entered World War I, Tokyo exploited American distraction to secure American acceptance of Japan's "special relations" with China in the 1917 Lansing-Ishii agreement and vigorously pressed its claims again during the 1919 peace conference. The long shadow of the Twenty-One demands crisis would fall coldly over the Treaty of Versailles.

Mexico

In addition to problems with China and Japan, Wilson faced revolution in Mexico during his first months in office (see Document 3.16). Although the revolution had actually begun in 1910, the situation grew critical in the weeks just before inauguration, when a military coup in Mexico City overthrew a short-lived democratic government. Victoriano Huerta, the new leader, was likely to be friendlier to foreign investors than his predecessor, but the brutality of his takeover made him unappealing. The outgoing Taft administration happily left Wilson to deal with the mess.

Wilson soon discovered not only that the dictator Huerta had seized power illegally and murdered his predecessor in the process, but that Taft's ambassador to Mexico had been in on Huerta's conspiracy. Appalled, Wilson declared, "I will not recognize a government of butchers." Recognition of Huerta, he argued, would betray the interests of the Mexican people, but, equally important, it would encourage "those who seek to seize the power of government to advance their own personal interests or ambition" (Cronon 1963, 6–7; Link and others 1978, 27:172). The issue was thus defined as a matter of principle from the outset.

Wilson at first tried indirect pressure to get rid of Huerta. He refused to recognize the Mexican government, asked other nations with interests in Mexico to do the same, and continued the Taft administration's ban on arms sales across the border. When several months of that policy produced no results, the president decided to take matters a step further. In the summer of 1913 he sent a special representative to Mexico City to demand that Huerta promise to call national elections in which he would not be a candidate. Huerta promptly rejected the demand and tightened his grip on power, whereupon Wilson dispatched another special agent to talk to a rebel group in northern Mexico calling themselves Constitutionalists.

The new agent sent encouraging news about the rebels. They were less interested in power, he reported, than in fundamental economic and social reform. Wilson welcomed that news but recognized that transforming Mexico would be neither quick nor easy. Probably a long, bloody civil war, with accompanying disorder and damage to foreign interests, lay ahead. "The real cause of the trouble in Mexico," Wilson warned the British ambassador, "was not political but economic," and at its root was "the land question." Resolving it, he said, would require "a fight to the finish" between the revolutionaries and the privileged elite, which outsiders could not control, for to intervene "would unite against the invading party all the patriotism and all the energies of which the Mexicans were capable" (Link and others 1979, 29:229–230). Social and economic justice for the masses of Mexican people strongly appealed to Wilson; this was, after all, the foundation of his own domestic policy.

Yet while Wilson recognized the pitfalls of intervention and warned others against it, it was tempting to think that the United States might be able to do something to speed up Mexico's transformation. Perhaps, at what the president later referred to as "a psychological moment," he might be able to tip the balance in favor of the rebels (Link and others 1979, 29:521). The opportunity arose in April 1914, when a minor confrontation between American sailors and Huertista soldiers created an incident that Wilson used as an excuse to order the U.S. Navy to occupy Huerta's main port at Veracruz. He was sure the rebels would see this as a gesture of support, and that Huerta would be correspondingly discouraged.

He was wrong. Huertistas and rebels joined in denouncing the American invasion, and cadets at the Mexican naval academy in Veracruz mounted a gallant but bloody and futile resistance to American forces. Within hours it was evident that the Veracruz landing had been a ghastly mistake. Wilson now faced a difficult choice. He could turn the landing into a full-scale invasion, as the military recommended, or he could try to get out before more damage was done. He chose the latter course, ordering the military simply to hold the city but not to advance and accepting an offer of mediation of the dispute by the "ABC nations"— Argentina, Brazil, and Chile. A mediation conference during the summer of 1914 at Niagara Falls, Ontario, settled nothing but provided the

Americans with a face-saving opportunity to end the disaster (see Document 3.17).

Wilson learned from the Veracruz experience that military intervention, no matter how benevolently intended, was dangerous and unpredictable. Thereafter his Mexican policy became more cautious. Americans with economic interests in Mexico, foreign countries concerned about their nationals in Mexico, Catholics appalled at Mexican anticlericalism, and Republicans all urged military intervention from time to time, but Wilson resisted the pressure. Although he used diplomatic means to encourage factions he hoped would implement economic and social reforms, he insisted that the Mexican people had the right to determine their own destiny without foreign interference.

The single notable exception to this reticence came in March 1916, when soldiers of a defeated rebel leader who blamed his failure on the Americans raided across the border into Columbus, New Mexico. Wilson quickly ordered American soldiers led by Gen. John J. Pershing to cross the border and hunt down the rebel leader, Pancho Villa. The president assumed that the weak Mexican government, to which he sent assurances that the United States was not challenging Mexican sovereignty or intervening politically, would acquiesce in the American action.

He again was wrong, and when the Americans penetrated deep into northern Mexico without catching Villa, Mexico City sent troops to push the Americans back. On June 21 a skirmish took place between the two forces, with casualties on both sides. Shocked, Wilson admitted that permitting American forces to advance so far into Mexico had been "an error of judgment," and he reassured the Mexicans that he had no intention of supporting "intervention of any kind in the internal affairs" of their country (Link and others 1981, 37:281; Link and others 1981, 36:298).

As with the Veracruz incident, Wilson stopped further advances by the American forces and invited the Mexican government to discuss means to improve security in the border area. A Mexican-American conference on this subject produced no results, but nevertheless, in February 1917 the last American troops were withdrawn from Mexico. After this Wilson refused even to listen to other schemes for intervention in Mexico.

Haiti and the Dominican Republic

The Mexican experience did not prevent Wilson from ordering invasions of Haiti and the Dominican Republic in 1915 and 1916. In these small and chronically chaotic states the president sent in the U.S. Marines after diplomacy failed to achieve lasting stability. Although possible threats to Americans and their economic interests played a part in his decisions, as did a genuine concern for the well-being of the peoples involved, fear of a potential European challenge to American strategic dominance of the Caribbean was the immediate cause of the actions. In an October 1913 speech at Mobile, Alabama, Wilson declared that the United States would "never again seek one additional foot of territory by conquest," but he had no such confidence in the Europeans (Link and others 1978, 28:451) (see Document 3.18).

The likely attraction in Haiti was the Mole St. Nicholas, a fine harbor on the country's north coast where some European power, using as its excuse Haiti's chronic failure to pay its foreign debts, might establish a naval base that could dominate the area and threaten the security of the Panama Canal, which was nearing completion. During 1914 and early 1915 the State Department attempted to negotiate an arrangement that would allow Americans to supervise Haiti's finances and thus deprive the Europeans of any excuse for intervention, but a rapidly changing series of Haitian governments rejected all proposals. In July 1915 when mob violence engulfed the capital, Port-au-Prince, Wilson ran out of patience. "I suppose there is nothing for it but to take the bull by the horns and restore order," he told Secretary of State Robert Lansing, and a few days later American sailors and marines landed and quickly secured control of the country (Link and others 1980, 34:78). The occupation would last nineteen years and leave Haiti with better roads, schools, and hospitals, and a functioning financial system, but neither political nor economic stability would long survive the American withdrawal. Wilson would undoubtedly have accounted the Haitian intervention as one of his administration's successes; a long-term view makes that judgment much more questionable.

In the Dominican Republic the situation was more complex but the result the same. American control over Dominican finances, imposed by Theodore Roosevelt in 1905, failed to secure political stability, and Wilson was afraid European creditors would intervene if civil war broke out. In an attempt to stabilize the situation, the Wilson administration arranged to supervise elections for the legislature in December 1913. The elections were a success, but a deadlock ensued between the legislature and the country's president that deteriorated into civil conflict. A second set of American-supervised elections in the autumn of 1914, accompanied by threats, created temporary order, but in May 1916 the government collapsed. "With the greatest reluctance," Wilson ordered in the marines the following November. It was, he said, "the least of the evils in sight" (Link and others 1982, 40:81). As in Haiti, an eight-year American military occupation produced short-term progress but failed to create the democratization and stability for which Wilson hoped (see Document 3.19).

FOREIGN POLICY LESSONS

In Mexico, Wilson was initially tempted into intervention in the hope of assisting democracy and self-determination. As he learned more about the Mexican rebels, however, he became convinced that they were genuinely committed to reform. Two bad experiences there suggested that imposing change from outside would be difficult at best.

But that did not mean Wilson entirely renounced intervention. In small, weak countries like Haiti and the Dominican Republic, where there were neither broad-based revolutionary movements to support nor serious obstacles to American domination, he yielded to the temptation to impose order. Although Wilson was not eager to intervene in either country, he gradually became convinced that action was necessary to avert dangerous consequences and to lay the foundations for future democracy. It would not be obvious until well after he left office that his hopes were vain.

In East Asia, distance and relative American weakness curtailed any inclination Wilson may have felt toward intervention. Although, as in Latin America, he was eager to promote democracy and self-determination for China, Japan's dominant influence put an activist policy out of reach, particularly during the war. Eight years after announcing that his administration would encourage a democratic China to take a leading role in Asia, Wilson's ideal of self-determination continued to resonate strongly in the region, but American policy had returned to the cautious, noninterventionist lines laid down by Wilson's predecessors. (For the discussion of World War I and the Treaty of Versailles controversy, see Chapter 4.)

BIBLIOGRAPHIC ESSAY

For overviews of Wilson's policies, see the works discussed in the bibliographic essay following the Introduction; for Wilson's own works, see the essay for Chapter 1. For the interpretations of two advisers who were particularly close to Wilson, see David F. Houston, *Eight Years with Wilson's Cabinet, 1913 to 1920, with a Personal Estimate of the President,* 2 vols. (Garden City, New York: Doubleday, Page & Co., 1926), and E. David Cronon, ed., *The Cabinet Diaries of Josephus Daniels* (Lincoln: University of Nebraska Press, 1963). Important aspects of specific policies are covered in a number of good articles and books: Frank Burdick, "Woodrow Wilson and the Underwood Tariff," *Mid-America* 50 (October 1968): 272–290; Robert Murray, "Public Opinion, Labor, and the Clayton Act," *Historian* 21 (May 1959): 255–270; Melvin Urofsky, "Wilson, Brandeis and the Trust Issue, 1912–1914," *Mid-America* 49 (January 1967): 3–28; G. Cullom Davis, "The Transformation of the Federal Trade Commission, 1914–1929," *Mississippi Valley Historical Review* 49 (December 1962): 437–455; William Letwin, *Law and Economic Policy in America: The Evolution of the Sherman Antitrust Act* (New York: Random House, 1965); Jerrold G. Van Cise, *The Federal Antitrust Laws* (Washington, D.C.: American Enterprise Institute, 1962); and James Livingston, *Origins of the Federal Reserve System: Money, Class, and Corporate Capitalism, 1890–1913* (Ithaca, N.Y.: Cornell University Press, 1986).

The history of the Keating-Owen Child Labor Act, one of the most notable elements of Wilson's 1916 program, is discussed in Walter I. Trattner, "The First Federal Child Labor Law (1916)," *Social Science Quarterly* 50 (December 1969): 507–524.

The two amendments passed during the Wilson administration, as well as the forces that shaped them, are detailed in the broader constitutional context in David E. Kyvig, *Explicit and Authentic Acts: Amending the U.S. Constitution, 1776–1995* (Lawrence: University Press of Kansas, 1996), chs. 10 and 11. Prohibition as part of American movement culture is examined in Richard F. Hamm, *Shaping the Eighteenth Amendment: Temperance Reform, Legal Culture, and the Polity, 1880–1920* (Chapel Hill: University of North Carolina Press, 1995). A synthesis on the topic is provided by Anne Firor Scott and Andrew MacKay Scott, *One Half the People: The Fight for Woman Suffrage* (Philadelphia: Lippincott, 1975), but useful insight into Wilson's gradual acceptance of the movement's goals is offered in Christine A. Lunardini and Thomas J. Knock, "Woodrow Wilson and Woman Suffrage: A New Look," *Political Science Quarterly* 95 (winter 1980–1981): 655–671.

Wilson's handling of race relations remains a matter of controversy, yet no synthesis has appeared to fill the gap. Two articles are useful: Henry

Blumenthal, "Woodrow Wilson and the Race Question," *Journal of Negro History* 48 (January 1963): 1–21; and Judson McLaury, "The Federal Government and Negro Workers under President Wilson" (paper delivered at meeting of the Society for History in the Federal Government, March 16, 2000, available at *www.dol.gov/asp/public/programs/history/ shfgpr00.htm*). Insight into the racial mindset of Wilson's generation is provided in Joel Williamson, *The Crucible of Race: Black-White Relations in the American South since Emancipation* (New York: Oxford University Press, 1984). The paradoxical relationship between progressive reform and race is explored in Jack Temple Kirby, *Darkness at the Dawning: Race and Reform in the Progressive South* (Philadelphia: Lippincott, 1972). The collision between the races during Wilson's second term is detailed in Elliott M. Rudwick, *Race Riot at East St. Louis, July 2, 1917* (Carbondale: Southern Illinois University Press, 1964); William H. Tuttle Jr., *Race Riot: Chicago in the Red Summer of 1919* (New York: Atheneum, 1970); and Robert L. Zangrando, *The NAACP Crusade against Lynching, 1909–1950* (Philadelphia: Temple University Press, 1980). Wilson's race relations in the broader context of civil rights are examined in Nell Irving Painter, *Standing at Armageddon: United States, 1877–1919* (New York: Norton, 1987). See Robert K. Murray, *Red Scare: A Study in National Hysteria, 1919–1920* (Minneapolis: University of Minnesota Press, 1955), or Harry N. Scheiber, *The Wilson Administration and Civil Liberties, 1917–1921* (New York: Cornell University Press, 1960) for discussion of the breakdown in Wilson era civil liberties.

Readers interested in Wilson's foreign policy will quickly discover that there is little agreement among historians about its basic objectives, but only a few samples of these differences can be provided here. Arthur S. Link, in *Woodrow Wilson: Revolution, War, and Peace* (Arlington Heights, Ill.: AHM, 1979), contends, for example, that Wilson's policies, sometimes derided as idealistic and impractical, would have promoted the development of a democratic, stable world that would have benefited nearly all nations and peoples. Frederick S. Calhoun, in *Power and Principle: Armed Intervention in Wilsonian Foreign Policy* (Kent: Kent State University Press, 1986), describes Wilson's policies as based upon a realistic understanding of the limits of force to achieve essentially altruistic goals. N. Gordon Levin and Lloyd Gardner, among others, have contended in a series of books and articles that Wilson's goals, whatever his rhetoric, were the extension of American economic and political hegemony. On this subject, see Levin,

Woodrow Wilson and World Politics: America's Response to War and Revo-
lution (New York: Oxford University Press, 1968); and Gardner, *Safe for*
Democracy: Anglo-American Responses to Revolution, 1913–1921 (New
York: Oxford University Press, 1984). Still other historians, such as Mark
Gilderhus and David Healy, have suggested that idealism and self-interest
often united in his policy. See, for example, Gilderhus, *Pan American*
Visions: Woodrow Wilson in the Western Hemisphere, 1913–1921 (Tucson:
University of Arizona Press, 1986) and Healy, *Drive to Hegemony: The*
United States in the Caribbean, 1898–1917 (Madison: University of Wis-
consin Press, 1988). A perceptive critique of recent scholarship on Wil-
son's foreign policy is provided in David Steigerwald, "Historiography:
The Reclamation of Woodrow Wilson?" *Diplomatic History* 23, (winter
1999): 79–99. The Department of State provides an invaluable docu-
mentary record, *Papers Relating to the Foreign Relations of the United*
States (Washington, D.C.: Government Printing Office, various years).

Roy Watson Curry's *Woodrow Wilson and Far Eastern Policy, 1913–1921*
(New York: Bookman, 1957); and Tien-yi Li's *Woodrow Wilson's China*
Policy, 1913–1917 (New York: Twayne, 1952) are the standard works on
Wilson's dealings with East Asia. The connection between idealism and
self-interest in the larger era's China policy is examined in Jerry Israel, *Pro-*
gressivism and the Open Door: America and China, 1905–1921 (Pittsburgh:
University of Pittsburgh Press, 1971). For an insider's perspective, see Paul
Reinsch's memoir, *An American Diplomat in China* (Garden City, N.Y.:
Doubleday, Page & Co., 1922).

Much has been written on the Wilson administration's relations with
Latin America. An older but still helpful survey of the period is Dana G.
Munro, *Intervention and Dollar Diplomacy in the Caribbean, 1900–1921*
(Princeton: Princeton University Press, 1964). A valuable overview of
Mexican-American relations is Mark T. Gilderhus, *Diplomacy and Revo-*
lution: U.S.-Mexican Relations under Wilson and Carranza (Tucson: Uni-
versity of Arizona Press, 1977). For intervention in the Dominican Repub-
lic and Haiti, see David Healy, *Gunboat Diplomacy in the Wilson Era: The*
U.S. Navy in Haiti, 1915–1916 (Madison: University of Wisconsin Press,
1976); Hans Schmidt, *The United States Occupation of Haiti, 1915–1934*
(New Brunswick: Rutgers University Press, 1971); and Bruce J. Calder,
The Impact of Intervention: The Dominican Republic during the U.S. Occu-
pation of 1916–1924 (Austin: University of Texas Press, 1984).

Document 3.1   Speech before Congress, April 8, 1913

In April 1913 Wilson broke a precedent dating to John Adams's presidency by going personally to the Capitol to address a special session of Congress that he had called to consider tariff reform. In his speech he commented on the novelty of the occasion and then went on to explain his reasons for believing reform was important.

I am very glad indeed to have this opportunity to address the two Houses directly and to verify for myself the impression that the President of the United States is a person, not a mere department of the Government hailing Congress from some isolated island of jealous power, sending messages, not speaking naturally and with his own voice—that he is a human being trying to cooperate with other human beings in a common service. After this pleasant experience I shall feel quite normal in all our dealings with one another. . . .

We have seen tariff legislation wander very far afield in our day—very far indeed from the field in which our prosperity might have had a normal growth and stimulation. . . . We long ago passed beyond the modest notion of "protecting" the industries of the country and moved boldly forward to the idea that they were entitled to the direct patronage of the Government. . . . Consciously or unconsciously, we have built up a set of privileges and exemptions from competition behind which it was easy by any, even the crudest, forms of combination to organize monopoly; until at last nothing is normal, nothing is obliged to stand the tests of efficiency and economy, in our world of big business, but everything thrives by concerted arrangement. Only new principles of action will save us from a final hard crystallization of monopoly and a complete loss of the influences that quicken enterprise and keep independent energy alive.

It is plain what those principles must be. We must abolish everything that bears even the semblance of privilege or of any kind of artificial advantage, and put our business men and producers under the stimulation of a constant necessity to be efficient, economical, and enterprising, masters of competitive supremacy, better workers and merchants than any in the world. Aside from the duties laid upon articles which we do not, and probably can not, produce, therefore, and the duties laid upon luxuries and merely for the sake of the revenues they yield, the object of the tariff duties henceforth laid must be effective competition, the whetting of American wits by contest with the wits of the rest of the world. It would be unwise to move toward this end headlong, with reckless haste, or with strokes that cut at the very roots of what has grown up amongst us by long process and at our own invitation. . . . We must make changes in our fiscal laws, in our fiscal system, whose object is development, a more free and wholesome development, not revolution or upset or confusion. We must build up trade, especially foreign trade. We need the outlet and the enlarged field of energy more than we ever did before. We must build up industry as well, and must adopt freedom in the place of artificial stimulation only so far as it will build, not pull down. . . .

It is best, indeed it is necessary, to begin with the tariff. I will urge nothing upon you now at the opening of your session which can obscure that first object or divert our energies from that clearly defined duty. At a later time I may take the liberty of calling your attention to reforms which should press close upon the heels of the tariff changes, if not accompany them, of which the chief is the reform of our banking and currency laws; but just now I refrain. For the present, I put these matters on one side and think only of this one thing—of the changes in our fiscal system which may best serve to open once more the free channels of prosperity to a great people whom we would serve to the utmost and throughout both rank and file.

Source: Arthur S. Link and others, eds., *The Papers of Woodrow Wilson, 1913* (Princeton: Princeton University Press, 1978), 27:269–272.

Document 3.2   Speech before Congress, June 23, 1913

In June 1913 Wilson again went to the Capitol to ask the members of Congress to extend the special session in order to pass banking and currency reform. In that age before air conditioning, Washington in the summer was a very unpleasant place; that he got his wish was evidence of his mastery over Congress. His speech also hints at the behind-the-scenes work he had done to arrive at a consensus with congressional leaders about the provisions of the proposed legislation.

It is under the compulsion of what seems to me a clear and imperative duty that I have a second time this session sought the privilege of addressing you in person. I know, of course, that the heated season of the year is upon us, that work in these chambers and in the committee rooms is likely to become a burden as the season lengthens, and that every consideration of personal convenience and personal comfort, perhaps, in the cases of some of us, considerations of personal health even, dictate an early conclusion of the deliberations of the session; but there are occasions of public duty when these things which touch us privately seem very small; when the work to be done is so pressing and so fraught with big consequence that we know that we are not at liberty to weigh against it any point of personal sacrifice. We are now in the presence of such an occasion. It is absolutely imperative that we should give the business men of this country a banking and currency system by means of which they can make use of the freedom of enterprise and of individual initiative which we are about to bestow upon them. . . .

We are about to set them free by removing the trammels of the protective tariff. . . . There will follow a period of expansion and new enterprise, freshly conceived. It is for us to determine now whether it shall be rapid and facile and of easy accomplishment. This it can not be unless the resourceful business men who are to deal with the new circumstances are to have at hand and ready for use the instrumentalities and conveniences of free enterprise which independent men need when acting on their own initiative. . . .

No man, however casual and superficial his observation of the conditions now prevailing in the country, can fail to see that one of the chief things business needs now, and will need increasingly as it gains in scope and vigor in the years immediately ahead of us, is the proper means by which readily to vitalize its credit, corporate and individual, and its originative brains. . . . The tyrannies of business, big and little, lie within the field of credit. We know that. Shall we not act upon the knowledge? . . . It is perfectly clear that it is our duty to supply the new banking and currency system the country needs, and it will need it immediately more than it has ever needed it before. . . .

The principles upon which we should act are also clear. The country has sought and seen its path in this matter within the last few years—sees it more clearly now than it ever saw it before—much more clearly than when the last legislative proposals on the subject were made. We must have a currency, not rigid as now, but readily, elastically responsive to sound credit, the expanding and contracting credits of everyday transactions, the normal ebb and flow of personal and corporate dealings. Our banking laws must mobilize reserves; must not permit the concentration anywhere in a few hands of the monetary resources of the country or their use for speculative purposes in such volume as to hinder or impede or stand in the way of other more legitimate, more fruitful uses. And the control of the system of banking and of issue which our new laws are to set up must be public, not private, must be vested in the Government itself, so that the banks may be the instruments, not the masters, of business and of individual enterprise and initiative.

The committees of the Congress to which legislation of this character is referred have devoted careful and dispassionate study to the means of accomplishing these objects. They have honored me by consulting me. They are ready to suggest action. I have come to you, as the head of the Government and the responsible leader of the party in power, to urge action now, while there is time to serve the country deliberately and as we should, in a clear air of common counsel. I appeal to you with a deep conviction of duty. I believe that you share this conviction. . . .

Source: Arthur S. Link and others, eds., *The Papers of Woodrow Wilson, 1913* (Princeton: Princeton University Press, 1978), 27:570–573.

Document 3.3   Speech before Congress, January 20, 1914

In January 1914 Wilson again addressed a joint session of Congress, this time to propose new antitrust legislation. Knowing how nervous businessmen were about new laws on this subject, he emphasized the conservative nature of his proposals and the prospective benefits of his plan for business.

In my report "on the state of the Union . . . ," on the 2d of December last, I ventured to reserve for discussion at a later date the subject of additional legislation regarding the very difficult and intricate matter of trusts and monopolies. The time now seems opportune to turn to that great question. . . .

Legislation is a business of interpretation, not of origination; and it is now plain what the opinion is to which we must give effect in this matter. It is not recent or hasty opinion. It springs out of the experience of a whole generation. It has clarified itself by long contest, and those who for a long time battled with it and sought to change it are now frankly and honorably yielding to it and seeking to conform their actions to it. . . .

The Government and businessmen are ready to meet each other half way in a common effort to square business methods with both public opinion and the law. The best informed men of the business world condemn the methods and processes and consequences of monopoly as we condemn them; and the instinctive judgment of the vast majority of businessmen everywhere goes with them. . . .

We are all agreed that "private monopoly is indefensible and intolerable," and our programme is founded upon that conviction. It will be a comprehensive but not a radical or unacceptable programme and these are its items, the changes which opinion deliberately sanctions and for which business waits:

It waits with acquiescence, in the first place, for laws which will effectually prohibit and prevent such interlockings of the personnel of the directorates of great corporations—banks and railroads, industrial, commercial, and public service bodies—as in effect result in making those who borrow and those who lend practically one and the same, those who sell and those who buy but the same persons trading with one another under different names and in different combinations, and those who affect to compete in fact partners and masters of some whole field of business. . . .

Such a prohibition . . . will bring new men, new energies, a new spirit of initiative, new blood, into the management of our great business enterprises. It will open the field of industrial development and origination to scores of men who have been obliged to serve when their abilities entitled them to direct. It will immensely hearten the young men coming on and will greatly enrich the business activities of the whole country.

In the second place, . . . [t]he country is ready . . . to accept, and accept with relief as well as approval, a law which will confer upon the Interstate Commerce Commission the power to superintend and regulate the financial operations by which the railroads are henceforth to be supplied with the money they need for their proper development to meet the rapidly growing requirements of the country for increased and improved facilities of transportation. . . .

The business of the country awaits also, has long awaited and has suffered because it could not obtain, further and more explicit legislative definition of the policy and meaning of the existing antitrust law. Nothing hampers business like uncertainty. Nothing daunts or discourages it like the necessity to take chances, to run the risk of falling under the condemnation of the law before it can make sure just what the law is. Surely we are sufficiently familiar with the actual processes and methods of monopoly and of the many hurtful restraints of trade to make definition possible, at any rate up to the limits of what experience has disclosed. These practices, being now abundantly disclosed, can be explicitly and item by item forbidden by statute in such terms as will practically eliminate uncertainty, the law itself and the penalty being made equally plain.

And the businessmen of the country desire something more than that the menace of legal process in these matters be made explicit and intelligible. They desire the advice, the definite guidance and information which can be supplied by an administrative body, an interstate trade commission.

The opinion of the country would instantly approve of such a commission. It would not wish to see it empowered to make terms with monopoly or in any sort to assume control of business, as if the Government made itself responsible. It demands such a commission only as an indispensable instrument of information and publicity, as a clearinghouse for the facts by which both the public mind and the managers of great business undertakings should be guided, and as an instrumentality for doing justice to business where the processes of the courts or the natural forces of correction outside the courts are inadequate to adjust the remedy to the wrong in a way that will meet all the equities and circumstances of the case. . . .

Inasmuch as our object and the spirit of our action in these matters is to meet business half way in its processes of self-correction and disturb its legitimate course as little as possible we ought to see to it, and the judgment of practical and sagacious men of affairs everywhere would applaud us if we did see to it that penalties and punishments should fall, not upon business itself, to its confusion and interruption, but upon the individuals who use the instrumentalities of business to do things which public policy and sound business practice condemn. . . .

I have laid the case before you, no doubt as it lies in your own mind, as it lies in the thought of the country. What must every candid man say of the suggestions I have laid before you, of the plain obligations of which I have reminded you? That these are new things for which the country is not prepared? No; but that they are old things, now familiar, and must of course be undertaken if we are to square our laws with the thought and desire of the country. . . .

Source: Arthur S. Link and others, eds., *The Papers of Woodrow Wilson, December 2, 1913–May 5, 1914* (Princeton: Princeton University Press, 1979), 29:153–158.

Document 3.4   Letter from Wilson to Charles Allen Culberson, July 30, 1914

In his speech to Congress on January 20, 1914, Wilson proposed a new law defining unfair competition, but the difficulties in specifying all the possible variations of anti-competitive methods had convinced him, by July 30, when this letter was written to Sen. Charles Allen Culberson, D-Texas, that the task was impossible.

. . . I venture to drop you this line to suggest my very grave doubt as to the advisability of attempting any definition whatever of unfair competition. It seems to me that we ought to leave it for the plotting out it will get by individual decisions with regard to particular cases and situations, just as we have been obliged to plot fraud out in the same way by the processes of experience and the examination of particular relationships. I think that what is most to be desired in the Legislation we are now contemplating is elasticity without real indefiniteness, so that we may adjust our regulation to actual conditions, local as well as national. . . .

Source: Arthur S. Link and others, eds., *The Papers of Woodrow Wilson, May 6–September 5, 1914* (Princeton: Princeton University Press, 1979), 30:320.

Document 3.5   Letter from Wilson to Carter Glass, May 12, 1914

Wilson came to recognize that creating equal economic opportunity for everyone required constant intervention and supervision by government, but he had difficulty in supporting measures that seemed to him to benefit only specific groups within society. In this letter to Rep. Carter Glass, D-Va., Wilson expressed his opposition to legislation that would benefit farmers.

. . . After our conference of this morning, I feel that it is really my duty to tell you how deeply and sincerely I feel that the Government should not itself be drawn into the legislation for credits based on farm mortgages. I think that the bill as it has been outlined would be very serviceable indeed without this feature and that the drawing of the Government into the purchase of land mortgages would launch us upon a course of experimentation in which we should have no guidance from experience either in this country or elsewhere because of the fundamental dissimilarity of conditions here and abroad. Moreover, I have a very deep conviction that it is unwise and unjustifiable to extend the credit of the Government to a single class of the community. . . .

Source: Arthur S. Link and others, eds., *The Papers of Woodrow Wilson, May 6–September 5, 1914* (Princeton: Princeton University Press, 1979), 30:24.

Document 3.6   Statement on Signing the Land Bank Bill, July 17, 1916

Wilson originally regarded measures like the Federal Land Bank Bill as unacceptable special interest legislation. This statement reveals the reasons he gave for changing his position. He supported the law because it was intended to rectify the special disadvantages under which farmers had been suffering, and thus was a measure to create equal opportunities for all.

. . . The farmers, it seems to me, have occupied hitherto a singular position of disadvantage. They have not had the same freedom to get credit on their real assets that others have had who were in manufacturing and commercial enterprises, and, while they sustained our life, they did not, in the same degree with some others, share in the benefits of that life. Therefore, this bill, along with very liberal provisions of the Federal Reserve Act, puts them upon an equality with all others who have genuine assets and makes the great credit of the country available to them. One cannot but feel that this is delayed justice to them, and cannot but feel that it is a very gratifying thing to play any part in doing this act of justice. I look forward to the benefits of this bill, not with extravagant expectations, but with confident expectations that it will be of very wide-reaching benefit; and, incidentally, it will be of advantage to the investing community, for I can imagine no more satisfactory and solid investments than this system will afford those who have money to use. . . .

Source: Arthur S. Link and others, eds., *The Papers of Woodrow Wilson, May 9–August 7, 1916* (Princeton: Princeton University Press 1981), 37:427–428.

Document 3.7   Wilson and Prohibition

The following are the Eighteenth Amendment to the Constitution, which provided for the prohibition of alcoholic beverages in the United States; excerpts from the Volstead Act, which defined alcoholic beverages and provided penalties for selling or possessing them; and excerpts from Wilson's message vetoing the Volstead Act, which was overridden by a vote of 175–55 in the House on October 27, 1919, and 65–20 in the Senate on October 28. Joseph Tumulty, Wilson's secretary, wrote the message with assistance and advice from Secretary of Agriculture David F. Houston. It is unlikely Wilson ever saw it.

AMENDMENT XVIII OF THE CONSTITUTION OF THE UNITED STATES

Section 1. After one year from the ratification of this article the manufacture, sale, or transportation of intoxicating liquors within, the importation thereof into, or the exportation thereof from the United States and all territory subject to the jurisdiction thereof for beverage purposes is hereby prohibited.

Section 2. The Congress and the several States shall have the concurrent power to enforce this article by appropriate legislation.

Section 3. This article shall be inoperative unless it shall have been ratified as an amendment to the Constitution by the legislatures of the several States, as provided in the Constitution, within seven years from the date of the submission hereof to the States by the Congress.

EXCERPTS FROM THE VOLSTEAD ACT

Be it enacted by the Senate and House of Representatives of the United States of America in Congress assembled, That the short title of this Act shall be the "National Prohibition Act."

Sec. 1. When used in . . . this Act (1) The word "liquor" or the phrase "intoxicating liquor" shall be construed to include alcohol, brandy, whisky, rum, gin, beer, ale, porter, and wine, and in addition thereto any spirituous, vinous, malt, or fermented liquor, liquids, and compounds, whether medicated, proprietary, patented, or not, and by whatever name called, containing one-half of 1 per centum or more of alcohol by volume which are fit for use for beverage purposes: *Provided,* That the foregoing definition shall not extend to dealcoholized wine nor to any beverage or liquid produced by the process by which beer, ale, porter or wine is produced, it if contains less than one-half of 1 per centum of alcohol by volume, and is made as prescribed in section 37 of this title, and is otherwise denominated than as beer, ale, or porter, and is contained and sold in, or from, such sealed and labeled bottles, casks, or containers as the commissioner may by regulation prescribe. . . .

Sec. 3. No person shall on or after the date when the eighteenth amendment to the Constitution of the United States goes into effect, manufacture, sell, barter, transport, import, export, deliver, furnish or possess any intoxicating liquor except as authorized in this Act, and all the provisions of this Act shall be liberally construed to the end that the use of intoxicating liquor as a beverage may be prevented. . . .

Sec. 29. Any person who manufactures or sells liquor in violation of this title shall for a first offense be fined not more than $1,000, or imprisoned not exceeding six months, and for a second or subsequent offense shall be fined not less than $200 nor more than $2,000 and be imprisoned not less than one month nor more than five years. . . .

Sec. 33. After February 1, 1920, the possession of liquors by any person not legally permitted under this title to possess liquor shall be prima facie evidence that such liquor is kept for the purpose of being sold, bartered, exchanged, given away, furnished, or otherwise disposed of in violation of this title. . . .

Source: U.S. Statutes at Large 41 [1919]: 305–317.

A VETO MESSAGE

To the House of Representatives:
    I am returning, without my signature, H.R. 6810, "An Act to prohibit intoxicating beverages. . . ."

I object to and can not approve [the] part of this legislation with reference to war-time prohibition. It has to do with the enforcement of an act which was passed by reason of the emergencies of the war and whose objects have been satisfied in the demobilization of the Army and Navy, and whose repeal I have already sought at the hands of Congress. Where the purposes of particular legislation arising out of war emergency have been satisfied, sound public policy makes clear the reason and necessity for repeal.

It will not be difficult for Congress in considering this important matter to separate these two questions and effectively to legislate regarding them, making the proper distinction between temporary causes which arose out of war-time emergencies and those like the constitutional amendment of prohibition which is now part of the fundamental law of the country. In all matters having to do with the personal habits and customs of large numbers of our people we must be certain that the established processes of legal change are followed. In no other way can the salutary object sought to be accomplished by great reforms of this character be made satisfactory and permanent.

Source: Arthur S. Link and others, eds., *The Papers of Woodrow Wilson, September 4–November 5, 1919* (Princeton: Princeton University Press, 1990), 63:601–602.

Document 3.8   Reply to National American Woman Suffrage Association, 1913

On December 8, 1913, Wilson met with a delegation from the National American Woman Suffrage Association. The group of fifty-five women, led by Anna Howard Shaw, hoped to convince the president either to ask Congress to send to the states an amendment permitting national woman suffrage or to insist that the House of Representatives establish a committee on the matter. In his reply, Wilson implied that he supported suffrage personally but evaded any promise of public action.

I want you ladies, if possible—if I can make it clear to you—to realize just what my present situation is. Whenever I walk abroad, I realize that I am not a free man; I am under arrest. I am so carefully and admirably guarded that I have not even the privilege of walking the street. That is, as it were, typical of my present transference from being an individual with his mind on any and every subject to being an official of a great government and, incidentally, or so it falls out under our system of government, the spokesman of a party. I set myself this very strict rule when I was Governor of New Jersey and have followed it as President, and shall follow it as President—that I am not at liberty to urge upon Congress in messages policies which have not had the organic consideration of those for whom I am spokesman. In other words, I have not yet presented any legislature my private views on any subject, and I never shall; because I conceive it to be part of the whole process of government that I shall be spokesman for somebody, not for myself. It would be an impertinence. When I speak for myself, I am an individual; when I am spokesman of an organic body, I am a representative. For that reason, you see, I am by my own principles shut out, in the language of the street, from "starting anything." I have to confine myself to those things which have been embodied as promises to the people at an election. That is the strict rule I set for myself.

I want to say that with regard to all other matters I am not only glad to be consulted by my colleagues in the two houses but I hope that they will often pay me the compliment of consulting me when they want to know my opinions on any subject. One member of the Rules Committee did come to me and ask me what I thought about this suggestion of yours of appointing a special committee of the House as the Senate has already appointed a special committee for consideration of the question of woman suffrage, and I told him that I thought it was a proper thing to do. So that so far as my personal advice has been asked by a single member of the committee, it has been given to that effect. I wanted to tell you that to show you that I am strictly living up to my principles. When my private opinion is asked by those who are cooperating with me, I am most glad to give it; but I am not at liberty until I speak for somebody besides myself to urge legislation upon the Congress.

Source: Arthur S. Link and others, eds., *The Papers of Woodrow Wilson, December 2, 1913–May 5, 1914* (Princeton: Princeton University Press, 1979), 29:21–22.

Document 3.9   Statement on Woman Suffrage, October 6, 1915
To drive home his belief that woman suffrage was a matter for the states, but at the same time signal his support of the vote for women, Wilson released this statement, urging the passage of a New Jersey referendum. Despite the president's support, the referendum did not pass, falling more than 46,000 votes short.

I intend to vote for woman suffrage in New Jersey because I believe that the time has come to extend that privilege and responsibility to the women of the state; but I shall vote, not as the leader of my party in the nation, but only upon my private conviction as a citizen of New Jersey called upon by the legislature of the state to express his conviction at the polls. I think that New Jersey will be greatly benefited by the change. My position with regard to the way in which this great question should be handled is well known. I believe that it should be settled by the states and not by the national government, and that in no circumstances should it be made a party question; and my view has grown stronger at every turn of the agitation.

Source: Arthur S. Link and others, eds., *The Papers of Woodrow Wilson, October 1, 1915–January 27, 1916* (Princeton: Princeton University Press, 1980), 35:28.

Document 3.10   Speech to the Senate, September 30, 1918

Wilson resisted a national woman suffrage amendment for a long time, but by 1918 he had come to see that it was essential to America's leadership among the democracies of the world, as he told the Senate in this speech urging the passage of the Nineteenth Amendment to the Constitution.

The unusual circumstances of a world war in which we stand and are judged in the view not only of our own people and our own consciences but also in the view of all nations and peoples will, I hope, justify in your thought, as it does in mine, the message I have come to bring you. I regard the concurrence of the Senate in the constitutional amendment proposing the extension of the suffrage to women as vitally essential to the successful prosecution of the great war of humanity in which we are engaged. I have come to urge upon you the considerations which have led me to that conclusion. It is not only my privilege, it is also my duty to apprise you of every circumstance and element involved in this momentous struggle which seems to me to affect its very processes and its outcome. It is my duty to win the war and to ask you to remove every obstacle that stands in the way of winning it.

I had assumed that the Senate would concur in the amendment because no disputable principle is involved but only a question of the method by which the suffrage is to be extended to women. There is and can be no party issue involved in it. Both of our great national parties are pledged, explicitly pledged, to equality of suffrage for the women of the country. Neither party, therefore, it seems to me, can justify hesitation as to the method of obtaining it, can rightfully hesitate to substitute federal initiative for state initiative, if the early adoption of the measure is necessary to the successful prosecution of the war and if the method of state action proposed in the party platforms of 1916 is impracticable within any reasonable length of time, if practicable at all. And its adoption is, in my judgment, clearly necessary to the successful prosecution of the war and the successful realization of the objects for which the war is being fought.

That judgment I take the liberty of urging upon you with solemn earnestness for reasons which I shall state very frankly and which I shall hope will seem as conclusive to you as they seem to me.

This is a peoples' war and the peoples' thinking constitutes its atmosphere and morale, not the predelections [*sic*] of the drawing room or the political considerations of the caucus. If we be indeed democrats and wish to lead the world to democracy, we can ask other peoples to accept in proof of our sincerity and our ability to lead them whither they wish to be led nothing less persuasive and convincing than our actions. Our professions will not suffice. Verification must be forthcoming when verification is asked for. And in this case verification is asked for,—asked for in this particular matter. You ask by whom? Not through diplomatic channels; not by Foreign Ministers. Not by the intimations of parliaments. It is asked for by the anxious, expectant, suffering peoples with whom we are dealing and who are willing to put their destinies in some measure in our hands, if they are sure that we wish the same things that they do. I do not speak by conjecture. It is not alone the voices of statesmen and of newspapers that reach me, and the voices of foolish and intemperate agitators do not reach me at all. Through many, many channels I have been made aware what the plain, struggling, workaday folk are thinking upon whom the chief terror and suffering of this tragic war falls. They are looking to the great, powerful, famous Democracy of the West to lead them to the new day for which they have so long waited; and they think, in their logical simplicity, that democracy means that women shall play their part in affairs alongside men and upon an equal footing with them. If we reject measures like this, in ignorance or defiance of what a new age has brought forth, of what they have seen but we have not, they will cease to believe in us; they will cease to follow or to trust us. They have seen their own governments accept this interpretation of democracy,—seen old governments like that of Great Britain, which did not profess to be democratic, promise readily and as of course this justice to women, though they had before refused it, the strange revelations of this war having made many things new and plain, to governments as well as to peoples.

Are we alone to refuse to learn the lesson? Are we alone to ask and take the utmost that our women can give,—service and sacrifice of every kind,—and still say we do not see what title that gives them to stand by our sides in the guidance of the affairs of their nation and ours? We have made partners of the women in this war; shall we admit them only to a partnership of suffering and sacrifice and toil and not to a partnership of privilege and right? This war could not have been fought, either by the other nations engaged or by America, if it had not been for the services of the women,—services rendered in every sphere,—not merely in the fields of effort in which we have been accustomed to see them work, but wherever men have worked and upon the very skirts and edges of the battle itself. We shall not only be distrusted but shall deserve to be distrusted if we do not enfranchise them with the fullest possible enfranchisement, as it is now certain that the other great free nations will enfranchise them. We cannot isolate our thought or our action in such a matter from the thought of the rest of the world. We must either conform or deliberately reject what they propose and resign the leadership of liberal minds to others. . . .

I tell you plainly that this measure which I urge upon you is vital to the winning of the war and to the energies alike of preparation and of battle. And not to the winning of the war only. It is vital to the right solution of the great problems which we must settle, and settle immediately, when the war is over. We shall need then in our vision of affairs, as we have never needed them before, the sympathy and insight and clear moral instinct of the women of the world. The problems of that time will strike to the roots of many things that we have not hitherto questioned, and I for one believe that our safety in those questioning days, as well as our comprehension of matters that touch society to the quick, will depend upon the direct and authoritative participation of women in our counsels. We shall need their moral sense to preserve what is right and fine and worthy in our system of life as well as to discover just what it is that ought to be purified and reformed. Without their counsellings [sic] we shall be only half wise. . . .

Source: Arthur S. Link and others, eds., *The Papers of Woodrow Wilson, September 14–November 8, 1918* (Princeton: Princeton University Press, 1985), 51:158–160.

Document 3.11   A Cabinet Discussion about Segregation in the Government, April 11, 1913

Wilson demonstrated insensitivity to civil rights issues early in his adminis-tration. Although he promised African Americans fair treatment during the 1912 campaign, once in office Wilson permitted several of his cabinet mem-bers to segregate their departments. Wilson's ambivalence toward segregation is apparent in this account of a cabinet discussion early in the administra-tion, as recorded by Secretary of the Navy Josephus Daniels.

. . . The Postmaster General brought up a matter that is always the hard-est matter to deal with—to wit: policies that are affected by race condi-tions. In the railway mail service there are a great many negroes who are employed and it often happens that there are four railway mail clerks in one car and when this happens, the white men might often have to do all the work. It is very unpleasant for them to work in a car with negroes where it is almost impossible to have different drinking vessels and differ-ent towels, or places to wash and he was anxious to segregate white and negro employees in all Departments of the Government, and he had talked with Bishop Walters and other prominent negroes and most of them thought it would be a great thing to do. Mr. Burleson thought the segre-gation would be a great thing as he had the highest regard for the negro and wished to help him in every way possible, but that he believed segre-gation was best for the negro and best for the Service. The matter then came up generally about negro appointments and how to use them. The President said he made no promises in particular to negroes, except to do them justice, and he did not wish to see them have less positions than they now have, but he wished the matter adjusted in a way to make the least friction. A negro is now Registrar of the Treasury, and Mr. Burleson, the Attorney [sic] General, thought it was wrong to have white clerks, men or women, under him, or any other negro. Secretary of the Treasury McAdoo doubted whether the Senate would confirm a negro even if the President appointed one for this place, and believed it would be very doubtful. As to the segregation of negro clerks in the Treasury Department under the Reg-istrar, Mr. McAdoo feared it would not work. The difference in salaries, etc., would operate against it. The up-shot of it all was that no action was taken, but Mr. Burleson said he would work out the matter in the Rail-way Mail Service in an easy way that would not go into effect at once and negroes would be employed on railway mail cars in sections where the appointment of negroes would not be objectionable.

Source: Arthur S. Link and others, eds., *The Papers of Woodrow Wilson, 1913* (Princeton: Princeton University Press, 1978), 27:290–291.

Document 3.12   Excerpt, Meeting between Wilson and William Monroe Trotter, November 12, 1914

William Monroe Trotter, editor and publisher of the Boston Guardian, *led a delegation of African Americans who came to the White House on November 12, 1914, to protest against segregation in federal offices. In this excerpt from the transcript of that meeting, Wilson defended the administration's policies. When Trotter disputed the accuracy of the president's facts, Wilson lost his temper and abruptly terminated the interview, an act he later regretted.*

WILSON: . . . Now, I think that I am perfectly safe in stating that the American people, as a whole, sincerely desire and wish to support, in every way they can, the advancement of the Negro race in America. They rejoice in the evidences of the really extraordinary advances that the race has made—in its self-support, in its capacity for independent endeavor, in its adaptation for organization, and everything of that sort. All of that is admirable and has the sympathy of the whole country.

But we are all practical men. We know that there is a point at which there is apt to be friction, and that is in the intercourse between the two races. Because, gentlemen, we must strip this thing of sentiment and look at the facts, because the facts will get the better of us whether we wish them to or not.

Now, in my view the best way to help the Negro in America is to help him with his independence—to relieve him of his dependence upon the white element of our population, as he is relieving himself in splendid fashion. And the problem, as I have discussed it with my colleagues in the departments, is this, for I had taken it very seriously after my last interview with a committee of this organization. If you will leave with me all the instances you have just cited, I will look into them again. But the point that was put to me, in essence, was that they were seeking, not to put the Negro employees at a disadvantage, but they were seeking to make arrangements which would prevent any kind of friction between the white employees and the Negro employees.

Now, they may have been mistaken in judgment. But their objective was not to do what you gentlemen seem to assume—to put the Negro employees at an uncomfortable disadvantage—but to relieve the situation that does arise. We can't blink the fact, gentlemen, that it does arise when the two races are mixed.

Now, of course color outside is a perfectly artificial test. It is a race question. And color, so far as the proposition itself, is merely an evidence of the development from a particular continent; that is to say, from the African continent. . . .

Now, I am perfectly willing to do anything that is just. I am not willing to do what may turn out to be unwise. Now, it is the unwise part that is debatable—whether we have acted in a wise way or not. If my colleagues have dealt with me candidly—and I think they have—they have not intended to do an injustice. They have intended to remedy what they regarded as creating the possibility of friction, which they did not want ever to exist. They did not want any white man made uncomfortable by anything that any colored man did, or a colored man made uncomfortable by anything that a white man did in the offices of the government. That, in itself, is essentially how they feel—that a man of either race should not make the other uncomfortable. It works both ways. A white man can make a colored man uncomfortable, as a colored man can make a white man uncomfortable if there is a prejudice existing between them. And it shouldn't be allowed on either end. . . .

I want to help the colored people in every way I can, but there are some ways, some things that I could do myself that would hurt them more than it would help them.

Now, you may differ with me in judgment. It is going to take generations to work this thing out. And mark these pages, it will come quickest if these questions aren't raised. It will come quickest if you men go about the work of your race, if you will go about it and see that the race makes good and nobody can say that there is any kind of work that they can't do as well as anybody else.

That is the way to solve this thing. It is not a question of intrinsic equality, because we all have human souls. We are absolutely equal in that respect. It is just at the present a question of economic equality—whether the Negro can do the same things with equal efficiency. Now, I think they are proving that they can. After they have proved it, a lot of things are going to solve them selves.

Now, that is the whole thing. We must not misunderstand one another in these things. We must not allow feelings to get the upper hands of our judgments. We must try to do what judgment demands now, as has been said to Mr. Trotter. I think you have the memoranda, and I will look into it again. I will look into it, and I accept the assurances that were given me, and I have repeated them to you. That is all I can do. . . .

TROTTER: Mr. President, we insist that the facts in the case bear us out in truth—that this segregation is not due to any friction between the races, but is due to race prejudice on the part of the official who puts it into operation.

Mr. President, citizens, as they are picked out, especially in a country where there are many races and many nationalities—and everyone is picked out to be subjected to a prejudice of theirs—they are going to be subjected to all kinds of mistreatment and persecution everywhere throughout the country. They are necessarily objects of contempt and scorn, because segregation is not only a natural order of things, but it is the way of progression and more segregation. The very fact of any racial element of government employees being by themselves is an invitation in the public mind. That fact cannot be denied nor disputed.

Now, Mr. President, this is a very serious thing with us. We are sorely disappointed that you take the position that the separation itself is not wrong, is not injurious, is not rightly offensive to you. You hold us responsible for the feeling that the colored people of the country have—that it is an insult and an injustice; but that is not in accord with the facts, Mr. President. We, if anything, lag behind. . . .

Source: Arthur S. Link and others, eds., *The Papers of Woodrow Wilson, September 6–December 31, 1914* (Princeton: Princeton University Press, 1979), 31:301–305.

Document 3.13   Diary Entry, Josephus Daniels, April 14, 1920

Secretary of the Navy Josephus Daniels kept a diary throughout the Wilson years, but it grew more abbreviated as time passed. In an April 14, 1920, entry he described the first cabinet meeting Wilson attended after his October 1919 stroke. At the meeting the cabinet discussed the mass arrests by Justice Department agents of alleged radicals that had taken place in the autumn of 1919 and January 1920. Attorney General A. Mitchell Palmer accused Assistant Secretary of Labor Louis F. Post of having released alien radicals who should have been deported, but Secretary of Labor William Wilson defended Post. This meeting may have been the first Wilson heard of the so-called Palmer Raids, but in any case, he certainly exercised no leadership on the subject.

Cabinet in WWs study at 10 o'clock. He was seated at his desk and did not rise when we entered as was his custom. He looked fuller in the face, lips seemed thicker & face longer, but he was bright and cheerful.

"I felt it well" he said "to put our heads together, not as the Chicago Aldermen who did so when they wished to make a solid pavement."

[Attorney General A. Mitchell] Palmer took up strike & attributed it to the Bolshevists led by [Soviet diplomat Ludwig] Martens and IWW [a radical labor union] who were the leaders of the strikes. [Labor Secretary] W[illiam] B[.] W[ilson] thought they of course promoted it but economic conditions & the h.c.l. [high cost of living] had some part. Also men were against authority.

Palmer said [Assistant Secretary of Labor Louis F.] Post, in absence of [Secretary] Wilson by sickness, had released alien anarchists who ought to be deported[.] WBW denied this – said all who committed overt acts or joined the Comm[unis]t Labor party by signing had been deported, but those whose Com[munis]t party all went over in a body had not been deported because, while they wished to change government, they were not lawless & expected to compass change by legal ways[.]

Palmer said if Post were removed from office it would end the strike. WBW thought might aggravate it.

Mrs. Wilson & Dr. Grayson came in & Mrs. W said "This is an experiment, you know" & [President Wilson] ought not to stay long

Open season for crtng [criticizing] Burleson, [the president] said with laugh. Told Palmer not to let the country see red[.]

Source: Arthur S. Link and others, eds., *The Papers of Woodrow Wilson, February 28–July 31, 1920* (Princeton: Princeton University Press, 1991), 65:186–188.

▬▬▬

Document 3.14   Diary Entry, Josephus Daniels, March 12, 1913
Suspicious of the intentions of foreign nations, and especially foreign bankers, Wilson and his advisers decided to discourage American participation in an

international banking consortium that had been arranged by the Taft administration to provide capital to China. On March 12, 1913, Secretary of the Navy Josephus Daniels recorded the cabinet's discussion in his diary.

The cabinet held its longest session to-day. It was called at the request of the Secretary of State to discuss the question of the Chinese loan. The European powers had agreed to furnish the new Republic of China money to pay its army and indebtedness upon condition that the money should be disbursed by or under the direction of the foreign governments. A group of American bankers, including what is known as the banker's trust, had stated to the Secretary of State that if requested by the administration they might take that portion of the loan allotted to this country. One of the stipulations made by those offering to make the loan was that if China wished to borrow more money it could be borrowed only from those making this loan. The Taft administration had approved the plan. The matter was discussed two hours, and was opened by Mr. Bryan who luminously stated the objections to the plan. The Secretary of the Treasury thought we could not agree to request the banker's trust to subscribe to the loan. Secretary Lane, who had made a long study of Chinese affairs, thought it would be a mistake to approve this old time favoritism method after China had declared for new ways, and that this country should not be a party to helping China upon condition that it should be beholden to a group of financiers in the biggest nations. Secy Redfield feared if we failed to help in some proper way, the loan would be made by the other nations, and America would lose the chance for building up a large trade. My idea was that we ought to find some way for this Government to help China coupled with the recognition of the Republic of China. The President was clear in his conviction that we could not request the trust group of bankers to effect the loan, and that we ought to help China in some better way. . . .

Source: Arthur S. Link and others, eds., *The Papers of Woodrow Wilson, 1913* (Princeton: Princeton University Press, 1978), 27:174–175.

Document 3.15   Twenty-One Demands

On January 18, 1915, the Japanese minister to Beijing followed up Japan's invasion of Kiaochow by presenting Chinese president Yuan Shikai with twenty-one demands that, if accepted, would have reduced China to a Japanese colony. Officials at the State Department in Washington, however, did not secure a complete listing of the demands until a month later.

ARTICLE I.

Proposed for the purpose of preserving peace in the far east and strengthening the friendly relations between the two countries.

1. China shall recognize the transfer of all the rights in Shantung acquired and enjoyed by Germany in accordance with treaty stipulations or other rights with reference to China, regarding which Japan expects to come to an agreement with Germany eventually.
2. China shall not lease to other countries any territory or island on the coast of Shantung.
3. China shall grant to Japan the right to construct a railway from Yentai or Lungkow to connect with the Kiaochow-Tsinan line.
4. China shall open without delay the principal important cities of Shantung to trade.

ARTICLE II.

Proposed for the purpose of securing to Japan a position of special dominance in South Manchuria and East Mongolia.

1. The lease of Port Arthur and Dairen, together with the South Manchurian Railway and the Mukden-Antung Railway, shall be extended to ninety-nine (99) years.
2. Japanese subjects shall have the right to rent and purchase land in South Manchuria and East Mongolia for uses connected with manufacture or agriculture.
3. Japanese subjects shall have the right to go freely to South Manchuria and East Mongolia for purposes of residence and trade.
4. The right to open and operate mines in South Manchuria and East Mongolia shall be granted to Japanese subjects.
5. China shall obtain the consent of the Japanese Government to actions of the following kinds:
   (a) Permitting citizens or subjects of other countries to build railroads in South Manchuria or East Mongolia, or negotiating for loans.

(b) Hypothecating the various revenues of South Manchuria and East Mongolia as security for foreign loans.

6. China shall consult Japan before employing advisers or instructors for conducting the administrative, financial or military affairs of South Manchuria and East Mongolia.

7. Japan shall have control of the Kirin-Changchun railway for ninety-nine (99) years.

ARTICLE III.

1. China and Japan shall agree to act jointly, not independently, in the contemplated formation of the Han-Yeh-Ping Company.

2. Without consent foreigners shall not be permitted to open and operate mines in the neighborhood of the Han-Yeh-Ping Company's property; and anything affecting the company directly or indirectly shall be decided jointly.

ARTICLE IV.

Proposed for the purpose of effectively protecting the territorial integrity of China.

1. China shall not alienate or lease to other countries any port, harbor, or island on the coast of China.

ARTICLE V.

1. The Central Government of China shall employ influential Japanese subjects as advisers for conducting administrative, financial and military affairs.

2. Japanese hospitals, missions, and schools established in the interior shall have the right to hold land in China.

3. China and Japan shall jointly police the important places in China, or employ a majority of Japanese in the police department of China.

4. China shall purchase from Japan at least half the arms and ammunitions used in the whole country or establish jointly in Japan factories for the manufacture of arms.

5. China shall permit Japan to build railroads connecting Wu Chang with Kiukiang and Nanchang, Nanchang with Hangchow, and Nanchang with Chiaochow (Swatow).
6. In case the Province of Fukien requires foreign capital for railway construction, mining, harbor improvements and shipbuilding Japan shall be first consulted.
7. Japan shall have the right to propagate religious doctrines in China.

Source: U.S. Department of State, *Papers Relating to the Foreign Relations of the United States, 1915* (Washington: Government Printing Office, 1924), 93–95.

Document 3.16   Statement on Latin America, March 12, 1913

Wilson issued this statement on relations with Latin America on March 12, 1913. It was widely interpreted as expressing his disapproval of revolutions such as that which had recently brought dictator Victoriano Huerta to power in Mexico.

. . . Cooperation is possible only when supported at every turn by the orderly processes of just government based upon law, not upon arbitrary or irregular force. We hold, as I am sure all thoughtful leaders of republican government everywhere hold, that just government rests always upon the consent of the governed, and that there can be no freedom without order based upon law and upon the public conscience and approval. We shall look to make these principles the basis of mutual intercourse, respect, and helpfulness between our sister republics and ourselves. We shall lend our influence of every kind to the realization of these principles in fact and practice, knowing that disorder, personal intrigue and defiance of constitutional rights weaken and discredit government and injure none so much as the people who are unfortunate enough to have their common life and their common affairs so tainted and disturbed. We can have no sympathy with those who seek to seize the power of government to advance their own personal interests or ambition. We are the friends of peace, but we know that there can be no lasting or stable peace in such circumstances. As friends, therefore, we shall prefer those who act in the interest of peace and honor, who protect private rights and respect the restraints of constitutional provision. Mutual respect seems to us the indispensable foundation of friendship between states, as between individuals.

The United States has nothing to seek in Central and South America except the lasting interests of the peoples of the two continents, the security of governments intended for the people and for no special group or interest, and the development of personal and trade relationships between the two continents which shall redound to the profit and advantage of both and interfere with the rights and liberties of neither. . . .

Source: Arthur S. Link and others, eds., *The Papers of Woodrow Wilson, 1913* (Princeton: Princeton University Press, 1978), 27:172.

Document 3.17   Wilson on the Veracruz Occupation, November 24, 1914

In April 1914, following a minor confrontation between American sailors and troops loyal to Mexican dictator Victoriano Huerta, Wilson ordered the U.S. Navy to occupy Veracruz. He was sure that rebels against Huerta would see it as a gesture of support. He was wrong. Both Huertistas and rebels joined in denouncing the American invasion. At a press conference on November 24, 1914, Wilson explained, off the record, both his reasons for authorizing the occupation and his determination that the Mexican people be accorded the right of self-determination.

. . . Mr. President, what, in your opinion, has been the big thing achieved by the taking and the evacuation of Veracruz?

Well, now, do you mean my own? If I speak to you, not for publication, that is the only way I can speak about it, because in the first place we are in there because of the action of a naval officer. Understand that we didn't go in on the choice of the administration, strictly speaking; but a situation arose that made it necessary for the maintenance of the dignity of the United States that we should take some decisive step; and the main thing to accomplish was a vital thing. We got Huerta. That was the end of Huerta. That was what I had in mind. It could not be done without taking Veracruz. It could not be done without some decisive step—to show the Mexican people that he was all bluff, that he was just composed of bluff and showed that; and that is all they ever got. . . . The very important thing—the thing I have got at heart now—is to leave those people free to settle their own concerns, under the principle that it's nobody else's business. Now, Huerta was not the Mexican people. He did not represent any part of them. He did not represent any part. He was nothing but a "plug ugly," working for himself. And the reason that the troops did not withdraw immediately after he was got rid of was that things were hanging at such an uneven balance that nobody had taken charge; that is, nobody was ready to take charge of things at Mexico City. . . .

Source: Arthur S. Link and others, eds., *The Papers of Woodrow Wilson, September 6–December 31, 1914* (Princeton: Princeton University Press, 1979), 31:351–352.

Document 3.18   Speech, October 27, 1913

During a visit to the Southern Commercial Congress at Mobile, Alabama, Wilson took the opportunity to explain that the struggle against monopoly, which he described as the basis of his domestic policy, would also be central to his foreign policy. In describing how foreign investors dominated Latin American governments and economies, he was one of the first world leaders to describe what modern social scientists call "dependency theory."

. . . The future, ladies and gentlemen, is going to be very different for this hemisphere from the past. These states lying to the south of us, which have always been our neighbors, will now be drawn closer to us by innumerable ties, and, I hope, chief of all, by the tie of a common understanding of each other. Interest does not tie nations together; it sometimes separates them. But sympathy and understanding does unite them, and I believe that by the new route that is just about to be opened [the Panama Canal], while we physically cut two continents asunder, we spiritually unite them. It is a spiritual union which we seek.

Do you not see now what is about to happen? These great tides, which have been running along parallels of latitude, will now swing southward athwart parallels of latitude, and that opening gate at the Isthmus of Panama will open the world to a commerce that she has not known before—a commerce of intelligence, of thought and sympathy between North and South. The Latin-American states, which, to their disadvantage, have been off the main lines, will now be on the main lines. . . .

There is one peculiarity about the history of the Latin-American states which I am sure they are keenly aware of. You hear of "concessions" to foreign capitalists in Latin America. You do not hear of concessions to foreign capitalists in the United States. They are not granted concessions. They are invited to make investments. The work is ours, though they are welcome to invest in it. We do not ask them to supply the capital and do the work. It is an invitation, not a privilege; and states that are obliged, because their territory does not lie within the main field of modern enterprise and action, to grant concessions are in this condition—that foreign interests are apt to dominate their domestic affairs: a condition of affairs always dangerous and apt to become intolerable. . . . [The Latin American nations] have had harder bargains driven with them in the matter of loans than any other peoples in the world. Interest has been exacted of them that was not exacted of anybody else, because the risk was said to be greater; and then securities were taken that destroyed the risk—an admirable arrangement for those who were forcing the terms! I rejoice in nothing so much as in the prospect that they will now be emancipated from these conditions, and we ought to be the first to take part in assisting in that emancipation. . . .

We must prove ourselves their friends and champions, upon terms of equality and honor. You cannot be friends upon any other terms than upon the terms of equality. You cannot be friends at all except upon the terms of honor. We must show ourselves friends by comprehending their interest, whether it squares with our own interest or not. It is a very perilous thing to determine the foreign policy of a nation in the terms of material interest. It not only is unfair to those with whom you are dealing, but it is degrading as regards your own actions. . . .

I want to take this occasion to say that the United States will never again seek one additional foot of territory by conquest. She will devote herself to showing that she knows how to make honorable and fruitful use of the territory she has; and she must regard it as one of the duties of friendship to see that from no quarter are material interests made superior to human liberty and national opportunity. . . .

We have seen material interests threaten constitutional freedom in the United States. Therefore, we will now know how to sympathize with those in the rest of America who have to contend with such powers, not only within their borders but from outside their borders also. . . .

This is not America because it is rich. . . . America is a name which sounds in the ears of men everywhere as a synonym with individual opportunity because a synonym of individual liberty. I would rather belong to a poor nation that was free than to a rich nation that had ceased to be in love with liberty. But we shall not be poor if we love liberty, because the nation that loves liberty truly sets every man free to do his best and be his best, and that means the release of all the splendid energies of a great people who think for themselves. A nation of employees cannot be free any more than a nation of employers can be.

In emphasizing the points which must unite us in sympathy and in spiritual interest with the Latin-American peoples, we are only emphasizing the points of our own life, and we should prove ourselves untrue to our own traditions if we proved ourselves untrue friends to them. . . . We dare not turn from the principle that morality, and not expediency, is the thing that must guide us, and that we will never condone iniquity because it is more convenient to do so. . . .

Source: Arthur S. Link and others, eds., *The Papers of Woodrow Wilson, 1913* (Princeton: Princeton University Press, 1978), 28:448–252.

Document 3.19 Wilson and the Caribbean

Although Wilson frequently asserted Mexico's right to self-determination, he did not apply the same principle to the smaller nations of the Caribbean, where he ordered American forces to intervene to bring to an end periods of revolution and political instability. The first document is his order for intervention in Haiti, sent to Secretary of State Robert Lansing on August 4, 1915; the second, also to Lansing, ordered intervention in the Dominican Republic on November 26, 1916.

ORDER FOR INTERVENTION IN HAITI

. . . These are serious matters, and my own judgment is as much perplexed as yours.

I fear we have not the legal authority to do what we apparently ought to do; and that if we did do what is necessary it would constitute a case very like that of Mr. Roosevelt's action in Santo Domingo, and have very much the same issue.

I suppose there is nothing for it but to take the bull by the horns and restore order. A long programme such as the enclosed letter suggests involves legislation and the cooperation of the Senate in treaty-making, and must therefore await the session of our Congress.

In the meantime this is plain to me:

1. We must send to Port au Prince a force sufficient to absolutely control the city not only but also the country immediately about it from

which it draws its food. I would be obliged if you would ascertain from the Secretary of the Navy whether he has such a force available that can reach there soon.

2. We must let the present [Haitian] Congress know that we will protect it but that we will not recognize any action on its part which does not put men in charge of affairs whom we can trust to handle and put an end to revolution.

3. We must give all who now have authority there or who desire to have it or who think they have it or are about to have it to understand that we shall take steps to prevent the payment of debts contracted to finance revolution: in other words, that we consider it our duty to insist on constitutional government there and will, if necessary (that is, if they force us to it as the only way) take charge of elections and see that a real government is erected which we can support. I would greatly value your advice as to the way in which all this can be done. . . .

ORDER FOR INTERVENTION IN THE DOMINICAN REPUBLIC

It is with the deepest reluctance that I approve and authorize the course here proposed, but I am convinced that it is the least of the evils in sight in this very perplexing situation. I therefore authorize you to issue the necessary instructions in the premises.

I have stricken out the sentence in the proposed proclamation which authorizes the commanding officer to remove judges and others in certain circumstances. It may be necessary to resort to such extreme measures, but I do not deem it wise to put so arbitrary an announcement in the proclamation itself.

Sources: Arthur S. Link and others, eds., *The Papers of Woodrow Wilson, July 21–September 30, 1915* and *November 20, 1916–January 23, 1917* (Princeton: Princeton University Press, 1980 and 1982), 34:78–79; 40:80–81.

Wilson and Colonel Edward M. House, his most trusted adviser. The title "Colonel" was honorary, given to him by one of the several governors of Texas whose election campaigns House had managed.

CHAPTER FOUR

Crises and Flashpoints

W orld War I challenged the United States militarily and economically and stalled the domestic reforms that had been Woodrow Wilson's reason for seeking the presidency, but it also opened a new, worldwide field for American reform ideals. Reflecting the desire of most Americans, Wilson struggled for almost three years to find a way to bring the war to an end without having the United States drawn in, only to find that economic and emotional ties to the Allies, and German submarine attacks on American ships, eventually made neutrality impossible.

In April 1917 the president asked Congress to declare war on Germany, going beyond a request for retribution for submarine attacks to argue that belligerency offered an opportunity to shape the postwar world and make another conflict impossible. He defined that goal more specifically in his "Fourteen Points" speech in January 1918, and he went to Paris in December following the armistice to push his plans at the peace conference personally. At the conference he won agreement on the creation of a League of Nations, which he saw as the foundation of a new international order. But in other ways the Treaty of Versailles, signed in June 1919, departed significantly from the vision set forth in the Fourteen Points. The departures made it vulnerable to liberal critics in the United States, while the inclusion of the League of Nations in the treaty alarmed conservatives reluctant to compromise American freedom of action. In the end, despite a supreme effort by the president that shattered his health, the treaty was defeated by the Senate.

BEGINNING OF WORLD WAR I

The outbreak of war in Europe in August 1914 found Woodrow Wilson at one of the lowest points of his presidential years. His wife Ellen, who had sustained the family through so many earlier crises, was gravely ill and died on August 6, 1914, just as the war was beginning. Although Wilson had sent his confidant, Edward M. House, to Europe in June in hopes of finding ways the United States could help to reduce growing international tensions, the president's mind was not really on diplomacy.

Fortunately, considering Wilson's distraction in August 1914, the first issues he had to confront regarding the war were straightforward. Americans overwhelmingly wanted to remain neutral, and when Wilson urged them to be "neutral in fact as well as in name. . . , impartial in thought as well as in action," most people seemed to approve (Link and others 1979, 30:393–394) (see Document 4.1). House, who thought from the outset that America's interest lay in a victory by the Allies (Britain, France, Russia, and Japan), complained that Wilson was "singularly lacking in appreciation of this European crisis." In fact, Wilson deliberately avoided thinking about the details of the conflict in order to retain his impartiality as a possible mediator (Link and others 1979, 31:95). Reflecting a widespread American belief that the causes of the war were obscure and perhaps trivial, he suggested that it would be best "if no nation gets the decision by arms," because only a compromise settlement would avert "the danger of an unjust peace, one that will be sure to invite further calamities" (Link and others 1979, 31:459).

Wilson's belief that neutrality would improve his chances of being accepted as a mediator was in tension with American economic interests, which pulled the country toward the Allies. Locked in a recession when the war began, American businessmen saw opportunities in the conflict. Less well prepared for war than the Central Powers (Germany and Austria-Hungary), the Allies were eager to buy American products, but two serious problems soon appeared. One was that the incredible cost of modern war rapidly exhausted Allied monetary reserves. If purchases of materiel were to continue, they would have to be on credit, which meant that American lenders would acquire a stake in an Allied victory.

A second problem was that the Germans would do everything in their power to prevent American supplies from getting to their enemies. Obviously, then, the longer the war continued, the more difficult it would be for the United States to maintain neutrality. Recognizing this reality, Wilson placed heavy emphasis on mediation. From the American point of view, almost any negotiated settlement was preferable to a continuation of the war (see Document 4.2).

Circumstances soon threatened both neutrality and mediation. At Secretary of State William Jennings Bryan's suggestion, the United States attempted to minimize its economic links to the belligerents by discouraging private loans to them. The so-called loan ban lasted only a few months, however, before it was overwhelmed by economic reality. In October 1914 the State Department announced that, although actual loans to the belligerents were still frowned upon, it would be acceptable to extend "credit" for purchases—a pointless distinction that, within a year, gave way to full freedom to loan. From October 1914 to March 1915 more than $80 million in credit was extended to the Allies, and by the beginning of 1917 the Allies were buying, usually on credit, $83 million of goods *a week* from the United States. In total, American bankers and businessmen advanced about $2 billion to the Allied governments between 1914 and 1917.

Allied purchases in the United States made it difficult for the Americans to retaliate against legally questionable British restrictions on neutrals' trade with the Central Powers. When the British laid mines in the North Sea, blacklisted American firms that traded with Germany, or seized shipments destined for the Central Powers, the State Department was hesitant about protesting, to avoid jeopardizing trade with the Allies. The British were well aware of this situation and shifted their policy as necessary to secure, as the British foreign secretary later explained, "the maximum of blockade that could be enforced without a rupture with the United States" (Grey 1925, 2:107). Among other stratagems, they arranged to buy most of the American cotton crop, to divert it from German purchasers without antagonizing the Americans.

SUBMARINE WARFARE AND THE *LUSITANIA*

The Germans saw the flow of American goods to their enemies as a major problem, but they had no navy capable of establishing a conventional

blockade of British and French ports. All they had were twenty-five fragile submarines, which were still largely untested in combat. On February 4, 1915, the German government, under pressure from its military
leaders to find some way to break the stalemate that had developed on
the battlefields of France, declared the waters around the British Isles a
"war zone" in which submarines would sink enemy vessels on sight and
might, through error, attack neutral ships as well. The implication was
that neutrals would be wise to keep their ships out of the war zone.

Prior to 1915 warfare at sea had been governed by a customary code
developed in the age of sail, under which warships could stop and search
merchant vessels on the high seas, and even seize them, but they could
not sink them without providing for the safety of passengers and crew.
Woodrow Wilson, hearing about the German announcement on February 5, was appalled. Their policy, he declared, was "unprecedented in
naval warfare." At his orders, the State Department sent a message to
Berlin declaring that the United States would hold Germany to "strict
accountability" for harm to American lives or property (Link and others 1980, 32:194–195) (see Document 4.3).

No one, including Wilson, knew what "strict accountability" meant,
but the policy was soon tested. On March 28 an American traveling on
a British passenger liner was killed in a submarine attack, and a month
later an American ship was slightly damaged by a bomb dropped by a
German plane. Both incidents were ambiguous—the former because the
ship involved was British, and the latter because the attack came from a
plane rather than a submarine. Real tests of "strict accountability" came
on May 1, when an American tanker, the *Gulflight,* was torpedoed,
killing three Americans. Six days later the British steamship, the RMS
Lusitania, was torpedoed off the Irish coast with a loss of 128 Americans. Colonel House, in London on a peace mission for the president,
predicted to the British that "a flame of indignation would sweep across
America, which would in itself probably carry us into the war" (quoted
in Link 1960, 370). On the other hand, Secretary Bryan, who had recommended banning American travel in the war zone, dreaded war and
was "thankful that a believer of peace is in the White House at this time"
(Link and others 1980, 33:134, 135).

Keenly aware of ethnic and political divisions within the country, Wilson feared that war would tear the nation apart. Initially at a loss for what
to do, he gradually began to forge a response to the attack; he would be

patient, calm, and detached. On May 10 he assured an audience of newly naturalized citizens in Philadelphia that "there is such a thing as a man being too proud to fight. There is such a thing as a nation being so right that it does not need to convince others by force that it is right" (Link and others 1980, 33:149). The speech pleased its immediate audience, but many other Americans read "too proud to fight" as "too cowardly to fight." The president's explanation the next day that his remarks represented merely a "personal attitude," not official policy, only made matters worse (Link and others 1980, 33:154).

Responding to public outrage, Wilson and his advisers drafted a sharp protest note to Germany that demanded an apology for the *Lusitania* sinking and insisted the Germans adhere to maritime rules in the future. Germany responded legalistically, implying that the sinking was justified because the British used neutral flags to disguise their ships, instructed their captains to ram submarines, and had been improperly carrying troops and munitions aboard the *Lusitania*. President Wilson was infuriated. In a second note early in June he demanded the Germans change their policy or abandon submarine warfare.

The second note brought a crisis within the administration. Bryan believed that Wilson's uncompromising position would lead to war, and rather than sign the note, he resigned on June 8 (see Document 4.4). His resignation removed from the cabinet the only person with the political stature necessary to challenge the president on fundamental policy. Moreover, it left Wilson completely on his own in maintaining the kind of aloofness from the war that Wilson himself wanted to underpin American policy. When Wilson decided to send the second *Lusitania* note, which was effectively an ultimatum to the Germans, control over the future of German-American relations shifted from Washington to Berlin. As Wilson himself admitted, "unless Germany yields—which, I fear, is most unlikely," war seemed probable (Link and others 1980, 34:8).

For a time, disaster was postponed. *Lusitania* notes traveled back and forth across the Atlantic, and although additional sinkings increased the tension, their circumstances were sufficiently ambiguous so that an open break was averted. The German government secretly ordered submarine commanders to avoid targeting passenger vessels in order to prevent conflict with the Americans. Ignorant of those orders, however, and keenly aware that peace was tenuous, Wilson had to prepare for the possibility that the United States could be drawn into the war at any moment.

Preparedness

Prior to this point the president had seen no need for a military build-up, but as tension with Germany increased, in July 1915 Woodrow Wilson instructed the secretaries of war and navy to prepare plans for strengthening the country's military. Three months later Congress adopted the administration's five-year, $500 million naval expansion plan, which seemed desirable even to isolationists in the South and West. On November 4 Wilson argued in a New York speech that preparedness was to protect neutrality, not to get ready for war. "We have it in mind to be prepared," he said, "not for war, but only for defense; and with the thought constantly in our minds that the principles we hold most dear can be achieved by the slow processes of history only in the kindly and wholesome atmosphere of peace, and not by the use of hostile force" (Link and others 1980, 35:169).

Although there was widespread support for the administration's naval preparedness program, many southern and western Democrats opposed Wilson's proposal to create a 400,000 man "continental army" that would provide a reserve in case of war. Since no one feared an invasion of the United States, such a force seemed expensive and unnecessary unless Wilson was contemplating intervention in the European war. A large army, declared former secretary of state Bryan, was "not only a menace to our peace and safety, but a challenge to the spirit of Christianity which teaches us to influence others by example rather than by exciting fear" (quoted in Link 1964, 33). Wilson defended his program, arguing that "[i]f our citizens are to fight effectively upon a sudden summons, they must know how modern fighting is done," but the continental army plan remained stalled in Congress through the autumn and winter of 1915–1916 (Link and others 1980, 35:297–298).

Early in 1916 congressional opponents of preparedness revived Bryan's idea about how to deal with submarines by introducing the Gore-McLemore Resolutions, which called on the State Department to deny a passport to anyone planning to travel into the war zone on an armed ship. The president was able to prevent passage of the resolutions, but the debate over them demonstrated the strong opposition within the Democratic Party to anything that might increase the risk of war.

In this context Wilson had little choice but to back away from the continental army proposal. During a speaking trip around the Midwest from January 21 to February 4, 1916, he made a persuasive case for some sort of preparedness but did not insist on the reserve army idea. After his return to Washington he indicated a willingness to accept federal control of the national guard instead of the continental army. On February 10 Secretary of War Lindley Garrison, who had been the strongest supporter of the continental army plan, resigned. Wilson chose as his replacement Newton D. Baker, whose near pacifist convictions were reassuring to southern and western Democrats. Baker's appointment cleared the way for congressional passage on June 3 of a National Defense Act that provided for expansion of the regular army to 175,000 men and authorized a national guard of 450,000 men that would come under federal control in a crisis.

The House-Grey Memorandum

The debate over preparedness demonstrated that there was no consensus within the United States about how to meet the risk of war with Germany that had resulted from the collision between German submarine warfare and Woodrow Wilson's insistence on America's rights as a neutral. The only way out of the dilemma seemed to be to secure a negotiated peace in the European war.

In February 1916 it appeared that Colonel House, then in Europe on another peace mission, might have discovered a route to that goal. Following up on hints the British had dropped the previous autumn, House talked to British foreign secretary Sir Edward Grey, and together the two drafted a memorandum stating that whenever Britain and France thought the moment "opportune," President Wilson would summon a peace conference. Should the Allies accept the proposal and Germany refuse it, the United States "would probably enter the war against Germany," but even if the Germans accepted and the conference failed, the Americans might enter on the Allied side (see Document 4.5). When House returned to the United States in March, Wilson rather casually approved the memorandum, merely altering it slightly to make the assurance of support to the Allies less definite.

Although it was not surprising that by 1916 House and Wilson assumed that if the United States entered the war it would be on the Allied side, it was remarkable that, given his recent experience with preparedness and the Gore-McLemore Resolutions, the president should think entry into the war on any terms was possible. In the absence of direct evidence about what Wilson was thinking as he initialed the memorandum, it is only possible to suggest two circumstances that may have shaped his outlook: (1) the American position on submarine warfare had created a crisis with Germany that might force the United States, ready or not, into war at any time; and (2) the memorandum, which included a British promise to consider postwar disarmament and an association of nations, offered Wilson the hope of securing a stable, lasting postwar settlement.

In short, the House-Grey memorandum gave Wilson a way to turn a situation over which he had little or no control into one where the outcome might be shaped by his ideas. Had the Allies ever invoked the House-Grey memorandum, it would have put Wilson in a very awkward situation with Congress, which jealously guarded its sole right to declare war, but he was evidently willing to take that chance. In the end, the Allies never invoked the memorandum's promise, preferring to hope for unaided victory rather than pay the price Wilson demanded.

The *Sussex* Pledge

On March 24, 1916, not long after Woodrow Wilson approved the House-Grey memorandum, a German submarine torpedoed the French steamer *Sussex,* killing eighty passengers, injuring several Americans, and reemphasizing the danger that the United States would be dragged into the war. On April 18 Wilson sent a sharp protest to Berlin, demanding that Germany "abandon its present methods of submarine warfare against passenger and freight-carrying vessels." If it did not, warned the note, the United States would "sever diplomatic relations," which would be just one step short of war (Link and others 1981, 36:496) (see Document 4.6).

Germany was not ready to risk conflict with the United States. Although they had more than doubled their submarine fleet since the beginning of the war, they still did not think they had enough to prevent the Americans, if they became belligerents, from moving men and equipment to France. Accordingly, on May 4 Germany issued the "*Sussex* Pledge," promising not to attack merchant vessels without warning, provided the Americans got the British to relax their blockade of Germany. Wilson, declaring that "responsibility in such matters is single, not joint or conditional, absolute, not relative," accepted the pledge but flatly denied any American obligation to force the British to change their blockade policies (Link and others 1981, 36:650). The Germans, who had apparently never really expected the Americans to put pressure on the British, ignored Wilson's reply, building more submarines and saying nothing.

Peace without Victory

The "*Sussex* Pledge" relieved the most serious threat to neutrality and enabled Americans to believe the United States was in control of events. Over the next several months President Wilson restored some balance to neutrality by protesting against British violations of American rights, and he further strengthened his hand by securing the passage of his preparedness program through Congress. By the time he launched his reelection campaign in the summer of 1916 he was able to claim plausibly that his policies had kept the nation out of war.

Nevertheless, Wilson understood perfectly that if conditions changed, American neutrality was fragile. Following the election he made a new, more urgent, push to find a diplomatic solution to the conflict. On December 18, 1916, he sent identical notes to the belligerents inviting them to state their war aims as a first step toward negotiations. In the notes he observed that the publicly stated aims of both sides were "virtually the same" and that both claimed to want to create a stable peace that would avert future wars (Link and others 1982, 40:274). That seemingly innocuous statement wrecked his peace initiative, if indeed it ever had a chance. The truth was that, although public peace aims on both sides were comparable, their secret goals, involving territorial seizures and punitive economic objectives, were totally incompatible. The Germans never even bothered to reply to Wilson, while in London the government and press complained bitterly and self-righteously that Wilson was equating the noble and selfless motives of the Allies with German imperialism.

Realizing that his December proposal had no chance of success, Wilson decided to suggest possible peace terms himself, in the hope that if he outlined a reasonable compromise, the belligerent governments would not dare prolong the slaughter. On January 22, 1917, he went before the Senate to deliver what has become known as the "peace without victory" speech (see Document 4.7). "Only a peace between equals can last," he said, and he proposed that the United States "join with the other civilized nations of the world in guaranteeing the permanence of peace" based upon mutual guarantees of territory, a concert of power instead of military alliances, governments resting on the consent of the governed, freedom of the seas, and restriction of armaments. In support of such a settlement he was prepared to ask that Americans give up their tradition of isolationism and "add their authority and their power to the authority and force of other nations to guarantee peace and justice throughout the world" (Link and others 1982, 40:534, 536, 538).

Wilson's speech was a remarkable challenge to both the warring nations and his own countrymen, but it never had a chance of succeeding. Two weeks before he spoke to the Senate, the German government had decided that they now had enough submarines to be able to cut off virtually all seaborne traffic to the British Isles. The Germans realized that doing so would almost certainly bring the Americans into the war, but they believed that economic strangulation of the Allies, combined with a new offensive in France, would win the war before the United States could mobilize. On January 31 the German ambassador delivered to the State Department a note announcing a new policy of unrestricted submarine warfare in which all ships, whether belligerent or neutral, were liable to be sunk in the war zone around the British Isles. "As usual," observed a British diplomat, the Germans had been "more stupid than ourselves in our dealings with the U.S." (quoted in Cooper 1976, 228).

THE UNITED STATES ENTERS THE WAR

The situation Woodrow Wilson had long feared—a German attack that would force action on the United States—had now arisen. He immediately severed diplomatic relations, as he had warned the Germans he would do in April 1916, but he still hoped to find some policy that would avoid war. His preferred option, a bill to arm American merchant vessels for self-defense, was filibustered to death in the Senate by what Wilson described as "a little group of willful men," but in truth deck guns manned by untrained merchant sailors would have been no threat to submerged German submarines (Link and others 1983, 41:320).

The pressure built over the next two months. On February 24 the British turned over to the Americans an intercepted message from German foreign minister Arthur Zimmermann to the Mexican government, proposing a German-Mexican-Japanese alliance in the event of war between Germany and the United States. Although the Mexican government quickly rejected the idea, it was further evidence of German hostility toward the United States and helped to arouse American public opinion. So, too, did the sinking of three American ships on March 18, with the loss of fifteen American lives. Secretary of State Robert Lansing thought that such acts amounted to "an announcement that a state of war exists," and House argued that since "we are already in the war," the country should "throw all our resources against Germany" (Link and others 1983, 41:425, 429).

On March 12 a sudden revolution in Russia overthrew the tsar and brought to power a democratic government. The transformation of the last of the major Allies into a democracy exerted an enormous appeal to Wilson, but still he said nothing about what he thought the country should do. Finally, on March 20, he summoned the cabinet to a special meeting to discuss the situation. As was his custom, he went around the table, asking each man to speak. One after the other, each recommended a declaration of war. Finally, he came to Secretary of the Navy Josephus Daniels, whose hatred of war equaled the president's. "Well, Daniels?" said Wilson. Daniels' eyes filled with tears, and his voice trembled, but he affirmed that even he could see no alternative to war. Wilson ended the meeting, giving no hint of what he meant to do. To Lansing, he said only that he would "sleep on it" (Link and others 1983, 41:442–443, 444).

The next day Wilson issued a call for a special session of Congress on April 2 and began work on his war message. Retreating into seclusion, he consulted with no one. The speech the president read in the packed House chamber on the rainy evening of April 2 was entirely his own (see Document 4.8). The "recent course of the Imperial German Government," he began, was "in fact nothing less than war against the government and people of the United States," and there was no choice but for Congress to "accept the status of belligerent" that had been thrust upon the nation. The nation would have to raise an army through conscription, increase taxes to pay the costs, authorize loans to the Allies, and do everything possible to increase agricultural and industrial production. Above all, the United States would have to commit itself without reserve to the defeat of "Prussian autocracy" with all its militarism and imperialism. The failed system of military alliances and balances of power would be replaced with a new international order: "The world must be made safe for democracy" (Link and others 1983, 41:521, 524, 525).

The war message was a stirring call to action, not only to strike back at Germany for its attacks on American ships, but also to restructure the whole international system and create a new order based on democracy and cooperation that instead of "peace without victory" would offer peace and the benefits of victory for everyone. But inspiration did not convert automatically into guns and soldiers. The German assumption that they could win the war before the Americans became a factor might well have been correct.

MOBILIZATION

Over the next months the administration labored frantically to turn the limited preparedness begun in 1915–1916 into real national mobilization. An army had to be created almost from nothing. To do so, camps to house and train the soldiers had to be built; uniforms, weapons, and ships to transport them had to be manufactured; and some means had to be devised to get the soldiers past the German submarines. At the same time, additional food and fuel had to be produced to feed and warm American and European soldiers as well as civilians. Finally, the transportation of these men and goods from farms, mines, and factories to their destinations had to be entrusted to an antiquated and disorganized railroad system prone to logjams and potential collapse. Worse still, the whole production task had to be at least doubled to compensate for the fact that America's allies had exhausted virtually all their own resources and were increasingly dependent upon American money, food, fuel, and industrial production. During the next year and a half the United States loaned nearly $7.5 billion to the Allies, mostly for purchases in the United States. The ordeal of mobilization was further complicated by social concerns. In a nation where one of every seven people was an immigrant, many from countries that were now America's enemies, some method had to be found to assure national unity and promote support for the war.

With such a recipe for disaster, it is no surprise that mobilization failed to go smoothly. An army was raised and trained, but the transport ships to France had to be supplied by the British and French because American shipyards had not begun production quickly enough. The Allies also provided the weapons for American soldiers and the planes for American airmen. The railroad system broke down and in December 1917 was nationalized for the duration of the war. At one point the defense industries east of the Mississippi had to be shut down for a week because the railroads were unable to deliver the coal they needed. Inefficiency and minor scandals so plagued the process that Congress seriously considered creating a special war cabinet to take over control from the president. The drive for national unity ran amok, and Congress passed the Espionage Act of 1917 and the Sedition Act of 1918, resulting in the suppression of virtually all dissent.

Despite so many problems, however, the nation achieved its main goal. Almost three million men were drafted and trained, and the navy devised a convoy system that virtually eliminated the German submarine threat, permitting the transportation of a million men to France, where they arrived in the spring of 1918 just in time to stop the last German offensive. Behind them came torrents of American food, fuel, and manufactured products, the mobilized resources of a continent. The achievement, observes historian Robert Ferrell, was "one of the great wonders of the present century" (Ferrell 1985, 15).

The method by which these miracles were achieved was uniquely American and reflected Wilson's conviction that government's role could be enlarged to meet the emergency without leading to a permanent expansion of federal power. Keeping to a minimum the growth of regular federal departments, he entrusted much of mobilization to specially created agencies whose charters stated clearly that they would go out of existence at the end of the war, and whose leaders were usually unpaid volunteers who fully intended to return to private life. A Railroad Administration operated the nationalized lines; Food and Fuel Administrations promoted production and conservation; a War Industries Board coordinated industrial production; a Shipping Board worked to build ships and use them efficiently; and a War Trade Board attempted to secure cooperation among the foreign purchasers of American products. On March 20, 1918, Wilson formalized the role of these various organizations by naming their heads to a War Cabinet, which met with him every Wednesday, and whose existence emphasized the point that all the special agencies drew their authority primarily from the president. His goal, as historian John Whiteclay Chambers notes, was "to create an American substitute for the expanded, modern, bureaucratic State," that would draw fully on all resources to meet the emergency but would shrink back to its normal size and powers when the crisis passed (Chambers 1987, 203).

In the midst of this turmoil Wilson stood as the central figure. His strength enabled Secretary of War Newton D. Baker to survive attacks on the inefficiency of mobilization; his decision to nationalize the railroads led to a resolution of the national transportation crisis; his words were used by the Committee on Public Information to build support for the war; it was his decision that the United States would fight as an "associated" power rather than as an Ally, so that American influence would not be corrupted by the rumored secret deals among the Allies. Above all, his speeches provided not only the goals around which Americans rallied, but also increasingly commanded admiration and support around the world, in enemy as well as allied nations, and among the millions of colonial peoples who prayed the war might free them finally from European imperialism.

THE FOURTEEN POINTS

Of these speeches, certainly the most important was the Fourteen Points address of January 8, 1918 (see Document 4.9). To attract the various national groups within Austria-Hungary, a multiethnic state, President Wilson proposed that the map of Europe be redrawn "along clearly recognized lines of nationality." For the Germans, surrounded by potentially hostile neighbors, he promised freedom of the seas, removal of economic barriers to trade, and reduction of armaments. For the colonial peoples of the world, as well as for the Germans who felt they had been prevented from securing access to the resources of the Third World by their lack of colonies, he proposed "a free, open-minded and absolutely impartial adjustment of all colonial claims" that would respect the interests of everyone involved. For the Allies, he proposed the evacuation of Russian, Belgian, and French territory occupied by the Germans; arms reduction; and the creation of "a general association of nations" to keep the peace in the future (Link and others 1984, 45:537–538).

As an argument for replacing the old international order with a new one that might meet everyone's needs better, the speech could hardly have been improved. Initial reactions in both the Allied states and the Central Powers were encouraging. The German and Austro-Hungarian chancellors even suggested publicly that Wilson's proposals might make peace possible. Then illusions of victory returned. On February 2, the Allied prime ministers, meeting in a Supreme War Council in France, declared that "the only immediate task before them lay in the prosecution with the utmost vigor . . . of the military effort" (quoted in Martin

1973, 164). A month later the Germans rejected Wilson's proposals in their own way, by imposing the harsh Treaty of Brest-Litovsk on the defeated Russians and throwing the forces freed from the Eastern Front into a great offensive in the West. German professions of a desire for peace, Wilson concluded sadly in the spring of 1918, had been shown to be totally "insincere" (Link and others 1985, 48:54). "There is, therefore, but one response possible from us," he declared at Baltimore on April 6, 1918: "Force, Force to the utmost, Force without stint or limit . . ." (Link and others 1984, 47:270).

Through the spring and early summer of 1918 it looked as if the German offensive might succeed, but then the hundreds of thousands of American soldiers landing in France every month began to make a difference. Gradually, the German attack slowed, then stopped, and a retreat began. Recognizing that defeat was imminent and eager to make the best possible deal, on October 6 the German government sent a note to Wilson proposing an immediate armistice based on the Fourteen Points (see Document 4.10). Suspicious of the sincerity of the German offer and unwilling to act without the agreement of the British and French, Wilson responded warily, but the collapse of the German government at the beginning of November persuaded him that victory was at hand. On November 11 American, British, and French officers joined German representatives in a railroad car in the French forest of Compiègne to sign an armistice.

The appearance of unity was deceptive, however. Although they had agreed reluctantly to accept the Fourteen Points as the basis of the armistice, the British and French were unconvinced by Wilson's argument that peace must be fair to be lasting. They intended to use the peace conference to impose a settlement that would weaken Germany so it could never again be a threat.

THE PEACE CONFERENCE

Suspecting that the Allies did not fully share his goals, President Wilson resolved to attend the peace conference himself. His status as spokesman of the hopes of the peoples of the world, he believed, could translate into power sufficient to secure a treaty that would not only end the war but also assure a just and therefore lasting peace. The decision was an enormous gamble, for it meant that the president's sole trump card—his international prestige as the spokesman of idealistic peace aims—would be on the table from the beginning of the negotiations. If he failed, there would be no one to appeal to.

Nor was the decision to go to Paris the only risk Wilson took. He also decided not to include among the members of the American delegation any well-known Republican, such as former president William Howard Taft or former secretary of state Elihu Root, or any member of the Senate from either party. Shortly before the fall congressional elections, smarting at Republican criticism of his conduct of the war, Wilson had urged Americans to endorse his program by electing a Democratic majority. His appeal further poisoned relations between the parties and, when it failed, made it almost impossible for him to invite any prominent Republican to join the delegation going to Paris. To Europeans it seemed evident that Wilson's leadership had been repudiated by his own countrymen even before he sailed to France.

The president's reception in Europe deflected doubts for a time, however. Two million French citizens cheered his entry into Paris on December 14, and huge throngs greeted him in London and Rome as well. He wanted desperately to believe that their cheers meant they approved his peace program, but the reality was otherwise. In Britain and France recent elections had reinforced leaders' commitment to squeezing everything possible out of the Germans. The crowds who lined the streets to see Wilson were celebrating the American intervention that had at last brought the war to an end, not his peace plans.

Wilson understood the difficulty of the task ahead, but thought he had certain advantages that might be decisive. Knowing that the Allied leaders were "determined to get everything out of the Germans that they can," he said privately that if a satisfactory agreement could not be reached, he was prepared to leave the conference and make a separate peace with the Germans (Link and others 1986, 53:336). He hoped, however, never to have to invoke that ultimate threat. He believed that his peace program would appeal to the people of the world and lead them to urge justice on their leaders, while on a practical level he was optimistic that the continuing dependence of the Allies on American food shipments and economic aid would help to "force them to our way of thinking," as he said to House (Link and others 1983, 43:238). Moreover, the advance of communism in Eastern Europe, and even in Germany, made stabilizing Europe seem urgent to everyone. Agreement among the Allies, British Prime Minister David Lloyd George declared, was "preferable to all sensible men to the alternative of Bolshevism" or to sending armies eastward to fight the Communists, as French Marshal Ferdinand Foch was suggesting (Link and others 1987, 56:262).

When the conference began in January 1919, the conferees quickly discovered that reconstructing the world order presented enormous practical problems. Twenty-seven Allied and associated nations sent official delegates, while dozens of other groups, from the Vietnamese to the Irish, sent representatives to plead their causes; the Central Powers were not invited, nor was the Bolshevik government of Russia. If anything was to get done, it was obvious that not everyone could have an equal voice, so the principal Allied leaders agreed that the main work of drafting a treaty would be carried on by a Council of Ten. When even that proved unwieldy, they reduced the leadership to a Council of Four, consisting of Georges Clemenceau of France, David Lloyd George of Great Britain, Vittorio Orlando of Italy, and Wilson of the United States. Others were to be consulted when decisions affecting their interests were made, and the work of the Council of Four was to be ratified by full plenary sessions, but the shape of the new world order was to be determined by the leaders of the great powers that had dominated the old order. Within that inner circle, only Wilson wanted real change.

It was obvious from the start of the conference that the Europeans had an agenda different from Wilson's. The first issue they wanted to discuss was what would happen to Germany's colonies. In the Fourteen Points Wilson had proposed self-determination for *all* identifiable national groups, including those living in colonies of the victorious as well as defeated European states. Applied literally, his proposal would have meant the end of European imperialism, but the victorious nations had no intention of permitting that. Before the conference met, they made it clear that any new colonial arrangements would apply only to German holdings, and even there, the Europeans wanted simply to follow the traditional practice of dividing up the loot among the victors. At the suggestion of South Africa's Jan Smuts they agreed to apply a fig leaf to their acquisitions by labeling them "mandates" whose progress toward independence would theoretically be supervised by the proposed League of Nations, but the difference was more in words than substance.

Wilson tried to use some of the supposed economic influence of the United States to counter European ambitions but soon found the situation had changed. Instead of buying more American products, the Europeans were canceling previous orders as prewar suppliers and markets were restored. American farmers and manufacturers, who had expanded production to meet the wartime demand, now found themselves with surpluses on their hands and nowhere to sell them. Plummeting prices and looming recession in the United States meant that the Europeans, not Wilson, held the economic power.

Even Wilson's ultimate threat, that he would leave the conference, proved illusory. After he left, there would be no one to call for moderation, and he was convinced that a harsh peace imposed on the Germans would soon lead to another war. But on the positive side, there was still one element of the treaty that might save the whole process. If an effective League of Nations could be constructed, there was hope that, when wartime passions cooled, it could rectify mistakes made in the treaty. As chairman of the conference's committee to draft a constitution for the league, Wilson was in a position to shape the organization.

The committee met ten times between February 3 and 13, 1919, to draft what Wilson would call the League "covenant," which he presented proudly to the full conference on February 14 (see Document 4.11). Key provisions created an assembly, in which all member states would be represented, and a council, made up of the four great powers and four other rotating members. Under Article 10 of the covenant, all members promised "to respect and preserve as against external aggression the territorial integrity and existing political independence of all States members of the League" (Link and others 1986, 55:132). Enforcement of the promise was left in the hands of the council, which had authority, provided its members were unanimous, to investigate threats to the peace and apply economic and even military sanctions. The conference's approval of the League Covenant and the inclusion of it as part of the peace treaty rather than putting it in a separate treaty, as some delegates wanted, were Wilson's greatest victories in Paris, although they cost him in terms of concessions on issues of interest to the Allied leaders.

Except for the League, the Fourteen Points did not fare well in the treaty. Instead of a peace with justice for all, Germany was required to acknowledge sole responsibility for the war and to promise to pay both for damage to civilian property and for pensions for Allied soldiers and their survivors. Portions of Germany's industrial heartland along the Rhine River were taken and put under French or international control.

Germany was shorn of its colonies, and the Austro-Hungarian Empire was dissolved into a series of small "successor states." Italy took territory from Austria that was populated largely by German speakers, and another large group of Germans was incorporated into the new state of Czechoslovakia. Japan's claim to German holdings in China was confirmed, and most of the remnants of the Ottoman Empire in the Middle East were taken over by the British and French. Nothing was said about disarmament, about freedom of the seas, or about the removal of economic barriers among nations, and Germany was forced to sign a blank check for "reparations" for the war with the total to be settled later.

Wilson's compromises in the treaty can be evaluated as either departures from principle or ameliorations of what would have happened without his influence. The same was true of the way the conference dealt, or failed to deal, with Russia. Wilson had said in the Fourteen Points that fair treatment of Russia would be the "acid test" of a postwar settlement. That was before the Russians withdrew from the war by signing the Treaty of Brest-Litovsk, and by the time the peace conference began, the president was no more eager to welcome the Bolshevik leaders of the Soviet Union as partners than were the Europeans. In July 1918 Wilson reluctantly agreed to commit a small number of American troops to take part in joint operations with the Allies in an area near Archangel to recover weapons that had been shipped to the Russians prior to Brest-Litovsk and to control the Trans-Siberian Railroad so that 70,000 Czech soldiers interned in Russia could escape to fight on the Western Front (see Document 4.12). The British and French, worried about the threat of communism in Europe, wanted to expand these limited operations into a full-scale effort to overthrow the Bolsheviks and restore the old regime. By the time of the peace conference, with the war over, the original excuse for intervention in Russia was gone, but the troops stayed. During meetings of the Council of Four Wilson was subjected to constant pressure from the others to support a major expansion of the intervention. He would have nothing to do with the proposal. "The seeds of Bolshevism," he declared, had sprouted in a soil manured by the failures of the tsarist regime. He did not believe that foreign troops could restore the old order, which in any case was "even more disastrous than the present one" (Link and others 1986, 54:102). Although his opposition saved the Soviets—and the Allies—from massive intervention in the Russian civil war, the continuation of the small operation into 1920 frustrated everyone. Wilson would never receive the credit he deserved for preventing a disaster.

As with Russia, there were few issues that arose in Paris where Wilson was able to dictate terms. He won popular acclaim as the spokesman of a humane, rational peace plan, but the European leaders were not awed. Wilson, said Clemenceau scornfully, "thought himself another Jesus Christ come upon the earth to reform men" (Link and others 1987, 56:517). It was not easy being an advocate for self-denial in an atmosphere of anger, bitterness, and desire for vengeance.

In addition to the constant strain of being outnumbered among the negotiators, Wilson also had his own problems. In March he left Colonel House as his stand-in while he returned to the United States for a month to attend to domestic issues. At this point, despite the fact that the conference had been in session for more than a month, little progress had been made in resolving such difficult issues as territorial settlements, German reparations, and future relations with the Soviet Union. The longer the negotiations dragged on, the more demanding the French seemed to become, and so House proposed to Wilson on the eve of his departure that House try to secure a "preliminary treaty" that would lock into place tentative agreements already reached on some of the disputed issues. When Wilson objected that this would take control out of his hands, House assured him that he intended only to have things in order so that final decisions could be made when Wilson returned. In the rush of the president's departure, House's exact assignment was never clearly defined. Over the next weeks Wilson complained that, because of a complicated new code and frequently garbled messages, he did "not really clearly know anything you are trying to tell me" (quoted in Floto 1973, 125).

The truth was that House thought he knew what Wilson wanted and was eager to take credit for having a nearly finished treaty awaiting when the president returned. For whatever reason, House accepted French demands for the transfer of German territory to France that Wilson had been resisting and accepted an Allied argument for enormous German reparations that the president strongly opposed. House reported all this to the president, but Wilson either did not receive it clearly or did not fully understand what House was telling him. Upon his return to Paris in mid-March Wilson obviously felt that House had betrayed him, and the two men were never close again (see Document 4.13).

The president's anger at House probably was compounded by the fact that Wilson was trying to undo House's work while at the same time asking the British and French for changes in the League of Nations agreement to meet objections that had come up in the American Senate (see Document 4.14). The other members of the Council of Four gave him what he needed but in return insisted that he concede on issues they cared about. Still other problems resulted from the fact that during an illness in April Wilson yielded on several issues where, had he been healthy, he might have held the line.

Although most of the departures from the Fourteen Points embodied in the final treaty grew out of deep-rooted clashes of national interests, it is difficult to know whether Wilson gained or lost from attending the conference personally. Being there permitted him to fight on a daily basis for his ideas, but sometimes he might have been better off to have allowed others to do the negotiating while he retained the power to approve or disapprove their decisions.

A draft of the treaty was finished by the beginning of May, and when it was given to the Germans on May 7 they had their first opportunity to propose changes. Not surprisingly, their strongest objections were rejected, but the Council of Four accepted some minor changes to strengthen the support of the German people for their new democratic government and to avoid the possibility that the Allies might have to occupy Germany for a prolonged period to impose the treaty. On June 28 the still-reluctant Germans were marched into the Hall of Mirrors of the royal palace at Versailles and compelled to sign the treaty. When the ceremony concluded, the delegates stepped outside to be cheered by a huge crowd in the gardens, where the fountains were splashing for the first time since the beginning of the war.

TREATY FIGHT IN THE UNITED STATES

President Woodrow Wilson was exhausted by six months of the hardest and most stressful work he had ever done in his life, which had been punctuated in the middle by a serious illness. He was only sixty-two, but his drawn, haggard face made him look old beyond his years. He was eager to go home. He tried to convince himself that the treaty, although "far from ideal," was "tolerably close to the lines laid down at the outset" (Link and others 1989, 61:204). On July 10, two days after landing in New York, the president presented the treaty to the Senate with a dramatic speech that implored Americans to accept "a new role and a new responsibility . . . to make the triumph of freedom and of right a lasting triumph in the assurance of which men might everywhere live without fear. . . . Dare we reject it," he asked, "and break the heart of the world?" (Link and others 1989, 61:434) (see Document 4.15).

If Wilson expected the Senate to see the treaty as he did and to give it quick approval, he was disappointed. Four months earlier Henry Cabot Lodge, R-Mass., Senate majority leader and chairman of the Foreign Relations Committee that would lead the Senate's review of the treaty, had circulated a "round robin" letter signed by enough senators to defeat the treaty. The letter had expressed doubt that American sovereignty was adequately protected by the treaty and criticized it for not explicitly recognizing such traditional American policies as the Monroe Doctrine. Wilson thought he had secured changes in the final treaty that met these objections, but Lodge and most other Republicans listened in stony silence to the president's speech. Although Lodge was not an isolationist and believed the United States needed to continue to cooperate with wartime allies Britain and France to keep the peace in Europe, he was dubious about the broad obligations the United States would have to undertake if the treaty were ratified. Under the treaty, he declared, the United States would be binding itself to use "military or economic force" to "guarantee the territorial integrity of the far-flung British Empire . . . of China or Japan, or of the French, Italian and Portuguese colonies in Africa" (quoted in Widenor 1980, 316, 319). Lodge argued that American interests needed to be protected through amendments or reservations added to the treaty. Eventually, Lodge proposed fourteen reservations to mock Wilson's Fourteen Points.

Lodge was a moderate in comparison to some other Republican senators who wanted nothing to do with the treaty in any form. The "Irreconcilables," as they came to be known, believed that American purity would inevitably be corrupted by association with other nations in the League of Nations. If the United States had any role to play in the world, it must be as an example for others to emulate. No amendments or reservations would be sufficient to win the support of this group. Outside Congress the Hearst newspapers beat the drums for "one-hundred-percent-Americanism" and traditional isolationism.

Also attacking the treaty were representatives of various nationalist groups such as Irish Americans, who were disappointed that Ireland had not received independence, or German Americans (although their voices were muted), who believed Germany had been treated unjustly. Liberals also expressed criticisms of the treaty's departures from the Fourteen Points, particularly because it did not force Japan to withdraw from the German territories it had seized in China, or because it failed what Wilson had called the "acid test" of fair treatment of the Soviet Union. Because of the secrecy in which the negotiations in Paris had been cloaked, few of these people understood the pressures that had forced Wilson into compromises; they tended to focus on specific defects of the treaty, not asking themselves whether the agreement as a whole was the best that could have been secured under the circumstances. This attitude prevailed even among some members of the American delegation, who had been largely cut out of the negotiations by Wilson. Russia expert William Bullitt criticized the omission of a settlement with Russia, and even Secretary of State Robert Lansing muttered behind the scenes about the injustice of the China provisions.

Wilson fought for the treaty during the summer, inviting uncommitted senators to the White House to talk about it and meeting for three hours with the entire Senate Foreign Relations Committee on August 19. None of these meetings seemed to have much effect, however, and as the lines hardened, it became obvious that Wilson did not have the two-thirds support in the Senate he needed. In private, he said that he was willing to consider "interpretive" reservations that might win over a few votes, but he told Senator Gilbert Hitchcock, the Democratic minority leader, that it was "premature" to propose specific language (*New York Times*, August 16, 1919, p.1). Instead, believing that most Americans favored the treaty but had been confused by the nit-picking of opponents, Wilson decided to take the issue to the people, hoping to create a groundswell of support that would sweep away minor objections. On September 3 he set out for a speaking trip through the West.

The speeches, which drew large, enthusiastic crowds, seemed to be effective. By the time the president reached the West Coast, treaty opponents were shadowing him with speakers of their own to try to counteract his influence. At his best, Wilson's pleas to Americans to join in leading "the world on the way to liberty," and his warnings that "you cannot disentangle the United States from the rest of the world," shifted attention from the imperfections of the treaty to its broad objectives. But as the trip continued, the daily grind of receptions and speeches took a toll

(Link and others 1990, 63:156). On September 25, after his speech at Pueblo, Colorado, President Wilson collapsed in his railroad car. Alarmed, his wife and physician insisted that he cancel the rest of the trip, and the train sped back to Washington. There he managed to walk to a waiting car to be driven to the White House, but on October 2 he suffered a massive stroke that left him paralyzed on his left side and largely blind in the center and left fields of both eyes.

Wilson's stroke took him out of the treaty fight six weeks before the Senate's vote. He was unable to lobby or to craft compromises as he had done so effectively in securing passage of his domestic program. Additionally, the disease narrowed his focus and reduced his ability to analyze issues rationally (see Document 4.16). Lying in his bed, cut off by his well-meaning wife and doctors from the details of the battle they feared might overstrain him, he became convinced that persistence would win the day. To supporters in the Senate who counseled acceptance of some reservations as a means of winning a few critical votes, he sent word that any compromise would be a "nullification of the Treaty and utterly impossible" (Grayson 1960, 102). "Let Lodge compromise," he told Sen. Gilbert M. Hitchcock of Nebraska, the Democratic minority leader (quoted in Weinstein 1981, 362). His attitude disorganized and confused his followers, and when the Senate voted on November 19 the treaty with Lodge's reservations was defeated on two separate votes, by 39–55 and 41–51, and defeated again when offered with no reservations, 38–53.

Wilson's stroke undoubtedly affected the outcome of the treaty struggle, but focusing on the president's health, longstanding personal enmity between Lodge and Wilson, partisan politics, and other factors that certainly played roles in the Senate's vote obscures the fact that there was a fundamental issue at stake. Wilson had argued that the United States would not endanger its sovereignty by joining the League of Nations, because the united power of the members would deter any aggressor from ever challenging them, thus making it less rather than more likely that America would ever have to use force. In this sense, membership in the League was not an "entangling" but a "disentangling" alliance "where all act in the common interest and are free to live their own lives under a common protection" (Link and others 1982, 40:539; 1981, 37:126).

Opponents of the treaty saw the matter differently. Their main fear was that the country was promising in advance to commit its forces whenever the Council ordered it to do so, regardless of the circumstances. In their view, the United States would be surrendering control over its military to an international organization. Wilson pointed out that the League Council "cannot give . . . advice without a unanimous vote. . . , without the affirmative vote of the United States," but opponents were unmoved (Link and others 1990, 63:158). It was worse, said Lodge, to make a promise and not intend to honor it than never to make it at all. That was the issue, complicated by Wilson's health and other matters that lay between the president and the opponents of the treaty, and there seemed no way to resolve it.

Americans were shocked by the defeat of the treaty by the Senate on November 19. In the weeks after the vote public demands for a reconsideration grew. In January, having recovered somewhat, Wilson declared his intention to make the election of 1920 "a great and solemn referendum" on the treaty (Link and others 1991, 64:258). On March 19 the Senate, in response to these pressures, took the unusual step of holding a second vote on the treaty, but despite the fact that some Democrats broke ranks with the president to vote for reservations, the 49–35 vote fell far short of the two-thirds majority needed for approval.

WILSON'S HEALTH

Woodrow Wilson remained in office, a pathetic and ruined invalid, for almost a year and a half after his stroke of October 2, 1919. During that time the administration drifted, with no one at the helm. Edith Wilson and the president's doctors, deceived by his "relatively well preserved intellectual function," severely underestimated the debilitating psychological effect of the stroke, which, argues a modern neurologist, left Wilson subject to "disorders of emotion, impaired impulse control, and defective judgment" (Park in Link and others 1991, 64:525). They saw no reason for him to resign, and no mechanism existed for removing him without his consent. Vice President Thomas R. Marshall, long excluded from the inner circle of the administration, was told little about the president's condition, and when Secretary of State Robert Lansing called cabinet meetings without the president's explicit consent, Wilson fired him (see Document 4.17). Until April 1920 Wilson did not meet with the cabinet at all, and most members had little idea just how ill he was.

Routine government business was carried on during Wilson's disability by the bureaucracy, but there was no leadership or creativity. Messages from cabinet members were or were not showed to the president at Edith's discretion and sometimes came back with her marginal notes indicating a decision, but no one knew whether Wilson had actually read or comprehended the documents. In any event, material came to him with little or no context so he could hardly have understood the implications of issues. Edith was not, as she has sometimes been called, "the first woman president." The situation was actually much worse than if she had taken real authority because she not only *refused* to make decisions but also, in the name of protecting Wilson from stress, kept information from him that might have enabled him to do his job, at least minimally.

In some cases, policies that went onto automatic pilot during this period worked out the way Wilson probably would have wanted. That was the case with the termination of the special agencies that had been created to deal with mobilization, which simply expired with the end of the war. Many of the people involved in these organizations believed that they had been so beneficial in planning and coordinating the development of the economy that they should be continued into the postwar period, but without Wilson's active support, the War Industries Board, Food Administration, and other wartime agencies closed early in 1919.

In other instances some established policies went astray during this period. The worst case was the suppression of dissent, which exploded out of control during the Red Scare of 1919–1920 under the leadership of Attorney General A. Mitchell Palmer. During the war Wilson had cautioned those who wanted to repress dissent to act "with the utmost caution and liberality," but his instructions were frequently ignored (Link and others 1983, 44:358). When, in the spring of 1919, a series of strikes and bombings struck the nation, Palmer abandoned all moderation. In a series of raids Justice Department agents rounded up more than four thousand suspected radicals, many of them aliens who often were arrested without warrants and deported without hearings or rights of appeal. Wilson's acceptance of wartime suppression of dissent created the soil in which the Palmer Raids grew, but the attorney general went far beyond anything Wilson had ever specifically authorized. Almost certainly the president never knew what was being done in his name.

During 1919 and 1920 the country stumbled from war to peace without help or guidance from the White House. Plagued by recession, strikes, and fear of radicalism, Americans seemed to regret only mildly the Senate's rejection of the Treaty of Versailles. What they longed for, in the words of Republican presidential candidate Warren G. Harding in 1920, was "not nostrums but normalcy." Wilson's era of challenging Americans to confront the abuses of big business and take on world responsibility was over, at least for the time being. For the next decade, national policy was controlled by those who believed more in limited than responsible government.

BIBLIOGRAPHIC ESSAY

American involvement with World War I has produced an enormous literature from which it is difficult to select a few titles. Three of the five volumes in Arthur Link's biographical series (Princeton: Princeton University Press, 1947–1965)—*Wilson: The Struggle for Neutrality, 1914–1915* (1960); *Wilson: Confusions and Crises, 1915–1916* (1964); and *Wilson: Campaigns for Progressivism and Peace, 1916–1917* (1965)—cover the period from 1914 to the declaration of war in 1917. John W. Coogan, *The End of Neutrality: The United States, Britain, and Maritime Rights, 1899–1915* (Ithaca, N.Y.: Cornell University Press, 1981); Robert Ferrell, *Woodrow Wilson and World War I, 1917–1921* (New York: Harper & Row, 1985); and Robert H. Zieger, *America's Great War: World War I and the American Experience* (Lanham, Md.: Rowman & Littlefield, 2000), offer good starting points and different interpretations.

The best analysis of the personal angle of the *Lusitania* tragedy, and its effect upon Wilson's understanding of World War I, remains Patrick Devlin's *Too Proud to Fight: Woodrow Wilson's Neutrality* (London: Oxford University Press, 1974). Devlin argues that Wilson's decision to intervene in 1917 was arbitrary, while the *Lusitania* would have provided an iron-clad reason for America to enter the war. His book then seeks to explain why Wilson did not ask for war in 1915, when he should have, and did ask some two years later, when he should not have. John Dos Passos's *Mr. Wilson's War* (New York: Doubleday, 1962) offers an impressionistic view of American neutrality and Wilson's reluctance to go to war, while Kendrick A. Clements's *William Jennings Bryan: Missionary Isolationist* (Knoxville: University of Tennessee Press, 1983) explains the break between Wilson and his first secretary of state.

The *Lusitania's* demise and the ensuing controversy have been detailed in Thomas A. Bailey, *The* Lusitania *Disaster: An Episode in Modern Warfare and Diplomacy* (New York: Free Press, 1975). More recently, Diana

Preston's *Lusitania: An Epic Tragedy* (New York: Walker & Co., 2002) has employed previously unused documentary evidence to reexamine the sinking and the many myths surrounding it.

Economic links between the United States and the British, a crucial factor in the American decision to go to war, are well analyzed in John Milton Cooper, "The Command of Gold Reversed: American Loans to Britain, 1915–1917," *Pacific Historical Review* 45, (May 1976): 209–230, and Kathleen Burk, *Britain, America and the Sinews of War, 1914–1918* (Boston: Allen & Unwin, 1985). The British position is described vividly in the memoirs of the foreign secretary, Sir Edward Grey, *Twenty-Five Years*, 2 vols. (New York: Frederick A. Stokes, 1925), and, from a different perspective, Lawrence Martin, *Peace without Victory: Woodrow Wilson and the British Liberals* (Port Washington, N.Y.: Kennikat, 1973).

Historians also have neglected the House-Grey Memorandum. Link's *Confusions and Crises* provides a useful narrative of the incident, but, perhaps due to its confused goals, the scheme has defied analysis. See, for a different perspective, John Milton Cooper, "The British Response to the House-Grey Memorandum: New Evidence and New Questions," *Journal of American History* 59 (March 1973): 958–966.

There is no single synthesis concerning preparedness. A fine book covering the administrative side is Paul A. C. Koistinen, *Mobilizing for Modern War: The Political Economy of American Warfare, 1865–1919* (Lawrence: University Press of Kansas, 1997), but the social and foreign policy implications of preparedness remain unexamined. A useful overview is Robert Ferrell's *Woodrow Wilson and World War I* (New York: Harper & Row, 1985), while Link devotes a chapter to the controversy in *Wilson: Confusions and Crises* (1964).

For the domestic side of the war, the place to begin is with David M. Kennedy, *Over Here: The First World War and American Society* (New York: Oxford University Press, 1980), while Edward M. Coffman's *The War to End All Wars: The American Military Experience in World War I* (New York: Oxford University Press, 1968), and John Whiteclay Chambers II, *To Raise an Army: The Draft Comes to Modern America* (New York: Free Press, 1987), are the best introductions to the military side of the war.

The Paris peace conference has likewise produced a flood of interpretation. Arthur Walworth's *Wilson and His Peacemakers: American Diplomacy at the Paris Peace Conference, 1919* (New York: Norton, 1986) provides a good one-volume overview of the subject. The official record of the conference is Paul Mantoux, *The Deliberations of the Council of Four, March 24–June 28, 1919: Notes of the Official Interpreter,* trans. and ed. by Arthur S. Link and Manfred F. Boemeke (Princeton: Princeton University Press, 1991), but students should supplement this by referring to the enormous amount of additional material included in the thirteen volumes of the *Papers Relating to the Foreign Relations of the United States: The Paris Peace Conference, 1919* (Washington, D.C.: Government Printing Office, 1942–1947). For interpretive disagreements about Wilson's role, see Lloyd Ambrosius, *Wilson and the American Diplomatic Tradition: The Treaty Fight in Perspective* (New York: Cambridge University Press, 1987); Thomas A. Bailey, *Woodrow Wilson and the Lost Peace* (New York: Macmillan, 1944); Herbert Hoover, *The Ordeal of Woodrow Wilson* (New York: McGraw-Hill, 1958); Thomas J. Knock, *To End All Wars: Woodrow Wilson and the Origins of the League of Nations* (New York: Oxford University Press, 1992); Margaret MacMillan, *Paris 1919: Six Months That Changed the World* (New York: Random House, 2002); and J. W. Schulte Nordholt, *Woodrow Wilson: A Life for World Peace* (Berkeley: University of California Press, 1991). Colonel House's controversial role at the conference, which contributed to a permanent break in his friendship with Wilson, is covered exhaustively by Inga Floto's *Colonel House in Paris: A Study of American Policy at the Paris Peace Conference 1919* (Princeton: Princeton University Press, 1973).

For the treaty fight in the United States, a standard account is Thomas A. Bailey, *Woodrow Wilson and the Great Betrayal* (New York: Macmillan, 1945). The most recent analysis of Wilson's struggle for the treaty is John Milton Cooper, *Breaking the Heart of the World: Woodrow Wilson and the Fight for the League of Nations* (New York: Cambridge University Press, 2001). William Widenor's *Henry Cabot Lodge and the Search for an American Foreign Policy* (Berkeley: University of California Press, 1980) makes it clear that critics of the treaty had a rational position that could not readily be reconciled with Wilson's. On the other hand, some historians, including Arthur Link, have argued that had Wilson not suffered a stroke in October 1919 he probably would have found a way to compromise with Lodge. This argument was made by Edwin A. Weinstein in *Woodrow Wilson: A Medical and Psychological Biography* (Princeton: Princeton University Press, 1981), and, in a somewhat different form, in Bert E. Park, *The Impact of Illness on World Leaders* (Philadelphia: University of Pennsylvania

Press, 1986). But the argument is sharply challenged by Alexander and Juliette George in essays in the *Political Science Quarterly* 96 (winter 1981–1982): 662–663, and the *Journal of American History* 71 (June 1984): 198–212, where they reaffirm the validity of their own psychological interpretation (see bibliographic essay for Chapter 2). For the discreet account of Wilson's personal physician, see Cary T. Grayson, *Woodrow Wilson: An Intimate Memoir* (New York: Holt, Rinehart and Winston, 1960). A famous biography of Wilson by Sigmund Freud and William C. Bullitt, *Thomas Woodrow Wilson: Twenty-Eighth President of the United States* (Boston: Houghton Mifflin, 1967) is useless because the factual material upon which it was based was distorted by Bullitt's hatred of Wilson.

▬▬▬▬▬▬

Document 4.1   Press Conference, August 3, 1914

When World War I broke out in August 1914, Wilson urged Americans to remain calm and avoid taking sides in the conflict. He also assured the nation that the war would not adversely affect the United States in the long run.

. . . I think that you will agree that we must all at the present moment act together as Americans in seeing that America does not suffer any unnecessary distress from what is going on in the world at large. The situation in Europe is perhaps the gravest in its possibilities that has arisen in modern times, but it need not affect the United States unfavorably in the long run. Not that the United States has anything to take advantage of, but her own position is sound, and she owes it to mankind to remain in such a condition and in such a state of mind that she can help the rest of the world. I want to have the pride of feeling that America, if nobody else, has her self-possession and stands ready with calmness of thought and steadiness of purpose to help the rest of the world. And we can do it and reap a great permanent glory out of doing it, provided we all cooperate to see that nobody loses his head. . . .

Source: Arthur S. Link and others, eds., *The Papers of Woodrow Wilson, May 6– September 5, 1914* (Princeton: Princeton University Press, 1979), 30:332.

Document 4.2   Speech, January 8, 1915

During the first two years of World War I Wilson believed that a major reason for maintaining American neutrality was to enable the United States to offer its services as an impartial mediator to the nations at war.

. . . Do you not think it likely that the world will some time turn to America and say: "You were right, and we were wrong. You kept your heads when we lost ours; you tried to keep the scale from tipping, but we threw the whole weight of arms in one side of the scale. Now, in your self-possession, in your coolness, in your strength, may we not turn to you for counsel and for assistance"?

Think of the deep-wrought destruction of economic resources, of life, and of hope that is taking place in some parts of the world, and think of the reservoir of hope, the reservoir of energy, the reservoir of sustenance that there is in this great land of plenty. May we not look forward to the time when we shall be called blessed among the nations, because we succored the nations of the world in their time of distress and of dismay?

I, for one, pray God that that solemn hour may come, and I know the solidity of character, I know the exaltation of hope, I know the high principle with which the American people will respond to the call of the world for this service. And I thank God that those who believe in America, who try to serve her people, are likely to be also what America herself from the first intended to be—the servant of mankind.

Source: Arthur S. Link and others, eds., *The Papers of Woodrow Wilson, January 1–April 16, 1915* (Princeton: Princeton University Press, 1980), 32:41.

Document 4.3   Draft of a Note to Germany about Submarine Warfare, February 6, 1915

Secretary of State Robert Lansing and President Wilson drafted this note to the American ambassador in Berlin about the German plan to use submarines to blockade the British Isles. Unfortunately, no one in the administration had a clear idea of what the United States would do if the Germans refused to modify their policy. (The words in parentheses were deleted by Wilson; the words in italics were inserted by him.)

Please immediately address a note to the German Government (in the sense of) to the following *effect:*

The Department (has) *having* had its attention directed to (a report in the press that) *the proclamation of* the German Admiralty *issued* on February fourth (issued a declaration) that the waters around the British Isles, including the whole of the English Channel, are to be (a war zone after the eighteenth instant) *considered as comprised within the seat of war;* that (every enemy ship) *all enemy merchant vessels* found in (this war zone) *those waters after the eighteenth instant* will be destroyed *although it may not always be possible to save crews and passengers;* and that neutral ships are in danger, as on account of the misuse of neutral flags ordered by the British Government on January thirty-first and the hazards of naval warfare, it cannot always be avoided that attacks meant for enemy ships endanger neutral ships. . . .

(Assuming that the report is officially confirmed.) The Government of the United States (would) *feels con[s]trained to inform the government of Germany in all frankness that it would* view with grave concern the critical situation in the relations between this country and Germany which (would) *might* arise if (a) *the* German naval force, in carrying out the policy (set forth) *foreshadowed* in the Admiralty's declaration, should destroy any merchant vessel of the United States or cause the death of American citizens.

The German Government must be aware that the sole right of a belligerent in dealing with neutral vessels on the high seas is limited to visit and search, unless a blockade is proclaimed and (efficiently) *effectively* maintained, which (has not been done) *this Government does not understand to be proposed* in the present case. To declare or exercise a right to attack and destroy any vessel entering a prescribed area of the high seas without first determining its belligerent nationality and the contraband character of its cargo would be (a wanton) *an* act (unparalleled) *so unprecedented* in naval warfare(.) *that this Government is reluctant to believe that the Government of Germany itself in this case contemplates it as possible.* . . .

If the Imperial German Government should act upon such presumption and destroy on the high seas an American vessel or the lives of American citizens, the Government of the United States could not but view the act as a flagrant violation of neutral rights, (as one) *seriously* offensive, if not (hostile,) *deliberately unfriendly* to the United States.

If such a deplorable situation should arise the Government of the United States would be constrained to hold the Imperial German Government to a strict accountability for (the) *such an* unwarranted act of their naval authorities and to take (the measures) *any steps it might be* necessary to *take to* safeguard American lives and property and to secure to American citizens the full enjoyment of their rights on the high seas.

The Government of the United States, in view of these considerations, expresses the confident hope and expectation that the Imperial German Government *can & will* give assurance that (the lives of) American citizens and their vessels will not be molested by the naval forces of Germany other than by visit and search though the vessels may be traversing the sea area (prescribed) *delimited* in the declaration of the German Admiralty.

Source: Arthur S. Link and others, eds., *The Papers of Woodrow Wilson, January 1–April 16, 1915* (Princeton: Princeton University Press, 1980), 32:194–195.

Document 4.4   Letter from William Jennings Bryan to Wilson, May 12, 1915

Wilson's insistence upon the rights of Americans to travel in the war zone, despite Germany's warnings, and his refusal to couple protests to Germany about the sinking of the Lusitania *with comparable protests to Great Britain about their blockade policy, seemed to Secretary of State Bryan to make war likely, as he said in this letter to the president. On June 8 Bryan resigned from the cabinet.*

Your more than generous note received with draft of protest to Germany.

I have gone over it very carefully and will give it to Mr Lansing at once, for I agree with you that it is well to act without delay in order to give direction to public opinion not see that you could have stated your position more clearly or more forcibly. . . .

But, my dear Mr President, I join in this document with a heavy heart. I am as sure of your patriotic purpose as I am of my own, but after long consideration, both careful and prayerful, I can not bring myself to the belief that it is wise to relinquish the hope of playing the part of a friend to both sides in the role of peace maker, and I fear this note will result in such a relinquishment—for the hope requires for its realization the retaining of the confidence of both sides. The protest will be popular in this country, for a time at least and possibly permanently, because public sentiment, already favorable to the allies, has been perceptibly increased by the Lusitania trajedy [*sic*], but there is peril in this very fact. Your position, being the position of the government, will be approved—the approval varying in emphasis in proportion to the feeling against Germany. There being no intimation that the final accounting will be postponed until the war is over, the jingo element will not only predict, but demand, war. . . . and the line will be more distinctly drawn between those who sympathize with Germany and the rest of the people. Outside of the country the document will be applauded by the allies, and the more they applaud the more Germany will be embittered, because we unsparingly denounce the retaliatory methods employed by her without condemning the announced purpose of the allies to starve the non-combattants [sic] of Germany and without complaining of the conduct of Great Britain in relying on passengers, including men, women and children of the United States, to give immunity to vessels carrying munitions of war—without even suggesting that she should convoy passenger ships as carefully as she does ships carrying horses and gasoline. . . .

Germany can not but construe the strong statement of the case against her, coupled with silence as to the unjustifiable action of the allies, as partiality toward the latter—an impression which will be deepened in proportion to the loudness of the praise which the allies bestow upon this government's statement of its position. . . . I am only giving you, my dear Mr President, the situation as it appears to me—and am praying all the while, that I may be wholly mistaken and that your judgment may be vindicated by events. . . .

Source: Arthur S. Link and others, eds., *The Papers of Woodrow Wilson, April 17–July 21, 1915* (Princeton: Princeton University Press, 1980), 33:165–166.

Document 4.5   The House-Grey Memorandum

On February 22, 1916, Edward House met with Sir Edward Grey and the two men initialed a memorandum that seemed to promise American entry into the war on the Allied side if Germany rejected an American-called peace conference or proved intransigent at a conference. After House returned to the United States, he and Wilson discussed the memorandum on March 6, and Wilson accepted it, with the single addition of the word probably *at a crucial point (enclosed in brackets and printed in italics). The British never called on the Americans to fulfill their promise.*

(Confidential) Colonel House told me that President Wilson was ready, on hearing from France and England that the moment was opportune, to propose that a Conference should be summoned to put an end to the war. Should the Allies accept this proposal and should Germany refuse it, the United States would probably enter the war against Germany.

Colonel House expressed the opinion that, if such a Conference met, it would secure peace on terms not unfavourable to the Allies; and, if it failed to secure peace, the United States would [*probably*] leave the Conference as a belligerent on the side of the Allies, if Germany was unreasonable. Colonel House expressed an opinion decidedly favourable to the restoration of Belgium, the transfer of Alsace and Lorraine to France, and the acquisition by Russia of an outlet to the sea, though he thought that the loss of territory incurred by Germany in one place would have to be compensated by concessions to her in other places outside Europe. If the Allies delayed accepting the offer of President Wilson, and if, later on, the course of the war was so unfavourable to them that the intervention of the United States would not be effective, the United States would probably disinterest themselves in Europe, and look to their own protection in their own way.

I said that I felt the statement, coming from the President of the United States, to be a matter of such importance that I must inform the Prime Minister and my Colleagues; but that I could say nothing until it had received their consideration. The British Government could, under no circumstances, accept or make any proposal except in consultation and agreement with the Allies. I thought that the Cabinet would probably feel that the present situation would not justify them in approaching their Allies on this subject at the present moment; but, as Colonel House had had an intimate conversation with M. Briand and M. Jules Cambon in Paris, I should think it right to tell M. Briand privately, through the French Ambassador in London, what Colonel House had said to us; and I should, of course, whenever there was an opportunity, be ready to talk the matter over with M. Briand if he desired it.

Source: Arthur S. Link and others, eds., *The Papers of Woodrow Wilson, January 27–May 8, 1916* (Princeton: Princeton University Press, 1981), 36:180.

━━━━━━

Document 4.6   American Protest against German Submarine Attack on the *Sussex*, April 16, 1916

This passage from the April 16, 1916, American note protesting a German submarine attack on the passenger ship Sussex *was drafted by Secretary of State Robert Lansing and revised by Wilson. It amounted to an ultimatum to Germany to cease submarine warfare. (Wilson substituted some of his own language, shown in italics, for Lansing's, shown in parentheses, in the final note.)*

. . . (The Government of the United States now owes it to a just regard for its own rights to declare that, if it is still the purpose of the Imperial) *If it is still the purpose of the Imperial* Government to prosecute relentless and indiscriminate warfare against vessels of commerce by the use of submarines without regard to what the Government of the United States must consider the sacred and indisputable rules of international law and the universally recognized dictates of humanity, the Government of the United States is at last forced to the conclusion that there is but one course it can pursue. (Unless the Imperial Government should now immediately declare its intention to abandon its present practices of submarine warfare and return to a scrupulous observance of the practices clearly prescribed by the law of nations,) *Unless the Imperial Government should now immediately declare its purpose to abandon its present methods of submarine warfare against passenger and freight-carrying vessels,* (It) *the Government of the United States* can have no choice but to sever diplomatic relations with the German Empire (until such time as the) *altogether. This action the Government of the United States contemplates with the greatest reluctance but feels constrained to take in behalf of humanity and the rights of neutral nations.*

Source: Arthur S. Link and others, eds., *The Papers of Woodrow Wilson, January 27–May 8, 1916* (Princeton: Princeton University Press, 1981), 36:496.

━━━━━━

Document 4.7   Address to the Senate, January 22, 1917

In an address to the Senate in January 1917, Wilson proposed a more active American role in the search for peace in the European conflict. Urging a "peace without victory," he suggested terms that he believed would provide a basis for a fair and lasting peace.

On the eighteenth of December last I addressed an identic note to the governments of the nations now at war requesting them to state, more definitely than they had yet been stated by either group of belligerents, the terms upon which they would deem it possible to make peace. I spoke on behalf of humanity and of the rights of all neutral nations like our own, many of whose most vital interests the war puts in constant jeopardy. The Central Powers united in a reply which stated merely that they were ready to meet their antagonists in conference to discuss terms of peace. The Entente Powers have replied much more definitely and have stated, in general terms, indeed, but with sufficient definiteness to imply details, the arrangements, guarantees, and acts of reparation which they deem to be the indispensable conditions of a satisfactory settlement. We are that much nearer a definite discussion of the peace which shall end the present war. We are that much nearer the discussion of the international concert which must thereafter hold the world at peace. In every discussion of the peace that must end this war it is taken for granted that that peace must be followed by some definite concert of power which will make it virtually impossible that any such catastrophe should ever overwhelm us again. Every lover of mankind, every sane and thoughtful man must take that for granted. . . .

It is inconceivable that the people of the United States should play no part in that great enterprise. To take part in such a service will be the opportunity for which they have sought to prepare themselves by the very principles and purposes of their polity and the approved practices of their Government ever since the days when they set up a new nation in the high and honourable hope that it might in all that it was and did show mankind the way to liberty. . . .

That service is nothing less than this, to add their authority and their power to the authority and force of other nations to guarantee peace and justice throughout the world. Such a settlement cannot now be long postponed. It is right that before it comes this Government should frankly formulate the conditions upon which it would feel justified in asking our people to approve its formal and solemn adherence to a League for Peace. I am here to attempt to state those conditions.

The present war must first be ended. . . .The treaties and agreements which bring it to an end must embody terms which will create a peace that is worth guaranteeing and preserving, a peace that will win the approval of mankind, not merely a peace that will serve the several interests and immediate aims of the nations engaged. . . .If the peace presently to be made is to endure, it must be a peace made secure by the organized major force of mankind. . . .

The question upon which the whole future peace and policy of the world depends is this: Is the present war a struggle for a just and secure peace, or only for a new balance of power? If it be only a struggle for a new balance of power, who will guarantee, who can guarantee, the stable equilibrium of the new arrangement? Only a tranquil Europe can be a stable Europe. There must be, not a balance of power, but a community of power; not organized rivalries, but an organized common peace.

Fortunately we have received very explicit assurances on this point. The statesmen of both of the groups of nations now arrayed against one another have said, in terms that could not be misinterpreted, that it was no part of the purpose they had in mind to crush their antagonists. But the implications of these assurances may not be equally clear to all,—may not be the same on both sides of the water. I think it will be serviceable if I attempt to set forth what we understand them to be.

They imply, first of all, that it must be a peace without victory. It is not pleasant to say this. I beg that I may be permitted to put my own interpretation upon it and that it may be understood that no other interpretation was in my thought. I am seeking only to face realities and to face them without soft concealments. Victory would mean peace forced upon the loser, a victor's terms imposed upon the vanquished. It would be accepted in humiliation, under duress, at an intolerable sacrifice, and would leave a sting, a resentment, a bitter memory upon which terms of peace would rest, not permanently, but only as upon quicksand. Only a peace between equals can last. . . . Right must be based upon the common strength, not upon the individual strength, of the nations upon whose concert peace will depend. . . .

And there is a deeper thing involved than even equality of right among organized nations. No peace can last, or ought to which does not recognize and accept the principle that governments derive all their just powers from the consent of the governed, and that no right anywhere exists to hand peoples about from sovereignty to sovereignty as if they were property. . . .

So far as practicable, moreover, every great people now struggling towards a full development of its resources and of its powers should be assured a direct outlet to the great highways of the sea. Where this cannot be done by the cession of territory, it can no doubt be done by the neutralization of direct rights of way under the general guarantee which will assure the peace itself. . . .

And the paths of the sea must alike in law and in fact be free. The free-dom of the seas is the *sine qua non* of peace, equality, and cooperation. . . . The free, constant, unthreatened intercourse of nations is an essential part of the process of peace and of development. . . .

There can be no sense of safety and equality among the nations if great preponderating armaments are henceforth to continue here and there to be built up and maintained. The statesmen of the world must plan for peace and nations must adjust and accommodate their policy to it as they have planned for war and made ready for pitiless contest and rivalry. The question of armaments, whether on land or sea, is the most immediately and intensely practical question connected with the future fortunes of nations and of mankind. . . .

I am proposing, as it were, that the nations should with one accord adopt the doctrine of President Monroe as the doctrine of the world: that no nation should seek to extend its polity over any other nation or people, but that every people should be left free to determine its own polity, its own way of development, unhindered, unthreatened, unafraid, the little along with the great and powerful.

I am proposing that all nations henceforth avoid entangling alliances which would draw them into competitions of power, catch them in a net of intrigue and selfish rivalry, and disturb their own affairs with influences intruded from without. There is no entangling alliance in a concert of power. When all unite to act in the same sense and with the same purpose all act in the common interest and are free to live their own lives under a common protection.

I am proposing government by the consent of the governed; that free-dom of the seas which in international conference after conference repre-sentatives of the United States have urged with the eloquence of those who are the convinced disciples of liberty; and that moderation of armaments which makes of armies and navies a power for order merely, not an instru-ment of aggression or of selfish violence.

These are American principles, American policies. We could stand for no others. And they are also the principles and policies of forward look-ing men and women everywhere, of every modern nation, of every enlight-ened community. They are the principles of mankind and must prevail.

Source: Arthur S. Link and others, eds., *The Papers of Woodrow Wilson, November 20, 1916–January 23, 1917* (Princeton: Princeton University Press, 1982), 40:533–539.

▬▬▬▬

Document 4.8   Request for Declaration of War, April 2, 1917

In January 1917 Germany announced a policy of unrestricted submarine warfare, and pressure for the United States to enter the war grew. At 8:30 p.m. on the rainy evening of April 2, 1917, Wilson asked a joint session of Congress for a declaration of war against Germany.

. . . On the third of February last I officially laid before you the extraordinary announcement of the Imperial German Government that on and after the first day of February it was its purpose to put aside all restraints of law or of humanity and use its submarines to sink every vessel that sought to approach either the ports of Great Britain and Ireland or the western coasts of Europe or any of the ports controlled by the enemies of Germany within the Mediterranean. That had seemed to be the object of the German submarine warfare earlier in the war, but since April of last year the Imperial Government had somewhat restrained the commanders of its undersea craft. . . . The new policy has swept every restriction aside. Vessels of every kind, whatever their flag, their character, their cargo, their destination, their errand, have been ruthlessly sent to the bottom without warning and without thought of help or mercy for those on board, the vessels of friendly neutrals along with those of belligerents. . . .

I was for a little while unable to believe that such things would in fact be done by any government that had hitherto subscribed to the humane practices of civilized nations. . . . This minimum of right the German Government has swept aside under the plea of retaliation and necessity and because it had no weapons which it could use at sea except these which it is impossible to employ as it is employing them without throwing to the winds all scruples of humanity or of respect for the understandings that were supposed to underlie the intercourse of the world. I am not now thinking of the loss of property involved, immense and serious as that is, but only of the wanton and wholesale destruction of the lives of noncombatants, men, women, and children, engaged in pursuits which have always, even in the darkest periods of modern history, been deemed innocent and legitimate. Property can be paid for; the lives of peaceful and innocent people cannot be. The present German submarine warfare against commerce is a warfare against mankind.

It is a war against all nations. American ships have been sunk, American lives taken, in ways which it has stirred us very deeply to learn of, but the ships and people of other neutral and friendly nations have been sunk and overwhelmed in the waters in the same way. There has been no discrimination. The challenge is to all mankind. . . . We must put excited feeling away. Our motive will not be revenge or the victorious assertion of the physical might of the nation, but only the vindication of right, of human right, of which we are only a single champion.

When I addressed the Congress on the twenty-sixth of February last I thought that it would suffice to assert our neutral rights with arms, our right to use the seas against unlawful interference, our right to keep our people safe against unlawful violence. But armed neutrality, it now appears, is impracticable. . . . There is one choice we cannot make, we are incapable of making: we will not choose the path of submission and suffer the most sacred rights of our nation and our people to be ignored or violated. The wrongs against which we now array ourselves are no common wrongs; they cut to the very roots of human life.

With a profound sense of the solemn and even tragical character of the step I am taking and of the grave responsibilities which it involves, but in unhesitating obedience to what I deem my constitutional duty, I advise that the Congress declare the recent course of the Imperial German Government to be in fact nothing less than war against the government and people of the United States; that it formally accept the status of belligerent which has thus been thrust upon it; and that it take immediate steps not only to put the country in a more thorough state of defense but also to exert all its power and employ all its resources to bring the Government of the German Empire to terms and end the war. . . .

While we do these things, these deeply momentous things, let us be very clear, and make very clear to all the world what our motives and our objects are. My own thought has not been driven from its habitual and normal course by the unhappy events of the last two months, and I do not believe that the thought of the nation has been altered or clouded by them. I have exactly the same things in mind now that I had in mind when I addressed the Senate on the twenty-second of January last; the same that I had in mind when I addressed the Congress on the third of February and on the twenty-sixth of February. Our object now, as then, is to vindicate the principles of peace and justice in the life of the world as against selfish and autocratic power and to set up amongst the really free and self-governed peoples of the world such a concert of purpose and of action as will henceforth ensure the observance of those principles. Neutrality is no longer feasible or desirable where the peace of the world is involved and the freedom of its peoples, and the menace to that peace and freedom lies in the existence of autocratic governments backed by organized force which is controlled wholly by their will, not by the will of their people. We have seen the last of neutrality in such circumstances. We are at the beginning of an age in which it will be insisted that the same standards of conduct and of responsibility for wrong done shall be observed among nations and their governments that are observed among the individual citizens of civilized states.

We have no quarrel with the German people. We have no feeling towards them but one of sympathy and friendship. It was not upon their impulse that their government acted in entering this war. It was not with their previous knowledge or approval. It was a war determined upon as wars used to be determined upon in the old, unhappy days when peoples were nowhere consulted by their rulers and wars were provoked and waged in the interest of dynasties or of little groups of ambitious men who were accustomed to use their fellow men as pawns and tools. . . .

A steadfast concert for peace can never be maintained except by a partnership of democratic nations. No autocratic government could be trusted to keep faith within it or observe its covenants. It must be a league of honour, a partnership of opinion. . . . Only free peoples can hold their purpose and their honour steady to a common end and prefer the interests of mankind to any narrow interest of their own.

Does not every American feel that assurance has been added to our hope for the future peace of the world by the wonderful and heartening things that have been happening within the last few weeks in Russia? Russia was known by those who knew it best to have been always in fact democratic at heart, in all the vital habits of her thought, in all the intimate relationships of her people that spoke their natural instinct, their habitual attitude towards life. The autocracy that crowned the summit of her political structure, long as it had stood and terrible as was the reality of its power, was not in fact Russian in origin, character, or purpose; and now it has been shaken off and the great, generous Russian people have been added in all their naive majesty and might to the forces that are fighting for freedom in the world, for justice, and for peace. Here is a fit partner for a League of Honour. . . .

We are glad, now that we see the facts with no veil of false pretence about them, to fight thus for the ultimate peace of the world and for the liberation of its peoples, the German peoples included: for the rights of nations great and small and the privilege of men everywhere to choose their way of life and of obedience. The world must be made safe for democracy. Its peace must be planted upon the tested foundations of political liberty. We have no selfish ends to serve. We desire no conquest, no dominion. We seek no indemnities for ourselves, no material compensation for the sacrifices we shall freely make. We are but one of the champions of the rights of mankind. We shall be satisfied when those rights have been made as secure as the faith and the freedom of nations can make them. . . .

It is a distressing and oppressive duty, Gentlemen of the Congress, which I have performed in thus addressing you. There are, it may be, many months of fiery trial and sacrifice ahead of us. It is a fearful thing to lead this great peaceful people into war, into the most terrible and disastrous of all wars, civilization itself seeming to be in the balance. But the right is more precious than peace, and we shall fight for the things which we have always carried nearest our hearts,—for democracy, for the right of those who submit to authority to have a voice in their own governments, for the rights and liberties of small nations, for a universal dominion of right by such a concert of free peoples as shall bring peace and safety to all nations and make the world itself at last free. To such a task we can dedicate our lives and our fortunes, everything that we are and everything that we have, with the pride of those who know that the day has come when America is privileged to spend her blood and her might for the principles that gave her birth and happiness and the peace which she has treasured. God helping her, she can do no other.

Source: Arthur S. Link and others, eds., *The Papers of Woodrow Wilson, January 24–April 6, 1917* (Princeton: Princeton University Press, 1983), 41:519–527.

Document 4.9   The Fourteen Points, January 8, 1918
Wilson's "Fourteen Points" address to a joint session of Congress was the first of a series of statements in which he attempted to spell out peace terms that would both appeal to the people of the Central Powers—Germany and Austria-Hungary—and also commit the Allies to principles he believed essential to a durable peace.

. . . Once more, as repeatedly before, the spokesmen of the Central Empires have indicated their desire to discuss the objects of the war and the possible bases of a general peace. . . .

There is no good reason why that challenge should not be responded to, and responded to with the utmost candor. We did not wait for it. Not once, but again and again, we have laid our whole thought and purpose before the world, not in general terms only, but each time with sufficient definition to make it clear what sort of definitive terms of settlement must necessarily spring out of them. . . .

We entered this war because violations of right had occurred which touched us to the quick and made the life of our own people impossible unless they were corrected and the world secured once for all against their recurrence. What we demand in this war, therefore, is nothing peculiar to ourselves. It is that the world be made fit and safe to live in; and particularly that it be made safe for every peace-loving nation which, like our own, wishes to live its own life, determine its own institutions, be assured of justice and fair dealing by the other peoples of the world as against force and selfish aggression. All the peoples of the world are in effect partners in this interest, and for our own part we see very clearly that unless justice be done to others it will not be done to us. The programme of the world's peace, therefore, is our programme; and that programme, the only possible programme, as we see it, is this:

I. Open covenants of peace, openly arrived at, after which there shall be no private international understandings of any kind but diplomacy shall proceed always frankly and in the public view.

II. Absolute freedom of navigation upon the seas, outside territorial waters, alike in peace and in war, except as the seas may be closed in whole or in part by international action for the enforcement of international covenants.

III. The removal, so far as possible, of all economic barriers and the establishment of an equality of trade conditions among all the nations consenting to the peace and associating themselves for its maintenance.

IV. Adequate guarantees given and taken that national armaments will be reduced to the lowest point consistent with domestic safety.

V. A free, open-minded, and absolutely impartial adjustment of all colonial claims, based upon a strict observance of the principle that in determining all such questions of sovereignty the interests of the populations concerned must have equal weight with the equitable claims of the government whose title is to be determined.

VI. The evacuation of all Russian territory and such a settlement of all questions affecting Russia as will secure the best and freest cooperation of the other nations of the world in obtaining for her an unhampered and unembarrassed opportunity for the independent determination of her own political development and national policy and assure her of a sincere welcome into the society of free nations under institutions of her own choosing; and, more than a welcome, assistance also of every kind that she may need and may herself desire. The treatment accorded Russia by her sister nations in the months to come will be the acid test of their good will, of their comprehension of her needs as distinguished from their own interests, and of their intelligent and unselfish sympathy.

VII. Belgium, the whole world will agree, must be evacuated and restored, without any attempt to limit the sovereignty which she enjoys in common with all other free nations. No other single act will serve as this will serve to restore confidence among the nations in the laws which they have themselves set and determined for the government of their relations with one another. Without this healing act the whole structure and validity of international law is forever impaired.

VIII. All French territory should be freed and the invaded portions restored, and the wrong done to France by Prussia in 1871 in the matter of Alsace-Lorraine, which has unsettled the peace of the world for nearly fifty years, should be righted, in order that peace may once more be made secure in the interests of all.

IX. A readjustment of the frontiers of Italy should be effected along clearly recognizable lines of nationality.

X. The peoples of Austria-Hungary, whose place among the nations we wish to see safeguarded and assured, should be accorded the freest opportunity of autonomous development.

XI. Rumania, Serbia, and Montenegro should be evacuated; occupied territories restored; Serbia accorded free and secure access to the sea; and the relations of the several Balkan states to one another determined by friendly counsel along historically established lines of allegiance and nationality; and international guarantees of the political and economic independence and territorial integrity of the several Balkan states should be entered into.

XII. The Turkish portions of the present Ottoman Empire should be assured a secure sovereignty, but the other nationalities which are now under Turkish rule should be assured an undoubted security of life and an absolutely unmolested opportunity of autonomous development, and the Dardanelles should be permanently opened as a free passage to the ships and commerce of all nations under international guarantees.

XIII. An independent Polish state should be erected which should include the territories inhabited by indisputably Polish populations, which should be assured a free and secure access to the sea, and whose political and economic independence and territorial integrity should be guaranteed by international covenant.

XIV. A general association of nations must be formed under specific covenants for the purpose of affording mutual guarantees of political independence and territorial integrity to great and small states alike.

In regard to these essential rectifications of wrong and assertions of right we feel ourselves to be intimate partners of all the governments and peoples associated together against the Imperialists. We cannot be separated in interest or divided in purpose. We stand together until the end. . . .

We have spoken now, surely, in terms too concrete to admit of any further doubt or question. An evident principle runs through the whole programme I have outlined. It is the principle of justice to all peoples and nationalities, and their right to live on equal terms of liberty and safety with one another, whether they be strong or weak. Unless this principle be made its foundation no part of the structure of international justice can stand. The people of the United States could act upon no other principle; and to the vindication of this principle they are ready to devote their lives, their honor, and everything that they possess. The moral climax of this the culminating and final war for human liberty has come, and they are ready to put their own strength, their own highest purpose, their own integrity and devotion to the test.

Source: Arthur S. Link and others, eds., *The Papers of Woodrow Wilson, November 11, 1917–January 15, 1918* (Princeton: Princeton University Press, 1984), 45: 534–539.

Document 4.10   Message from German Government to Wilson, October 6, 1918

In October 1918 Germany's military regime was replaced by a new government led by Prince Max of Baden, who sent this message to Wilson. The Germans hoped that by approaching Wilson they could secure a peace based on the Fourteen Points rather than the more punitive terms they feared the British and French would demand.

The German government requests the President of the United States of America to take steps for the restoration of peace, to notify all belligerents of this request, and to invite them to delegate Plenipotentiaries for the purpose of taking up negotiations. The German government accepts, as a basis for the peace negotiations, the program laid down by the President of the United States in his message to Congress of January 8, 1918, and in his subsequent pronouncements, particularly in his address of September 27, 1918. In order to avoid further bloodshed the German government requests to bring about the immediate conclusion of a general armistice on land, on water, and in the air.

Source: Arthur S. Link and others, eds., *The Papers of Woodrow Wilson, September 14–November 8, 1918* (Princeton: Princeton University Press, 1985), 51:253.

Document 4.11   Excerpts, League of Nations Covenant

Although Article X of the League of Nations Covenant became the center of controversy during the American ratification debate, Articles XI–XIII and XV–XVI actually spelled out the enforcement mechanisms of the organization. Following are those articles as Wilson presented and explained them to the Third Plenary Session of the peace conference on February 14, 1919.

Mr. Chairman: I have the honor and as I esteem it the very great privilege of reporting in the name of the commission constituted by this conference on the formulation of a plan for the league of nations. I am happy to say that it is a unanimous report, a unanimous report from the representatives of fourteen nations—the United States, Great Britain, France, Italy, Japan, Belgium, Brazil, China, Czecho-Slovakia, Greece, Poland, Portugal, Roumania, and Serbia. I think it will be serviceable and interesting if I, with your permission, read the document as the only report we have to make. . . .

ARTICLE X

"The High Contracting Parties undertake to respect and preserve as against external aggression the territorial integrity and existing political independence of all States members of the League. In case of any such aggression or in case of any threat or danger of such aggression the Executive Council shall advise upon the means by which this obligation shall be fulfilled.

ARTICLE XI

"Any war or threat of war, whether immediately affecting any of the High Contracting Parties or not, is hereby declared a matter of concern to the League, and the High Contracting Parties reserve the right to take any action that may be deemed wise and effectual to safeguard the peace of nations.

"It is hereby also declared and agreed to be the friendly right of each of the High Contracting Parties to draw the attention of the Body of Delegates or of the Executive Council to any circumstances affecting international intercourse which threaten to disturb international peace or the good understanding between nations upon which peace depends.

ARTICLE XII

"The High Contracting Parties agree that should disputes arise between them which cannot be adjusted by the ordinary processes of diplomacy, they will in no case resort to war without previously submitting the questions and matters involved either to arbitration or to inquiry by the Executive Council and until three months after the award by the arbitrators or a recommendation by the Executive Council: and that they will not even then resort to war as against a member of the League which complies with the award of the arbitrators or the recommendations of the Executive Council.

"In any case under this Article, the award of the arbitrators shall be made within a reasonable time, and the recommendation of the Executive Council shall be made within six months after the submission of the dispute.

ARTICLE XIII

"The High Contracting Parties agree that whenever any dispute or difficulty shall arise between them which they recognize to be suitable for submission to arbitration and which cannot be satisfactorily settled by diplomacy, they will submit the whole subject matter to arbitration. For this purpose the Court of arbitration to which the case is referred shall be the court agreed on by the parties or stipulated in any Convention existing between them. The High Contracting Parties agree that they will carry out in full good faith any award that may be rendered. In the event of any failure to carry out the award, the Executive Council shall propose what steps can best be taken to give effect thereto. . . .

ARTICLE XV

"If there should arise between States members of the League any dispute likely to lead to a rupture, which is not submitted to arbitration as above, the High Contracting Parties agree that they will refer the matter to the Executive Council; either party to the dispute may give notice of the existence of the dispute to the Secretary-General, who will make all necessary arrangements for a full investigation and consideration thereof. . . .

"Where the efforts to [*sic*] the Council lead to the settlement of the dispute, a statement shall be published indicating the nature of the dispute and the terms of settlement. . . . If the dispute has not been settled, a report by the Council shall be published, setting forth with all necessary facts and explanations the recommendation which the Council think just and proper for the settlement of the dispute. If the report is unanimously agreed to by the members of the Council other than the parties to the dispute, the High Contracting Parties agree that they will not go to war with any party which complies with the recommendation and that, if any party shall refuse so to comply, the Council shall propose the measures necessary to give effect to the recommendation. If no such unanimous report can be made, it shall be the duty of the majority and the privilege of the minority to issue statements indicating what they believe to be the facts and containing the recommendations which they consider to be just and proper. . . .

ARTICLE XVI

"Should any of the High Contracting Parties break or disregard its covenants under Article XII, it shall thereby *ipso facto* be deemed to have committed an act of war against all the other members of the League, which hereby undertake immediately to subject it to the severance of all trade or financial relations, the prohibition of all intercourse between their nationals and the nationals of the covenant-breaking State, and the prevention of all financial, commercial, or personal intercourse between the nationals of the covenant-breaking State and the nationals of any other State, whether a member of the League or not.

"It shall be the duty of the Executive Council in such case to recommend what effective military or naval force the members of the League shall severally contribute to the armed forces to be used to protect the covenants of the League. . . ."

Now, as to the character of the document. While it has consumed some time to read this document, I think you will see at once that it is, after all, very simple, and in nothing so simple as in the structure which it suggests for the League of Nations—a Body of Delegates, an Executive Council, and a Permanent Secretariat. . . .

[Y]ou will notice that this body has unlimited rights of discussion—I mean of discussion of anything that falls within the field of international relationship—and that it is specially agreed that war or international misunderstandings or anything that may lead to friction and trouble is everybody's business, because it may affect the peace of the world. . . .

[T]hroughout this instrument we are depending primarily and chiefly upon one great force, and that is the moral force of the public opinion of the world—the cleansing and clarifying and compelling influences of publicity—so that intrigues can no longer have their coverts, so that designs that are sinister can at any time be drawn into the open, so that those things that are destroyed by the light may be properly destroyed by the overwhelming light of the universal expression of the condemnation of the world.

Armed force is in the background in this program, but it is in the background, and if the moral force of the world will not suffice, the physical force of the world shall. But that is the last resort, because this is intended as a constitution of peace, not as a league of war.

The simplicity of the document seems to me to be one of its chief virtues, because, speaking for myself, I was unable to foresee the variety of circumstances with which this League would have to deal. I was unable, therefore, to plan all the machinery that might be necessary to meet differing and unexpected contingencies. Therefore, I should say of this document that it is not a straitjacket, but a vehicle of life. A living thing is born, and we must see to it that the clothes we put upon it do not hamper it—a vehicle of power, but a vehicle in which power may be varied at the discretion of those who exercise it and in accordance with the changing circumstances of the time. . . .

So I think I can say of this document that it is at one and the same time a practical document and a humane document. There is a pulse of sympathy in it. There is a compulsion of conscience throughout it. It is practical, and yet it is intended to purify, to rectify, to elevate. . . .

Many terrible things have come out of this war, gentlemen, but some very beautiful things have come out of it. Wrong has been defeated, but the rest of the world has been more conscious than it ever was before of the majesty of right. People that were suspicious of one another can now live as friends and comrades in a single family, and desire to do so. The miasma of distrust, of intrigue, is cleared away. Men are looking eye to eye and saying; "We are brothers and have a common purpose. We did not realize it before, but now we do realize it, and this is our Covenant of fraternity and of friendship."

Source: Arthur S. Link and others, eds., *The Papers of Woodrow Wilson, February 8–March 16, 1919* (Princeton: Princeton University Press, 1986), 55:164, 167–169, 174–178.

Document 4.12   Press Release on Allied Intervention in Russia, August 3, 1918

When the Russians and Germans signed the Treaty of Brest-Litovsk on March 3, 1918, withdrawing Russia from the war against Germany, the British and French put intense pressure on Wilson to agree to joint intervention in Russia that might restore a noncommunist government and bring Russia back into the war. Wilson, insisting upon the Russians' right of self-determination, resisted this pressure until the summer of 1918, when he reluctantly approved a limited intervention. In a memorandum to the governments of Great Britain, France, and Italy on July 17, 1918, and in this press release on August 3, 1918, he explained his point of view.

In the judgment of the Government of the United States,—a judgment arrived at after repeated and very searching considerations of the whole situation,—military intervention in Russia would be more likely to add to the present sad confusion there than to cure it, and would injure Russia rather than help her out of her distresses. Such military intervention as has been most frequently proposed, even supposing it to be efficacious in its immediate object of delivering an attack upon Germany from the east, would, in its judgment, be more likely to turn out to be merely a method of making use of Russia than to be a method of serving her. Her people, if they profitted [*sic*] by it at all, could not profit by it in time to deliver them from their present desperate difficulties, and their substance would meantime be used to maintain foreign armies, not to reconstitute their own or to feed their own men, women, and children. We are bending all our energies now to the purpose, the resolute and confident purpose, of winning on the western front, and it would in the judgment of the Government of the United States be most unwise to divide or dissipate our forces.

As the Government of the United States sees the present circumstances, therefore, military action is admissible in Russia now only to render such protection and help as is possible to the Czechoslovaks against the armed Austrian and German prisoners who are attacking them and to steady any efforts at self-government or self-defence in which the Russians themselves may be willing to accept assistance. Whether from Vladivostock or from Murmansk and Archangel, the only present object for which American troops will be employed will be to guard military stores which may subsequently be needed by Russian forces and to render such aid as may be acceptable to the Russians in the organization of their own self-defence. . . .

Source: Arthur S. Link and others, eds., *The Papers of Woodrow Wilson, July 18–September 13, 1918* (Princeton: Princeton University Press, 1985), 49:170–171.

Document 4.13   House and the Treaty of Versailles, November 24 and 27, 1919

Although Edward M. House later remarked that "my separation from Woodrow Wilson was and is to me a tragic mystery, a mystery that now can never be dispelled, for its explanation lies buried with him," most historians have concluded that Wilson felt betrayed by House's concessions to the Allies in Paris (Seymour 1928, 4:518). With that in mind, and given Wilson's physical and mental state in late November 1919, House's letters to Wilson on November 24 and 27, 1919, which proposed acceptance of some of the Senate's reservations, fell on deaf ears and went unanswered.

I hesitate to intrude my views upon you at such a time, but I feel that I would be doing less than my duty if I did not do so, since so much depends upon your decision in regard to the Treaty. Its failure would be a disaster not less to civilization than to you.

My suggestion is this: Do not mention the Treaty in your message to Congress, but return it to the Senate as soon as it convenes. In the mean time, send for Senator Hitchcock and tell him that you feel that you have done your duty and have fulfilled your every obligation to your colleagues in Paris by rejecting all offers to alter the document which was formulated there, and you now turn the Treaty over to the Senate for such action as it may deem wise to take.

I would advise him to ask the Democratic Senators to vote for the Treaty with such reservations as the majority may formulate, and let the matter rest with the other signatories of the Treaty. I would say to Senator Hitchcock that if the Allied and Associated Powers are willing to accept the reservations which the Senate see fit to make, you will abide by the result being conscious of having done your full duty.

The Allies may not take the Treaty with the Lodge Reservations as they now stand, and this will be your vindication. But even if they should take them with slight modifications, your conscience will be clear. After agreement is reached, it can easily be shown that the Covenant in its practical workings in the future will not be seriously hampered and that time will give us a workable machine.

A great many people, Democrats, Progressives, and Republicans, have talked with me about ratification of the Treaty and they are all pretty much of one mind regarding the necessity for its passage with or without reservations. To the ordinary man, the distance between the Treaty and the reservations is slight.

Of course, the arguments are all with the position you have taken and against that of the Senate, but, unfortunately, no amount of logic can alter the situation; therefore my advice would be to make no further argument, but return the Treaty to the Senate without comment and let Senator Hitchcock know that you expect it to be ratified in some form, and then let the other signatories decide for themselves whether they will accept it.

The supreme place which history will give you will be largely because you personify in yourself the great idealistic conception of a league of nations. If this conception fails, it will be your failure. To-day there are millions of helpless people throughout the world who look to you and you only to make this conception a realization.

I am wondering if I made myself clear to you in my letter of the other day.

I wish to emphasize the fact that I do not counsel surrender. The action advised will in my opinion make your position consistent and impregnable.

Any other way out that now seems possible of success would be something of a surrender.

Practically every one who is in close touch with the situation admits that the Treaty cannot be ratified without substantial reservations. You must not be a party to those reservations. You stood for the Treaty as it was made in Paris, but if the Senate refuses to ratify without reservations, under the circumstances, I would let the Allies determine whether or not they will accept them.

This does not mean that no effort will be made by those Senators and others who favor the Treaty as it is to make the reservations as innocuous as possible. Neither does it mean that the Allies will accept the Treaty as the Senate majority have desired it.

If you take the stand indicated, it will aid rather than hinder those working for mild reservations. It will absolutely ensure the passage of the Treaty and probably in a form acceptable to both you and the Allies.

I did not make the suggestion until I had checked it up with some of your friends in whom I felt you had confidence, for the matter is of such incalculable importance that I did not dare rely solely upon my own judgment.

In conclusion, let me suggest that Senator Hitchcock be warned not to make any public statement regarding your views. When the Treaty is ratified, then I hope you will make a statement letting your position become known.

I feel as certain as I ever did of anything that your attitude would receive universal approval. On the one hand your loyalty to our Allies will be commended, and, on the other, your willingness to accept reservations rather than have the Treaty killed will be regarded as the act of a great man.

Source: Charles Seymour, ed., *The Intimate Papers of Colonel House* (New York: Houghton Mifflin, 1928), 4:509–511.

Document 4.14   Round Robin Resolution, March 3, 1919

On the eve of the expiration of the 65th Congress, Sen. Henry Cabot Lodge, R-Mass., who would become the chairman of the Senate Foreign Relations Committee in the incoming 66th Congress, introduced what was known as the "Round Robin" resolution expressing the opposition of more than one-third of senators and senators-elect to the peace treaty as it was then taking shape in Paris. Lodge's opposition forced Wilson to ask the other conferees for changes in the treaty to meet American objections, and they, in return, secured concessions from Wilson on issues of interest to their countries.

Whereas under the Constitution it is a function of the Senate to advise and consent to, or dissent from, the ratification of any treaty of the United States, and no such treaty can become operative without the consent of the Senate expressed by the affirmative vote of two-thirds of the Senators present; and

Whereas owing to the victory of the arms of the United States and of the nations with whom it is associated, a peace conference was convened and is now in session at Paris for the purpose of settling the terms of peace; and

Whereas a committee of the conference has proposed a constitution for a league of nations and the proposal is now before the peace conference for its consideration: Now, therefore, be it

Resolved by the Senate of the United States in the discharge of its constitutional duty of advice in regard to treaties, That it is the sense of the Senate that while it is their sincere desire that the nations of the world should unite to promote peace and general disarmament, the constitution of the league of nations in the form now proposed to the peace conference should not be accepted by the United States; and be it

Resolved further, That it is the sense of the Senate that the negotiations on the part of the United States should immediately be directed to the utmost expedition of the urgent business of negotiating peace terms with Germany satisfactory to the United States and the nations with whom the United States is associated in the war against the German Government, and that the proposal for a league of nations to insure the permanent peace of the world should be then taken up for careful and serious consideration. [Signed by thirty-seven senators and senators-elect]

Source: Congressional Record, 65th Cong., 3d sess., 4974.

Document 4.15   Speech to the Senate, July 10, 1919

In his speech presenting the Treaty of Versailles to the Senate, one of his most dramatic, Wilson called upon America to forsake isolationism and join with other nations in the League of Nations to prevent future wars.

. . . The United States entered the war upon a different footing from every other nation except our associates on this side of the sea. We entered it, not because our material interests were directly threatened or because any special treaty obligations to which we were parties had been violated, but only because we saw the supremacy, and even the validity, of right everywhere put in jeopardy and free government likely to be everywhere imperiled by the intolerable aggression of a power which respected neither right nor obligation and whose very system of government flouted the rights of the citizens as against the autocratic authority of his governors. And in the settlements of the peace we have sought no special reparation for ourselves, but only the restoration of right and the assurance of liberty everywhere that the effects of the settlement were to be felt. We entered the war as the disinterested champions of right and we interested ourselves in the terms of the peace in no other capacity.

The hopes of the nations allied against the central powers were at a very low ebb when our soldiers began to pour across the sea. There was everywhere amongst them, except in their stoutest spirits, a sombre foreboding of disaster. The war ended in November, eight months ago, but you have only to recall what was feared in midsummer last, four short months before the armistice, to realize what it was that our timely aid accomplished alike for their morale and their physical safety. . . . Thereafter the Germans were to be always forced back, back, were never to thrust successfully forward again. . . . The mere sight of our men,—of their vigour, of the confidence that showed itself in every movement of their stalwart figures and every turn of their swinging march, in their steady comprehending eyes and easy discipline, in the indomitable air that added spirit to everything they did,—made everyone who saw them that memorable day realize that something had happened that was much more than a mere incident in the fighting, something very different from the mere arrival of fresh troops. A great moral force had flung itself into the struggle. The fine physical force of those spirited men spoke of something more than bodily vigour. They carried the great ideals of a free people at their hearts and with that vision were unconquerable. . . .

And the compulsion of what they stood for was upon us who represented America at the peace table. It was our duty to see to it that every decision we took part in contributed, so far as we were able to influence it, to quiet the fears and realize the hopes of the peoples who had been living in that shadow, the nations that had come by our assistance to their freedom. It was our duty to do everything that it was within our power to do to make the triumph of freedom and of right a lasting triumph in the assurance of which men might everywhere live without fear. . . .

It had been our privilege to formulate the principles which were accepted as the basis of the peace, but they had been accepted, not because we had come in to hasten and assure the victory and insisted upon them, but because they were readily acceded to as the principles to which honourable and enlightened minds everywhere had been bred. They spoke the conscience of the world as well as the conscience of America. . . .

That there should be a league of nations to steady the counsels and maintain the peaceful understandings of the world, to make, not treaties alone, but the accepted principles of international law as well, the actual rule of conduct among the governments of the world, had been one of the agreements accepted from the first as the basis of peace with the central powers. The statesmen of all the belligerent countries were agreed that such a league must be created to sustain the settlements that were to be effected. . . .

[T]he most practical, the most skeptical among them turned more and more to the League as the authority through which international action was to be secured, the authority without which, as they had come to see it, it would be difficult to give assured effect either to this treaty or to any other international understanding upon which they were to depend for the maintenance of peace. The fact that the Covenant of the League was the first substantive part of the treaty to be worked out and agreed upon, while all else was in solution, helped to make the formulation of the rest easier. The Conference was, after all, not to be ephemeral. . . .

[The League] . . . validated itself in the thought of every member of the Conference as something much bigger, much greater every way, than a mere instrument for carrying out the provisions of a particular treaty. It was universally recognized that all the peoples of the world demanded of the Conference that it should create such a continuing concert of free nations as would make wars of aggression and spoliation such as this that has just ended forever impossible. . . . War had lain at the heart of every arrangement of the Europe,—of every arrangement of the world,—that preceded the war. Restive peoples had been told that fleets and armies, which they toiled to sustain, meant peace; and they now knew that they had been lied to: that fleets and armies had been maintained to promote national ambitions and meant war. They knew that no old policy meant anything else but force, force,—always force. And they knew that it was intolerable. . . . The League of Nations was not merely an instrument to adjust and remedy old wrongs under a new treaty of peace; it was the only hope for mankind. . . . Shall we or any other free people hesitate to accept this great duty? Dare we reject it and break the heart of the world? . . .

Our participation in the war established our position among the nations and nothing but our own mistaken action can alter it. It was not an accident or a matter of sudden choice that we are no longer isolated and devoted to a policy which has only our own interest and advantage for its object. It was our duty to go in, if we were indeed the champions of liberty and of right. . . . It is thus that a new role and a new responsibility have come to this great nation that we honour and which we would all wish to lift to yet higher levels of service and achievement.

The stage is set, the destiny disclosed. It has come about by no plan of our conceiving, but by the hand of God who led us into this way. We cannot turn back. We can only go forward, with lifted eyes and freshened spirit, to follow the vision. It was of this that we dreamed at our birth. America shall in truth show the way. The light streams upon the path ahead, and nowhere else.

Source: Arthur S. Link and others, eds., *The Papers of Woodrow Wilson, June 18–July 25, 1919* (Princeton: Princeton University Press, 1989), 61:426–436.

Document 4.16   Wilson's Stroke

On October 2, 1919, Wilson suffered a massive stroke. This account, from an unpublished and undated memoir by Irwin Hood ("Ike") Hoover, the White House head usher, describes events on that day and makes it clear that for the remainder of his term, Wilson was not physically or mentally competent to exercise the powers of the presidency. The spelling and punctuation are original.

Dr. Grayson attempted to walk right in but the door was locked. He knocked gently and upon [it] being opened he entered. I continued on to wait in the outer hall. In about ten minutes Dr. Grayson came out and with raised arms, said "My God the President is paralized, send for Dr. Stitt and the nurse," mentioning the name of the latter, the same one who had been in attendance upon the first Mrs. Wilson and who was with her when she died. . . .

There were doctors everywhere. A consultation of them all together was held about four oclock. An aire of secrecy had come over things during the day. Those outside the room could find out nothing, including family and employes. It was during this time the beginning of the deception practiced on the American people had its inception. Never was a conspiracy so pointedly and so artistically formed. After events but bore out this conclusion to the mind of all in a position to observe and have any interest in the fate of the patient. It was my privilege to go in the room in the late afternoon. Some rearrangement of the furnishings of the room had to be made and the domestic attendants on the floor were not looked upon with favor for this purpose. So, Dr. Grayson, the nurse and myself did the job.

The President layed stretched out on the large Lincoln bed. He looked as if dead. There was not a sign of life. His face bore a long cut about the temple from which the signs of blood were still evident. His nose also bore a long cut lengthwise. This too looked red and raw. There was no bandage. He was just gone as far as one could judge from appearances, especially when one had been told as I had that he was paralized.

Soon after I made confidential inquiry as to how and when it all happened. I was told and know it to be right that he had went to the bath upon arising in the morning and was sitting on the stool when the affliction overcame him. That he tumbled over on the floor, striking his head on the sharp plumbing of the bath tub in his fall. That, Mrs. Wilson hearing groans from the bath went in and found him in an unconscious condition. She dragged him to the bed in the room ajourning [adjoining] and came out in the hall to call over the 'phone for the doctor as before mentioned.

For the next three or four days the White House was like a hospital. There were all kinds of medical aparatus and more doctors and more nurses. Day and night this went on. . . .

This condition just seemed to go on indefinately. It was perhaps three weeks or more before an[y] change seemed to come over things. I had been in and out of the room many times during this period and I saw very little change. He just lay helpless. True, he had been taking nourishment but the working the doctors had been doing on him had just about sapped his remaining vitality. All his natural functions had to be artifically helped and relieved and he appeared just as helpless as one could possibly be and live.

Still he lived and what a triumph that was and what an incentive to those most interested, personally, materially and otherwise. And he lived on but oh what a wreck of his former self. He did grow better but that does not say much. I was with him every day at some time for some purpose and saw him, even unto the end, at his private residence. There was never a moment during all that time when he was but a shadow of his former self. He had changed from a giant to a pigmy in every wise that one would rate in a fair reckoning. He was physically, almost incapicated, mentally but a guisser [guesser?] compared to the normal understanding of his great mind. Could articulate but indistinctly and think but feebly. It was so sad that those of us about him, who almost universally admired him would turn our head away when he came along or we went near to him. . . .

This orignal stroke or whatever it was simply put the President out of business, mentally & physically for at least a month. At the end of that time he could be lifted from the bed, placed in a chair beside the bed and chair and man moved to another part of the room. After a few days of this an invalid rolling chair was tried but it soon proved a failure. He could not sit upright. It was evident that more rigid braces for the poor old deformed body was necessary. The writer suggested one of the single person rolling chairs like the ones used on the board walk at Atlantic City. This was agreed too. . . . This chair was used every time the President got out of bed for the remaining days at the White House. . . .

If there was ever a man in bad shape he was. There was no comparison with the President that went to Paris and before. He was changed in every way and every one about him recognized and understood it to be so. He could not talk plain, mumbled more than he articulated, was helpless and looked awful. Everybody tried to help him realizing he was so dependent for everything. The stories in the papers from day to day may have been true in their way but never was deception so universally practiced in the White House as it was in those statements being given out from time to time. And the strange part to me was that the President in his feeble way, entered into the scheme. He permitted himself to be camaflouged like on occassions of his socalled Cabinet Meetings and his meeting of the Congressional Committee from the Senate. At all of the Cabinet meetings held he would be rolled into the Cabinet room in his old chair and fixed up prior to the coming of the Cabinet members. He sat there during all the meetings as one in a trance, the Cabinet members doing all the talking. He would have agreed to about anything they said for the thought of ending the meeting was the paramount one in his mind if there were any thoughts there at all. . . .

Source: Arthur S. Link and others, eds., *The Papers of Woodrow Wilson, September 4–November 5, 1919* (Princeton: Princeton University Press, 1990), 63:634–637.

Document 4.17   Tumulty and Succession

Joseph Tumulty remained loyal to his "governor," as he had referred to Wilson since their days together at Trenton, to the end of the administration. Following Wilson's stroke in October 1919, Tumulty's devotion led him to oppose Secretary of State Lansing's suggestion that the vice president take over the president's duties, as the following extract from Tumulty's memoir shows.

I am convinced that only the President's illness a few days later prevented an immediate demand on his part for the resignation of Mr. Lansing.

That there was no real devotion on the part of Mr. Lansing for the President is shown by the following incident.

A few days after the President returned from the West and lay seriously ill at the White House, with physicians and nurses gathered about his bed, Mr. Lansing sought a private audience with me in the Cabinet Room. He informed me that he had called diplomatically to suggest that in view of the incapacity of the President we should arrange to call in the Vice-President to act in his stead as soon as possible, reading to me . . . the following clause of the United States Constitution:

"In case of the removal of the President from office, or his death, resignation, or inability to discharge the powers and duties of the said office, the same shall devolve upon the Vice-President."

Upon reading this, I coldly turned to Mr. Lansing and said: "Mr. Lansing, the Constitution is not a dead letter with the White House. I have read the Constitution and do not find myself in need of any tutoring at your hands of the provision you have just read." When I asked Mr. Lansing the question as to who should certify to the disability of the President, he intimated that that would be a job for either Doctor Grayson or myself. I immediately grasped the full significance of what he intimated and said: "You may rest assured that while Woodrow Wilson is lying in the White House on the broad of his back I will not be a party to ousting him. He has been too kind, too loyal, and too wonderful to me to receive such treatment at my hands." Just as I uttered this statement Doctor Grayson appeared in the Cabinet Room and I turned to him and said: "And I am sure that Doctor Grayson will never certify to his disability. Will you, Grayson?" Doctor Grayson left no doubt in Mr. Lansing's mind that he would not do as Mr. Lansing suggested. I then notified Mr. Lansing that if anybody outside of the White House circle attempted to certify to the President's disability, that Grayson and I would stand together and repudiate it. I added that if the President were in a condition to know of this episode he would, in my opinion, take decisive measures. That ended the interview.

It is unnecessary to say that no further attempt was made by Mr. Lansing to institute ouster proceedings against his chief.

Source: Joseph P. Tumulty, *Wilson as I Know Him* (Garden City, N.Y.: Doubleday, 1921), 443–444.

Henry Cabot Lodge, a Republican senator from Massachusetts, was one of Wilson's greatest adversaries. During World War I, Lodge chaired the Senate Foreign Relations Committee and was highly critical of Wilson's peace policies. In 1918, Lodge became Senate majority leader and used his powerful position to oppose Wilson's plan for U.S. participation in the League of Nations.

CHAPTER FIVE

Institutional Relations

In his dealings with other branches of the government, as well as his own cabinet, the military, and outside forces like the media, President Woodrow Wilson adhered closely to his theory that the president should be the focal point of government power. But as a seasoned administrator he also knew that successful leaders relied on their subordinates and that a collegial atmosphere was more productive than one dominated from the top. Within the executive, he chose cabinet members who were competent enough that they could be delegated considerable authority but who deferred to Wilson on matters of basic policy. He kept the military, which he considered little more than an extension of the president's diplomatic prerogative, on a short leash, harshly upbraiding navy and army commanders when they acted outside his instructions.

Congress and the Supreme Court were a different matter. Wilson entered office with the outlines of a legislative plan in mind but without the constitutional power to institute it. As a result, he collaborated closely with Congress in the drafting of legislation that would be acceptable to all parties concerned and thus quickly and efficiently passed. The Supreme Court required less finesse because it did not take a leading role—either by its support or its opposition—in Progressive Era reforms and because Wilson focused on Congress and the presidency as instruments of change. His three appointments to the bench reflected his ambivalence both toward Court power and toward government expansion. One group with which Wilson was always at odds was the press. Wilson the statesman never quite mastered the use of the media as an ally in forwarding his reforms; Wilson the man resented the press's constant probing so much that he cultivated with it his worst presidential relationship.

RELATIONSHIP WITH HIS CABINET

Despite Woodrow Wilson's earlier enthusiasm for parliamentary-style "cabinet government," he used his own cabinet in traditionally American ways. Its members were appointed to pay political debts or to woo important factions in the Democratic Party. While members were given great autonomy to run the routine business of their departments, the president determined basic policy directions and sometimes took control of important issues personally (see Document 5.1).

During the first seven months of Wilson's first term the cabinet met twice a week, but early in the autumn of 1913 Wilson discovered that one of the cabinet members, Secretary of the Interior Franklin K. Lane, was an incurable gossip who could not refrain from dropping broad hints to journalists about what had been said in cabinet meetings. Wilson liked Lane so well that he kept him in the cabinet despite the leaks, but the president cut meetings back to once a week and frequently discussed sensitive issues only in private with the most directly affected cabinet member. He was impatient with people who were longwinded or repeated the same points several times, so he kept cabinet meetings relatively brief, but even after they were limited to once a week he often brought up important issues for general discussion. His usual method was to go around the table, starting with a different person each time, inviting each to express his opinion while the president listened (see Document 5.2). No votes were ever taken, and Wilson seldom expressed his own opinion, although at the end he might sum up the discussion.

Occasionally cabinet members grumbled about not knowing what was going on in other departments, but most of them were enthusiastic about Wilson's goals, impressed by his intellect and grasp of issues, and pleased by their personal relationships with the president. "I took my [War Department] problems to him," said Secretary of War Newton D. Baker in a typical comment, "and always came away with the feeling that he had sought and considered my views and then exercised his clear and powerful mind to the utmost to help me in their solution" (quoted in Link 1956, 76).

The president kept a close watch on major policy issues before the various departments and sometimes assumed control over policy himself if he thought an issue was delicate or important. For crucial foreign policy issues, for example, he often drafted dispatches on his own typewriter. On the other hand, he gave cabinet members virtually complete freedom to deal with routine matters and backed them loyally, even when their decisions were embarrassing for the administration. During the war such support also extended to the heads of the various mobilization organizations, such as the Food Administration, where Wilson backed Herbert Hoover's frequently controversial price-setting policies. Although such freedom for cabinet members to set policy sometimes created embarrassments, as did the segregation policies pursued in some departments or the Post Office Department's suppression of various publications during the war, overall it was important and valuable to the administration that its major officers were confident of the president's backing. In the rare cases when there was a serious disagreement between cabinet member and president, as with Secretary of State William Jennings Bryan's belief that neutral rights could be compromised in 1915 and the controversy over preparedness involving Secretary of War Lindley M. Garrison in 1916, there was no alternative but for the cabinet member to resign (see Document 5.3).

Wilson's massive stroke in October 1919 might have thrust new responsibilities on the cabinet, but quite the opposite happened. Because Wilson did not meet with the cabinet between October 1919 and April 1920, and the president's wife and physicians concealed the extent of Wilson's incapacitation from the cabinet as well as the general public, there was little the secretaries could do. Departments continued to take care of routine business, but without leadership from the White House, cabinet members dared not initiate new policies, particularly after Wilson fired Secretary of State Robert Lansing in February 1920 merely for calling cabinet meetings without specific authorization from the president. Instead of filling in for the ill president, the cabinet was nearly as paralyzed as he by his stroke.

Cabinet Members

Wilson surrounded himself with some of the ablest administrators and most popular politicians of his day. For his secretary of state, usually the president's right-hand man, Wilson chose William Jennings Bryan. Initially the choice was entirely political. As the Democratic presidential candidate in 1896, 1900, and 1908, Bryan had built a fiercely loyal following, and Wilson appointed him to the cabinet to secure the support of that wing of the Democratic Party for his domestic program. But Wilson and Bryan gradually discovered they had much in common. Like Wilson, Bryan was inexperienced in foreign policy (although he had traveled far more extensively), and both shared a deep Christian faith and a belief that America had a mission to extend peace and democracy throughout the world. Bryan also proved to be a rock of support for the administration's domestic program. Bryan's rumpled clothes, refusal to serve wine at diplomatic functions, and naive faith that all international conflicts could be solved through investigation sometimes made it difficult to take him seriously, but Wilson came to rely on the secretary and, as time passed, Bryan and Wilson grew very fond of each other. Wilson and Bryan's cordial personal relationship even outlasted their disagreement over policy toward German submarines and Bryan's resignation in June 1915.

Bryan's successor, Robert Lansing, who was the State Department's legal adviser under Bryan, was promoted largely because Wilson expected to handle foreign policy himself and saw no need for a strong secretary. Although Lansing was more experienced than Bryan, Wilson never treated him as an equal, as he had Bryan. Lansing served for five years, despite disagreeing with the president's policy on Mexico, neutrality, and the Treaty of Versailles. Wilson was aware of some of these differences but did nothing about them until February 1920, when a report reached him that Lansing had called cabinet meetings without specific authorization. Considering that Wilson's illness made him incapable of running the government, Lansing's action was entirely justified, but the president seized the excuse to fire him. Lansing's replacement by the inexperienced but fiercely loyal Bainbridge Colby was evidence that Wilson, perhaps thinking in prime ministerial terms, never wanted an independent secretary of state.

The need to win the support of Bryan's followers for the new administration also accounted for the appointment of an old Bryan loyalist, Albert S. Burleson, as postmaster general. As was traditional in the position, Burleson, a Texan with a long record in the House of Representatives, was the administration's chief liaison with Congress, where the political appointments at his command made him popular. Although Burleson was a narrow, intolerant man whose racial prejudices and persecution of dissenters during the war drew criticism from many progressives, Wilson valued him for his loyalty and political skills.

Wilson also wanted to reward his own closest supporters, but that caused a major problem in the days just after the 1912 election. Wilson's campaign manager, William F. McCombs, expected a cabinet office, but other advisers thought he was too mentally unstable for a major appointment. During a long and painful meeting in New York, Wilson finally told McCombs that he would not be named to the cabinet, but that he could have the ambassadorship to France. Correctly interpreting this offer as more exile than honor, McCombs turned it down but agreed as a compromise to stay on as chairman of the Democratic National Committee.

The cabinet post McCombs craved, that of secretary of the Treasury, went instead to his rival during the campaign, William Gibbs McAdoo. McAdoo became one of Wilson's strongest cabinet members. He served as secretary from 1913 to 1918, and then as Railroad Administrator for the remainder of the administration. In the cabinet, he played a major part in shaping one of the administration's most important achievements, the creation of the Federal Reserve System, and in organizing the financing of World War I. Wilson respected him as an administrator but never liked him very well personally, particularly after McAdoo, who was then forty-one, married Wilson's favorite daughter, twenty-five-year-old Eleanor, in May 1914. Wilson thought the widowed McAdoo was too old for Eleanor, and personal relations between the two men were strained thereafter. In 1920, despite the fact that McAdoo was well qualified for the Democratic presidential nomination, Wilson refused to support him.

In the course of his administration, Wilson appointed three men to the position of attorney general. The first, James C. McReynolds, seemed a good choice because of his strong support of the antitrust laws. But despite McReynolds' skill and zeal in trust litigation, he was so rude and unpleasant that he alienated everyone in the cabinet. When Supreme Court Justice Horace Lurton died in 1914, Wilson appointed McReynolds to his seat, reportedly just to get him out of the cabinet. By contrast, McReynolds' successor, Thomas W. Gregory, was a loyal and able administrator who provided a consistently moderate voice on issues that came before the cabinet. When he resigned in January 1919, Wilson said that he had never met a man "whose gifts and character I have admired more" (quoted in Heckscher 1991, 528). To replace Gregory, the president turned reluctantly to A. Mitchell Palmer, an early supporter from Pennsylvania who had served during the war as alien property custodian and had the support of party leaders. Wilson did not like or trust Palmer, but busy at the peace conference, he could come up with no viable alternative. In the autumn of 1919, when Palmer responded to a Red Scare with thousands of arbitrary arrests and deportations, Wilson's uneasiness was proved prescient.

Of all Wilson's cabinet choices, none seemed stranger to contemporaries than his selection of near-pacifists for the navy and war departments. Secretary of the Navy Josephus Daniels, a North Carolina newspaperman, was a longtime backer of Bryan and an early supporter of Wilson. The president quickly came to appreciate the North Carolinian's personal qualities and loyalty. Naval officers were initially suspicious of this rank outsider, but his competence and integrity gradually won their support. He served efficiently through both of Wilson's terms. The other near-pacifist, Newton D. Baker, became secretary of war in 1916 after Wilson's first appointee, Lindley M. Garrison, a New Jersey judge recommended by Tumulty, resigned because he thought the president's plan to expand the army was inadequate. Baker was a leader of the reform movement in Ohio, and in 1913 Wilson had asked him to become secretary of the interior, but Baker had declined in order to continue his reform work in Cleveland. Invited into the cabinet a second time in 1916, he did not feel he could refuse. Once in office he became one of Wilson's most trusted advisers, and to the surprise of the military, a strong advocate for what the generals said they needed. The president backed him consistently, despite political attacks on his department during the war.

Two other important members of the cabinet, Secretary of the Interior Franklin K. Lane and Secretary of Agriculture David F. Houston, were appointed largely on recommendation of Wilson's friend, Edward M. House. When Newton Baker declined his first appointment, Wilson accepted House's suggestion of Lane for the Department of the Interior because, as a Californian, he was acceptable to westerners who thought that federal conservation policies had restricted development. The two men did not meet until inauguration day, but Lane turned out to be so likable that Wilson even overlooked the secretary's love of gossip (see Document 5.4). Houston, on the other hand, was recommended by House and strongly approved by Wilson, who had met the economist when Houston was serving as chancellor of Washington University in St. Louis, Missouri. As fellow academics and university administrators, Wilson and Houston had common backgrounds and got along well from the start. Although his position as secretary of agriculture was not very important in the cabinet, Houston was often consulted by Wilson on a variety of subjects. In 1920 the president finally recognized Houston's expertise, appointing him to succeed Carter Glass as secretary of the Treasury (see Document 5.5).

Except for Bryan, no member of Wilson's cabinet was well known to the public, and some, such as Daniels and Baker, seemed poor fits for the positions they occupied. Yet on the whole the cabinet served Wilson well. Daniels, Burleson, Houston, and Secretary of Labor William B. Wilson served all eight years, as did McAdoo (although not in the cabinet the whole time), and Lane would have also if failing health had not forced him to resign in 1920. Their longevity suggests that they suited the president and that they, in turn, approved his policies and were grateful for his support (see Appendix C). As historian John Milton Cooper concludes, "In administrative and political talent . . . Wilson's cabinet stacked up well against . . . any other" (Cooper 1976, 240).

Special Advisers

Like most presidents, Woodrow Wilson also sought advice from outside the cabinet, but his options were limited. The White House staff, aside from domestic servants, numbered just ten during his presidency, most of them clerks and typists. Only one staff member, Joseph Tumulty, the secretary to the president, actually had an advisory role on political issues such as appointments or how to appeal to a member of Congress whose vote was needed. From time to time Wilson sought political assistance from members of the Democratic National Committee, such as Vance McCormick, but for advice on more substantive issues he could only turn to the cabinet or to unofficial advisers, such as his friends Louis D. Brandeis and Col. Edward M. House. He met both men early in the 1912 campaign, and both became trusted advisers. No one had a greater influence on domestic policy in the first administration than Brandeis, whose distrust of large corporations and belief that genuine economic competition could be restored echoed and clarified Wilson's own ideas. Wilson hoped to appoint Brandeis as attorney general, but politics prevented this; he was later able to appoint Brandeis to the Supreme Court.

House, whom Wilson first met in the autumn of 1911, quickly became his closest friend and confidant. "Mr. House is my second personality," Wilson once said. "He is my independent self. His thoughts and mine are one. If I were in his place I would do just as he suggested . . ." (Seymour 1928, 1:114). That, it seems clear, was precisely the impression that House wanted the president to have, but in most instances the Texan was more important as a friend than a manipulator of policy. Wilson appreciated his unfailing discretion, which enabled the president to explore ideas with no fear of their leaking to the press, and Wilson often used House as a political go-between in sounding out possible appointees about their opinions, feeling out members of Congress whose votes were needed, and tending to minor business to relieve Wilson's burden (see Document 5.6). House was the one man with whom Wilson could relax completely and be himself, and the Texan's talent for flattery helped to cement his place in the president's affections.

House's influence on domestic policy was limited, as the president came into office with clearly defined ideas of what he wanted to achieve. House took a more overt role in the field of foreign policy, where Wilson initially had less experience and less interest, and where he did not have full confidence in either Secretary of State Bryan or his successor, Robert Lansing. Not surprisingly, House thought that the administration should put greater emphasis on foreign affairs. "To my mind," he wrote in his diary in June 1915, "the President has never appreciated the importance of our foreign policy and has laid undue emphasis upon domestic affairs . . ." (Seymour 1928, 1:177).

House moved to center stage with the beginning of World War I. When the president wanted an informal method of exploring opportunities for American mediation, he turned to House, and at his request the colonel traveled to Europe in 1914 even before the war began and then again in 1915 and 1916. In 1919 House served in his only official capacity for the administration as a member of the American delegation to the Paris peace conference. His skill at ingratiating himself with everyone he met served him well in diplomacy, but his foreign initiatives also gradually exposed the fact that he did not understand Wilson's goals as well as he thought he did. The two men remained close until the spring of 1919, when Wilson returned from Europe to the United States to deal with domestic business, leaving House in charge of the American delegation at the peace conference. During the president's absence House made what Wilson considered unwarranted concessions to the Allies, and Wilson never forgave him. After the end of the peace conference, the two never met again.

RELATIONSHIP WITH THE MILITARY

Although Woodrow Wilson had relatively little interest in foreign policy in 1912, he made it absolutely clear from the time he entered the White House that he meant to exercise tight civilian control over the military. He was reluctant to use military force unless it was absolutely necessary, and once decided upon its use, he was determined to combine it with diplomacy and other forms of influence for purposes and under rules that he defined personally and precisely. As historian Frederick Calhoun has observed, "He allowed the military little freedom of action, for he expected it to fight only when he ordered it, only for the reasons he felt worthy of battle, and only until he decided to quit" (Calhoun 1986, 35). Some of Wilson's political rivals, such as former president Theodore Roosevelt and Sen. Henry Cabot Lodge, R-Mass., derided him as a pacifist. They were misled by his refusal to authorize massive intervention in Mexico or by his reluctance to enter World War I. In fact, the Wilson administration used force, albeit in a limited and controlled way, more often than any of its predecessors.

Wilson's insistence on civilian control of the military was made clear within months after the new administration took power. In the spring of 1913 the California legislature passed a law designed to prevent land ownership by Asian immigrants. Humiliated and outraged by this discrimination, the Japanese government protested strongly. U.S. Army and Navy commanders, well aware of American weakness in the Pacific, and particularly in the Philippines, warned that the Japanese might attack without warning and recommended moving American gunboats from China to the Philippines to strengthen the islands' defenses. Secretary of War Lindley M. Garrison supported the commanders, while Secretary of the Navy Josephus Daniels argued that moving the ships would be provocative and dangerous. After a heated discussion of the issue at a cabinet meeting on May 16, the president concurred with Daniels (see Document 5.7).

The next day, to Wilson's astonishment, the Joint Board of the Army and Navy, the planning agency for the two services, met and recommended strongly that ships from California be sent to Hawaii to reinforce the fleet there. Wilson was furious. "After we talked this matter over in Cabinet Friday and you and [the] Secretary of War informed these Navy and Army gentlement [sic] that there was to be no movement now," he told Daniels, "they had no right to hold a meeting at all and discuss these matters. . . . I wish you would say to them that if this should occur again, there will be no General or Joint Boards. They will be abolished" (Cronon 1963, 68). Thereafter there was no doubt who would control the administration's policy.

Yet while Wilson was insistent on civilian control, he was not antimilitary. He gave officers whom he trusted, such as Admiral Frank F. Fletcher and General Hugh L. Scott, considerable latitude to conduct diplomatic as well as military operations in Mexico, and he appointed General Tasker H. Bliss to represent the United States on the Supreme War Council in Europe in 1917 and on the peace delegation in Paris in 1919. In 1915 General Leonard Wood and his civilian allies, including Theodore Roosevelt, advocated a "preparedness" policy under which all able-bodied young men would receive short-term military training and then be required to enlist in a reserve. Wilson was concerned that such a policy would lead to a permanent standing army, but he realized that the growing conflict with Germany necessitated some preparations for defense. Under the National Defense Act of 1916 he secured federal funding for voluntary reserve officer training programs and greater federal control over the national guard, a system which he believed would provide a corps of well-trained officers who, in times of crisis, could train and command volunteer soldiers. He also supported a substantial expansion of the navy, including the construction of a number of battleships and heavy cruisers. Unfortunately, by the time the United States entered the war in April 1917 neither of these programs was sufficiently advanced to make much difference.

Secretary of War Garrison regarded Wilson's 1916 preparedness program as inadequate and resigned in protest. Wilson replaced him with Newton D. Baker, who agreed completely with Wilson's commitment to a "citizen army." Although there was widespread criticism of the way Baker handled mobilization, Wilson consistently supported him and the officers he appointed to fight the war. Ultimately, despite all difficulties,

Baker managed to raise, train, equip, and transport to France an American army of a million men, all within an amazingly short time. In large part Baker's success came from his ability to select and support able officers, including Quartermaster General George W. Goethals, Army Chief of Staff Peyton C. March, and John J. Pershing, commander of the American expeditionary force in France.

During the war Wilson left the fighting to the military, but he kept close supervision over general strategy (see Document 5.8). Nearly every day he would go to Baker's office in the old State-War-Navy Building across from the White House and there talk with the secretary, read dispatches from Europe, and issue orders about what needed to be done. Among other things, Wilson insisted that because the army was made up of civilian draftees, it must be more in tune with civilian attitudes, providing educational and entertainment facilities and a more liberal Code of Military Justice.

Similar reforms were also implemented in the navy, where even before the war Secretary Daniels banned liquor aboard ships and modernized discipline. Wilson and Daniels worked well together, but their joint inexperience led to one mistake. They agreed to the navy's requests for the construction of large warships in the 1916 preparedness program, only to discover after the nation entered the war that what was really needed were merchant vessels and smaller, speedy ships capable of convoy duty and antisubmarine warfare. Although the construction program was reoriented in 1917, disappointingly few of the smaller ships got into service before the end of the war.

In addition, despite his resolution not to intervene in strictly military matters, Wilson found himself drawn into a major dispute within the navy over how to combat submarines. One faction recommended convoys; another proposed using only mines; a third demanded that scarce ships be kept near home to protect American coasts. Irritated at this dispute among the supposed experts, Wilson eventually decided in favor of convoys, although the method was radical. He consoled himself that "nobody ever before conducted a war like this and therefore nobody can pretend to be a professional in a war like this . . ." (quoted in May 1960, 116).

Despite all the blunders and muddles of mobilization in 1917 and 1918, the United States achieved near-miracles in World War I, creating a modern army and navy where virtually none had existed a year previously. As military historian Edward Coffman concludes, "In World War

I, within the limited sphere of military activity, the Americans were successful in mobilizing the nation and making their force a factor on the Western Front. The Allies could not have won without their help" (Coffman 1968, 364). That was what Wilson had set out to do.

In addition to the enormous commitment of World War I, the Wilson administration also applied military force as an instrument of policy in a number of other cases. American forces intervened in Mexico in 1914 and 1916, occupied Haiti in 1915 and the Dominican Republic in 1916, and joined with Allied forces in Russia in 1918 (see Chapter 3). In all these cases Wilson intended to use force in a strictly limited way, but events sometimes outran his ability to control them. The disastrous interventions in Mexico, for instance, made Wilson deeply skeptical about the efficacy of military intervention in a revolutionary situation, particularly in a large country. When the Allies pressed Wilson in 1918 to help them invade Russia—a similarly vast and revolutionary country— and restore a government that would return Russian troops to the Eastern Front, Wilson dug in his heels. He had learned during his time in office that American military force rarely succeeded at correcting other countries' internal problems, let alone establishing stable and democratic governments. In that instance, Wilson consented to sending troops specifically to protect Allied munitions at Archangel and to open the Trans-Siberian Railroad to Czech troops who had been stranded in Western Russia, but the action poisoned Russian-American relations for years afterward. Had Wilson lived to witness the ultimate results of his military involvement in the Caribbean, he would have seen yet another example of the futility of such interventions. The military could build roads and schools, but it could not build democracy or goodwill. Wilson learned after every intervention that armies alone could not make the world safe for democracy.

It is certainly possible to criticize Wilson as commander in chief, even to deride him as historian Robert Ferrell has done, as "a complete misfit as commander in chief" (Ferrell 1993, 67). Having come to office with little interest in foreign policy, no experience with the military, and a deep hatred of war, Wilson initially had little to guide him in dealing with the military beyond general principles. The officers through whom he had to work were generally elderly and unimaginative, and the structures of supply and command in the services were bureaucratic nightmares. Wilson's opposition to militarism made him unwilling to make large changes before the war, and when the United States entered the conflict in April 1917 the system broke down almost completely. Overconfidence also led to blunders in Latin America, but Wilson learned from his mistakes and held, throughout, to the basic principle that military force must be a flexible instrument and not a determinant of national policy. Despite missteps, he established a model for his successors of "principled applications of power in the relations between nations" (Calhoun 1986, x).

RELATIONSHIP WITH CONGRESS

Historian and political scientist James MacGregor Burns argues that Wilson's leadership of Congress offers a model for twentieth century presidents. As Burns puts it, "Wilson exercised leadership in the simplest, most direct way. He stated his program, presented it to the public, conferred early and often with his congressional lieutenants and advisers, carefully timed the programming of the measures in Congress, maintained pressure on the leaders and rank and file, soothed hurt feelings, and stood firm behind the principles of his bills while allowing some changes in details." His first year's leadership, concludes Burns, "has become the classic example of presidential marshaling of support behind a predetermined program" (Burns 1966, 198). Wilson, concludes political scientist Marshall Dimock, was "a master strategist and at the same time one of the most successful tacticians ever to occupy the White House" (Dimock 1957, 9).

Wilson had not always thought of the president as the leader of the federal government. Growing up during the late nineteenth century when Congress was dominant, his early academic work focused on ways to secure responsible leadership in Congress that would seriously address national problems (see Chapter 1). Not until the twentieth century, when Presidents William McKinley and Theodore Roosevelt began to revive presidential leadership in foreign and domestic policy, did Wilson shift the focus of his study from Capitol Hill to the White House. By 1908 he had come to see the president not only as an important but as a *dominant* part of the government. In New Jersey, Wilson had been what he called an "unconstitutional governor," an executive who constantly took issues to the public and invited them specifically to endorse his programs and thus strengthen his influence over the legislature. As he entered the

White House in 1913, he expected to lead Congress in a similar way (see Document 5.9).

Wilson's brief experience in New Jersey gave him little preparation for Washington, where he knew few people and where even his academic knowledge was twenty years out of date. Moreover, although the Democrats controlled both the legislature and executive for the first time since the 1890s, their majorities were no guarantee of achievement. Congressional Democrats were more accustomed to opposing than drafting and passing legislation. In addition, two of the Democratic Party's main congressional leaders, Sen. Oscar W. Underwood of Alabama and Speaker of the House James Beauchamp "Champ" Clark of Missouri, had been Wilson's rivals for the presidential nomination. It did not prove easy for the new president to translate his theory of leadership into practice.

The pleasure Democrats felt at having a Democrat and a southerner in the White House gave Wilson a temporary advantage that he exploited shrewdly. During the months prior to the inauguration he met extensively with congressional leaders, particularly Clark, Underwood, and Rep. Carter Glass, D-Va. They were familiar with the general outlines of his program from the campaign, and Wilson suggested the order in which he thought that measures should be taken up, but he flattered them by inviting them to draft specific legislation and by consulting them on how to gather the votes needed (see Document 5.10). Congressional leaders were delighted that the new president seemed disposed to pay them the deference they expected.

Yet even as Wilson seemed to pay homage to Congress, he also found ways to assert his leadership. Among the most effective was the personal message to Congress. On April 8, 1913, at the opening of a special session that Wilson called to consider tariff reduction, he went personally to the Capitol to speak to a joint session of Congress, something no president since John Adams had done (see Document 5.11). Although he joked during his speech that his goal was merely to prove that he was a real person, not a disembodied office, the event captured headlines across the country. While appearing to honor Congress by coming to them, in fact Wilson was turning the spotlight of publicity on the legislators and increasing the pressure for action. It was a tactic that he would use with good effect throughout his presidency, and that all subsequent presidents have adopted.

Wilson also revived another old custom that, again, seemed to honor Congress but in fact strengthened his leadership. No president since Ulysses S. Grant had gone to Capitol Hill to meet with a congressional committee until Wilson did so on April 9, 1913, when he met with the Senate Finance Committee to discuss the tariff. By meeting first with a Senate committee, Wilson paid special respect to the senior chamber, and at the same time he focused public attention on the body where opposition to tariff reform was the strongest. Recognizing that it was important not to give the impression that the executive was subservient to the legislature, Wilson did not often go to Capitol Hill to meet with committees, but his willingness to do so occasionally enhanced his relationship and influence with Congress. At other times he used a similar technique by inviting individual legislators or small groups of them to the White House for what he called "common counsel."

Given Wilson's conviction that government should be responsible to the public's wishes, it is not surprising that he also used the press to push congressional action. Although his relationship with reporters was often strained, he successfully used press conferences to arouse public interest in an issue. For example, in May 1913, when the tariff bill stalled in the Senate, he declared at a press conference that Washington was "swarming with lobbyists" who were spending "money without limit" in order "to overcome the interests of the public for their private profit" (Link and others 1978, 27:472, 473). He seems to have had no basis for his claim, but the resulting controversy embarrassed some Senators who appeared to be profiting from protectionism and increased public pressure for reform.

When necessary, Wilson showed great skill in shaping the compromises that were sometimes essential to achieving a broad objective. One of the most dramatic cases of this sort arose during the drafting of the Federal Reserve Act in the late spring of 1913. Although there was bipartisan agreement that reform of the banking and currency system was needed (see Chapter 3), there was serious disagreement about whether the new system would be publicly or privately controlled. Wilson at first favored private control, but when influential Democrats objected, he quickly endorsed a public system. His flexibility united the party and assured the success of the legislation.

The same flexibility was evident in the president's willingness to change his position on antitrust law when shown that his original approach was unworkable. In 1912 he had opposed Theodore Roosevelt's suggestion of a federal regulatory agency with discretionary authority to regulate business and called instead for passage of a law that would spell out, in detail, anticompetitive practices. Presidential adviser Louis D. Brandeis argued that such a law was probably unworkable, however, and by the time of the election Wilson was changing his mind. The administration supported the Clayton Act of 1914, which banned specific business practices, to please Democrats who favored that method, but Wilson had really come to prefer the regulatory approach embodied in the Federal Trade Commission Act of the same year. He might have chosen to push one bill and abandon the other, but favoring either would have alienated some reformers. His choice to endorse *both* of the somewhat incompatible approaches to the problem provided a unique compromise and assured the success of both pieces of legislation.

The president's relations with Congress were not always harmonious, of course. He enjoyed remarkable success during his first term, but the second was more troubled. War aroused powerful tensions within American society, and there was probably no way Wilson could have avoided all controversy, but the administration's handling of mobilization was sometimes inept. Minor corruption and major inefficiency drew Congress's attention, and Wilson's enemies seized on the opportunity to demand the creation of a special civilian body to take control of the process away from the president. He maneuvered cleverly to head off the threat by securing congressional authorization to reorganize the whole executive (which was more than even the most ardent critics wanted), but this particular criticism subsided only with the end of the war (see Document 5.12).

War's end exacerbated rather than ended Wilson's most notable battle with Congress. Beginning with an ill-advised decision to ask Americans to support his foreign policy by electing Democrats in the 1918 congressional elections, Wilson appeared to be on a collision course with the Senate over the terms of the peace that would follow the war. Confrontation became probable when the Republicans won control of both Houses, and Wilson departed for Europe without taking with him any important Republicans or any members of the Senate who would vote on the peace treaty. During the summer of 1919, after the president submitted the Treaty of Versailles to the Senate, he courted undecided senators and even met for three hours with the Senate Foreign Relations

Committee (chaired by Henry Cabot Lodge), but the methods that had served him so well earlier now failed. Even his most reliable technique of the past, an appeal directly to the people through a series of speeches, did not assure success in this case. In November the Senate rejected the treaty.

The spectacular disaster of the treaty fight contrasts markedly with the president's previously harmonious relationship with Congress. Wilson's health (he suffered a major stroke during the campaign for the treaty), wartime tensions between president and Congress, partisanship, and personal animosity between Wilson and the new Republican majority leader (Senator Lodge) all contributed to the debacle, but ultimately an issue of principle divided Wilson and his critics: he was prepared to compromise American sovereignty to achieve collective security; they were not (see Chapter 4 for details). Wilson's failure in this case overshadowed in the minds of succeeding generations all his previous successes.

Despite the League of Nations disaster, Wilson ranks among the most effective twentieth-century presidents in his relations with Congress. Not only did he make effective use of familiar techniques, such as setting priorities and negotiating with legislators, but he also pioneered what has proved to be the modern president's most effective tool: the mobilization of public opinion behind his program. When in 1908 Wilson declared that if a president could "once win the admiration and confidence of the country . . . no other single force can withstand him," the concept must have seemed far-fetched to listeners who had never experienced such leadership (Wilson 1908, 68). Wilson's successors, however, built on his advice to create what sixty years later would be referred to as an "imperial presidency."

RELATIONSHIP WITH THE SUPREME COURT

The Supreme Court did not have a major influence on the United States during the Wilson years. One reason for this situation was that the chief justice, Edward Douglass White (first appointed to the Court in 1894 and elevated to chief justice by President William Howard Taft in 1910), was sixty-eight at the start of Wilson's presidency and not very forceful. Another was that the Court, which at this point lacked the authority to decide what cases it would hear, was buried under a large number of trivial cases. The huge backlog of cases waiting to be decided often meant that the Court's long-delayed rulings seemed outdated and irrelevant. The Court did not actively oppose reforms, as it did during the New Deal of the 1930s, but neither was it an active force for change during most of the Progressive Era.

The White Court's decisions, much like Wilson's presidency, illustrate ambivalence about increased federal power. A string of cases throughout the Wilson administration forced the Court constantly to review the boundaries of congressional power, as well as the power of agencies like the Interstate Commerce Commission (ICC). In the *Shreveport Rate Cases* (1914), for instance, the ICC had argued that railroad rates within states could not be less than rates *between* states for travel of equal distance. Although the commission was statutorily allowed to set interstate rates, the case questioned whether it could, by extension, also set intrastate rates. The Court ruled in favor of Congress and therefore in favor of the ICC. Perhaps reflecting the waning of the Progressive Era, six years later, in *Federal Trade Commission v. Gratz* (1920), the Court ruled *against* the FTC, arguing that such agencies could not determine the nature of the term *fair competition*. In the *Selective Draft Law Cases* (1918), the Court affirmed the federal government's use of the draft, but only a few months later, in *Hammer v. Dagenhart* (1918), it struck at federal power by declaring unconstitutional the Keating-Owen Act of 1916, which had outlawed child labor.

A secondary development linked to the increase in federal power was the concomitant decrease in state power. The White Court struggled to draw a line between the federal and state spheres, but the distinction was increasingly less important in an era of massive federal expansion and nationalized problems. In 1920, faced with the confusing language of enforcement included in the Eighteenth Amendment, the Court effectively ruled in the *National Prohibition Cases* (1920) that state power no longer existed, it having been subsumed by another authority regulating "throughout the length and breadth of the United States, without reference to state lines or the distinctions between state and federal power" (quoted in Pratt 1999, 230). That conflation of state and federal power was repeated in *Missouri v. Holland* (1920). In that instance, a 1918 treaty with Great Britain required the establishment of a federal protection program for birds migrating between the United States and Canada. The Court, however, had previously argued that that authority belonged to the states. Here the Court argued that the federal program took precedence, deriving its power from the treaty clause of the Constitution.

A second broad set of cases tried by the Court dealt with labor-capital relations. In *Coppage v. Kansas* (1915) the Court supported the right of T. B. Coppage to require future employees to agree not to be a part of a union. Kansas had made this practice illegal in 1903, but the Court argued that government had no power to prevent individuals entering into contracts. The ruling in *Hitchman Coal & Coke Company v. Mitchell* (1917) was much the same, but in both cases dissenting opinions argued that, without a union to protect him, a worker could not be an equal party in contracts made with an employer.

Finally, and perhaps most important, the Court ruled on cases relating to race relations and freedom of speech. With regard to the former, *Buchanan v. Warley* (1917) was a landmark case in that it struck down a Louisville, Kentucky, law allowing segregation in residential areas. Although the Court argued in blacks' favor by invoking violations of traditional contract law, and opponents of the ruling found ways to get around it, the case pointed toward the future. The verdict in *South Covington & Cincinnati Street Railway Co. v. Kentucky* (1920), however, which affirmed segregation on railroad cars, pointed just as clearly into the past.

With regard to freedom of speech, the Court delivered some of its most famous verdicts. In *Schenck v. United States* (1919) the Court voted unanimously in support of convictions resulting from the wartime Espionage Act of 1917. In defending the Court's opinion, Justice Oliver Wendell Holmes wrote, "When a nation is at war many things that might be said in time of peace are such a hindrance to its effort that their utterance will not be endured so long as men fight and that no Court could regard them as protected by any constitutional right" (quoted in Pratt 1999, 216). Similar opinions appeared in *Frohwerk v. United States* (1919) and *Debs v. United States* (1919), the latter upholding the arrest of three-time Socialist Party presidential candidate Eugene V. Debs. Argued in the subsequent session of the Court, however, *Abrams v. United States* (1919) and *Schaefer v. United States* (1920) hinted at a break with earlier decisions, sharply dividing the Court over what constituted free speech. Nevertheless, the Court upheld those earlier rulings when Minnesota's 1917 sedition law was challenged in *Gilbert v. Minnesota* (1920) by the pacifist Joseph Gilbert. In an important dissent, however, Justice Brandeis challenged the states' power to override First Amendment rights. Brandeis found it hard to believe that the Constitution could protect, among other things, the right of employers to discriminate against workers who belonged to unions, yet it "does not include liberty to teach, either in the privacy of the home or publicly, the doctrine of pacifism; so long, at least, as Congress has not declared that the public safety demands its suppression" (quoted in Pratt 1999, 254).

Wilson had the opportunity to appoint three justices to the Supreme Court. His appointments reflected the tension in Wilsonian progressivism between a belief that any concentration of power, whether in private hands or under government control, was dangerous and a desire to make the government responsive to the public's wish for strong federal policies to rectify problems. His first appointee, James C. McReynolds, although generally depicted by historians as a conservative, even a reactionary, wanted to curtail the powers of *both* government and corporations. Like Wilson himself, although in a far more extreme form, McReynolds straddled the gulf between nineteenth-century Democratic principles of localism, state rights, and laissez faire and the Progressive Era party's embrace of federal authority to correct distortions of the economic and social order caused by the unchecked power of giant corporations. Wilson's other two appointees, Louis D. Brandeis and John Hessin Clarke, clearly represented the progressive belief that the federal government should attack social and economic inequities.

McReynolds grew up in Kentucky and graduated from Vanderbilt University and the University of Virginia Law School and practiced law in Tennessee. In 1903 he was appointed to the Justice Department, where he made a reputation as an antitrust crusader. Regarding monopolies as "essentially wicked," he won a major case against the large tobacco companies for violations of the Sherman Act, and it was this record that led Wilson to appoint him attorney general (quoted in Friedman and Israel 1969, 2026). McReynolds was an able lawyer but an unpleasant person, and he soon won the hearty dislike of his cabinet colleagues. When Justice Harold Lurton died on July 12, 1914, Wilson welcomed the opportunity to move McReynolds from the cabinet to the Supreme Court.

On the Court, where he was no more popular than he had been in the cabinet, McReynolds gained a reputation as an erratic dissenter, but there was a common thread in his opinions. He favored individualism and local autonomy, and he distrusted size and centralization, whether it was in industry or in government. Thus he believed strongly that antitrust laws must be enforced vigorously to prevent the growth of monopolies, but he was equally suspicious of the discretionary power of the Federal Trade Commission. In his opinion in *Federal Trade Commission v. Gratz* (1920) he argued that the courts, not the commission, must decide what were unfair methods of competition (see Document 5.13). Insofar as possible, he sought to achieve a totally free market, liberated from the domination of either government or big business. Historians have generally argued that, from Wilson's perspective, McReynolds's "appointment was a lost one in terms of policy influence" (Handberg 1976, 366), but Wilson shared McReynolds' ambivalence about the use of federal power to rectify economic problems.

Wilson's second appointee to the Court, Louis D. Brandeis, was also born in Kentucky, but he could hardly have been more different from McReynolds. The son of Jewish immigrants, Brandeis studied in Germany and at Harvard, and within a few years after graduating from Harvard Law School in 1877 he became a very successful private attorney. Turning increasingly to public interest cases, he earned a national reputation as a crusader against monopolies and for consumers. His admirers often referred to him as "the people's attorney." In 1908, in *Muller v. Oregon,* he helped convince the Supreme Court to accept for the first time sociological and statistical evidence. Wilson sought out Brandeis in 1912 for advice on antitrust policy and based much of his campaign position on the lawyer's arguments, but he did not have the courage to bring Brandeis into his cabinet in the face of unified opposition from New England's intellectual and business elite.

When Justice Joseph R. Lamar died on January 2, 1916, however, the president decided to name Brandeis to the Court. Wilson was well aware that the nomination would outrage conservatives and anti-Semites, but he also believed it would send a message that it was time for the Supreme Court to move away from a rigid, literal reading of the Constitution. "The Constitution, like the Sabbath, was made for man and not man for the Constitution," he said a few months later. "And men must be put forward whose whole comprehension is that law is subservient to life and not life to law" (quoted in Link 1964, 324).

Wilson's appointment of Brandeis was primarily a matter of principle, but it was also smart politics. By naming Brandeis, Wilson indicated his support for the left wing of the progressive movement and won the applause of groups ranging from Theodore Roosevelt's supporters to the Socialists. The nomination helped to create and solidify the coalition that would secure Wilson's reelection that autumn (see Document 5.14).

Conservatives were as passionate in their opposition to Brandeis as progressives were enthusiastic, but they could find little substance to support their position. Although they declared that he was "not scrupulous in the methods he adopts," the charge referred not to any actual misbehavior but to Brandeis's belief that the technical requirements of the law, and even the Constitution, must be less sacred than the people's needs— exactly what Wilson liked about him (quoted in Pratt 1999, 141). Brandeis was confirmed by the Senate on June 1, 1916, by a 47–22 vote. He would have a long and distinguished career on the bench, acting as an advocate of the individual American in the face of growing centralization of the government and industry.

The third of Wilson's appointees to the Supreme Court, made as a result of Charles Evans Hughes's decision to resign to run for president in 1916, was John Hessin Clarke. Born in 1857 in Ohio, Clarke attended Western Reserve College, studied law under his father, and in 1878 was admitted to the bar. In 1880 he became part owner of a newspaper in Youngstown, Ohio, and over the next several years also built a successful law practice. In 1914 Wilson appointed him to the Federal District Court of the Northern District of Ohio, probably at Secretary of War Newton Baker's recommendation. Lawyers who practiced before his court disliked him, finding him impatient and abrupt, but they admitted he was a good judge. When Hughes resigned, Wilson considered several possible replacements but rejected them all for various reasons and eventually turned to Clarke as a reliable progressive. He was confirmed by the Senate by a voice vote on the same day Wilson nominated him, July 24, 1916.

Clarke made no strong impression on his new colleagues. McReynolds thought he was stupid and refused even to speak to him. Others regarded him as pleasant but sometimes muddled in his thinking. For the most part he voted with the minority on the Court who supported the expansion of federal power, joining Brandeis in dissent on *Hammer v. Dagenhart* (1918) and joining the majority to uphold the constitutionality of the federal inheritance tax in *New York Trust Co. v. Fisner* (1921) (see Document 5.15). He gave progressives one of their last victories in 1921 when he wrote the opinion for the majority in the so-called Hardwood Lumber Case, *American Column and Lumber Co. v. United States*, in which the Court ruled that antitrust law applied to trade associations as well as individual companies. In other opinions he strongly supported organized labor's right to strike, picket, and boycott, and he upheld state laws designed to set maximum hours and improve working conditions. As one observer has noted, he led all members of the Court, including Brandeis, "in his support of the economic underdogs of society" (Handberg 1976, 366). To the surprise and annoyance of liberals, however, on September 1, 1922, Clarke abruptly resigned from the Court to campaign for American membership in the League of Nations.

Taken together, Wilson's appointees to the Court suggest some patterns within his version of progressivism. Brandeis and Clarke clearly exemplified the trend toward greater federal activism in dealing with social and economic problems, while McReynolds, with his suspicion of both big business and big government, revealed a lingering commitment to traditional Democratic values of individualism, limited government, and local autonomy. Between the belief that government should be both responsive to the needs and wishes of the people and limited in size and scope there was never a clear reconciliation in Wilson's policy, any more than there was between McReynolds and Brandeis.

RELATIONSHIP WITH THE MEDIA

In the spring of 1911, when Woodrow Wilson made his first campaign trip to the West, he was annoyed to discover that his assistant, Frank Parker Stockbridge, had scheduled two daily interviews with the press in each city he was to visit. After the first session, during which Wilson was barely able to conceal his anger at being asked questions about his wife and family rather than about his ideas and proposals, he asked Stockbridge, "Do I have to go through that again?" Stockbridge, who understood perfectly the interest of reporters and their readers in the private life of a possible president, and the importance of Wilson appearing open and approachable, answered frankly, "Everywhere we stop, Governor" (Juergens 1981, 126).

The story captures the essence of Wilson's relationship with the press. He saw its value to him as a means of communicating his message to the public, which was essential to his style of leadership, but he did not understand that the reporters' questions were indicators of public opinion, and he rejected entirely their right to inquire into matters he considered private. He wanted the reporters to act as publicity agents, not investigators, and when they did not do as he wished, he could be testy. On March 19, 1914, for example, when Ellen Wilson was ill with what would prove to be a terminal illness and his daughter Eleanor was about to get married, he came to a press conference in a towering rage.

> I am a public character for the time being, but the ladies of my household are not servants of the government and they are not public characters. I deeply resent the treatment they are receiving at the hands of the newspapers at this time. . . . I do not see why I should permit representatives of those papers who treat the ladies of my household in this way to have personal interviews with me. . . . I cannot act altogether as an individual while I occupy this office. But I must do something. The thing is intolerable. Every day I pick up the paper and see some flat lie, some entire invention. . . . (Link and others 1985, 50:418–419)

Wilson could not imagine the possibility that a limited revelation of his personal life might add to his popularity and political influence.

Wilson was the first president to hold formal press conferences, meeting with reporters once or twice a week for more than two years, until he suspended the conferences on grounds of national security after the sinking of the *Lusitania* in May 1915. Thereafter he did not meet reporters formally for a year and held only three press conferences during his entire second term.

At press conferences Wilson admitted all accredited reporters, not just a favored few, and did not require that questions be submitted in advance. Although this method occasionally produced angry confrontations, the president's intimate knowledge of administration policy impressed the reporters. Unfortunately, some of the good effect was undone by his tendency to answer questions with academic lectures directed to pupils he obviously did not consider very bright. Also, he sometimes dealt with subjects he did not want to discuss by giving answers that, while technically accurate, gave a misleading impression. Soon after the 1912 election, for example, reporters asked him if he planned to make a speech at a large dinner in New York. He replied truthfully that he did not but failed to mention that he was not even planning to attend the dinner. Reporters who spent the evening racing around the city trying to locate the president-elect were furious, and thereafter if they suspected he was "grazing the truth," they might try to ask a question several different ways (quoted in Smith 1990, 27). That angered Wilson almost as much as personal questions, and he sometimes snapped at those who did it. His private stenographer, Charles Swem, observed, "The truth is the President didn't *enjoy* the conferences, he submitted to them" (quoted in Juergens 1981, 142).

Wilson's greatest asset in dealing with the press was his secretary, Joseph Tumulty. Tumulty grew up in an Irish-American family in Jersey City, New Jersey, and learned his politics there, but he hated the corruption of the political machines. When Wilson burst on the scene, Tumulty embraced him whole-heartedly. As secretary to the new president, Tumulty admitted he "felt terrified at the prospect of being interviewed" by the Washington press corps, but soon found he had nothing to fear (quoted in Stein 1969, 55). When the reporters learned that he would hold press briefings practically every day, that he would make himself available to them night or day if there was news, and that he gave them reliable information, they treated him with courtesy and consideration. They also appreciated his talent as a story-teller and his willingness to say frankly if he had no information on a subject or was forbidden to answer a question. "If Joseph P. Tumulty will not tell you all you want to know," said one reporter, "he will not mislead you nor tell you what is not so" (quoted in Juergens 1981, 160–161).

Soon after Wilson was reelected in 1916, Edward House and Edith Wilson, who never liked or trusted Tumulty, persuaded the president to replace him. Reporters, who fully understood Tumulty's importance to the administration as well as his value to them, intervened and managed to save the secretary's job, but the incident seriously damaged the relationship between the two men. When Wilson went to Paris in 1918 to attend the peace conference, he left Tumulty behind and instead took as his press representative George Creel, head of the Committee on Public Information, which had been set up in 1917 to handle wartime propaganda. That was a mistake. Creel may have known more about the issues than Tumulty, but he had less influence with Wilson and less understanding of the importance of public gestures by the president. Although Tumulty bombarded Wilson with cables urging him to visit soldiers in the field and in hospitals and to mix with ordinary people so he would not be seen "as an official living in a palace and guarded by soldiery," the overworked president never understood the importance of the advice (quoted in Stein 1969, 64).

Instead of courting the reporters, as Tumulty advised, Wilson bowed to French insistence that the deliberations of the peace conference be secret, which allowed them, through carefully manipulated leaks, to slant newspaper coverage to their advantage. The president met with reporters in France only twice—on February 14, 1919, just after the conference approved the covenant of the League of Nations, and on June 27, 1919, the day before the treaty was formally signed at Versailles. In both cases it was apparent to everyone that Wilson's only reason for speaking to the press was to promote support for the League and the treaty. In short, his relations with the press at Paris were, as one observer put it, "a dismal flop" (Stein 1969, 64).

One of Tumulty's least known but most important functions during the early part of the Wilson administration was as a conduit of public opinion to the president. Every day he had his staff clip articles from newspapers and magazines across the country, and each evening he took them home with him to read. If he detected patterns or trends in the stories, he made sure Wilson knew about them, and he did the same thing with confidential reports from friends among the reporters and with the gossip he picked up in the White House. His talent for gathering and winnowing an enormous amount of information, and then seeing its significance, was invaluable to Wilson, who had no other reliable method of assessing public opinion. After 1916, when Wilson and Tumulty's relations became more distant, the president was increasingly isolated.

Throughout his public career Wilson's relations with the press embodied a paradox. He believed strongly in the importance of public scrutiny of government activities as a means of holding officials accountable for their acts, and, even more important, his basic philosophy of government held that the president must be the spokesman of the national will—a role he could play only if there was full and clear communication in each direction. Yet he never found a comfortable or even a tolerable relationship with reporters. With few exceptions he regarded them as hostile and insensitive, and he made his feelings all too clear. He told George Creel, when Creel urged him to resume his press conferences in 1917:

It is a waste of time. I came to Washington with the idea that close and cordial relations with the press would prove of the greatest aid. I prepared for the conferences as carefully as for any lecture, and talked freely and fully on all large questions of the moment. Some men of brilliant ability were in the group, but I soon discovered that the interest of the majority was in the personal and trivial rather than in principles and policies. (quoted in Juergens 1981, 150–151)

That comment, with its revelation about how he regarded reporters and his description of press conferences as opportunities for "lectures" on "large questions," illustrated why his relations with the press were a failure.

BIBLIOGRAPHIC ESSAY

A number of Wilson's cabinet members left records of their roles in the administration. These include: William Jennings Bryan and Mary Baird Bryan, *The Memoirs of William Jennings Bryan* (Chicago: Winston, 1925); E. David Cronon, ed. *The Cabinet Diaries of Josephus Daniels, 1913-1921,* (Lincoln: University of Nebraska Press, 1963); Josephus Daniels, *The Wilson Era,* 2 vols. (Chapel Hill: University of North Carolina Press, 1944, 1946); David F. Houston, *Eight Years with Wilson's Cabinet, 1913 to 1920,* 2 vols. (Garden City, N.Y.: Doubleday, Page, 1926); Anne Wintermute Lane and Louise Herrick Wall, eds. *The Letters of Franklin K. Lane, Personal and Political,* (Boston: Houghton Mifflin, 1922); Robert Lansing, *The Peace Negotiations: A Personal Narrative* (Boston: Houghton Mifflin, 1921); and William Gibbs McAdoo, *Crowded Years: The Reminiscences of William G. McAdoo* (Boston: Houghton Mifflin, 1931). Accounts by other advisers include: William F. McCombs, *Making Woodrow Wilson President* (New York: Fairview, 1921); Charles Seymour, *The Intimate Papers of Colonel House,* 4 vols. (Boston: Houghton Mifflin, 1926–1928); and Joseph Tumulty, *Woodrow Wilson as I Know Him* (Garden City, N.Y.: Doubleday, Page, 1921). McCombs, embittered and unbalanced when he wrote his book, is not to be trusted, and House's claims about his influence on Wilson tend to be exaggerated. Seymour's selections and linking narrative always put House in the best possible light and should be used with caution. Previously cited works quoted in this section include Arthur S. Link, *Wilson: The New Freedom;* August Heckscher, *Woodrow Wilson;* and John Milton Cooper, *The Warrior and the Priest* (see Works Cited).

David F. Trask, and Arthur Link and John Whiteclay Chambers II, have essays assessing various aspects of Wilson's relationship with the military in Richard H. Kohn, ed., *The United States Military under the Constitution of the United States, 1789–1989* (New York: New York University Press, 1991). Chambers is also the author of an excellent book on the World War I draft, *To Raise an Army: The Draft Comes to Modern America* (New York: Free Press, 1987). For the American military in World War I, see Edward Coffman, *The War to End All Wars: The American Military Experience in World War I* (New York: Oxford University Press, 1968), while the more general context of Wilson's military and diplomatic policy is explored in Arthur S. Link, ed., *Woodrow Wilson and a Revolutionary World, 1913–1921* (Chapel Hill: University of North Carolina Press, 1982).

Contrasting evaluations of Wilson as commander in chief are provided by Frederick S. Calhoun (see bibliographic essay for Chapter 3); Ernest R. May, ed., "Wilson (1917–1918)," *The Ultimate Decision: The President as Commander in Chief* (New York: George Braziller, 1960); and Robert H. Ferrell, "Woodrow Wilson: A Misfit in Office?" in *Commanders in Chief: Presidential Leadership in Modern Wars*, ed. Joseph G. Dawson III (Lawrence: University Press of Kansas, 1993). Paul A. C. Koistinen, *Mobilizing for Modern War: The Political Economy of American Warfare, 1865–1919* (cited in Chapter 4), is a masterful analysis of the relationship among the military, politics, and the economy.

Wilson's remarkable success in securing the passage of his legislative program is analyzed in some detail in Marshall E. Dimock, "Woodrow Wilson as Legislative Leader," *Journal of Politics* 19 (February 1957): 3–19. James MacGregor Burns looks at the same subject in the broader context of the history of the presidency in *Presidential Government: The Crucible of Leadership* (Boston: Houghton Mifflin, 1966). For Wilson's own ideas about presidential leadership, as he expressed them in 1908, see his *Constitutional Government* (cited in Chapter 1).

Wilson's appointees to the Supreme Court—James McReynolds, Louis Brandeis, and John H. Clarke—are the subjects of good, brief biographies in Leon Friedman and Fred L. Israel, eds., *The Justices of the United States Supreme Court, 1789–1969, Their Lives and Major Opinions* (New York: Chelsea House, 1969), vol. 3; Walter F. Pratt Jr., *The Supreme Court under Edward Douglass White, 1910–1921* (Columbia: University of South Carolina Press, 1999); and Roger Handberg Jr., "Decision-Making in a Natural Court, 1916–1921," *American Politics Quarterly* 4 (July 1976): 357–378, provide valuable perspective on the Court in the Wilson era.

Henry J. Abraham, *Justices and Presidents: A Political History of Appointments to the Supreme Court* (New York: Oxford University Press, 1985) discusses the relationship between politics and Supreme Court appointments. Joan Biskupic and Elder Witt, *Guide to the U.S. Supreme Court*, 3rd ed., 2 vols. (Washington, D.C.: Congressional Quarterly, 1997), and Kermit L. Hall et al., eds., *The Oxford Companion to the Supreme Court of the United States* (New York: Oxford University Press, 1992) provide concise information on cases, opinions, justices, and other topics related to the Court. Henry Abraham and Barbara A. Perry, *Freedom and the Court: Civil Rights and Liberties in the United States*, 7th ed. (New York: Oxford University Press, 1998), is a good introduction to this important issue as it developed during and after World War I. Arthur Link's *Wilson: Confusions and Crises* (cited in Chapter 2) covers the Brandeis appointment.

Robert C. Hilderbrand did a remarkable job of reconstructing and editing the transcripts of Wilson's press conferences in Volume 50, *The Complete Press Conferences, 1913–1919* (1985) of Link and others, eds., *The Papers of Woodrow Wilson*. George Juergens, *News from the White House: The Presidential-Press Relationship in the Progressive Era* (Chicago: University of Chicago Press, 1981), is both entertaining and authoritative. Also useful on Wilson's relations with the press are: Carolyn Smith, *Presidential Press Conferences: A Critical Approach* (Westport, Conn.: Praeger, 1990), and M. L. Stein, *When Presidents Meet the Press* (New York: Julian Messner, 1969). Jeffrey Tulis, *The Rhetorical Presidency* (Princeton: Princeton University Press, 1987), makes a persuasive case that Wilson, more than any other early twentieth-century president, invented the dominant presidency with which we are all familiar, in which the chief executive articulates public desires, translates those wishes into policies, and presents Congress with a specific legislative agenda to implement his program. The negative side of this formidable power is, of course, that the president is blamed if things go wrong.

For all these topics, valuable additional material may be found in the sources discussed in the bibliographical essay following the Introduction.

Document 5.1   Relations with the Cabinet

Wilson gave his cabinet members great autonomy to run the routine business of their departments, but he determined basic policy directions and sometimes took personal control of important issues. Writing to Sen. James A. O'Gorman on May 5, 1913, Wilson proffered his interpretation of the relationship between the president and his cabinet.

You spoke the other day of the Secretary of the Treasury as a "subordinate." I do not look upon any member of the Cabinet as a subordinate. The offices they occupy are of the first dignity and consequence. Moreover, an "Administration" must be a unit in spirit and in action or it will fail and come to naught. If I were inclined to ignore the members of my Cabinet in these matters, or in any others that affected the administration and efficiency of their several departments, there could be no Administration at all. Men of pride and of reputation would not serve in the Cabinet. I have had long experience in cooperative administrative action where the partners were men of spirit and of parts, and I know that I must support my colleagues as loyally as they support me and must defer to them in every matter in which I do not disagree with them in principle or upon grounds of large public policy. It would be folly for me not to attach the greatest possible weight to the judgment and preference in respect of their subordinates, especially their chief subordinates, even if I were inclined to do so—except when I think them radically mistaken in their men. I must be guided by them so far as possible, if I am to have an efficient and successful administration. But they are men of sense and discretion and good feeling and are as ready to defer to my wish and judgment as I could wish them to be.

Source: Arthur S. Link and others, eds., *The Papers of Woodrow Wilson, 1913* (Princeton: Princeton University Press, 1978), 27:400.

Document 5.2   Cabinet Meetings

In this account by Robert Lansing of the March 20, 1917, cabinet meeting that preceded the declaration of war against Germany, Lansing illustrates how Wilson conducted cabinet meetings.

He [Wilson] said that the two questions as to which he wished to be advised were—

Should he summon Congress to meet at an earlier date than April 16th, for which he had already issued a call?

Second. What should he lay before Congress when it did assemble?

He then spoke in general terms of the political situations in the belligerent countries, particularly in Russia where the revolution against the autocracy had been successful, and in Germany where the liberal element in the Prussian Diet was grumbling loudly against their rulers. He also spoke of the situation in this country, of the indignation and bitterness in the East and the apparent apathy of the Middle West.

After the President had finished [Secretary of the Treasury William Gibbs] McAdoo was the first to speak. He said that war seemed to him a certainty and he could see no reason for delay in saying so and acting accordingly; that we might just as well face the issue and come out squarely in opposition to Germany, whose Government represented every evil in history; that, if we did not do so at once, the American people would compel action and we would be in the position of being pushed forward instead of leading, which would be humiliating and unwise. He further said that he believed that we could best aid the Allies against Germany by standing back of their credit, by underwriting their loans, and that they were sorely in need of such aid. He felt, however, that we could do little else, and doubted whether we could furnish men.

McAdoo spoke with great positiveness in advocating an immediate call of Congress. His voice was low and his utterance deliberate, but he gave the impression of great earnestness.

[Secretary of Agriculture David F.] Houston, who followed, said that he agreed with McAdoo that it would create a most unfortunate, if not disastrous, impression on the American public as well as in Europe if we waited any longer to take a firm stand now that Germany had shown her hand. He said that he doubted whether we should plan to do more than to use our navy and to give financial aid to the Allies; that to equip an army of any size would divert the production of our industrial plants and so cut off from the Allies much needed supplies; and he thought that we ought to be very careful about interfering with their efficiency. He concluded by urging the President to summon Congress at once because he felt that a state of war already existed and should be declared.

[Secretary of Commerce William] Redfield followed Houston with his usual certainty of manner and vigor of expression. He was for declaring war and doing everything possible to aid in bringing the Kaiser to his knees. He made no points which particularly impressed me; and, as he had so often shown his strong pro-Ally sentiments, I was sure his words made little impression upon the President.

[Secretary of War Newton] Baker was the next to express an opinion and he did so with the wonderful clearness of diction of which he is master. He said that he considered the state of affairs called for drastic action with as little delay as possible, and that he believed Congress should meet before April 16th. He said that the recent German outrages showed that the Germans did not intend to modify in the least degree their policy of inhumanity and lawlessness, and that such acts could mean only one thing, and that was war.

Since we were now forced into the struggle he favored entering it with all our vigor. He advocated preparing an army at once to be sent to Europe in case the Allies became straightened in the number of their men. He said that he believed the very knowledge of our preparations would force the Central Powers to realize that their cause was hopeless. He went on to discuss the details of raising, equipping and training a large force.

I followed Baker and can very naturally remember what I said better and more fully than I can the remarks of others.

I began with the statement that in my opinion an actual state of war existed today between this country and Germany, but that, as the acknowledgment of such a state officially amounted to a declaration of war, I doubted the wisdom as well as the constitutional power of the President to announce such fact or to act upon it; that I thought that the facts should be laid down before Congress and that they should be asked to declare the existence of a state of war and to enact the laws necessary to meet the exigencies of the case. I pointed out that many things could be done under our present statutes which seriously menaced our national safety and that the Executive was powerless to prevent their being done. I referred in some detail to the exodus of Germans from this country to Mexico and Cuba since we severed diplomatic relations, to the activities of German agents here, to the transference of funds by Germans to Latin American countries, to the uncensored use of the telegraph and the mails, &c.

For the foregoing reasons I said that I felt that there should be no delay in calling Congress together and securing these necessary powers.

In addition to these reasons which so vitally affected our domestic situation I said that the revolution in Russia, which appeared to be successful, had removed the one objection to affirming that the European War was a war between Democracy and Absolutism; that the only hope of a permanent peace between all nations depended upon the establishment of democratic institutions throughout the world; that no League of Peace would be of value if a powerful autocracy was a member, and that no League of Peace would be necessary if all nations were democratic; and that in going to war at this time we could do more to advance the cause of Democracy than if we failed to show sympathy with the democratic powers in their struggle against the autocratic government of Germany.

I said that the present time seemed to me especially propitious for action by us because it would have a great moral influence in Russia, because it would encourage the democratic movement in Germany, because it would put new spirit in the Allies already flushed with recent military successes, and because it would put an end to the charges of vacillation and hesitation, which were becoming general and bring the people solidly behind the President.

"The time for delay and inaction," I said, "has passed. Only a definite, vigorous and uncompromising policy will satisfy or ought to satisfy the American people. Of this I am convinced. We are at war now. Why not say so without faltering? Silence will be interpreted abroad as weakness, at home as indecision. I believe that the people long for a strong and sure leadership. They are ready to go through to the very end. If we enter this war, and there is not the slightest doubt but that we will enter if not today then tomorrow, the Government will lose ground which can never regain by acting as if it was uncertain of its duty or afraid to perform that duty, a duty which seems to me very plain."

I said a good deal more in the same vein and urged the propriety of taking advantage of the aroused sentiment of the people since it would have a tremendous influence in keeping Congress in line. I said that I would not permit my judgment to be swayed by this sentiment but that as a matter of expediency in affecting congressional action it ought to be used. I must have spoken with vehemence because the President asked me to lower my voice so that no one in the corridor could hear.

The President said that he did not see how he could speak of a war for Democracy or of Russia's revolution in addressing Congress. I replied that I did not perceive any objection but in any event I was sure that he could do so indirectly by attacking the character of the autocratic government of Germany as manifested by its deeds of inhumanity, by its broken promises, and by its plots and conspiracies against this country.

To this the President only answered, "Possibly."

Whether the President was impressed with the idea of a general indictment of the German Government I do not know. I felt strongly that to go to war solely because American ships had been sunk and Americans killed would cause debate, and that the sounder basis was the duty of this and every other democratic nation to suppress an autocratic government like the German because of its atrocious character and because it was a menace to the national safety of this country and of all other countries with liberal systems of government. Such an arraignment would appeal to every liberty-loving man the world over. This I said during the discussion, but just when I do not remember.

When I had finished, Secretary [of Labor William] Wilson in his usual slow but emphatic way said: "Mr. President, I think we must recognize the fact that Germany has made war upon this country and, therefore, I am for calling Congress together as soon as possible. I have reached this conviction with very great reluctance, but having reached it I feel that we should enter the war with the determination to employ all our resources to put an end to Prussian rule over Germany which menaces human liberty and peace all over the world. I do not believe we should employ half-measures or do it half-heartedly."

In view of the fact that Wilson had on previous occasions shown a disposition to temporize with the German Government and had opposed war because of submarine attacks, I was surprised at his frank assertion in favor of radical measures. There is this to be said of Secretary Wilson, he never speaks at haphazard; he is slow to express an opinion but very firm in it when it is once declared. When I have disagreed with him I have always had to acknowledge the soundness of his reasoning unless the subject was Labor, as to that he is biased. I consider him a valuable adviser because he is equipped with an abundance of commonsense.

[Attorney General Thomas] Gregory, who had been listening with much attention although on account of his deafness I am sure only heard his neighbors at the table, gave it as his opinion that it was useless to delay longer, and that he was in favor of assembling Congress as soon as possible, of enacting all necessary legislation, and of pursuing as aggressive action toward Germany as we were able. He went on to speak of German intrigues here, of the departure of German reservists and of the helplessness of his Department under existing laws. He said that every day's delay increased the danger and Congress ought to be called on to act at once.

After Gregory had given his views the President said, "We have not yet heard from Burleson and Daniels."

[Postmaster General Albert] Burleson spoke up immediately and said: "Mr. President, I am in favor of calling Congress together and declaring war; and when we do that I want it to be understood that we are in the war to the end, that we will do everything we can to aid the Allies and weaken Germany with money, munitions[,] ships and men, so that those Prussians will realize that, when they made war on this country, they woke up a giant which will surely defeat them. I would authorize the issue of five billions in bonds and go the limit." He stopped a moment and then added, "There are many personal reasons why I regret this step, but there is no other way. It must be carried through to the bitter end."

The president then turned his head toward [Secretary of the Navy Josephus] Daniels who sat opposite Burleson and said: "Well, Daniels?" Daniels hesitated a moment as if weighing his words and then spoke in a voice which was low and trembled with emotion. His eyes were suffused with tears. He said that he saw no other course than to enter the war, that do what we would it seemed bound to come, and that, therefore, he was in favor of summoning Congress as soon as possible and getting their support for active measures against Germany.

Burleson had at previous meetings resisted an aggressive policy toward Germany, and he had, as late as the Cabinet meeting on Friday, the 16th, advocated very earnestly taking a radical stand against Great Britain on account of detention of the mails.

Whenever I had called attention to the illegal acts of Germany he would speak of British wrong-doings. I felt sure that he did this to cause a diversion of attention from the German violations of law. Possibly I misjudged him, and there was no such motive. His words at this meeting indicated hostility to Germany and a desire for drastic action, so I may have been mistaken.

As for Daniels his pacifist tendencies and personal devotion to Mr. Bryan and his ideas were well known. It was, therefore, a surprise to us all when he announced himself to be in favor of war. I could not but wonder whether he spoke from conviction or because he lacked strength of mind to stand out against the united opi[ni]on of his colleagues. I prefer to believe the former reason, though I am not sure.

The President said, as Daniels ceased speaking: "Everybody has spoken but you, Lane."

[Secretary of the Interior Franklin K.] Lane answered that he had nothing to add to what had been said by the other members of the Cabinet, with whom he entirely agreed as to the necessity of summoning Congress, declaring war and obtaining powers. He reviewed some of the things which had been said but contributed no new thought. He emphasized particularly the intensity of public indignation against the Germans and said that he felt that the people would force us to act even if we were unwilling to do so.

Knowing the President's mental attitude as to the idea of being forced to do *anything* by popular opinion, these remarks by Lane seemed to me unwise and dangerous to the policy which he advocated. I could almost feel the President stiffen as if to resist and see his powerful jaw set as Lane spoke. Fortunately before the President had time to comment Lane kept on in his cool and placid way drifting into another phase of the subject which was more to the President's taste since it appealed to his conception that he must be guided by the principle of right and by his duty to this country and to all mankind. Thus what might have been a dangerous incident was avoided.

The foregoing is a brief outline of the debate which occupied over two hours and which frequently was diverted into other channels such as the effectiveness of armed guards on merchant ships, the use of patrol boats, German plots in Latin America, the danger of riots and vandalism in this country, the moving of interned vessels, the need of censors, &c., &c.

When at last every Cabinet officer had spoken and all had expressed the opinion that war was inevitable and that Congress ought to be called in extraordinary session as soon as possible, the President in his cool, unemotional way said: "Well, gentlemen, I think that there is no doubt as to what your advice is. I thank you."

The President, during the discussion or at the close, gave no sign what course he would adopt. However as we were leaving the room he called back Burleson and me and asked our views as to the time of calling a session if he so decided. After some discussion we agreed that to prepare the necessary legislation for submission to Congress would take over a week and that, therefore, Monday, April 2nd, would be the earliest day Congress could conveniently be summoned. I asked the President if he would issue a proclamation that afternoon so it would appear in the morning papers on Wednesday. He replied smilingly: "Oh, I think I will sleep on it."

Thus ended a Cabinet meeting the influence of which may change the course of history and determine the destinies of the United States and possibly of the world. The possible results are almost inconceivably great. I am sure that every member of the Cabinet felt the vital importance of the occasion and spoke with a full realization of the grave responsibility which rested upon him as he advised the President to adopt a course which if followed can only mean open and vigorous war against the Kaiser and his Government. The solemnity of the occasion as one after another spoke was increasingly impressive and showed in every man's face as he rose from the council table and prepared to leave the room. Lane, Houston and Redfield, however, did not hide their gratification, and I believe we all felt a deep sense of relief that not a dissenting voice had been raised to break the unanimity of opinion that there should be no further parley or delay. The ten councillors of the President had spoken as one, and he—well, no one could be sure that he would echo the same opinion and act accordingly.

Source: Arthur S. Link and others, eds., *The Papers of Woodrow Wilson, January 24–April 6, 1917* (Princeton: Princeton University Press, 1983), 41:438–444.

Document 5.3   Lindley Garrison's Resignation, January 14, 1916

Secretary of War Lindley Garrison learned in February 1916, as had William Jennings Bryan six months previously, that a difference of principle with Wilson necessitated resignation. Garrison's staunch advocacy of raising a national reserve force came into conflict with Wilson's negotiations with Congress. Wilson was not wedded to any particular plan, but Garrison's inflexibility stood in the way of what the president perceived as the broader goal: the beginning of mobilization. Wilson's insistence on cooperating with Congress rather than forcing a plan on it, which would then be rejected, led to the parting of the ways, with Garrison tendering his resignation on February 10. The following letter to Wilson, drafted some three weeks earlier, explains Garrison's decision.

What you said to-day by way of response to my letter of the 12th requires me to make my position perfectly clear to you.

You stated that Mr. Hay [Wilson's contact in Congress] told you that your proposal of Federal volunteers could not be procured, and that the same end for which you were striving could be procured by other means—by utilizing the State troops as the basis of the policy and making appropriations of pay to the States conditioned on Federal control of the State troops.

You stated to him that you were not interested in any particular program or means of accomplishing the purpose of securing the men, and would accept his proposal if it accomplished that purpose.

Since the policy that was recommended to you and adopted by you discarded as absolutely impossible a military system based upon State troops, and asserted that the only possible basis for a military policy was National forces, it is entirely clear that the proposals are diametrically opposed to each other and are irreconcilable.

Those who are conscientiously convinced that nothing but National forces can properly be the basis of a policy of national defense, cannot possibly accept a policy based upon State forces. It not only does not in itself offer an acceptable solution, but acts to prevent any proper solution.

If those who are thus convinced are faced with the necessity of declaring their position on the matter, they can only show their sincerity and good faith by declining to admit the possibility of compromise with respect to this essential, fundamental principle.

I am thus convinced.

I feel that we are challenged by the existing situation to declare ourselves promptly, openly and unequivocally, or be charged properly with lack of sincerity and good faith.

We cannot hope to see our program, based on this essential principle, succeed if we admit the possibility of compromise with respect to it.

Yours is the ultimate responsibility; yours is the final determination as to the manner in which the situation shall be faced and treated. I fully realize this and I do not desire to cause you the slightest embarrassment on my account; if, therefore, my withdrawal from the situation would relieve you, you should not hesitate for a moment on that account.

Source: Arthur S. Link and others, eds., *The Papers of Woodrow Wilson, October 1, 1915–January 27, 1916* (Princeton: Princeton University Press, 1980), 35:480–481.

Document 5.4   Franklin Lane on the Wilson Administration

Writing to his friend, John H. Wigmore, on March 9, 1913, Franklin Lane expressed his excitement over the possibilities and responsibilities offered by the newly inaugurated Wilson administration.

MY DEAR JOHN, —I want you as my First Assistant. It is absolutely essential that I should have you!! I am aiming to gather around me the largest men whom I can secure and to form a cabinet of equals. Four years of this life here would bring a great deal of satisfaction to you. You would meet the distinguished men of the world. It is the center of all the great law movements of the world,—for peace, international arbitration, reform in procedure, and such matters. Beside that, we have two or three of the greatest problems to meet and solve that have ever been presented to the American people. First in the public mind is the land problem. How can we develop our lands and yet save the interest of the Nation in them? Second, and I think perhaps this should be first, is the Indian problem. Here we have thousands of Indians, as large a population as composes some of the States, owning hundreds of millions of dollars' worth of property which is rapidly rising in value. I am their guardian. I must see that they are protected. They have schools over which we have absolute control— the question of teachers that they are to have, the question of the kind of education that they are to be given, the question of industry that they are to pursue. Their morals, I understand, are in a frightful state, largely owing to our negligence and the lack of enforcement of our laws. We can save a great people; and the First Assistant has this matter as his special care. I do not know of any place in the United States which calls for as much wisdom and for as great a soul as this particular job. I will give you men under you over whom you will have entire control and who will be to your liking. I will give you men to sit beside you at the table who will be of your own class. You can do more good in four years in this place than you can possibly do in forty where you are now. There are a lot of men who can teach law, and lots of men who can write the philosophy of the law, but there are few men who can put the spirit of righteousness into the business, social, and educational affairs of an entire race. Think of that work! Beside that you have the constructive work in framing and helping to frame a line of policy as to the disposition of our national lands—the opening of Alaska.

Now, John, I have looked over the entire United States and you are the only man that I want. The salary is five thousand a year. You can live on that here without embarrassment. The President will be delighted to have you, and you will find him treating you with the same consideration and giving you the same dignity that he does all the members of his Cabinet; all the Supreme Court. I have never seen a man more considerate, more reasonable. Dr. Houston, who has become Secretary of Agriculture, left Washington University in St. Louis, under an arrangement by which he can return at the end of his term. You, doubtless, could make a similar arrangement, and if you wish to, you will have plenty of opportunity to give one or two courses of lectures in the University during the year.

I have thought seriously of going out to see you, but with Cabinet conditions as they are it is impossible, for we are passing upon important questions now that prevent that. I am very selfish in urging you to this, but I am also giving you an opportunity to do work that will be more congenial than any you have ever done, and to be with a more congenial lot of people. If there is any doubt in your mind let me know, but don't say "No" to me. The country needs you. You have done a great work. There is nothing higher to be done in your line. Now come here and help in a great constructive policy.

Source: Anne Lane and Louise Wall, eds., *The Letters of Franklin K. Lane* (New York: Houghton Mifflin, 1922), 131–133.

Document 5.5   David Houston on Wilson

David Houston was one of Wilson's most loyal advisers, even after the president left the White House, and his memoir provides valuable insight into decisions Wilson made during his eight years in office. The following extract from a chapter Houston devoted to a "Personal Estimate of Woodrow Wilson," details Houston's impression of Wilson's reasons for entering World War I.

It was pure tragedy that a man like Wilson, who knew what war means, who had witnessed the horrors of its aftermath, who detested it as a method of settling difficulties and thought it stupid, should have been called upon to lead this nation into war. He spoke from his heart and experience when he said to Congress, in his War Message: "It is a fearful thing to lead this great nation into war"; and he held back more than two and a half years for many reasons. I thought at the time, and still think, that he was right in his thinking and his action at each stage of the developments. At no point did I think the time had come for us to strike till we did strike; and I anxiously watched every step with utter sympathy for the Allies. I did not always agree with every part of Wilson's reasoning, but I accepted and endorsed his conclusions and course of action. I was influenced neither by the desires nor by the criticisms of the Allies of our course; and I was not disturbed by the mutterings of the pro-Ally Americans. I said frequently during the course of the developments that the Allies would continue to criticize us as long as we did not do exactly what they desired us to do, just as they would furiously applaud us if we did act according to their notions, and especially if we entered the war. My sole concern was what was our duty as Americans. Going in or staying out of the war and the time of it were matters solely for us to determine as American citizens, in the light of America's interests. . . .

Wilson led the nation into war at the right moment—the moment when Germany abandoned all pretences, broke her promises, declared her intention to resume unrestricted submarine warfare, and undertook to dictate the course we should follow. Then Uncle Sam rolled up his sleeves and made it plain that he was "free, white, and twenty-one" and would see whether anybody could tell him what he could or could not do. From this moment, Wilson had back of him a united and determined people, and he knew it.

Wilson hated the thought of war. He knew what it meant, but he accepted the challenge with the same poise and calm courage that he had manifested in the more difficult former trial of maintaining peace.

Wilson's knowledge of the meaning of war and what the new task involved and his boldness were made manifest at the outset and were evident at each stage of the development, from first to last. There was no hesitating. He did not waver for an instant, and he had at no time any doubt as to the issue. With him, it was a foregone conclusion. There was in him the spirit of the Crusader and the Roundhead. He would have immediate and good execution of the enemy, for the good of their souls and for the glory of God.

Source: David F. Houston, *Eight Years with Wilson's Cabinet, 1913 to 1920* (Garden City, N.Y.: Doubleday, Page & Co., 1926), 2:230–231, 244–245.

Document 5.6   Wilson and Edward M. House

Colonel House often acted as an adjunct to President Wilson, handling interviews with industrialists and labor leaders, evaluating possible appointments, and generally keeping Wilson up to date on the opinions of businessmen and other public leaders. The following extracts from House's diaries, compiled by Charles Seymour, show a few such instances.

March 22, 1913: Mr. Frick came at eleven. He wished to know whether I thought it was possible to settle the United States Steel Corporation suit outside of the courts. He declared that he came of his own initiative and no one knew he was doing so. He wanted the matter kept confidential, excepting the President and Attorney-General. We discussed the matter at some length. I pointed out the difficulties, with which he concurred. He seemed fair. I promised to mention the matter and to see what could be done. . . .

March 24, 1913: I told him [Wilson] about Mr. Frick's call and his suggestion in regard to the United States Steel Corporation suit. Before the President replied, I said, "You had better let me tell Frick that you referred me to the Attorney-General and suggested that whatever proposal came to you should come through the Attorney-General's Office." The President smiled and said, "You may consider it has been said."

We discussed it at some length. The President thought that the Steel Corporation should have the same consideration as any other, neither more nor less, and that they should be allowed to make a proposition for an agreement as to a decree of court in the suit. . . .

April 18, 1913: I went to the White House early and met the President on his way to the memorial service held for the late President of the Honduras. I found a large number of people waiting, Mitchell Palmer being one of them. I asked if I could not attend to his matters for him, explaining how busy the President was and how uneasy we were for his health if the pressure continued. He said he wanted to know about Guthrie's chances for an ambassadorship. I was able to tell him that the President had him down for Japan. I asked, "What next?" He wished to know about Berry for Collector of the Port of Philadelphia. I was able to tell him that McAdoo and I had threshed that out the day before and we would both recommend his appointment.

After that he wanted to know about Graham, who wishes to go in the Attorney-General's Office. I told him that McReynolds and I had discussed that the day before and that he intended to appoint him. This satisfied Palmer and he went back to the Capitol.

Jerry Sullivan from Iowa was waiting to see the President, and I treated him as I did Palmer. He had just been appointed on the Appraisers' Court in New York. . . . He was uncertain as to whether he ought to leave Iowa and wished to know how much time he could have to decide. . . . I asked him not to bother the President, but to take it up with me and I would thresh it out with the Attorney-General and take it to the President in concentrated form. He had several other desires, which I advised him to put in writing and to send to me at his convenience.

I wish I could always be here to do these things for the President and give him time to devote himself to the larger problems which confront the country. . . .

August 2, 1913: John Mitchell, President of the Federation of Miners, and Timothy Healy, President of the International Brotherhood of Stationary Firemen, lunched with me to-day. I talked to them earnestly concerning the future of labor. I urged upon them the necessity of taking a broad view, and not letting the unimportant things of to-day interfere with the larger ones which are to come. . . .

November 19, 1913: I lunched with Charles Grasty of the Baltimore *Sun*. The other guest was Mr. Daniel Willard of the Baltimore and Ohio. I found Willard had a clear knowledge of railroad rates. Many of the facts given me by Secretary Lane, Commissioner Marble, and Frank Trumbull are misleading. Mr. Willard is very agreeable. He used the tablecloth instead of paper to make diagrams and to illustrate his points, and he ate no lunch to speak of, but talked all the time, though not tiresomely. . . .

Source: Charles Seymour, ed., *The Intimate Papers of Colonel House* (New York: Houghton Mifflin Co., 1926), 1:128-130.

Document 5.7   Civilian Control of the Military

Wilson's insistence on civilian control of the military is demonstrated in Secretary of the Navy Josephus Daniels's account of the cabinet meeting of May 16, 1913, in which the possibility of preparing for war with Japan was debated.

. . . In the Cabinet Meeting Friday, this matter came up and was threshed out after lengthy discussion. Secretary Garrison presented his view with ability of the action of the Joint Board. I presented, briefly, the reasons why I could not agree with the Joint Board and while [why] I believed at this time any such action which might inflame the passions of the people of Japan and lead to a war which we would all regret. Secretary Redfield was strongly supporting Secretary Garrison as did Secretary McAdoo. The Secretary of State and the Secretary of Labor took strong grounds against moving any ships in the Pacific and helped me hold up my end of the argument. Secretary Lane also indicated that it might be unwise to move the ships at this time. Attorney General McReynolds was inclined to agree with the Secretary of War. The Secretary of Agriculture took my side. I do not recall that the Postmaster General had any statement to make but I gathered that he was with me. On Mr. Bryan's earnest advocacy of peace, he could not approve any movement now that might make war. Most of the time of the discussion was taken up with the arguments of those who wished to withdraw the ships. When all was said and done the President said, "The Joint Board, of course, has presented the military aspect of the situation as it sees it and it may be right, but we are considering this matter with another light, on the diplomatic side, and must determine the policy. I do not think any movement should be made at this time in the Pacific Ocean and I will, therefore, take the responsibility of holding the ships where they are at present." He spoke at more length and made me very happy to find that he was in accord and agreement with the views I had made in supporting me in his clear and logical power.

In the afternoon the President and his wife held a garden party in the White House grounds, and I was made very happy by his taking me aside and saying, "I think we did right today. At one time I think we had a majority of the Cabinet against us, but when I looked down the table and saw you upholding what you thought was the right course, it cheered my heart, We must not have war except in an honorable way and I fear the Joint Board made a mistake."

Source: David Cronon, ed., *The Cabinet Diaries of Josephus Daniels, 1913–1921* (Lincoln: University of Nebraska Press, 1963), 66.

Document 5.8 Wilson and the Military during World War I
As he demonstrated in his dealings with his cabinet, Wilson was content to set guidelines for policy and delegate authority to trusted administrators. His handling of the war effort was no different, as this March 27, 1918, letter to Gordon Auchincloss, son-in-law and private secretary to Col. House, regarding British questions about war plans, indicates.

. . . I have been expecting a cable from [Secretary of War] Baker, but none has come. I think the reason plain. All the decisions asked for can be much better and more wisely made on the other side of the water than on this and Baker, [General] Bliss and [General] Pershing have full authority to make them,—acting, of course, as they should act, under the authority of the Executive Committee or Board of the Supreme War Council. I wish them to make these decisions and will accept any plan they determine. The possible execption [exception] is the suggestion about sending only infantry from this country instead of full-quota divisions; but even with regard to that I shall act upon the advice of Baker and Bliss in consultation with the Executive Board of the Supreme War Council.

Source: Arthur S. Link and others, eds., *The Papers of Woodrow Wilson, March 13–May 12, 1918* (Princeton: Princeton University Press, 1984), 47:158.

Document 5.9 Presidential Leadership in Congress
In this campaign speech at West Chester, Pennsylvania, on October 28, 1912, Wilson explained what type of leadership he would offer, and how partisanship would relate to it. Here Wilson argues that parties are irrelevant except inasmuch as they allow candidates to offer a program to be endorsed or rejected by voters. Voting the Democratic ticket in 1912, Wilson seemed to say, amounted to a vote in favor of activism rather than the paralysis advocated by the Republicans.

I do not feel that this is an ordinary political campaign, and it does not make any difference to me now whether a man is a Democrat, or has been a Republican, or is something now for which he has not found a label. Because I find a good many men confused to find out what they are by description. They are, as a friend of mine said, between sizes in politics, and nothing seems to fit them. That is because we have come into a new age in which we must do new things, and think new things, and get together in order to agree upon a common policy, no matter what party we have belonged to. I would rather, therefore, have an audience like this, made up, as I believe, of men ready to vote according to their convictions, than speak to a body of mere partisans who already know how they are going to vote, or rather do not know anything except that they are going to vote as they were told to vote. I do not want anybody to vote for me because somebody else told him to vote for me. I want him to vote for me because he believes this. And every man in his senses in America believes this because he believes that we have come to a time of imperative change, that to wait for that change for four years would be folly, because the change, when it came at the end of four years, might not be thoughtful and deliberate,—that we have got to have change now.

It is better to have it now under an organized force, moderately and intelligently guided, than to have it four years from now under forces which we cannot foresee or calculate. Where but in the Democratic party will you find a force big enough, organized enough, united enough, to do this work for you now—while we are still calm, while we are still deliberate, while we are still under the leadership of men who have been thoughtful about affairs, and who have taken the pains to understand the business of the country? Where else will you find a force? Everywhere I go, I find men admitting that the next House of Representatives is going to be Democratic. Nobody doubts that. Very few people doubt that the next Senate is going to be Democratic. Well, then, is it not wise that you should have a Democrat as President also? Because only a Democrat can drive that team. Where else, I ask you in candor, are you going to find a President who can manage the forces that are going to assemble in Washington in the next Congress? The present President has not even tried to manage them. A very honest man, he has felt that his honesty was safest when safeguarded by absolute inactivity. He has thought that a House that was Democratic and a Senate that was not entirely standpat Republican ought not to be trusted to do anything, and that, therefore, the only safe thing was to save the

United States and veto everything. Do you want a policy of inaction like that for another four years, with all the forces gathering that you have seen in your own communities, that any man with vision sees all over the United States? The people of this country are infinitely impatient that they have been unable to get what their consciences and their principles demand. And if you make them wait another four years, or if you give them a four years in which they will be guessing every month which way they are going, why, at the end of those four years, you will have something that you cannot control, and that no man can now calculate or foresee.

Source: Arthur S. Link and others, eds., *The Papers of Woodrow Wilson, 1912* (Princeton: Princeton University Press, 1978), 25:465–466.

Document 5.10   Working with Congress

The following two excerpts from letters written by Rep. Carter Glass, chairman of the House Banking and Currency Committee, depict the interplay between Wilson and members of Congress in constructing legislation, even before Wilson's inauguration. On December 26, 1912, Wilson met with Glass and Henry Parker Willis to discuss legislation leading to currency reorganization. Willis had argued for a highly decentralized reserve system, but Wilson thought that too uncoordinated. What he wanted was a hybrid system delegating broad discretionary powers to a central organ, under strict federal oversight. In the first excerpt, Glass expresses his fear that bankers would dominate a too-decentralized system like that proposed by the Aldrich bill. In the second, from Glass to Willis, Glass discusses how to translate Wilson's ideas into legislation that will satisfy both Wilson and Congress.

GLASS TO WILSON, DECEMBER 29, 1912

I have been thinking much about the subject of our interview at Princeton on Thursday and am trying in my mind to reduce the suggestions there made to something tangible in order that the hearings before my subcommittee, beginning January 7th, may be directed to a definite, even though tentative, plan of currency reform. . . . I have some very distinct notions about the lines we should pursue and especially about the situation that will confront us at Washington. On this latter point there is some illumination in a letter I have just received from one of the great New

York bankers invited to the hearings of my sub-committee. There is this paragraph:

> "The American Bankers Association, as a body, at its meeting in New Orleans a year ago, endorsed the Aldrich bill. It would seem, therefore, impossible for us as members of the Currency Commission of the American Bankers Association, to take any other position or do anything else before your committee than to endorse that bill, if we were to appear before you officially."

I felt certain before receiving this letter that we would encounter this difficulty. The bankers intend to fight for the Aldrich plan as it is drafted in order to get the same thing in a different form. They do not intend that the $350,000 expended by the Monetary Commission and the additional $300,000 expended by the Citizens League in "educational work" shall be wasted. I much apprehend that "educational work" with some of these gentlemen means ability to organize influences and to bring pressure to bear to drive schemes through Congress merely because they want them and not entirely because they should have them. Might it not be well to draft a bill on the Regional Reserve Bank lines, taking care of all the details discussed last Thursday, and put on the advocates of the Aldrich bill the burden of showing that a central superstructure should be imposed, requiring them to suggest a superstructure that shall not possess the evils of bank monopoly and the dangers of centralized power? We may ourselves have in readiness such a "capstone" as I understood you to suggest, having the wholesome powers of a central supervisory control.

If I might have a further brief talk with you some day at your convenience before we begin hearings, I think matters would be decidedly facilitated. I know how busy you are and I dislike to take up any part of your time; but I likewise know what a powerful factor you must be in the solution of this problem if we are to have any currency legislation at all.

GLASS TO HENRY PARKER WILLIS, DECEMBER 29, 1912
. . . It is clear to me that Mr. Wilson has been written to and talked to by those who are seeking to mask the Aldrich plan and give us dangerous centralization; but we shall have to keep quiet on this point for the present. . . . We should make the alterations that you and I have talked over and should so alter certain sections of the bill as to meet the tentative views expressed

by President-elect—that is if you understand what they are. You will recall that he would take away from the individual banks the right of issue; but was disposed to compromise on my suggestion to lodge the right of issue with the divisional reserve bank instead of centralizing it at Washington. As I recall he also took kindly to the suggestion that there should be no inducement for the country banks to keep money on deposit in New York beyond their actual needs for exchange purposes and that, therefore, it would be well not to permit payment of interest by banks on bank deposits. Then there is the matter of divisional reserve bank organization. I mean the method of appointing directors and the character of men who are to direct. We shall have to hit upon some distinction between "bankers" and "business men," perhaps defining the former as men whose "chief business" is that of banking.

I did not get the impression that Mr. Wilson at this time is opposed to the guarantee of deposits. I have no doubt, however, that great pressure will be brought to bear to put him against that feature of the bill; but I am disposed to insist. Very likely you will recall my remark that, speaking for myself, I would cheerfully go with the President-elect for some body of central *supervisory* control, if such a body can be constituted and divested of the practical attributes of a central bank. In my judgment this is the point of danger. This is where the bombardment will be directed. If we can devise a superstructure or, to use Mr. Wilson's phrase, a "capstone," for the plan we have as it shall be revised, it would be well to be prepared for that emergency.

I would like the best in the world to get another hour or two with Mr. Wilson. . . . I have some very definite ideas, not only on the currency itself, but on the practical situation at Washington and on this line I would like a further discussion with President-elect. I shall write to him immediately and suggest this.

Source: Arthur S. Link and others, eds., *The Papers of Woodrow Wilson, 1912* (Princeton: Princeton University Press, 1978), 25:641–644.

Document 5.11   Wilson on Capitol Hill

As was characteristic of his collegial style of leadership, in early April 1913, Wilson went to Capitol Hill to meet with legislators regarding tariff reform. Below is an article published in the New York World *on April 10, describing the meeting.*

PRESIDENT VISITS CAPITOL AGAIN TO MEET SENATORS

Meets the Democratic Members of the Senate Finance Committee and Talks Over the Tariff Bill with Them for an Hour and a Half with the Object of Insuring Harmony and Keeping Party Promises.

WASHINGTON, April 9.—In a dignified and characteristically Wilsonian way, the President to-day jolted custom and woke up sleeping precedent by visiting the Capitol for a conference with the lawmakers on pending legislation. For an hour and a half he had a friendly consultation with the Democratic members of the Senate Finance Committee in the President's Room, which is located in the Senate wing. In so doing he revived a procedure that has lain dormant since the days of Grant, and at the same time he carried out his announced intention of frequently occupying the room and holding pleasant conferences with the Senators. That it was a profitable conference was proved when it was all over and the President confidently said: "We don't see any difficulty in standing together on any sort of party programme."

The Tariff bill was the sole topic of discussion. The President sought to reach an amicable arrangement by which necessary amendments could be added to the measure with the least possible friction, both in the House and after it reaches the Senate.

In order to provide the maximum degree of harmony and prevent possible wrangling during debate on the Tariff bill, the President urged that every Senator be requested to advise him personally just what amendments he desires to have incorporated in the measure. He would give them careful consideration and either explain that they did not meet his approval or he would request their insertion in the bill. He desires that no amendments be proposed in the Senate by Democrats except those offered by the Finance Committee.

At the request of the President, the ten members of the Finance Committee present at the meeting promised to say nothing regarding the conference, but refer all anxious inquirers to the President.

When approached for information on the questions pending during the ninety minutes passed in the President's room, and before any interrogations could be propounded, Mr. Wilson said:

"I suppose you fellows think this is another national crisis." Being assured to the contrary, the President continued:

"This conference was to discuss the tariff. I am glad I had it and I hope the Senators will let me come and consult them frequently. The net result of this meeting is that we don't see any sort of difficulty about standing firmly on our party programme."

"Will there be one bill or several? Will the sugar schedule be considered separately?" the President was asked.

"That is for the other house to decide," replied the President.

"Will the House be guided by the wishes of the Senate?" was the final inquiry.

"I haven't asked them," answered the President, as he moved away.

The sole purpose of the President's visit was to secure the greatest degree of harmony in the matter of amendments and to lessen those proposed by the Senate to the smallest possible number. The President frankly said that some amendments were absolutely essential. If these were not made in the House he desired the Finance Committee to take the subject up and remedy the apparent defects in the bill as printed. . . . He sought team work between the Senate and House in enacting the new tariff measure.

The Senators present replied that it was utterly impossible to give any pledge of the character indicated. They said the constitutional right of amending all House bills rested with the Senate and could neither be waived nor abrogated.

No resentment was manifested by the President at this plain statement of the situation. He received the announcement seriously and said all these matters could be adjusted at conferences which would follow in the future.

Source: Arthur S. Link and others, eds., *The Papers of Woodrow Wilson, 1913* (Princeton: Princeton University Press, 1978), 27:278–280.

Document 5.12   The Overman Act, May 20, 1918

In the Overman Act of 1918, the Wilson administration gained a great victory for its ability to control the war effort. The act, which gave the president wide discretionary powers to reorganize the executive branch, prevented the creation of a civilian board that would have taken control over mobilization away from Wilson.

Chap. 78.—An Act Authorizing the President to coordinate or consolidate executive bureaus, agencies, and offices, and for other purposes, in the interest of economy and the more efficient concentration of the Government.

Be it enacted by the Senate and House of Representatives of the United States of America in Congress assembled, That for the national security and defense, for the successful prosecution of the war, for the support and maintenance of the Army and Navy, for the better utilization of resources and industries, and for the more effective exercise and more efficient administration by the President of his powers as Commander in Chief of the land and naval forces the President is hereby authorized to make such redistribution of functions among executive agencies as he may deem necessary, including any functions, duties, and powers hitherto by law conferred upon any executive department, commission, bureau, agency, office, or officer, in such manner as in his judgment shall seem best fitted to carry out the purposes of this Act, and to this end is authorized to make such regulations and to issue such orders as he may deem necessary, which regulations and order shall be in writing and shall be filed with the head of the department affected and constitute a public record: *Provided,* That this Act shall remain in force during the continuance of the present war and for six months after the termination of the war by the proclamation of the treaty of peace, or at such earlier time as the President may designate: *Provided further,* That the termination of this Act shall not affect any act done or any right or obligation accruing or accrued pursuant to this Act and during the time that this Act is in force: *Provided further,* That the authority by this Act granted shall be exercised only in matters relating to the conduct of the present war.

SEC. 2. That in carrying out the purposes of this Act the President is authorized to utilize, coordinate, or consolidate any executive or administrative commissions, bureaus, agencies, offices, or officers now existing by law, to transfer any duties or powers from one existing department, commission, bureau, agency, office, or officer to another, to transfer the personnel thereof or any part of it either by detail or assignment, together with the whole or any part of the records and public property belonging thereto.

SEC. 3. That the President is further authorized to establish an executive agency which may exercise such jurisdiction and control over the production of aeroplanes, aeroplane engines, and aircraft equipment as in his judgment may be advantageous; and, further, to transfer to such agency, for its use, all or any moneys heretofore appropriated for the production of aeroplanes, aeroplane engines, and aircraft equipment.

SEC. 4. That for the purpose of carrying out the provisions of this Act, any moneys heretofore and hereafter appropriated for the use of any executive department, commission, bureau, agency, office, or officer shall be expended only for the purposes for which it was appropriated under the direction of such other agency as may be directed by the President hereunder to perform and execute said function.

SEC. 5. That should the President, in redistributing the functions among the executive agencies as provided in this Act, conclude that any bureau should be abolished and it or their duties and functions conferred upon some other department or bureau or eliminated entirely, he shall report his conclusions to Congress with such recommendations as he may deem proper.

SEC. 6. That all laws or parts of laws conflicting with the provisions of this Act are to the extent of such conflict suspended while this Act is in force.

Upon the termination of this Act all executive or administrative agencies, departments, commissions, bureaus, offices, or officers shall exercise the same functions, duties, and powers as heretofore or as hereafter by law may be provided, any authorization of the President under this Act to the contrary notwithstanding.

Approved, May 20, 1918.

Source: U.S. Statutes at Large 40 (1918), 556–557.

Document 5.13   Justice James McReynolds's Opinion in *Federal Trade Commission v. Gratz* **(1920)**

In the case of Federal Trade Commission v. Gratz, *Justice James McReynolds challenged the commission's power to determine what was or was not fair competition. Since the FTC was one of the great accomplishments of Wilson's tenure, the decision has been interpreted as a kind of repudiation of Wilsonianism.*

It is unnecessary now to discuss conflicting views concerning validity and meaning of the act creating the commission and effect of the evidence presented. The judgment below must be affirmed, since, in our opinion, the first count of the complaint is wholly insufficient to charge respondents with practicing "unfair methods of competition in commerce" within the fair intendment of those words. We go no further and confine this opinion to the point specified. . . .

The words "unfair method of competition" are not defined by the statute and their exact meaning is in dispute. It is for the courts, not the commission, ultimately to determine as matter of law what they include. They are clearly inapplicable to practices never heretofore regarded as opposed to good morals because characterized by deception, bad faith, fraud, or oppression, or as against public policy because of their dangerous tendency unduly to hinder competition or create monopoly. The act was certainly not intended to fetter free and fair competition as commonly understood and practiced by honorable opponents in trade.

Count 1 alleges, in effect: That Warren, Jones & Gratz are engaged in selling, either directly to the trade or through their correspondents, cotton ties produced by the Carnegie Steel Company and also jute bagging manufactured by the American Manufacturing Company. That P. P Williams & Co., of Vicksburg, and C. O. Elmer, of New Orleans, are the selling and distributing agents of Warren, Jones & Gratz, and as such sell and distribute their ties and bagging to jobbers and dealers, who resell them to retailers, ginners, and farmers. That with the purpose and effect of discouraging and stifling competition in the sale of such bagging all the respondents for more than a year have refused to sell any of such ties unless the purchaser would buy from them a corresponding amount of bagging—six yards with as many ties.

The complaint contains no intimation that Warren, Jones & Gratz did not properly obtain their ties and bagging as merchants usually do; the amount controlled by them is not stated; nor is it alleged that they held a monopoly of either ties or bagging or had ability, purpose or intent to acquire one. So far as appears, acting independently, they undertook to sell their lawfully acquired property in the ordinary course, without deception, misrepresentation, or oppression, and at fair prices, to purchasers willing to take it upon terms openly announced.

Nothing is alleged which would justify the conclusion that the public suffered injury or that competitors had reasonable ground for complaint. All question of monopoly or combination being out of the way, a private merchant, acting with entire good faith, may properly refuse to sell, except in conjunction, such closely associated articles as ties and bagging. If real competition is to continue, the right of the individual to exercise reasonable discretion in respect of his own business methods must be preserved. . . .

The first count of the complaint fails to show any unfair method of competition practiced by respondents and the order based thereon was improvident.

Source: The Supreme Court Reporter 40: November 1919–July 1920. (St. Paul, Minn.: West Publishing Company, 1921), 574–575.

Document 5.14   Justice Louis Brandeis's Dissent in *Hitchman Coal & Coke Company v. Mitchell* (1917)

Justice Louis Brandeis voiced his support for labor unions in Hitchman Coal & Coke Company v. Mitchell. *In the case, the Court's majority affirmed an injunction against the United Mine Workers' coercive attempt "to induce plaintiff's employees to join the union and at the same time to break their agreement with plaintiff by remaining in its employ after joining; and this for the purpose not of enlarging the membership of the union, but of coercing plaintiff, through a strike or the threat of one, into recognition of the union." Brandeis's dissent is given below.*

It is urged that a union agreement curtails the liberty of the operator. Every agreement curtails the liberty of those who enter into it. The test of legality is not whether an agreement curtails liberty, but whether the parties have agreed upon something which the law prohibits or declares otherwise to be inconsistent with the public welfare. The operator by the union agreement binds himself: (1) To employ only members of the union; (2) to negotiate with union officers instead of with employees individually the scale of wages and the hours of work; (3) to treat with the duly constituted representatives of the union to settle disputes concerning the discharge of men and other controversies arising out of the employment. These are the chief features of a "unionizing" by which the employer's liberty is curtailed. Each of them is legal. To obtain any of them or all of them men may lawfully strive and even strike. And, if the union may legally strike to obtain each of the things for which the agreement provides; why may it not strike or use equivalent economic pressure to secure an agreement to provide them?

It is also urged that defendants are seeking to "coerce" plaintiff to "unionize" its mine. But coercion, in a legal sense, is not exerted when a union merely endeavors to induce employees to join a union with the intention thereafter to order a strike unless the employer consents to unionize his shop. . . . The employer is free either to accept the agreement or the disadvantage. Indeed, the plaintiff's whole case is rested upon agreements secured under similar pressure of economic necessity or disadvantage. If it is coercion to threaten to strike unless plaintiff consents to a closed union shop, it is coercion also to threaten not to give one employment unless the applicant will consent to a closed non-union shop. The employer may sign the union agreement for fear that labor may not be otherwise obtainable; the workman may sign the individual agreement, for fear that employment may not be otherwise obtainable. But such fear does not imply coercion in a legal sense.

In other words an employer, in order to effectuate the closing of his shop to union labor, may exact an agreement to that effect from his employees. The agreement itself being a lawful one, the employer may withhold from the men an economic need—employment—until they assent to make it. Likewise an agreement closing a shop to non-union labor being lawful, the union may withhold from an employer an economic need—labor—until he assents to make it. . . .

As persuasion, considered merely as a means, is clearly legal, defendants were within their rights if, and only if, their interference with the relation of plaintiff to its employees was for justifiable cause. The purpose of interfering was confessedly in order to strengthen the union, in the belief that thereby the condition of workmen engaged in mining would be improved; the bargaining power of the individual workingman was to be strengthened by collective bargaining; and collective bargaining was to be insured by obtaining the union agreement. It should not, at this day, be doubted that to induce workingmen to leave or not to enter an employment in order to advance such a purpose, is justifiable when the workmen are not bound by contract to remain in such employment.

Source: The Supreme Court Reporter 38: November 1917–July 1918. (St. Paul, Minn.: West Publishing Company, 1918), 78, 79–80.

Document 5.15 Justice John Hessin Clarke's Opinion in *Abrams v. United States* (1919)

Justice John Hessin Clarke was known as a liberal, but in Abrams v. United States, *his best known majority opinion, he upheld the wartime Espionage and Sedition Acts rather than individual civil rights. The case concerned radicals who had distributed literature calling for the overthrow of the United States government to workers in the defense industry.*

This is not an attempt to bring about a change of administration by candid discussion, for no matter what may have incited the outbreak on the part of the defendant anarchists, the manifest purpose of such a publication was to create an attempt to defeat the war plans of the government of the United States, by bringing upon the country the paralysis of a general strike, thereby arresting the production of all munitions and other things essential to the conduct of the war. . . .

That the interpretation we have put upon these articles, circulated in the greatest port of our land, from which great numbers of soldiers were at the time taking ship daily, and in which great quantities of war supplies of every kind were at the time being manufactured for transportation overseas, is not only the fair interpretation of them, but that it is the meaning which their authors consciously intended should be conveyed by them to others is further shown by the additional writings found in the meeting place of the defendant group and on the person of one of them. One of these circulars is headed: "Revolutionists! Unite for Action!"

. . . It concludes with this definite threat of armed rebellion:

"If they will use arms against the Russian people to enforce their standard of order, *so will we use arms,* and they shall never see the ruin of the Russian Revolution."

These excerpts sufficiently show, that while the immediate occasion for this particular outbreak of lawlessness, on the part of the defendant alien anarchists, may have been resentment caused by our government sending troops into Russia as a strategic operation against the Germans on the eastern battle front, yet the plain purpose of their propaganda was to excite, at the supreme crisis of the war, disaffection, sedition, riots, and, as they hoped, revolution, in this country for the purpose of embarrassing and if possible defeating the military plans of the government in Europe. A technical distinction may perhaps be taken between disloyal and abusive language applied to the *form* of our government or language intended to bring the *form* of our government into contempt and disrepute, and language of like character and intended to produce like results directed against the President and Congress, the agencies through which that form of government must function in time of war. But it is not necessary to a decision of this case to consider whether such distinction is vital or merely formal, for the language of these circulars was obviously intended to provoke and to encourage resistance to the United States in the war. . . .

Source: The Supreme Court Reporter 40: November 1919–July 1920. (St. Paul, Minn.: West Publishing Company, 1921), 19–20.

On the occasion of Warren G. Harding's inauguration on March 4, 1921, Wilson rides to the Capitol with Harding; Joseph G. Cannon, R-Ill., former Speaker of the House; and Sen. Philander C. Knox, R-Pa.

CHAPTER SIX

After the White House
Wilson in Retirement

W oodrow Wilson left the White House a broken man. Essentially an invalid during his final year in office as a result of his 1919 stroke, his life after the White House revolved around the struggle against physical and mental impairment. Symbolic of Wilson's condition was his quiet acceptance, in December 1920, of the Nobel Peace Prize for 1919. "[E]verybody must admit," enthused Albert George Schmedeman, the American minister to Norway and Wilson's proxy at the acceptance ceremony, that the peace prize "is but your due for your efforts" (Link and others 1992, 66:478). But for the remainder of Wilson's life that cause ran a disappointing parallel to his physical infirmity; his inability to attend the ceremony or respond to the award with one of his famous, rousing speeches was proof that he was incapable of leading his supporters (see Document 6.1). For the next three years, until his death in February 1924, those who had seen in his League of Nations the possibility of a better world would look to Wilson to champion their cause—and he would prove unable to rise to the challenge.

AN INAUGURATION JOURNEY

On March 4, 1921, Wilson left the White House for the last time to ride to the Capitol with Warren G. Harding, to the president-elect's inauguration and toward their own separate entrances into history. They rode in silence most of the way, until Harding, discussing pets, joked that he would like to own an elephant. Wilson shot back, with the wit only rarely manifested after his collapse, "I hope it won't turn out to be a white elephant!" (quoted in Smith 1964, 184). Nonplussed but glad to fill the conversational vacuum, Harding gregariously related to Wilson his missionary sister's story of an elephant in its death throes, crying out for its master. When they were eventually united, the elephant encircled him with its trunk, able to die in peace with its friend there. The ever-jovial Harding was horrified when he turned to see Wilson's reaction and discovered the outgoing president in tears. They were approaching the Capitol and the crowds assembled for the inauguration, and Harding wondered whether he should wipe Wilson's face clean for the crowds, but Wilson recovered and produced a handkerchief in time. For all its pathos, the incident revealed that the ex-president still had some fight left in him. Despite his disability and the disappointing recent rejection of the League of Nations by the Senate, Wilson's wry wit, passion, and almost prophetic vision would persist well after leaving the White House. Indeed, though few probably imagined it that March day, the shrunken and defeated figure accompanying Harding would not only outlive his successor, but his principles and spirit would continue to influence the course of American politics for the rest of the century.

At the Capitol Wilson took an infrequently used freight elevator to the President's Room, where he approved a last few bills, met with his cabinet one final time, and dismissed Congress. Asked to observe the swearing-in of the new vice president, Calvin Coolidge, Wilson eyed the three perilous steps to the Senate chamber and growled, "The Senate has thrown me down, but I don't want to fall down" (quoted in Smith 1964, 185). Harding explained to the president that he did not have to join him in the stands outside, and Wilson reluctantly agreed, proffering to his successor "all the luck in the world" (quoted in Smith 1964, 186). Then Wilson divested himself of his presidential seal and, accompanied for the last time by his faithful Secret Service agent Edmund Starling, rode with his wife, Edith; his physician, Cary Grayson; his former secretary, Joseph Tumulty; and his valet, Arthur Brooks, to what was then the outskirts of Washington. There, on S Street, the Wilsons officially moved into the Georgian-styled house, number 2340, they had purchased a few months before for $150,000, two-thirds of which was provided by ten close friends. One of those, financier Bernard Baruch, bought the neighboring lot and let it grow wild to give the Wilsons added privacy. Opulently designed, the house was fitted with built-in shelves to house the ex-president's massive library and an elevator to allow him access to the three of four stories he would inhabit. Eschewing the inaugural ceremony at the Capitol, a crowd of around 2,000 waited for Wilson to arrive. After he was installed at S Street, they cheered him. Overwhelmed by emotion, or perhaps simply too weak to talk, the former president indicated his throat and waved to the crowd from the second floor of the house before disappearing from public view.

In the thirty-five months Edith and Woodrow lived at S Street together, they adhered rigidly to a tedious routine. After breakfast in bed or in the solarium adjoining the gardens at the rear of the house, Wilson would hobble downstairs to answer mail with his secretary, John Randolph Bolling (Edith's brother). After lunch, again taken in the ex-president's bedroom, perhaps with a guest but usually with Edith feeding him by hand, he would nap and, later, perhaps receive a visitor if none had been present for lunch. Grayson limited Wilson's interviews to one a day, and then only for a half an hour. In late afternoon, Wilson went for his usual drive, then Edith and he would retire to the library for a light dinner. Evening entertainment consisted of Edith reading aloud from a book—perhaps one of the mysteries he liked—or viewing a movie, before preparing for bed. They usually played cards together, with Wilson doing most of the winning, until he drifted off to sleep. It was a mundane schedule for two who had once consorted with kings and statesmen, but one that Wilson's health demanded.

Because Americans had never been informed adequately of the extent of Wilson's illness, after his retirement he was inundated with correspondence demanding opinions on a variety of subjects or requesting a personal appearance. Although the fees proffered were often quite high, Wilson neither cared to comment nor possessed the ability to do so. One publisher inquiring about a possible memoir from the ex-president received the curt reply, "There ain't going to be none" (quoted in Smith 1964, 195). Wilson remained open to mail from friends, the amount of which vastly increased now that he was free of the White House. Finally a private citizen again himself, Wilson relished expressing his often unflattering private opinions of public personalities to his friends. Letters from ex-soldiers and children also gave him great pleasure. But beyond correspondence, that wider world Wilson had striven to reform remained largely unreachable. When the Washington Order of the Merry Men, a naturalist group and one of the many organizations seeking his membership after his presidency, inducted him as an honorary member, Wilson replied from his sickbed, "I wish that I could wander about the woods with you" (quoted in Smith 1964, 198).

Wilson's removal from the outside world briefly ended in November 1921. On November 11 the body of the Unknown Soldier was to be buried at Arlington National Cemetery, and Wilson was included in the funeral procession leading there. The half-paralyzed ex-president could not walk, so arrangements were made to transport him in the parade in a horse carriage. Dressed all in black, wearing a poppy in his buttonhole, Wilson joined the cortege at Pennsylvania Avenue behind the coffin of the Unknown. The parade was planned to run for seventeen blocks. Setting off for Arlington, the crowds were silent and impassive. Then, as they caught sight of Wilson, people lined up along the streets began to murmur among themselves. Gradually applause and cheers overtook the funereal atmosphere. At the White House, where Wilson would exit the parade, leaving officials to go on to Arlington, the crowds closed in on the carriage. Polite applause and whispered approval grew into outright cheers. Then Wilson the invalid acknowledged the applause with a stiff wave of his top hat.

When the carriage headed out of the city, toward S Street, a crowd followed, accumulating more followers until it reached a few thousand strong. At 2340, the crowd shouted for its erstwhile leader, crying, "Three cheers for the League of Nations!" "Three cheers for the greatest soldier of them all!" and "Three cheers for Woodrow Wilson!" (Link and others 1992, 67:450). The clamor persuaded Wilson to limp out onto the front stoop, where, with the assistance of his new valet, Isaac Scott, he clambered down to shake the hands of three crippled veterans. Hamilton Holt, an acquaintance and fervent advocate of the League, addressed Wilson: "We wish to congratulate you—a wounded soldier of the war—on your regaining your health. We also wish to pledge to you our honor and our respect. Your work shall not die" (Link and others 1992, 67:451). The crowd quieted when it appeared Wilson would speak. Falteringly, eyes streaming with tears, he croaked, "I wish that I had the voice to reply and to thank you for the wonderful tribute that you have paid me. I can only say God bless you" (Link and others 1992, 67:451). Then he doffed his silk hat, blew them kisses, and returned to the isolation of the house. Outside, the crowd sang a rendition of "My Country, 'Tis of Thee" and remained the better part of the day before drifting away. That Armistice Day was a turning point for Wilson, a first step in his reconciliation with the public whom he thought had rejected him and perhaps to a return to his former self.

The Wilson/Colby Law Firm

A somewhat less successful reentry into public life was the short-lived law partnership between Wilson and former secretary of state Bainbridge Colby. Opened in the summer of 1921, the law offices in Washington and New York commanded a great deal of high profile, international business. But Wilson refused to employ his former public status for private purposes, despite the fact that that was *why* the firm was receiving the custom in the first place, so work with the United States government and with the League of Nations was turned down.

Colby was alarmed at the caliber of business slipping through their hands, but his devotion to Wilson prevented him voicing his disapproval. Unlike Tumulty, who probably would have brought Wilson gently around to the reality of the situation, Colby hid his concern, ending up several thousand dollars in debt from expenses to which he refused to allow his senior partner to contribute. By November 1922, Colby had had enough and asked Wilson if there was a way they could refashion their partnership to accommodate the ex-president's stringent limitations on the types of cases they could accept. Wilson went a step further. Sensing Colby's frustration, he had suggested dissolution of the firm in the summer; now he suggested it again. Writing to his partner on November 29, Wilson asked that it be made clear to the public "that this dissolution of our partnership had come about through no dissatisfaction on the part of either of us by the actions or influence of the other" (Link and others 1993, 68:213). The Wilson and Colby firm offered the former president a sense of participation in the outside world and the camaraderie of partnership. Wilson wanted to retain those qualities, even if the partnership had to be dissolved.

Moved by Wilson's words and decision to step down in favor of his junior partner, Colby wired on December 1, "You are the dearest man in the world[.] I want to come down [and] just take you by the hand[.] I like to feel that there is no hurry about the next move[.] I feel all broken up" (Link and others 1993, 68:214). Almost two weeks later, Colby released a statement to the press dissolving the firm on December 31. Stressing the continued good relations between the two partners, it went on to attribute the breakup to Wilson's improved health, which beckoned him toward more pressing and profound issues than mere litigation. Such optimism about Wilson's health and the possibility of his renewed involvement in national issues belied the situation.

POLITICS PUBLIC AND PRIVATE

Friends of Wilson who would not cooperate in the charade of optimism were quickly ejected from his inner circle. Edith was constantly aware of her husband's fragility but remained convinced that he should not have to confront that fact. The result was an S Street version of Wilson's last year at 1600 Pennsylvania Avenue, in which Edith ruthlessly protected her husband from disruptions, often at the expense of longstanding friendships and occasionally of his own good.

Such was the case when, in April 1922, Edith seems to have precipitated a break between Joseph Tumulty and her husband. Edith had never liked Tumulty; indeed, she had tried to oust him from her husband's side as early as 1916. But Tumulty, ever loyal to his "Governor," as he had called Wilson since their days in Trenton, had ensured his usefulness to the Wilsons in 1919 by assisting the first lady in maintaining the sham of the president's recovery after his collapse, and he remained attached when the Wilsons moved to S Street.

The Democratic Party's annual Jefferson Day dinner was to be held on April 8, 1922, and Tumulty asked his former chief to send the Democrats assembled there a salutation. Wilson responded that the event was not "a specially appropriate one for breaking my silence" (quoted in Smith 1964, 205). Refusing to give up, Tumulty asked Edith to help him convince her husband to change his mind, but she stood by his decision. Tumulty then requested an interview with Wilson, joining his old boss at S Street as his allotted afternoon guest. As Tumulty later reported it, the interview consisted of a "casual conversation with me at Mr. Wilson's home on Friday last when he remarked he would support any candidate who stood for justice for all" (quoted in Smith 1964, 206).

Tumulty passed this message on to the Democrats, who read it aloud at the banquet in New York along with other messages from Democrats not present. It was mere coincidence that the message immediately preceded the keynote address delivered by James M. Cox, the party's 1920 candidate, but reporters nonetheless misconstrued Wilson's message as an endorsement of Cox for 1924. It was not, and though Tumulty and the Democrats dismissed the incident as a misunderstanding, Wilson bristled at this supposed breach of confidence, telling Tumulty that he had no intention of supporting Cox, "whose renomination would in my judgment be an act of deliberate suicide. I shall do everything that I honourably can to prevent it" (Link and others 1993, 68:10). Although apparently not at fault, Tumulty still wrote S Street twice to apologize but was ignored, and soon after the banquet the message—and by extension its messenger—were denounced in a public letter signed by Woodrow Wilson.

The episode severely wounded Tumulty, particularly since he believed it was Edith and not his "Governor" who had rejected him. Tumulty explained to reporters that the mistake was his own if Wilson had not authorized the banquet message, but to Edith he quoted dialogue from the play, *Liliom:* "It is possible, dear, that some one whom you love may beat you and beat you and beat you—and not hurt you at all." Then he assured her that "I shall always be around the corner when you or yours need me. I expect no reply to this letter. I shall understand" (quoted in Smith 1964, 207).

For his part, Wilson seemed proud of the denunciation of his old friend, telling Cary Grayson, "If Tumulty had been my son and had acted as he did, I would have done the same thing" (Link and others 1993, 68:60). Nevertheless, it was a blow Wilson could little afford. Tumulty had always provided a kind of practical dimension to Wilson's world. That talent might have been of great use as Wilson surfaced from his illness and tried to make himself in some way relevant again to American politics. Instead, the loss of Tumulty's advice cut Wilson away from one of his few anchors to reality, allowing Edith and Woodrow to sail off together into a neverland of adoring crowds, lost ideals, and mutual devotion. As at Paris in 1919, ignoring Tumulty drove the ex-president farther into his own isolation.

The estrangement from Tumulty and refusal to support James Cox did not jeopardize Wilson's standing as the conscience of the nation and the spiritual leader of reformers in the Democratic Party. Friends and admirers had already set up the Woodrow Wilson Foundation in his honor in 1921, to promote with grants "democracy, public welfare, liberal thought and peace through justice" (quoted in Smith 1964, 216). A year later, in late April 1922, advocates of a similar cause sought him out. A thousand delegates, from the Women's Pan-American Conference on reform and world peace, joined the former president at S Street. Many found his appearance shocking, a fact Wilson himself recognized and made light of, joking as he had during the 1912 campaign, "I'm not much to look at." Though he declined because of weakness to make an address, he did recite a favorite, if perhaps bittersweet, limerick:

> For beauty I am not a star;
> There are others more handsome by far.
>   But my face, I don't mind it,
>   For I am behind it;
> It's the people in front that I jar.

In the mail the following day he received a reply:

> Your courage is nobler by far
> Than mere beauty e'en though like a star.
>   And your face? Why, we find it
>   Just right! You're behind it.
> So we people in front cry "Hurrah!" (quoted in Smith 1964, 216)

Later that year, on Armistice Day 1922, a large crowd gathered outside the front door of the S Street house, and Wilson again emerged to greet them. Seeming much stronger, he condemned those senators who preferred, for "personal partisan motives," an incomplete armistice to a proactive peace: "and we are so bent on a cessation of fighting that we are even throwing our arms away." This was not the way, Wilson believed; America had to throw its full weight, moral and military, behind peace before full resolution of the war could be had. "America has always stood for justice and always will stand for it. Puny persons who are now standing in the way will presently find that their weakness is no match for the strength of a moving Providence." Begging his audience's pardon for putting on his hat, joking that "I will promise not to talk through it," Wilson said, "I think, then, we may renew today our faith in the future though we are celebrating the past. The future is in our hands, and if we are not equal to it the shame will be ours and none other[']s" (Link and others 1993, 68:186–187).

THE DOCUMENT

Writing to John Hessin Clarke, by then retired from the Supreme Court to which Wilson had appointed him, Wilson remarked that the previous "Tuesday's elections [in which the Republicans were partially repudiated] make it easier to turn the thoughts of the country in the right direction and to make ready for the great duty of 1924" (Link and others 1993, 68:189). Cheated of his third bid for the presidency in 1920 because of ill-health, Wilson flirted with the notion of a nomination for the coming election. But building the correct platform—one that would sweep away the Republicans in 1924—was a measured process. Wilson had been thinking about that platform as early as June 1921 and approached Louis D. Brandeis, Bainbridge Colby, and Thomas L. Chadbourne Jr. that month hoping to compile a set of progressive principles to guide the party, with the ulterior motive of using it as his own platform in a 1924 election bid.

Over the next eighteen months, the collaborators consulted others for statements on taxation, agriculture, and railroad management, but what became known as "The Document" remained in large measure a very vague but very personal polemic against the Republican Party. Wilson's request to his old friend, David Houston, was illustrative: "Will you not be generous enough to send me something which will be a concise characterization of the taxation of the Republicans, and of the better way we should wish to follow?" (Link and others 1992, 67:477). This was not the Wilson of old, partisan but insistent upon finding the most efficient solution to any problem. "The Document" was the expression of a once complex and mobile mind stripped down to its crude constituent parts. The clever and multifaceted Wilson of 1913 would have depended upon party politics as a surgical instrument to gain greater goals; now partisanship was all that remained, a blunt instrument wielded by a blunted intellect.

Houston duly sent his old boss a statement on taxation, but thought it sounded "bromidic." This was a good description of "The Document" in general. Its generic calls for reform and increased internationalism; attacks on the Senate as "partisan, prejudiced, ignorant and unpatriotic" because of its rejection of the Treaty of Versailles; and implied (and sometimes not so implied) criticisms of the Republicans harked back to the Republicans' 1920 platform of bromidic "normalcy." When he wrote to Brandeis that the "vital importance of such a document in the near future seems to me more and more evident as the days, empty of all political achievement, go by," Wilson revealed just how much a product of bitterness "The Document" actually was (Link and others 1992, 67:507).

There were, however, some reminders of the old Wilson in "The Document." One plank, for instance, called for collaboration between the executive and Congress when legislation affected areas administered by the former. Another advocated creation of a transport secretary and transportation board, which together would centralize, render more efficient, and oversee financial matters for the national transportation network. The platform called for better treatment of farmers and laborers, and congratulated President Harding for advocating entrance of the United States into the World Court (although Wilson viewed Harding's action as only a first step that had to be augmented by complete entry into the League of Nations). All in all, "The Document" could hardly claim to represent the "definite principles and purposes" to which Wilson referred when he fantasized about how he would accept the Democratic nomination in 1924 (Link and others 1993, 68:541) (see Document 6.2). Nor had the notion of a Wilsonian platform been palatable to Democratic leaders when he presented the idea to them in May 1922. So Wilson worked on his project in isolation, and it joined the illusions of improved health and a triumphal return to politics in his ever-deepening fantasy world (see Document 6.3).

THE ROAD AWAY FROM REVOLUTION

Other intellectual endeavors came just as painfully to him. Garbled notes typed out in May 1922 for a history of the United States petered out after a brief and facile outline (see Document 6.4). A year later, in spring 1923, Wilson began to dictate to Edith, line by line, the short article that would be his last published work: "The Road away from Revolution." The essay, which friends had prompted him to write, argued simply that reform and social justice were essential characteristics of democratic government, and that—if placed in conflict with each other—capitalism mattered less to civilization than human sympathy. Sent to George Creel, who had been chairman of the Committee on Public Information during

Wilson's administration, to assess its viability for publication, "The Road away from Revolution" was disappointing. Creel wrote confidentially to Edith that "the article is far from being what it should be in view of the significance that will be attached to it as Mr. Wilson's first public writing since his illness and also as the signal of his return to active public life." The writing was not poor, but "what the article lacks is *body*." Neither Creel, nor an editor friend from *Collier's* whom he had asked for advice on the matter, believed that the article was publishable. At the same time, however, both men believed that a rejection would crush the former president. Creel had secured from *Collier's* a pledge to buy the article for $2,000 and "handle it handsomely and with dignity," but newspapers refused to syndicate it. Creel urged Edith to destroy the letter explaining all this, enclosing another, glowing with its promise of a *Collier's* printing and its denunciation of newspaper "huckstering" (Link and others 1993, 68:342–343).

Edith was torn. Naturally she wanted to protect her husband's reputation as a writer, but she also feared exposing him to upsetting criticism. One day in mid-April, she, Wilson, and Stockton Axson, Wilson's friend and brother-in-law through his first wife, were talking in the limousine on Wilson's daily ride. There Mrs. Wilson broached the subject that she had been "greatly dreading." She related what Creel had said, "that the article simply wouldn't do. It didn't do justice to him—it didn't reason out what he had to say, and the old touch wasn't there at all; and just for his own sake they did not want to publish it." Frustrated, Wilson lashed out at those who had pushed him to break his silence: "They kept after me to do this thing, and I did it." Attempting to calm him, Edith said the article needed "expansion, reasoning out the case more." Wilson replied, "I have done all I can, and all I am going to do. I don't want those people bothering me any more." For Edith, the article provided the breaking point, and after they returned to S Street Axson found her sitting alone, weeping. "All I want to do is just to help in any way I can. I am not urging him to do things he doesn't want to do. I just want to help and I just don't know how to help. I don't know what to do" (Link and others 1993, 68:349n1).

Axson offered to edit the article, telling her that fleshing it out was the wrong way to go about it, and that "it needs to be shorter. This is not an argument, it is a challenge, and that is all it is." Axson recommended chopping two paragraphs from the end to tighten up the argument, and Wilson agreed wholeheartedly: "Why you see exactly the point. Fix it"

(Link and others 1993, 68:349n1). Edith then wrote Creel a brittlely cheery note on April 24, 1923, explaining that her husband welcomed his suggestions but that Creel had the wrong idea. "The Road away from Revolution" was not an article requiring greater exposition, nor was it ever intended to be; it was "simply a short essay in the form of a '*challenge*'—to quote from his last paragraph which is the keynote of it all." Moreover, not only did Wilson not think it needed to be longer, he thought it should be "even *shorter.*" "So much for that!" Edith then instructed Creel to approach *The Atlantic Monthly,* where all Wilson's earlier essays had been published, and this "challenge" saw print there in August 1923 (Link and others 1993, 68:347–348).

Despite its troubled birth, "The Road away from Revolution" was an eloquent work that offered a brief and final glimpse of the Woodrow Wilson who had risen to national and world attention. In the article Wilson charged that revolutions like that in Russia were caused by the harsh greed of capitalism and that an uncritical commitment to such an economy was myopic. Revolutions, he argued, resulted when governments failed to be responsible to the needs of their constituents. The Russian Revolution was, therefore, less an attack on capitalism than a violent rebellion against a negligent government. Wilson's alternative to these extremes, a middle road between capitalism or revolution, was for individuals "to forego self-interest in order to promote the welfare, happiness, and contentment of others and of the community as a whole." But that path had to be found within, in a spiritual commitment to justice and fair play rather than in a solution imposed from above. The road away from revolution was thus an individual and internal journey of understanding that would free society of the discontent that would feed a revolution. Wilson's last imploring words—"Shall we not all earnestly cooperate to bring in the new day?"—provided a fitting conclusion to Wilson's intellectual career. A thoughtful counterpoint to the vagueness of "The Document," "The Road away from Revolution" remains the best short summation of Wilsonianism ever written (Link and others 1993, 68:395) (see Document 6.5).

WILSON'S LAST DAYS

The article was the apex of Wilson's post-White House existence. For many, like old friend William Jennings Bryan, it testified to Wilson's improving health, but by August 1923 Wilson was declining drastically. Edith, too, struggled to maintain the brave face she had been keeping for nearly four years. The shadow of mortality fell over both of them that month when, on August 2, 1923, young and dynamic Warren Harding suddenly died. Wilson had not been a friend of Harding, but they had been cordial. And Wilson himself probably did not expect to outlive his successor. Edith and Woodrow joined the funeral procession in their Pierce-Arrow limousine and returned briefly to the White House on August 8 for the service. Even there in the company of old servants, and in the comfort of old memories, unhappy intrusions could still occur. Waiting for the funeral to begin, a cavalry officer rushed up and asked, "Mr. Wilson, do you know where I can find Senator Lodge [Wilson's foe in the battle over the League]?" Wilson replied, "I am not Senator Lodge's keeper." The incident was a cruel reminder of the past, but it was also a kind of wake-up call: even if Wilson somehow achieved a messianic 1924 return to power, Lodge or others would still be there to thwart him. When the officer had dashed away, Wilson asked, "What asylum did that Colonel escape from?" (quoted in Smith 1964, 225).

The funeral provided another wake-up call for Wilson. Seeing his wife gradually breaking down, he convinced Edith to get away from S Street for a while. She went to Massachusetts in late August and stayed with some friends there, walking on beaches and taunting reporters asking after her husband. When she returned, rejuvenated, she finally saw how bad her husband's condition was. Nevertheless, intensely devoted to his wife, Wilson arranged with a friend to take Edith to play cards once a week, just to get her away from the house. In a noticeable departure from the dutiful companionship Edith had offered her husband since the beginning of his illness, in October she elected to take a weekend trip alone, to stay with friends in New York.

In November 1923, just three months before his death, Wilson reluctantly consented to deliver a radio address for the fifth anniversary of Armistice Day. Speaking to the country on November 10 through a transmitter brought to S Street, via a radio network crossing the entire continent, Wilson called Armistice Day "our day, a day above those early days of that never-to-be-forgotten November which lifted the world to the high levels of vision and achievement upon which the great war for democracy and right was fought and won" (Link and others 1993, 68:466). But the memories of that day, he warned, would be blemished forever by the United States' failure to join with its fellow nations in a league of peace. Only by "resolving to put self-interest away and once more formulate and act upon the highest ideals and purposes of international policy" could the country redeem itself and the lives of soldiers lost in the Great War (Link and others 1993, 68:467) (see Document 6.6).

The speech was like an epitaph in more ways than one. It represented closure for Wilson, a last national statement on the League of Nations and the essential forces that drove Wilson to support it. But to listeners around the country, the ex-president's faltering speech, and his need for prompting by Edith, marked him as a dying man. "That is all, isn't it?" he asked Edith meekly at the end of the speech, and the transmitter at S Street asked the question of an entire nation of listeners (quoted in Smith 1964, 229). The following day 20,000 admirers came to see their former president at his home. Supported by former secretary of the Treasury Carter Glass and the loyal servant, Isaac Scott, Wilson came out of the house to greet them, just as he had in 1921 and 1922. When the crowd had calmed down, Glass read a statement he had prepared:

> To you, sir, it must be a source of infinite satisfaction to observe on each recurring anniversary of Armistice Day that the American people of all persuasions are coming more and more to realize what a shocking mistake it was to have permitted a conspiracy of racial animosities and selfish politics to cheat the nation of honorably participating in that permanent guarantee of peace for which our boys died and the country sacrificed. (Link and others 1993, 68:470)

Overcome by emotion, Wilson thanked the crowd and Glass for their words, but shifted the congratulations to the soldiers of World War I. "Thank you with all my heart for your kindness," he added, then muttered, "That's about all I can do." As he was escorted into the house again, he stopped, turned back to the crowd, which had just started singing "How Firm a Foundation."

> Just one word more. I cannot refrain from saying it: I am not one of those that have the least anxiety about the triumph of the principles I have stood for. I have seen fools resist Providence before and I have seen the destruction, as will come upon these again—utter destruction and contempt. That we shall prevail is as sure as that God reigns. Thank you. (Link and others 1993, 68:469)

After Armistice Day, Wilson's health declined dramatically. At Christmas some friends purchased for him a black Rolls-Royce pinstriped with Princeton orange, the design of which offered better access for him with his disability, but he had little time to make use of it. A charming limerick written for him by Richard Linthicum, a fellow Democrat, nevertheless captured the brittle pretense that he was growing better by the day:

> On S Street resides a great sage
> Whose name brightens history's page.
>   Is he old? Fiddlesticks!
>   One year past sixty-six —
> A very young age for a sage. (quoted in Smith 1964, 233)

On January 16, 1924, Wilson met with the Democratic National Committee (DNC), inviting two hundred men and women into the S Street library to shake the hand of each one. The DNC had that day resolved to congratulate the ex-president for his administration's high ideals and to wish him good health. Four days later Wilson met with Raymond Fosdick, an old friend and a vocal supporter of American entry into the League of Nations. Fosdick asked after his health, and Wilson replied, as John Quincy Adams had once replied to the same question near the end of his own life: "John Quincy Adams is all right, but the house he lives in is dilapidated, and it looks as if he would soon have to move out" (quoted in Smith 1964, 234). As he departed, Fosdick pledged that his generation would advance the cause of the League in the United States, and left Wilson alone and in tears.

At the end of January 1924, Wilson's health declined further. Lethargy seemed to overtake him and, after finding him "very sick," Edith decided it was time to recall Grayson, who was on a shooting trip in South Carolina. Although from the symptoms Grayson dismissed Wilson's case as "another indigestive attack," he agreed to return to Washington (Link and others 1993, 68:549). Wilson spent the day in bed on January 30 and 31 and, although Grayson still did not believe his patient was seriously ill, another doctor was called in for a second opinion. The second doctor, Sterling Ruffin, who had consulted with Grayson back in 1919, believed that Wilson was very ill indeed and told Grayson to stay the night at S Street. On February 1 Edith told her brother she thought her husband was dying, and she wanted to notify his three daughters.

Duly, telegrams were sent to Margaret in New York; Jessie, who was with her husband in Thailand; and Nell, who lived in California with McAdoo.

Somehow word of Wilson's condition got out and a three-day vigil ensued—with crowds forming one last time not only around the Wilsons' home but also all around the country. Grayson came out to the front step regularly to give updates to those assembled, but for two days it was the same: the former president was gradually declining. Reporters gathered at the door to 2340 S Street, hoping to be the first to tell their respective papers of the former president's demise. Telegrams began to filter in from around the country expressing support and love for Woodrow Wilson. Callers filed in and out of the house, expressing their concern and best wishes; taken together they were a roll call of the many lives and places Wilson had touched in his life. Even Joseph Tumulty came to pay his respects, but though Grayson invited him in, Tumulty never made it to his "Governor's" bedside.

On the evening of Saturday, February 2, Grayson explained to the crowd outside the Wilsons' house: "There has been no radical change in Mr. Wilson's condition during the day, but rather a gradual wearing-away process" (quoted in Smith 1964, 241). Scott, however, was instructed to ask the crowds to disperse. A little later, Edith had left her husband's bedside for a moment when a cry came from him: "Edith!" It was his last word. Woodrow Wilson died the following morning, February 3, 1924, at 11:15 a.m.

As Edith made ready for the funeral services, an outpouring of grief swept the country. More telegrams came to S Street, this time expressing words of sorrow rather than hope. On Monday President Calvin Coolidge instructed government offices to lower flags to half-mast for thirty days, and, after it appointed several of its members to attend the funeral, the Senate suspended operations for three days. One appointed attendee was Sen. Henry Cabot Lodge. When she discovered this, Edith wrote him coldly that, "As the funeral is private and not official and realizing that your presence would be embarrassing to you and unwelcome to me I write to request that you do *not* attend" (Link and others 1993, 68:574). Lodge replied meekly that he would not want to embarrass the one-time First Lady.

Edith and the family had considered burying Wilson in Staunton, Virginia, where he was born, or Columbia, South Carolina, where his father and mother lay, but neither of these places seemed proper. Wilson himself had not wanted to be buried at Arlington. So eventually it was decided to inter him in the newly built Washington National Cathedral. The funeral took place on February 6, a dark and wet day punctuated by the thunder of guns firing around the country—around the clock, all day long. It began at three o'clock with a simple service at S Street, and at that moment the whole country paused in memory. Then Wilson's body was taken by hearse to the cathedral where, after a second, brief, public service, the body was interred in its temporary resting place. It was later moved to a more permanent crypt when the cathedral was completed. Burial there was especially appropriate for the only president up to that time who had made Washington his home after leaving the White House. A newspaper best summed up the connection between man and city on the day the former president died:

> Mr. Wilson was always popular in Washington, but after retiring, broken in health, he seemed to touch their hearts more than ever. Everywhere Mr. Wilson went he was cheered by the Washington people, and this seemed to give him courage to keep up the fight for the League of Nations. (Link and others 1993, 68:569)

LEGACY

Except in time of war, nineteenth-century presidents were relatively minor figures in Washington, their main function being to carry out the orders of Congress, which held the real power. In his first book, *Congressional Government,* published in 1885, Wilson deplored this situation, arguing that it made the government irresponsible and prey to special interests. By the time he became president in 1912, however, Theodore Roosevelt had focused new attention on the White House and familiarized the country with vigorous presidential leadership. During his own administrations Wilson adopted Roosevelt's methods of taking issues to the country and added a new dimension of direct leadership of Congress as well, which has become a model for his successors. Together, Roosevelt and Wilson transformed the presidency into the center of the federal government.

Like Roosevelt, Wilson also expanded the influence of the federal government over citizens' daily lives. This was particularly true during World War I, when a number of special wartime agencies mobilized the military and economic power of the nation, becoming models for future administrations to deal with national emergencies, such as the Great Depression and World War II. But even before the United States entered the war in April 1917, Wilson enlarged the power of the federal government. He created the Federal Reserve System to manage the monetary and banking systems and the Federal Trade Commission to control national corporations, mandated the first eight-hour day for workers on the railroads and the first workman's compensation system for federal workers, established a nationwide system of county agricultural agents and banks for farmers, and signed the first federal law banning child labor.

While Wilson responded to a national demand for federal control over an increasingly nationalized economy, he also tried to limit federal power to the minimum needed to accomplish necessary reforms. His desire for a government that would be responsible to public wishes but also as limited as possible was particularly evident in regard to wartime agencies, which were mandated to expire at the end of the war. But it was also evident in the county agent system and a 1916 federal highways act in which Washington shared authority with local governments. Although Wilson grew less rather than more conservative as he became older, he retained throughout his career a conservative skepticism about federal action as a panacea for problems and a strong belief in the importance of individual initiative and opportunity.

In foreign policy Wilson's greatest legacy was his proposal for the creation of a League of Nations that would bring the United States into a system of collective security designed to eliminate the causes of war by providing a mechanism for gradual, controlled change and the rectification of injustices through investigation and reasoned discussion. The world honored him for his achievement with the 1919 Nobel Peace Prize, but the U.S. Senate rejected American membership in the League. Nevertheless, millions of Americans remained convinced that Wilson had been right, and in 1945, long after his death, the United States seized a "second chance" by not only joining the United Nations but inviting it to establish its headquarters in New York City.

Less well known but equally important was Wilson's championship of the right of national self-determination, a troublesome but vital principle for a world then beginning to emerge from the bondage of European colonialism. Although he violated his own principle in his relations with Mexico, Russia, and the Caribbean nations, Wilson's concept of self-determination was eagerly embraced by nationalist leaders from Ireland to Indonesia and provided legitimacy for their longing for independence. What was perhaps even more important than the idea of political self-determination was the concept of economic self-determination, under which Wilson fought to free Asian and Latin American nations of their dependence on inequitable and exploitive relations with foreign investors and businessmen. In recognizing that this form of indirect empire might be as burdensome as the more obvious political type, Wilson opened discussion of a problem that remains into the twenty-first century.

In later years Wilson would often be remembered as a dreamer of great but impractical dreams—an image perhaps reinforced by his failure to win the approval of the Senate for the Treaty of Versailles and the futility of his last years. But that was not how he saw his own legacy. Just as in "The Road away from Revolution" he refused to be drawn into the debate over whether Bolshevism was evil and instead focused on urging the correction of the political and economic failures that gave it an opportunity to grow, so he saw his legacy in both domestic and foreign policy as the application of practical solutions to practical problems. Principles, he argued, "must hold water, real wet water, or they must be mended so they will," and Wilson was confident that his principles *did* hold water (Link and others 1972, 12:362). From the conception of responsible but limited government to the League of Nations, he challenged Americans to address problems in innovative ways that, seventy-five years later, still have the power to stir debate, stimulate imaginations, and even influence policy.

BIBLIOGRAPHIC ESSAY

Of all the periods of Wilson's life, this last segment needs the most critical attention. Professional historians have largely eschewed study of Wilson's postpresidential years, leaving the subject to journalistic accounts. The best of these is Gene Smith's *When the Cheering Stopped: The Last Years of Woodrow Wilson* (New York: William Morrow and Company, 1964). A moving and detailed account of Wilson's breakdown in 1919, the book provides a narrative running through Wilson's final days and touches briefly on the lives of his family after his death. Although Smith avoids any strong analytic framework, he is highly critical of Edith Wilson's hold over her husband. Other useful accounts include William Allen White, *Woodrow*

Wilson: The Man, His Times, and His Task (New York: Houghton Mifflin Company, 1924); Ray Stannard Baker, *American Chronicle* (New York: Charles Scribner's Sons, 1945); and Arthur Walworth, *American Prophet* (New York: Longmans, Green and Company, 1958). A rather harsh portrayal of Edith's supposed control over the presidency and the broken man who occupied it, Phyllis Lee Levin's recent book, *Edith and Woodrow: The Wilson White House* (New York: Scribner, 2001), briefly covers the S Street years.

Personal accounts of the period provide probably the best insight into Wilson's condition. Among the most lively and useful are Cary Grayson's *Woodrow Wilson: An Intimate Memoir* (New York: Holt, Rinehart, & Winston, 1960), and Joseph Tumulty's *Woodrow Wilson as I Know Him* (Garden City, N.Y.: Doubleday, Page, & Co., 1921). Edith Wilson's autobiography, *My Memoir* (New York: Bobbs-Merrill Company, 1938), offers a rather selective and jaundiced view of her husband's last years.

See also the sources cited in the bibliography for the Introduction.

Document 6.1   Nobel Prize Acceptance Speech

The following note is Wilson's acceptance speech for the Nobel Prize for peace awarded him by the Nobel Peace Committee of the Norwegian Storting. As indicated by the first passage, the acceptance speech, delivered as a telegram, was drafted by Norman Davis, Wilson's adviser. It is difficult to say whether the recently invalided Wilson even saw the draft, and in any case only a few words were altered before the telegram was "Approved by President" and dispatched. The American minister to Norway, Albert George Schmedeman, wrote Wilson after accepting the award for the president that "this has been one of the most gratifying occasions of my life, and I appreciate unspeakably the honor of receiving on your behalf this token of a nation's recognition of your high purpose towards mankind." (The words in parentheses were deleted by Wilson; the words in italics were inserted by him.)

Dear Mr. President: [Washington] Dec 8–20.

In spite of your instructions I hesitate to send this message on your behalf without your seeing it. As it must go forward today may I ask that you let me know if it is satisfactory?

Cordially yours

Norman H. Davis

Approved by President

ENCLOSURE

Washington, December 8, 1920.

RUSH. Your December 4.

The President has directed me to authorize you [that is, George Schmedeman] to receive the award of the Nobel Committee and in reply to the speech made in announcing it you are instructed to convey the following message from the President:

QUOTE: In accepting the honor of your award, I am moved not only by a profound gratitude for the recognition of my earnest efforts in the Cause of Peace, but also by a very poignant humility before the vastness of the work still called for by this Cause.

May I not take this occasion to express my respect for the far-sighted wisdom of the Founder in arranging for a continuing system of awards? If there were but one such prize or if this were to be the last, I could not of course accept it. For mankind has not yet been rid of the unspeakable horror of war. I am convinced that our generation has despite its wounds made notable progress. But it is the better part of wisdom to consider our work as only begun. It will be a continuing labor. In the indefinite course of years before us, there will be *abundant* opportunity (a plenty) for others to distinguish themselves in the Crusade against hate and fear and war.

There is indeed a peculiar fitness in the grouping of these Nobel rewards. The Cause of Peace and the Cause of Truth are of one family. Even as those who love Science and devote their lives to physics or chemistry, even as those who would create new and higher ideals for mankind in literature, even so with those who love Peace, there is no limit set. Whatever has been accomplished in the past is petty compared to the glory and promise of the future.

Davis Acting

Source: Arthur S. Link and others, eds., *The Papers of Woodrow Wilson, August 2–December 23, 1920* (Princeton: Princeton University Press, 1992), 66:492–493.

▬▬▬▬▬

Document 6.2   Wilson's Vision for Reelection, 1924

Wilson believed the Democrats could not fail to win the 1924 election, and that a third term as president was in his immediate future. Both written near the end of January 1924, the first document below consists of his outline for his speech accepting the Democratic nomination for that office, while the second is a set of notes for his third inaugural address. Readers should note that all typographical errors are Wilson's own, the result in part of the loss of the use of his left hand.

Notes and Passages for an Acceptance Speech
Analysis.
Overwhelming honour.
Why should it be offered?
Because the Democratic party has proved an effective instrument of public service by its close integration and its frank acceptance of leadership and does not wish to change its organization or its habit and spirit of action. (See Burke on party)
We wish greatly to add to the services it has already rendered.
It is a united body devoted to definite principles and purposes.
It has by practiced association and action qualified itself to fulfil that famous and now classical definition of a political party which I shall take the loberty of quoting in the incomparable English of Edmund Burke (I., 530)

◆

The failure of the Republican party&:
Began by forecasts of policy; ended in inanition, neglect, and mere drift
High time that its place should be taken by a party of well defined purposes and practiced action.
THE United States were at the front of the new forces of diplomacy wh. united and liberated the world. The Republican administration has transferred them to the old forces, which enslaved free peoples and kept governments at loggerheads.

◆

The complete and disastrous failure of the Republicans ca cannot be a proper subject of gratification to any thoughtful man. It has in fact been a great disappointment to the Republicn party not only but also to thinking men of every party throughout the country. It was sinister in origin and sinister in issue. It came at perhaps the most critical juncture in the social and political history of mankind, when, therefore, it was sure to b be most harmful and most dispiriting to the whole world; and by it the world has lost at least a generation of progress

◆

I am sure that in the High Court of Honour and true Loyalty it must be held to be as deep and heinous a treason that a great and holy cause whose success has been bought by the blood of thousands of your fellow countrymen should be betrayed in the moment od its triumph as that the armies of the nation should be betrayed on the field of battle.

Notes and Passages for a Third Inaugural Address

3rd Inaugural

Yearning of peoples the world over for Liberty, Justice, Brotherhood. The duty of the U. S.—to lead
(1) By example of moderation and constructive plan
and
(2) To fight and defeat all—aggression—all Reaction and thus bring light and hope back into the world of affairs whence they have fled.

◆

Our fathers lighted a torch and placed it at the front of the nations wh. shall never thr. any fault of mine be extinguished or removed from its place There
America, the champion of Right and Justice, the "nearest friend" of free peoples

◆

Putting all partisanship and self-interest firmly aside, let us address ourselves with true singleness of mind and sincerity of devotion to the high and sacred task of Justice

◆

Objects and motives of the nation in the great wa war: Our entrance was an unexampled instance of heroic disinterestedness on the part of a great free people, who wished to. serve, not to profit,—devoting the lives of its men and the whole body of its resources to save the peoples of Europe from an arrogant and odious dominion which would have been destructive of their liberties and of their happiness.

◆

Present objects and motives: to establish an order in which labour shall have assumed the greater dignity and capital acquired the greater vigour and advantage by the practice of justice

◆

I summon to my side andbeg the counsel and suppo support of every man and every woman who loves justice and believes no sacrifice too great which promises to set it up as the rule of life in the community, whether local or national. We can have it so if we will but sincerely turn our purpose to it.

JUSTICE.
Closing passage of third inaugural

Bustice is the only, certain insurance against revolution and the only invariable stimulant to any kind of successful action in any field of human activity. Without justice labour must be disheartened and industry unfruitful. Without justice society must break up into hostile groups,—even into hostile individuals, and go utterly to pieces.

Source: Arthur S. Link and others, eds., *The Papers of Woodrow Wilson, April 8, 1922–February 6, 1924* (Princeton: Princeton University Press, 1993), 68:541–543.

Document 6.3   "The Document"

"The Document" was the last gasp of Wilson's political career. Completed in the concluding weeks of January 1924, it was meant to form the basis for Wilson's triumphal return to politics. Instead, despite much intelligent input from old friends like David Houston and Bainbridge Colby, it was more a manifesto for Wilson's hatred of all things Republican in the 1920s. It is printed in its entirety. Readers should note that all typographical errors are Wilson's own, the result in part of the loss of the use of his left hand.

CONFIDENTIAL DOCUMENT

1. We recognize the fact that the complex, disturbing and for the most part destructive results of the great war have made it necessary that the progressive countries of the world should supply for the reconstruction of its life a programme of law and reform which shall bring it back to health and effective order; and that it lies with the political party which best understands existing conditions, is in most sympathetic touch with the mass of the people, and is ready and best qualified to carry a constructive programme through to take the initiative in making and pressing affirmative proposals of remedy and reform.

2. In this spirit and with this great purpose we, as representatives of the Democratic party of the United States put forth, in deep earnestness, the following declaration of principle and purpose and thereby seek to serve America and, through America, liberal men throughout the world who seek to serve their people.

3. "AMERICA FIRST" is a slogan which does not belong to any one political party; it is merely a concise expression of what is in the heart of every patriotic American. We enthusiastically incorporate it into this our declaration of principles and purposes. But it means different things in different mouths and requires definition. When uttered by the present leaders of the Republican party it means that America must render no service to any other nation or people which she can reserve for her own selfish aggrandizement. When we use it we mean that in every international action or organization for the benefit of mankind America must be foremost; that America by developing within her own citizenship and acts a

sensitive regard for justice in all the relations of men, must lead the world in applying the broadest conceptions of justice and peace, of amity and respect, to the mutual relations of other peoples, and in rendering them material aid in the realization of those ideals.

4. We are suffering in common with other nations of the world from the industrial and commercial prostration which followed the great war. Bound up with world conditions from which we could not extricate ourselves, the Republican Administration nevertheless committed itself to a policy of isolation. It blindly persisted in the delusion that we are unaffected by the world's all-encompassing perils and calamities and that, although we have great accumulated strength and matchless resources, we have no responsibility for and need not interest ourselves in efforts to discover and apply safeguards and remedies. It still refuses to take the lead or to cooperate with the Governments of other nations in the adoption of measures which would improve our own situation or that of our customers and debtors.

The Republican Administration has no economic policy, domestic or foreign. In economic matters it is trying to go in several opposite directions at the same time. It declares its desire to stimulate foreign trade and to revive shipping and yet, under pressure of special interests and for their benefit, it erects a high tariff barrier to lessen imports and therefore to limit or destroy foreign trade. It recklessly ignores the fact that we have more than half of the gold of the world; that other nations cannot pay us in gold, that it would not benefit us to receive it if they could, and that we cannot sell our surplus products of the farm and factory and collect our debts unless our customers and debtors can produce and sell their goods.

That it would be worse than stupid to try to maintain a merchant fleet by direct and indirect subsidies to carry freight and then to destroy trade by excluding commodities, does not enter the minds of the Old Guard Republican leaders who are in charge of the Government. They assert their eagerness to reduce taxes and the cost of living and yet ought to know, in their hearts, if they had any intelligent conception of the situation that they add to both by the tariff programme, based on greed. They preach economy and yet press legislation for new undertakings and obligations involving hundreds of millions of dollars. They profess to be concerned about the laborers' standard of living, and at a time when the beneficiaries of their tariff policy are omitting nothing to reduce wages they are devising measures to increase the laborers' cost of living. They clamour for the stabilization of trade and exchange and by their course contribute to the conditions which render stabilization impossible. They are blind to the fact that the protection which the American farmers and manufacturers need is that which would be afforded by a great foreign market, and that this can be secured only by measures which will bring peace to the world, stimulate the forces of production everywhere, and make possible through legitimate business ventures this nation's assistance to Europe through loans and investments.

5. We demand the immediate resumption of our international obligations and leadership—obligations which were shamelessly repudiated and a leadership which was incontinently thrown away by the failure of the Senate to ratify the Treaty of Versailles and the negotiation of separate treaties with the central powers. We heartily approve and endorse the proposal of President Harding that the United States officially adhere to the permanent international court of justice established under the auspices of the League of Nations, but the proposal is manifestly only a fragment of a policy which is incomplete and which ought to be frankly and courageously rounded out and made self-consistent. We deem it essential to the maintenance of the dignity of the United States, to the vindication of our national honour and to the final confirmation of the good faith of our Government towards the nations with whom we were associated in the recent war that the United States should become a member of the League of Nations, assuming the same responsibilities that the other members assume for the organization and maintenance of peace.

6. We condemn the group of men who brought about these evil results as the most partisan, prejudiced, ignorant and unpatriotic group that ever misled the Senate of the United States.

7. We call attention to the lamentable record of incompetence, evasion and political truckling of the last Congress, dominated in both the Senate and House of Representatives by a commanding Republican majority. No step has been taken toward the redemption of

the pledges made by the Republican party. Despite the crying needs of the hour and the hopes of the people, it has not enacted a single piece of constructive or ameliorative legislation, although for the last three years it has controlled both houses of Congress.

8. The demand for a revision of the tax laws, made three years ago by a Democratic President upon the conclusion of the armistice, is still unheeded, and the burdensome and unequal taxes, born of and justified only by a great emergency, still persist, thwarting the normal processes of economic recovery, and robbing the frugality and industry of the people of their just rewards.

9. We believe that the President and the members of his cabinet should be accorded the right to places on the floor of the Senate and the House of Representatives whenever those bodies have under discussion affairs which are entrusted by the Constitution or the laws to the executive branch of the Government; that they should also be accorded the right to take part in such discussions; and that they should be required to answer upon the floor all proper questions addressed to them concerning matters dealt with by the Executive.

10. We call attention to the fact that a budget still unbalanced, and distended beyond the requirements of efficient and economical administration in time of peace, shows no sign of contraction, and every day brings the report of some fresh conspiracy against the public treasury. We promise studious and disinterested approach to the problems of national relief and rehabilitation and condemn the callousness and levity with which the Republican party has subordinated the duty of intelligent attention to these vital problems to petty considerations of partisan politics.

11. We shall use every legitimate means to advance to the utmost the industrial and commercial development of the United States. That development has already made the people of the United States the greatest economic force in the world. It is as convincing proof of their practical genius as their free institutions are proof of their political genius. It is their manifest opportunity and destiny to lead the world in these great fields of endeavor and achiev[e]ment. Our opponents have sought to promote the accumulation of wealth as an instrument of power in the hands of individuals and corporations. It is our object to promote it as a means of diffused

prosperity and happiness and of physical and spiritual well being on the part of the great working masses of our people.

12. Without the systematic coordination, cooperation and interchange of services by the railroads the expanding, varying and changeable commerce and industry of the country cannot be properly served. All of these conditions are now lacking because our present laws deal with the railroads without system and altogether by way of interference and restriction. The result is a confusion which is constantly made worse almost to the point of paralysis by the multiplicity and intermittent conflict of regulative authorities, local and national.

13. The Eighteenth Amendment made prohibition the law of the Nation. The Volstead Act prescribed for the Nation what liquor should be deemed intoxicating. But the people, when adopting the Amendment, recognized fully that the law could not be enforced without the co-operation of the States within the Nation. Hence it provided in Section 2 that "The Congress and the several States shall have concurrent power to enforce this article by appropriate legislation." The intention was that such government should perform that part of the task for which it was peculiarly fitted. The Federal Government's part is to protect the United States against illegal importation of liquor from foreign countries and to protect each State from the illegal introduction into it of liquor from another State. To perform that part of the task effectively required centralized, unified action and the employment of the large federal powers and resources. Experience has demonstrated that to perform adequately this part of the task will require all the resources which Congress makes available for enforcement of this law. To this part of the whole task of enforcement the Federal Government should, therefore, devote its entire energies. The protection of the people of a State against the illegal sale within it of liquor illegally manufactured within it, is a task for which the State Governments are peculiarly fitted, and which they should perform. That part of the task involves diversified governmental action and adaptation to the widely varying conditions in, and the habits and sentiments of the people of, the several States. It is a task for which the Federal Government is not fitted. To relieve the States from the duty of performing it, violates our traditions; and threatens the best

interests of our country. The strength of the Nation and its capacity for achiev[e]ment is, in large measure, due to the federal system with its distribution of powers and duties.

There should be frank recognition of the fact that the prime duty of the Federal Government is to protect the country against illegal importation from abroad and from illegal introduction of liquor from one State into another; that the full performance of this duty will tax the resources of the Federal Government to the uttermost; and that, for the rest, the people of each State must look to their state governments. But the Eighteenth Amendment should remain unchanged. And the Volstead Act should remain unchanged.

14. We need a Secretary of Transportation who shall rank with the heads of other great federal cabinet departments and who shall be charged with the formulation and execution of plans for the coordinated use and full development of the transportation systems of the country. He should be associated with a federal Transportation Board which should be invested with all the powers now lodged with the Interstate Commerce Commission and, in addition, with the authority to determine the occasions and the conditions of all loans floated and of all securities issued by the several railway and steamship lines. This Board should have the same powers of supervision and regulation over the steamship lines of the United States that are now exercised by the Interstate Commerce Commission over the railways.

15. The present menace to political liberty and peaceful economic prosperity lies, not in the power of kings or irresponsible governments, but in hasty, passionate and irrational programmes of revolution. The world has been made safe for democracy, but democracy has not yet made the world safe against irrational revolution. It is the privilege and duty of ours, the greatest of all democracies, to show the way. It is our purpose to defeat the irrational programmes of revolution beforehand by sober and practical legislative reforms which shall remove the chief provocations to revolution.

16. Among these we hold the following to be indispensable:

A practical plan for a veritable partnership between capital and labour, in which the responsibilities of each to the other, and of both to the nation, shall be stressed quite as much as their respective rights. Our industrial system must command the interest and respect of the wage earners as an avenue to those liberties and opportunities for self-development which it is the nature of free men to desire. Justice must reign over it, and its dignity as one of the foundations of the national vigour and as a great training school for democratic citizenship must be recognized and cultivated.

A plan by which the raw materials of manufacture and the electrical and other motive power now universally necessary to industry shall be made accessible to all upon equitable and equal terms.

Such legal requirements of the manufacturer and the merchant as will serve to bring cost of production and retail price into a clearly standardized relationship made known to the purchaser.

17. We heartily endorse and believe in the efforts which the farmers and certain other producers are making to set up and administer cooperative organizations for purchase and sale in all the markets which they serve or which serve them, and we earnestly advocate the fullest possible assistance of all our State legislatures in making these efforts successful and effective.

18. We unqualifiedly condemn the action of the Republican administration in interrupting and in large part destroying the work of creating and developing an American merchant marine so intelligently begun and so efficiently carried forward by the Democratic administration, and we demand the immediate rehabilitation of the Shipping Board and such appropriations for its use and such additions to its powers as may be necessary to put its work upon a permanent footing and assure its energetic and successful completion. An efficient and adequate merchant marine is vital to the nation's safety, and indispensable to the life and growth of its commerce.

19. In close relation to the upbuilding of our overseas trade is the development of our inland waterways. We demand therefore the unprejudiced and scientific study of this vastly important field of national expansion, and the prompt inauguration of adequate and effective measures to bring to the service of our producers in the interior States a systemized, cheap and efficient transportation by inland water routes, including the development of ship canal communication with the Atlantic seaboard.

19. Inasmuch as access by all upon equitable and equal terms to the fuel supply and to the raw materials of manufacture and also the availability to all upon fair and equal terms of the motive power

supplied by electrical power companies and other similar privately owned and controlled agencies are indispensable to the unhampered development of the industries of the country, we believe that these are matters which should be regulated by federal legislation to the utmost limit of the constitutional powers of the federal government.

Source: Arthur S. Link and others, eds., *The Papers of Woodrow Wilson, April 8, 1922–February 6, 1924* (Princeton: Princeton University Press, 1993), 68:535–541.

Document 6.4   Draft of a History of the United States, 1922
One of Wilson's final intellectual activities was to begin drafting, in May 1922, the outline for the masterwork on American government that he had been planning since the 1890s. The historical interpretations sketched by Wilson in the plan printed below, however, owe more to his experiences in the 1910s and the 1920s than to reasoned scholarly analysis. Nevertheless, the notes provide insight into Wilson the historian's view of the United States' role in the world, but as it was colored both by his successes and failures as president. Readers should note that all typographical errors are Wilson's own, the result in part of the loss of the use of his left hand.

DEDICATION.

To my incomparable wife, Edith Bolling Wilson, whose gentle benefits to me are beyond all estimation, this book, which is meant to contain what is best in me, is, with deep admiration and gratitude, lovingly dedicated.

◆

PREFACE

In the following pages I have set forth as clearly and truly as I could the ideals and principles which have governed my life, and whihch have also (such is my faith)governed the life of the nation, although they have. not always been articulately avowed or always audibly uttered amidst the niose [noise] of events

◆

FOREWORD

I have tried in this articleand in one or two articles which are to follow the following pages to set dorth as fullyand faithfully as possible the ideals and principles which have governed my life. They are the same (such is my assured faith) that have governed the action and deve,opment of the nation itself.

◆

THE DESTINY OF THE REPUBLIC.

I.
The Vision and Purpose of the Fathers (Founders)
    II.
    III
"he Great Opportunity.
    III.
Afterwards.

◆

I.
THE PLAN
    II.
THE OPPORTUNITY.
    III.
AFTERWARDS.
    IV.
LOOKING FORWARD.

◆

The Vision and Purpose of the Founders.
    Unlike the government of every other great state, ancient or modern, the government of the United Stateswas set up for the benefit of mankind as well as for the benefit of its own people,—a most ambitious enterprise, no doubt, but undertaken with high purpose, with clear vision, and with

thoughtful and deliberate unselfishness, and undertaken by men who were no amateurs but acquainted with the world they lived in, practiced in the conduct of affairs, who set the new government up with an ordiliness and self-possession which marked them as men who were proud to serve liberty with the dignity and restraint of true devotees of a great ideal.

But their experiment was not welcomed by their contemporaries. Seasoned observers and sophisticated politicians must have marvelled at the profound sensation which this event in distant America occasioned in Europe. The new state had no material power that any European government need have feared. And yet it was almost everywhere looked upon with dislike and suspicion. Mankind were, of course, everywhere. under e established governments; and established g governments looked with deep concern upon this new thing in the West, heard with unconcealed alarm this new and confident voice of liberty

◆

To follow opening sentence:

Mem.

But mankind were everywhere under governments and established governments looked with deep concern upon this new thing in the West, heard with unconcealed alarm this new and confident voice of liberty

Note how Europe looked on and pondered (de Toqueville.)

The Holy Alliance

The Monroe Doctrine, hated and feared ever since.

American influence everywhere the yeast.

◆

III.

AFTERWARDS.

Effects on the world politically and economicelly

Effects on the United States,

Its influence internationally

Its financial and commercial power

"o recover?

Show that America, knows how to lead the world in the solution of modern political and industrial problems, and thus vindicate democracy.

◆

It was not the possible physical power of the new republicthat was feared. Statesmen oversea feared the effect, rather, which its principles and example would have on their own people. No old government felt confident that it could justify itself in the midst of a public opinion aroused and free to ask questions.

France, the while, caught in a luminous fog of political theory, was groping her way from revolution to revolution in bewildered search of firm ground upon which to build a permanent government.

◆

France, the while, was groping her way through irridescent mists of politilal theory from revolution to revolution in bewildered search of firm ground upon which to build a permanent government.

◆

France the while was groping her way through a luminous fog of political theory from revolution to revolution in bewildered search of firm ground upon which to build a permanent government.

W. W.

per E B W

Source: Arthur S. Link and others, eds., *The Papers of Woodrow Wilson, April 8, 1922–February 6, 1924* (Princeton: Princeton University Press, 1993), 68:39–42.

Document 6.5   "The Road away from Revolution," August 1923

"The Road away from Revolution" was Woodrow Wilson's last published work. It is reproduced here in full. Although this version of the article differed little from the original draft, it omitted two paragraphs that Wilson's brother-in-law and editor, Stockton Axson, advised should be cut to strengthen its argument and tone. Those paragraphs have been reinstated in italics below,

from Wilson's first draft. The essay was originally printed in The Atlantic Monthly, *August 1923, 145–146.*

THE ROAD AWAY FROM REVOLUTION

In these doubtful and anxious days, when all the world is at unrest and, look which way you will, the road ahead seems darkened by shadows which portend dangers of many kinds, it is only common prudence that we should look about us and attempt to assess the causes of distress and the most likely means of removing them.

There must be some real ground for the universal unrest and perturbation. It is not to be found in superficial politics or in mere economic blunders. It probably lies deep at the sources of the spiritual life of our time. It leads to revolution; and perhaps if we take the case of the Russian Revolution, the outstanding event of its kind in our age, we may find a good deal of instruction for our judgment of present critical situations and circumstances.

What gave rise to the Russian Revolution? The answer can only be that it was the product of a whole social system. It was not in fact a sudden thing. It had been gathering head for several generations. It was due to the systematic denial to the great body of Russians of the rights and privileges which all normal men desire and must have if they are to be contented and within reach of happiness. The lives of the great mass of the Russian people contained no opportunities, but were hemmed in by barriers against which they were constantly flinging their spirits, only to fall back bruised and dispirited. Only the powerful were suffered to secure their rights or even to gain access to the means of material success.

It is to be noted as a leading fact of our time that it was against "capitalism" that the Russian leaders directed their attack. It was capitalism that made them see red; and it is against capitalism under one name or another that the discontented classes everywhere draw their indictment.

There are thoughtful and well-informed men all over the world who believe, with much apparently sound reason, that the abstract thing, the system, which we call capitalism, is indispensable to the industrial support and development of modern civilization. And yet everyone who has an intelligent knowledge of social forces must know that great and widespread reactions like that which is now unquestionably manifesting itself against capitalism do not occur without cause or provocation; and before we commit ourselves irreconcilably to an attitude of hostility to this movement of the time, we ought frankly to put to ourselves the question, Is the capitalistic system unimpeachable? which is another way of asking, Have capitalists generally used their power for the benefit of the countries in which their capital is employed and for the benefit of their fellow men?

Is it not, on the contrary, too true that capitalists have often seemed to regard the men whom they used as mere instruments of profit, whose physical and mental powers it was legitimate to exploit with as slight cost to themselves as possible, either of money or of sympathy? Have not many fine men who were actuated by the highest principles in every other relationship of life seemed to hold that generosity and humane feeling were not among the imperative mandates of conscience in the conduct of a banking business, or in the development of an industrial or commercial enterprise?

And, if these offenses against high morality and true citizenship have been frequently observable, are we to say that the blame for the present discontent and turbulence is wholly on the side of those who are in revolt against them? Ought we not, rather, to seek a way to remove such offenses and make life itself clean for those who will share honorably and cleanly in it?

The world has been made safe for democracy. There need now be no fear that any such mad design as that entertained by the insolent and ignorant Hohenzollerns and their counselors may prevail against it. But democracy has not yet made the world safe against irrational revolution. That supreme task, which is nothing less than the salvation of civilization, now faces democracy, insistent, imperative. There is no escaping it, unless everything we have built up is presently to fall in ruin about us; and the United States, as the greatest of democracies, must undertake it.

The road that leads away from revolution is cleanly marked, for it is defined by the nature of men and of organized society. It therefore behooves us to study very carefully and very candidly the exact nature of the task and the means of its accomplishment.

The nature of men and of organized society dictates the maintenance in every field of action of the highest and purest standards of justice and of right dealing; and it is essential to efficacious thinking in this critical matter that we should not entertain a narrow or technical conception of justice. By justice the lawyer generally means the prompt, fair, and open application of impartial rules; but we call ours a Christian civilization, and a Christian conception of justice must be much higher. It must include sympathy and helpfulness and a willingness to forego self-interest in order to promote the welfare, happiness, and contentment of others and of the community as a whole. This is what our age is blindly feeling after in its reaction against what it deems the too great selfishness of the capitalistic system.

Many grave and even tragical mistakes have been made, practically all of which have been illustrated in the course of the Russian revolution; but they need not be repeated, and many of them can be retrieved.

A friend of mine, on a visit to the country, was one day standing beside a farmer, his host, leaning on the fence of a pig-sty, watching a number of pigs eat out of a trough. The usual things were happening. The pigs all had their forefeet in the trough; were slopping its contents out on the ground; and were getting as much of the food in their faces and on their hides as into their throats,—making a mess of their performance in every possible way. Presently the farmer turned to my friend, a philosophical light in his eye, and observed "Well, Sir, they're all well named pigs: they eat like pigs." I am told that in Russian the word Bolshiviki means the Minority, and I am tempted to echo the farmer's reflection and observe, "Well, Sirs, they are well named the Minority: they act like a minority, with the haste, ignorance and passion characteristic of a minority suddenly come into possession of all the machinery of power and free to do as they please, obliged to respect no opposition either of reason or of force from any quarter." But the mistakes which have been made need not be repeated, and we can move on towards right ends by right means, if only we think clearly and act unselfishly.

The sum of the whole matter is this, that our civilization cannot survive materially unless it be redeemed spiritually. It can be saved only by becoming permeated with the spirit of Christ and being made free and happy by the practices which spring out of that spirit. Only thus can discontent be driven out and all the shadows lifted from the road ahead.

Here is the final challenge to our churches, to our political organizations, and to our capitalists–to everyone who fears God or loves his country. Shall we not all earnestly cooperate to bring in the new day?

Source: Arthur S. Link and others, eds., *The Papers of Woodrow Wilson, April 8, 1922–February 6, 1924* (Princeton: Princeton University Press, 1993), 68: 322–324, 393–395.

Document 6.6   Speech, November 10, 1923

Around 8:30 p.m. on November 10, 1923, Wilson gave his last public speech, via radio, to commemorate the fifth anniversary of Armistice Day. Transmitted across the country from a microphone set up in Wilson's library at S Street, it was estimated by the New York Times *the following morning that the address might have been heard by "millions." Writing the next day from New York City, the president's daughter Margaret exclaimed, "Your speech was a wonder. Every word was clear and easily heard. There were no statics to mar it. A group of us who heard it together were deeply stirred and I was so happy" (Link and others 1993, 68:471).*

The anniversary of Armistice Day should stir us to great exaltation of spirit because of the proud recollection that it was our day, a day above those early days of that never-to-be-forgotten November which lifted the world to the high levels of vision and achievement upon which the great war for democracy and right was fought and won; although the stimulating memories of that happy time of triumph are forever marred and embittered for us by the shameful fact that when the victory was won—won, be it remembered—chiefly by the indomitable spirit and ungrudging sacrifices of our incomparable soldiers—we turned our backs upon our associates and refused to bear any responsible part in the administration of peace, or the firm and permanent establishment of the results of the war—won at so terrible a cost of life and treasure—and withdrew into a sullen and selfish isolation which is deeply ignoble because manifestly cowardly and dishonorable.

This must always be a source of deep mortification to us and we shall inevitably be forced by the moral obligations of freedom and honor to retrieve that fatal error and assume once more the role of courage, self-respect and helpfulness which every true American must wish to regard as our natural part in the affairs of the world.

That we should have thus done a great wrong to civilization at one of the most critical turning points in the history of the world is the more to be deplored because every anxious year that has followed has made the exceeding need for such services as we might have rendered more and more evident and more and more pressing, as demoralizing circumstances which we might have controlled have gone from bad to worse.

And now, as if to furnish a sort of sinister climax, France and Italy between them have made waste paper of the Treaty of Versailles and the whole field of international relationship is in perilous confusion.

The affairs of the world can be set straight only by the firmest and most determined exhibition of the will to lead and make the right prevail.

Happily, the present situation in the world of affairs affords us the opportunity to retrieve the past and to render mankind the inestimable service of proving that there is at least one great and powerful nation which can turn away from programs of self-interest and devote itself to practising and establishing the highest ideals of disinterested service and the consistent maintenance of exalted standards of conscience and of right.

The only way in which we can worthily give proof of our appreciation of the high significance of Armistice Day is by resolving to put self-interest away and once more formulate and act upon the highest ideals and purposes of international policy.

Thus, and only thus, can we return to the true traditions of America.

Source: Arthur S. Link and others, eds., *The Papers of Woodrow Wilson, April 8, 1922–February 6, 1924* (Princeton: Princeton University Press, 1993), 68: 466–467.

Appendix A
Notable Figures of the Wilson Presidency

Alexander, Joshua Willis (1852–1936, b. Cincinnati, Ohio)
Secretary of commerce, 1919–1921
Joshua Alexander was an attorney in Gallatin, Missouri. He served in local government and the state legislature before becoming a judge for the 7th Judicial Circuit Court of Missouri in 1901. In 1906 he was elected to Congress as a Democrat, serving in the House until December 11, 1919, when he resigned to become secretary of commerce for the last months of the Wilson administration, after which he returned to the practice of law in Missouri.

Axson, Isaac Stockton Keith, II (1867–1935, b. Rome, Georgia)
National secretary of the Red Cross, 1917–1919
Stockton Axson, Ellen Axson Wilson's younger brother, became one of Woodrow Wilson's best friends. He taught English literature at the University of Vermont (1892–1894), Adelphi College (1896–1899), Princeton (1899–1913), and Rice University (1913–1935). During World War I he served as national secretary of the Red Cross (1917–1919).

Baker, Newton Diehl (1871–1937, b. Martinsburg, West Virginia)
Secretary of war, 1916–1921
Newton Baker met Wilson while he was an undergraduate at the Johns Hopkins University and Wilson was a visiting lecturer. An attorney, he served as city solicitor of Cleveland from 1902 to 1912 and then was elected mayor (1912–1916). Wilson invited him to join his original cabinet, but Baker wanted to complete his work as mayor. When Wilson asked him to become secretary of war in March 1916, however, Baker accepted, although his Quaker religion seemed to make him an odd choice. Despite controversy about his handling of mobilization during the war, he enjoyed Wilson's full support and served until the end of the administration in March 1921.

Baruch, Bernard Mannes (1870–1965, b. Camden, South Carolina)
Adviser, 1916–1921
Bernard Baruch became wealthy as an investor on the New York Stock Exchange and was semiretired by the beginning of World War I. In 1916 Wilson asked him to serve as a member of the Advisory Committee of the Council of National Defense. He became chairman of the successor agency, the War Industries Board,

in 1918, and in that capacity earned a reputation as someone who, without much official authority, nevertheless succeeded in securing efficient cooperation among companies providing raw materials and manufactured goods for the war effort. In 1919 he was a member of Wilson's First Industrial Conference. During the 1920s he served in various advisory capacities to federal agencies, and during World War II he again returned to Washington as an expert on mobilization.

Bliss, Tasker Howard (1853–1930, b. Lewisburg, Pennsylvania)
Chief of staff, 1917

Tasker Bliss, a West Point graduate, was a career army officer, becoming a brigadier general in 1902. He served in the military government of Cuba, 1898–1902; on the army general staff, 1903–1905; and in the administration of the Philippines, 1906–1909. During the Wilson administration he served on the Joint Army and Navy Board, and from September 23, 1917, until his retirement at the end of the year, as chief of staff. Wilson extended his service by special order, however, so he could serve as the American representative on the Supreme War Council in France during the war. Wilson then asked him to serve as a member of the American Peace Commission in Paris, 1918–1919.

Brandeis, Louis Dembitz (1856–1941, b. Louisville, Kentucky)
Associate justice of the Supreme Court, 1916–1939

Louis Brandeis was widely referred to as the "people's attorney" because of his advocacy of the public interest during his career in Massachusetts, where he settled after his graduation from Harvard Law School. In 1912 he campaigned for Robert La Follette, but when Wilson secured the Democratic nomination, Brandeis became his most important adviser on antitrust issues in particular. Wilson wanted to appoint him to his cabinet but was dissuaded by the opposition of powerful figures in Massachusetts. In January 1916 Wilson seized an opportunity to name him as an associate justice of the U.S. Supreme Court, where he served with distinction until his retirement in 1939.

Bryan, William Jennings (1860–1925, b. Salem, Illinois)
Secretary of state, 1913–1915

William Jennings Bryan began his career as an attorney in Illinois, but moved to Lincoln, Nebraska, in 1887. He was elected to the House of Representatives in 1890 and served two terms. In 1896, 1900, and 1908 he was the Democratic candidate for president. Wilson appointed him secretary of state largely because he thought that Bryan would be helpful in winning congressional support for the president's domestic program. The friendship that grew between the two men even survived Bryan's resignation over Wilson's policy toward Germany in June 1915. Bryan campaigned for Wilson in 1916 and supported the ratification of the Treaty of Versailles in 1919. In the 1920s Bryan became a prominent spokesman for fundamentalist Christianity. At the time of his death in 1925 he had taken part in the prosecution of a Tennessee public school teacher, John Scopes, for instructing students about evolution.

Burleson, Albert Sidney (1863–1937, b. San Marcos, Texas)
Postmaster general, 1913–1921
Albert S. Burleson began his career as an attorney and local politician in Austin, Texas. He was elected to the House of Representatives in 1898 and served there until 1913, when he resigned to become postmaster general in the Wilson administration. His political skills and ties to members of Congress served the administration well in securing the passage of legislation, but Burleson became controversial during World War I when he stretched his powers to the limit to ban from the mails magazines and newspapers he deemed disloyal. His segregation policy in the Post Office Department also drew criticism from liberals and civil rights supporters.

Clark, James Beauchamp ("Champ") (1850–1921, b. Anderson County, Kentucky)
U.S. House of Representatives, Missouri, 1893–1920; Speaker of the House, 1911–1918
Champ Clark practiced law and entered local politics in Bowling Green, Missouri. He was elected to the Missouri House of Representatives in 1888 and to Congress in 1892, where he served until his death in 1921. He became minority leader in 1904 and Speaker of the House of Representatives in 1911, serving in that position until the Republicans won control of Congress in the election of 1918. In 1912 Clark was Wilson's principal competitor for the Democratic presidential nomination, leading through the first twenty-seven ballots at the convention. Although he and Wilson were never close, they worked together well during Wilson's administration.

Clarke, John Hessin (1857–1945, b. Lisbon, Ohio)
Associate justice of the Supreme Court, 1916–1922
John Hessin Clarke was Wilson's third appointee to the Supreme Court. He was elevated from the U.S. District Court for the Northern District of Ohio in July 1916 when Charles Evans Hughes resigned from the Court to run for president. Wilson did not know Clarke personally and seems to have chosen him largely on the recommendation of Newton Baker. Clarke did not make much mark on the Court and resigned in September 1922 to become president of the League of Nations Non-Partisan Association and a trustee of the World Peace Foundation.

Colby, Bainbridge (1869–1950, b. St. Louis, Missouri)
Secretary of state, 1920–1921
Bainbridge Colby became actively involved in the progressive movement as a lawyer in a number of antitrust cases. He was a supporter of Theodore Roosevelt in 1912 and a founder of the Progressive Party that year. In 1914 he ran unsuccessfully for the Senate as a Progressive Party candidate in New York. During World War I,

while he was a member of the U.S. Shipping Board, he and Wilson became friends, and on March 22, 1920, Wilson named him secretary of state to succeed Robert Lansing. He served for the remainder of the administration, becoming one of Wilson's most ardent admirers. After Wilson left office they formed a short-lived partnership (1921–1923) to practice international law.

Cox, James Middleton (1870–1957, b. Jacksonburg, Ohio)
Democratic presidential candidate, 1920
James M. Cox, the Democratic presidential candidate in 1920, was a newspaperman and publisher. He served in Congress, 1909–1913, and as governor of Ohio, 1913–1915 and 1917–1921. In 1920 he loyally if unenthusiastically supported American membership in the League of Nations and went down to defeat with the cause to the Republican nominee, Warren G. Harding.

Creel, George C. (1876–1953, b. Lafayette County, Missouri)
Chairman, Committee on Public Information, 1917–1920
George Creel, a newspaperman and prolific author, was appointed by Wilson to be chairman of the Committee on Public Information during World War I. The committee's mission, at which it was remarkably successful, was to "sell" World War I to the American people, to popularize Wilsonian ideas in America and around the world, to manage and control the flow of news from the battlefields, and to promote national unity. The committee recruited large numbers of scholars, journalists, advertising executives, moviemakers, and a host of speechifying "Four-Minute Men" to broadcast American war aims far and wide. Admirers thought Creel did a wonderful job; critics accused his committee of arousing intolerance and promoting the violation of civil liberties.

Daniels, Josephus (1862–1948, b. Washington, D.C.)
Secretary of the navy, 1913–1921
Josephus Daniels, secretary of the navy throughout the Wilson administration, began his career as a journalist in North Carolina. He was a member of the Democratic National Committee (DNC) from North Carolina from 1896 to 1916 and an enthusiastic supporter, first of William Jennings Bryan and then of Wilson. As secretary of the navy he liberalized discipline and helped to modernize the service's purchasing and support services. His diaries and books about the Wilson years remain valuable sources for historians. During the administration of Franklin Roosevelt, who had been assistant secretary of the navy during Wilson's term, Daniels became ambassador to Mexico.

Garfield, Henry (Harry) Augustus (1863–1942, b. Hiram, Ohio)
Fuel administrator, 1917–1919
Harry Garfield, son of President James A. Garfield, became one of Wilson's admirers when he taught at Princeton (1903–1908), and their friendship continued after

Garfield left Princeton to become president of Williams College (1908–1934). During World War I Wilson asked Garfield to become fuel administrator, a job made particularly difficult because the country's main fuel, coal, was produced by an inefficient mining system and shipped on antiquated and badly run railroads that became almost completely paralyzed during blizzards in the winter of 1917–1918. In the midst of national mobilization, Garfield was forced to close down most factories east of the Mississippi for five days to straighten out the transportation mess. Thereafter the fuel administration effectively secured and distributed fuel for American homes, factories, and ships and even provided a surplus to ship to Europe for the Allies.

Garrison, Lindley Miller (1864–1932, b. Camden, New Jersey)
Secretary of war, 1913–1916
Lindley M. Garrison, although a New Jersey attorney and vice-chancellor of the state (1904–1913), seems to have been unknown to Wilson before he was named secretary of war at the recommendation of Wilson's secretary, Joseph Tumulty. Sharp-tongued and truculent, Garrison did not get along well with his fellow cabinet members. He resigned on February 10, 1916, after Wilson decided on an expansion of the national guard rather than the creation of a 400,000—man, federally controlled, "continental army" that Garrison proposed as a reserve force. By that time, most members of the administration were not sorry to see him go.

Glass, Carter (1858–1946, b. Lynchburg, Virginia)
Secretary of the Treasury, 1918–1920
Carter Glass deserves as much as anyone to be called the father of the Federal Reserve System. A newspaperman in Virginia in his early years, he was elected to the U.S. House of Representatives in 1902 and served until December 1918, when he resigned to become secretary of the Treasury. While in the House he served as chairman of the Committee on Banking and Currency, which developed the Federal Reserve Act in close collaboration with Wilson and his advisers. In February 1920 Glass resigned from the cabinet to accept an appointment to the Senate by the governor of Virginia, where he served until his death in 1946.

Gompers, Samuel (1850–1924, b. London, England)
Labor leader, 1886–1924
Samuel Gompers, the founder and first president of the American Federation of Labor (AFL), early formed a close relationship with Wilson, with whom he carried on an extensive correspondence on a variety of subjects. Gompers was pleased when the Clayton Act (1914) exempted unions from the antitrust laws, and he worked closely with the administration to minimize strikes during World War I. He served as a member of the Advisory Committee of the Council of National Defense, as the representative of the AFL at the peace conference in Paris, and as a member of Wilson's First Industrial Conference in the autumn of 1919.

Grayson, Cary Travers (1878–1938, b. Culpepper County, Virginia)
Wilson's personal physician, 1913–1924
Cary Grayson received his medical training at the Medical College of Virginia and the U.S. Naval Medical School. He served as attending and consulting physician to both Presidents Theodore Roosevelt and William Howard Taft, and became Wilson's personal physician in 1913. Grayson put the president on a healthy diet and encouraged him to get regular exercise, which contributed to one of the longest periods of sustained good health during Wilson's life. Wilson promoted Grayson to rear admiral in August 1916. The two men were friends and frequent golfing partners, as well as patient and doctor. When Wilson suffered his stroke in October 1919, Grayson called in as consultants the foremost specialists in the country. If Grayson erred, it was not in his treatment of Wilson but in yielding to the insistence of Edith Wilson that the president should not resign.

Gregory, Thomas Watt (1861–1933, b. Crawfordsville, Mississippi)
Attorney general, 1914–1919
Thomas Watt Gregory earned a reputation in the early 1900s as a prosecutor of businesses that violated the Texas antitrust laws. In 1913 Attorney General James McReynolds brought him to Washington to assist in the prosecution of the New York, New Haven, and Hartford Railroad for antitrust violations. When Wilson appointed McReynolds to the Supreme Court, he asked Gregory to become attorney general. Gregory served in that position from August 29, 1914, to March 4, 1919, when he resigned to become a partner in a Washington law firm. Wilson regarded Gregory as rational and moderate and often sought his advice on policy. In 1919–1920 Gregory served as a member of Wilson's Second Industrial Conference.

Harvey, George Brinton McClellan (1864–1935, b. Peacham, Vermont)
Publisher
George Harvey began his career in journalism as a reporter for the *Springfield Republican* and rose to become managing editor of the New York *World*. In 1899, after becoming wealthy as a builder and operator of electric railroads, he purchased the *North American Review* and served as its editor for the next twenty-seven years, also becoming the president of Harper and Brothers publishers. A conservative Democrat who supported Grover Cleveland in the 1890s, he believed that William Jennings Bryan was a dangerous radical and hoped to find an attractive, conservative Democrat to challenge Bryan's party dominance. This search led him to Woodrow Wilson, and in 1906 Harvey began to promote Wilson as a possible presidential candidate. In 1910 he was instrumental in securing the New Jersey Democratic gubernatorial nomination for Wilson and also managed his successful campaign that year. By 1911, however, as Wilson began supporting policies that Harvey regarded as too liberal, he and Wilson had a well-publicized falling out.

Hitchcock, Gilbert Monell (1859–1934, b. Omaha, Nebraska)
U.S. senator, Nebraska, 1911–1923
Gilbert Hitchcock began his career as an attorney in Omaha. In 1885 he purchased the Omaha *Evening World* and four years later bought the *Morning World,* merging the two papers into the Omaha *World-Herald,* of which he became the publisher. A long time rival of Democrat William Jennings Bryan in Nebraska politics, Hitchcock served in the House of Representatives from 1903 to 1905 and from 1907 to 1911. In 1910 he was elected to the Senate, serving in that body until 1923. In 1918, when the Republicans took control of the Senate, Hitchcock became minority leader, and in that position he had the unenviable task of trying to craft a compromise on the Treaty of Versailles that would be accepted by the president and a two-thirds majority of the senators. Wilson's stubborn rejection of everything Hitchcock proposed led to the defeat of the treaty.

Hoover, Herbert Clark (1874–1964, b. West Branch, Iowa)
U.S. food administrator, 1917–1919
Herbert Hoover was orphaned at an early age and grew up with his aunt and uncle in Oregon. After graduating from Stanford University in 1895, he began a successful career as a mining engineer that took him all over the world and made him a multimillionaire before he was forty. Retiring from business in 1914, he organized the Commission for the Relief of Belgium, which provided food for millions of Belgians and other European civilians during World War I. In June 1917, after the United States entered the war, Wilson asked Hoover to become American food administrator, in charge of securing conservation and increased production of food. Later in the war Hoover was also a member of the Interallied Food Council and the Supreme Economic Council of the wartime allies. At the end of the war Hoover accompanied Wilson to France, where he provided relief for the defeated Germans, as well as for many of the people of Eastern Europe and Russia. In 1919–1920 he was vice chairman of Wilson's Second Industrial Conference. During the 1920s he served as secretary of commerce under Presidents Harding and Calvin Coolidge, and in 1928 he was elected president.

House, Edward Mandell (1858–1938, b. Houston, Texas)
Adviser, 1911–1919
Edward M. House was a wealthy and liberal Texan who wanted political power but was prevented by fragile health from running for office. In November 1911 House met Wilson, who was then seeking the presidency, and decided that by influencing Wilson he could shape policy indirectly. Wilson soon came to regard House as his best friend, valuing him for his wide political acquaintance, shrewd advice, and unfailing discretion. Declining any office, House nevertheless became Wilson's most important adviser on both foreign and domestic policy. In 1914, 1915, and 1916, House traveled to Europe as Wilson's private emissary to try to avert or end

World War I. In September 1917 Wilson asked him to organize a group of experts, later known as the Inquiry, who would gather and organize information in preparation for a postwar peace conference. A year later, in November 1918, House served as an American representative in negotiating an armistice to end the war, and he was a member of the American Peace Commission in Paris in 1919. When Wilson returned to the United States in March 1919, House became the chief American negotiator at the peace conference. For reasons that are not completely clear, Wilson lost trust in House after this period, and although they corresponded occasionally, the two men never met again after the end of the peace conference.

Houston, David Franklin (1866–1940, b. Monroe, North Carolina)
Secretary of agriculture, 1913–1920; Secretary of treasury 1920–1921
David F. Houston was, like Wilson, trained as a political scientist and had an academic career before entering politics. He taught at Harvard and the University of Texas, among other places, and served as president of the University of Texas and chancellor of Washington University in St. Louis. Edward M. House secured Houston's appointment as secretary of agriculture, where he served from 1913 to 1920, leaving that post in 1920 only to become secretary of the Treasury. He was one of Wilson's most trusted advisers in the cabinet, and Wilson often asked his advice about issues that ranged far beyond agriculture.

Hurley, Edward Nash (1864–1933, b. Galesburg, Illinois)
Chairman, U.S. Shipping Board, 1917–1919
Edward N. Hurley was a pioneer in the manufacture of pneumatic tools in the United States and England, making his fortune in that industry before turning to banking and the manufacture of machine tools. A friend of Secretary of Commerce William Redfield, Hurley served as an American trade representative in Latin America and then as chairman of the Federal Trade Commission. When the United States entered the war, Wilson appointed him chairman of the U.S. Shipping Board and president of the Emergency Fleet Corporation, which were set up to build and buy merchant vessels to transport men and materiel to Europe.

Kitchin, Claude (1869–1923, b. Scotland Neck, North Carolina)
U.S. House of Representatives, North Carolina, 1901–1924; majority leader, 1914–1918
Claude Kitchin, an attorney, was first elected to Congress as a Democrat in 1911, where he quickly emerged as a progressive and party leader. A friend of William Jennings Bryan, Kitchin became an important supporter of Wilson's domestic program, particularly after he became majority leader in 1914, a position he retained until the Republicans regained control of the House in 1918. Although he opposed Wilson's preparedness program and eventually voted against the war resolution, he worked loyally to pass bills to finance the conflict.

Lane, Franklin Knight (1864–1921, b. Charlottetown, Prince Edward Island, Canada)
Secretary of the interior, 1913–1920
Franklin K. Lane worked for several years as a reporter before being admitted to the California bar in 1889. He worked for the San Francisco city government until Theodore Roosevelt appointed him to the Interstate Commerce Commission in 1905. In 1913 Wilson, seeking a progressive acceptable to westerners, asked Lane to join his cabinet as secretary of the interior. Although Lane's inability to keep secrets from reporters soon forced Wilson to reduce the frequency of cabinet meetings and curtail discussion of sensitive issues, Lane was so lovable that he was forgiven his indiscretions. Had ill health not forced his resignation on March 1, 1920, he would certainly have served to the end of Wilson's second term.

Lansing, Robert (1864–1928, b. Watertown, New York)
Secretary of state, 1915–1920
Robert Lansing was the son-in-law of John W. Foster, who had been secretary of state under Republican president Benjamin Harrison, and began a career in international law partly with the aid of his father-in-law's influence. Between 1896 and 1914 he represented the United States on a series of international arbitration panels and claims commissions, including the Alaska Boundary Tribunal in 1903. It was this experience, rather than his political views (which were extremely conservative), that led to his appointment as counselor of the State Department on March 20, 1914. When William Jennings Bryan resigned in June 1915, Wilson named Lansing as Bryan's successor, largely because Wilson saw Lansing as technically competent but unlikely to seek to influence policy. Lansing, it turned out, disagreed with Wilson's Mexican policy, thought the United States should have entered the war long before Wilson wanted to do so, and let it be known in the summer of 1919 that he believed Wilson had bungled the negotiation of the Treaty of Versailles. Nevertheless, despite this record of disloyalty, Wilson did not actually fire Lansing until February 13, 1920, when the president accused the secretary (erroneously) of having improperly convened cabinet meetings during Wilson's illness.

Marshall, Thomas Riley (1854–1925, b. North Manchester, Indiana)
Vice president, 1913–1921
Thomas Marshall, vice president during both of Wilson's terms, had little influence on policy and is mainly remembered for allegedly saying that "what this country needs is a good five-cent cigar." An Indiana lawyer and politician, he served as governor of Indiana from 1909 to 1913. He became the Democratic vice presidential candidate in 1913 largely as a reward to the Indiana machine for its support of Wilson in the late balloting at the Democratic convention.

McAdoo, William Gibbs (1863–1941, b. near Marietta, Georgia)
Secretary of the Treasury, 1913–1918
William Gibbs McAdoo began his career as a lawyer but achieved wealth and prominence mainly as the president of the Hudson and Manhattan Railroad Company, which in 1908 opened the first tunnel between New York and New Jersey under the Hudson River. In the summer of 1911 he volunteered his services to the Wilson presidential campaign, and by the autumn of 1912 he was effectively Wilson's campaign manager. Wilson appointed him secretary of the Treasury in 1913, and his informal influence on the administration was strengthened when he married Wilson's favorite daughter, Eleanor, on May 7, 1914. He played a crucial role in the development of the Federal Reserve System in 1914 and was largely responsible for planning and organizing the immense increase of government spending that accompanied World War I. On December 28, 1917, when the nation's railroad system all but collapsed under the weight of mobilization and a series of terrible blizzards, Wilson asked McAdoo to become director of a nationalized railroad system. Although McAdoo was clearly one of the most competent members of Wilson's administration and the president's logical successor for the Democratic presidential nomination in 1920, Wilson declined to support him, perhaps because the president cherished illusions of running for a third term. One of the most ardent segregationists in the administration, McAdoo drew attacks from civil rights supporters.

McCombs, William Frank (1875–1921, b. Hamburg, Arkansas)
Chairman, Democratic National Committee, 1912–1916
William McCombs, a New York lawyer and former student of Wilson's at Princeton, was an early and active supporter of Wilson's presidential campaign. Although he suffered from physical and mental problems that would contribute to his early death, McCombs was an enthusiastic and energetic political organizer, and Wilson named him his campaign manager and later chairman of the Democratic National Committee. As the 1912 campaign progressed, it became clear that McCombs was neither a good fund-raiser nor adept at managing people. In the later stages of the campaign he was gently pushed aside and William Gibbs McAdoo largely took over as manager. Following the election, Wilson offered McCombs an ambassadorship to France rather than the cabinet position he wanted. Hurt and offended, McCombs declined the ambassadorship but retained the chairmanship of the DNC until 1916, when Wilson maneuvered him out of that post, as well.

McCormick, Vance Criswell (1872–1946, Harrisburg, Pennsylvania)
Adviser, 1911–1919
Vance McCormick, a newspaper publisher and mayor (1902–1905) in Harrisburg, Pennsylvania, was an early Wilson supporter in that large and politically important state. He helped to organize and finance Wilson's first campaign trip in the spring of 1911 and became one of Wilson's inner circle of campaign advisers. In

1916, when Wilson eased William McCombs out of the chairmanship of the Democratic National Committee, McCormick became his successor. That same year Wilson named him as a director of a Federal Reserve bank, and during the war he served as the chairman of the War Trade Board, as a member of a special trade mission to England and France, and after the war as an economic adviser to Wilson at the peace conference in Paris.

McReynolds, James Clark (1862–1946, b. Elkton, Kentucky)
Associate justice of the Supreme Court, 1914–1941
James McReynolds practiced law in Nashville, Tennessee, for several years before being named an assistant attorney general by Theodore Roosevelt in 1903 because of his reputation as an opponent of "trusts." At the end of the Roosevelt administration he moved to New York City, where he practiced until he was named to Wilson's cabinet in 1913 as attorney general. Wilson appointed him without meeting him first, and that proved a mistake. McReynolds was abrasive and rude to everyone he thought inferior to him, which included almost everyone, and he soon became the most unpopular man in the cabinet. In August 1914 Wilson seized an opportunity to get him out of the cabinet by appointing him as an associate justice of the U.S. Supreme Court.

Meredith, Edwin Thomas (1876–1928, b. Avoca, Iowa)
Secretary of agriculture, 1920–1921
E.T. Meredith spent most of his career as the publisher of newspapers and magazines for farmers and as a director of midwestern banks. In 1914 he was the unsuccessful Democratic candidate for U.S. senator in Iowa, and in 1916 he was again unsuccessful as a candidate for governor. He was a member of Wilson's First Industrial Conference in 1919, and in January 1920 he succeeded David F. Houston as secretary of agriculture, serving until the end of the administration.

Palmer, Alexander Mitchell (1872–1936, b. Moosehead, Pennsylvania)
Attorney general, 1919–1921
A. Mitchell Palmer was perhaps the most controversial member of Wilson's administration because of his role during the "Red Scare" of 1919–1920. Palmer, a lawyer, became active in Pennsylvania politics as a progressive in the early 1900s and was elected to Congress in 1908, where he served until 1915. He was an early and vigorous advocate of Wilson's presidential nomination in 1912 and a strong supporter of Wilson's New Freedom Program in Congress. Following a failed bid for the Senate in 1914, Wilson appointed him to the U.S. Court of Claims in 1915 and as alien property custodian after the United States entered World War I in 1917. Despite Palmer's record of loyalty, Wilson did not entirely trust his judgment, and it was only because he was focused on the peace conference that he agreed to Palmer's appointment as attorney general in March 1919. Wilson's uncertainty was soon borne out when a wave of strikes and bombings that spring created a national panic to which

Palmer responded by authorizing mass and often illegal arrests of native and foreign-born people suspected of being radicals. Most of those arrested were later freed by the courts, but several hundred aliens were deported without hearings.

Payne, John Barton (1855–1935, b. Pruntytown, Virginia [now West Virginia])
Secretary of the interior, 1920–1921
John Barton Payne practiced law and served as a judge in West Virginia and Chicago between 1876 and 1917. In 1917 he came to Washington to serve as general counsel for the U.S. Railroad Administration and the U.S. Shipping Board, of which he became chairman in 1919. From February 1920 until the end of the administration he was secretary of the interior, and from May 18, 1920, until April 1921 he was also director general of the nationalized railroads. From October 1, 1921, until his death he was chairman of the American Red Cross.

Pershing, John Joseph (1860–1948, b. Linn County, Missouri)
General; commander, American Expeditionary Force, 1917–1918
"Black Jack" Pershing, commander of the American Expeditionary Force (AEF) during World War I, graduated from the U.S. Military Academy at West Point in 1886 and served in campaigns against Indians in the West in the late 1880s and 1890s, in Cuba during the Spanish-American War, and in the Philippines during the insurrection. Later, he served as a military attaché in Tokyo and on the general staff in Washington. In March 1916 he commanded the American forces sent into Mexico in pursuit of Pancho Villa, and he was the obvious candidate to command the AEF when the United States entered the war in 1917. Like Wilson, he believed strongly that American forces in Europe should fight as independent units, not be subsumed into armies commanded by the British and French.

Redfield, William Cox (1858–1932, b. Albany, New York)
Secretary of commerce, 1913–1919
William C. Redfield was a successful businessman in New York when he was elected to the House of Representatives in 1910 as a Democrat. He caught Wilson's attention because of his support for tariff reduction, which was unusual for a businessman, and the two corresponded before Wilson was elected president. It was largely because of Redfield's stand on the tariff that Wilson invited him to become secretary of commerce. In that position Redfield served as a liaison with the business community and as a vigorous advocate of expanding American foreign trade and overseas investments.

Roosevelt, Franklin Delano (1882–1945, b. Hyde Park, New York)
Assistant secretary of the navy, 1913–1921
Franklin Delano Roosevelt followed in the footsteps of his cousin, Theodore, by serving in the New York legislature, as governor of New York, as assistant secretary

of the navy under Wilson from 1913 to 1921, and as candidate for the vice presidency in 1920. Wealthy, charming, and the bearer of a famous name, Roosevelt achieved greater prominence in the Wilson administration than was usual for an assistant secretary, but he did not much influence policy.

Tumulty, Joseph Patrick (1879–1954, b. Jersey City, New Jersey)
Wilson's private secretary, 1910–1921
Joe Tumulty was born into an Irish immigrant family and entered politics in Jersey City, in the middle of one of the most boss-ridden areas of the state, yet he retained his integrity and became a dedicated reformer. He served in the New Jersey legislature from 1907 to 1910, when he became Wilson's private secretary and political adviser, following his beloved boss to the White House in 1913. Aside from clerks, typists, and domestic workers, he was virtually the whole White House staff during the Wilson era, serving as press secretary, legislative liaison, political adviser, and in a host of other capacities. He was so close to the president that Edith, Wilson's second wife, became jealous of him and tried to get Wilson to fire him in 1916. Fortunately, more politically astute advisers prevented that from happening, and Tumulty served throughout the remainder of the administration, though the relationship between the two men was less close than it had been previously.

Underwood, Oscar Wilder (1862–1929, b. Louisville, Kentucky)
U.S. senator, Alabama, 1915–1927
Oscar W. Underwood was the key figure in Congress in shaping and passing the Wilson administration's tariff reduction bill, which also included the first income tax provision under the recently passed Sixteenth Amendment to the Constitution. Although trained as a lawyer, Underwood was primarily a politician, entering Democratic Party affairs in Alabama in the 1880s and being elected to Congress in 1894. He served in the House until 1914, when he was elected to the Senate, serving there until 1927. In 1912 Underwood was a serious candidate for the Democratic presidential nomination. When it became clear at the Democratic convention that Underwood could not secure the nomination himself, he formed an alliance with Wilson's supporters to deny it to Champ Clark, eventually releasing his supporters to vote for Wilson when it became obvious he could not win. During Wilson's first term Underwood was chairman of the House Ways and Means Committee and majority leader, so his support of the administration's programs was crucial. He drafted and managed the House's passage of the administration's tariff bill, the Underwood-Simmons Act.

Wilson, Edith Bolling Galt (1872–1961, b. Wytheville, Virginia)
First lady
Edith Wilson, Woodrow Wilson's second wife, grew up in a traditional family in southwestern Virginia. In 1896 she married Norman Galt, owner of a Washington

jewelry store. When he died in 1908 she ran the store herself, proving to be a good businesswoman. Following her husband's death, she supplemented her scanty formal education with reading and travel, especially in Europe, and was regarded in Washington social circles as an intelligent and entertaining conversationalist. In March 1915 Wilson's cousin introduced her to the president, and they quickly became close. They were engaged secretly in late June but did not announce it to the public until October. The wedding took place on December 18, 1915. Edith was less interested in social issues than Ellen, but, from the outset, Wilson consulted her about policy. She was jealous of Wilson's close relations with Edward M. House and Joseph Tumulty and used her influence to distance her husband from them. Following Wilson's stroke in October 1919, she and the doctors were virtually the only people who saw the president regularly, and she not only controlled his visitors but also decided what documents he would see. Often papers were returned to their senders with marginal notes in her handwriting, giving what purported to be the president's decision on the matter in question. Her decision that it would be bad for the president's health to resign kept him in office despite his inability to perform his duties most of the last year and a half of his term. Following his death in February 1924, she became the guardian of their house on S Street in Washington, which she kept just as it had been when he lived there, and the protector, insofar as she was able, of his reputation.

Wilson, Ellen Louise Axson (1860–1914, b. Savannah, Georgia)
First lady
Ellen Wilson was the rock upon which Wilson built his life prior to her death in 1914. The daughter of a Presbyterian minister, she was a talented portrait and landscape painter, a devoted wife and mother, and a gentle but effective voice for social reform. When Wilson was governor of New Jersey, she encouraged him to make reform of the state systems for the care of prisoners and the insane a priority. In Washington, she became president of the Women's Department of the National Civic Association, and at the time of her death a bill she had promoted for the improvement of living conditions for African Americans in Washington was pending in Congress.

Wilson, William Beauchop (1862–1934, b. Blantyre, Scotland)
Secretary of labor, 1913–1921
William Wilson came with his family to the United States in 1870 and the next year went to work in the Pennsylvania coal mines. He joined a miners' union in Pennsylvania in 1888 and was an organizer of the United Mine Workers in 1890. He served in Congress from 1907 to 1913, when Samuel Gompers recommended him to Wilson to head the new Department of Labor, which had recently been separated from the Department of Commerce. He held the position throughout the eight years of the Wilson administration.

Appendix B
Key Events in Wilson's Life

1849
June 7 Joseph Ruggles Wilson and Janet Woodrow are married in Steubenville, Ohio.
1851
October 20 Marion Williamson Wilson is born.
1853
September 8 Annie Josephine Wilson is born.
1855
Wilson family moves to Staunton, Virginia, where Joseph Ruggles Wilson becomes pastor of the First Presbyterian Church.
1856
December 28–29 Thomas Woodrow Wilson is born near midnight in the Presbyterian Manse at Staunton, Virginia.
1858
January Wilson family moves to Augusta, Georgia.
1861–1865
Civil War.
1867
July 20 Joseph Ruggles Wilson Jr. is born.
1870
Wilson family moves to Columbia, South Carolina, where Joseph Ruggles Wilson joins the faculty of the Columbia Theological Seminary.
1873
July 5 Wilson becomes a member of Columbia's First Presbyterian Church.
1873–1874
Wilson attends Davidson College.
1874
Joseph Ruggles Wilson resigns his faculty position at the Columbia Theological Seminary and accepts a call to the First Presbyterian Church of Wilmington, North Carolina.
1874–1875
Wilson studies at home in Wilmington.
1875–1879
Wilson attends the College of New Jersey at Princeton (later Princeton University), receiving a B.A. in 1879.

1879

August Wilson's first major article, "Cabinet Government in the United States," is published in the *International Review.*

1879–December 1880

Wilson attends the University of Virginia Law School.

1881–1882

Wilson completes his study of the law at home.

Summer 1882–Summer 1883

Wilson practices law in Atlanta in partnership with Edward I. Renick; passes the Georgia Bar Examination in October 1882.

1883

ca. April 8 Wilson meets Ellen Axson in Rome, Georgia.

September 14 Ellen and Woodrow are engaged.

1883–1885

Wilson is a student in the Ph.D. program in history and political science at the Johns Hopkins University in Baltimore.

1885

January Congressional Government: A Study in American Politics is published.

June 24 Wilson marries Ellen Axson in Savannah, Georgia.

1885–1888

Wilson is a faculty member at Bryn Mawr College.

1886

April 16 Margaret Woodrow Wilson is born.

Wilson awarded a Ph.D. by Johns Hopkins.

1887

July "The Study of Administration" is published in *Political Science Quarterly.*

August 28 Jessie Woodrow Wilson is born.

1888

April 14 Wilson's mother, Janet Woodrow Wilson, dies.

1888–1890

Wilson is a faculty member at Wesleyan University, Middletown, Connecticut.

1888–1896

Wilson is a guest lecturer on administration at Johns Hopkins.

1889

October 16 Eleanor Randolph Wilson is born.

Autumn The State: Elements of Historical and Practical Politics, A Sketch of Institutional History and Administration is published.

1890

August 14 Wilson's sister, Marion Wilson (Kennedy), dies.

1890–1902

Wilson is professor of jurisprudence and political economy at Princeton.

1893

Division and Reunion, 1829–1889, is published.

1896

George Washington (biography) is published.

ca. May 27 Wilson suffers a possible cerebral stroke.

Summer Wilson's first trip to England.

October 21 Princeton becomes a university and Wilson delivers the major address, "Princeton in the Nation's Service."

1898

Spanish-American War.

1899

Summer Wilson's second trip to England.

1901

September President William McKinley is assassinated.

1902

A History of the American People is published in five volumes.

June 9 Wilson elected president of Princeton; inaugurated October 25.

1903

January 21 Wilson's father, Joseph Ruggles Wilson, dies.

1904

May–June Wilson suffers temporary partial paralysis of his right arm.

December Wilson has operation for intestinal hernia.

1905

January–February Wilson is bedridden because of phlebitis following his hernia operation.

1906

February 3 In a speech at the Lotos Club in New York, George Harvey suggests nominating Wilson for the presidency.

May 28 Wilson suffers a possible stroke with temporary blindness in one eye.

July–August Wilson's third trip to Great Britain.

December Wilson presents plan to trustees to house students in quadrangles.

1907

January Wilson's first trip to Bermuda.

November Wilson's right arm is again temporarily paralyzed during an attack he labels "neuritis."

1908

January Wilson's second trip to Bermuda.

Constitutional Government in the United States is published.

1910

September 15 Wilson receives Democratic nomination for governor of New Jersey.

November 8 Wilson elected governor of New Jersey.

December 20 Wilson resigns presidency of Princeton.

1911

January 17 Wilson inaugurated as governor of New Jersey.

January 25 Democratic Party boss James Smith admits defeat in his attempt to be reelected to the Senate from New Jersey.

March–April Wilson travels to the West and South to campaign for presidential nomination.

May *World's Work* magazine publishes a "Wilson edition," with the governor's picture on the cover and articles on his presidential candidacy.

November Republicans regain control of New Jersey legislature.

November 24 Wilson first meets Edward M. House.

1912

January 8 At a Jackson Day dinner in Raleigh, North Carolina, Wilson and William Jennings Bryan patch up any differences resulting from the publication of the 1907 "Joline letter."

June 20 Democratic Convention meets in Baltimore.

July 2 Wilson nominated for the presidency on the forty-sixth ballot.

August 6 Theodore Roosevelt accepts the presidential nomination of the Progressive Party.

November 5 Wilson is elected president.

1913

February 25 The 16th Amendment to the Constitution, authorizing a national income tax, goes into effect.

February 28 A subcommittee (the "Pujo Committee") of the House Committee on Banking and Currency reports on the increasing concentration of power within the banking industry, thus making Wilson's proposed reforms more urgent.

March 1 Wilson resigns as governor of New Jersey.

March 4 Wilson inaugurated as president.

March 11 Wilson issues a statement on Latin America in which he stresses that the United States will support only legal and democratic governments.

March 18 Wilson announces the withdrawal of administration support for the participation of American bankers in an international consortium to loan money to China because he believes that concessions demanded by foreign lenders undermine Chinese sovereignty.

April 8 After calling a special session of Congress to pass tariff reform, Wilson breaks a precedent dating to the presidency of John Adams by delivering his speech on the topic personally to a joint session of the two houses.

Spring A risk of war with Japan arises when California adopts a law banning land ownership by Asian aliens. Wilson refuses to move warships into forward positions as proposed by the navy and sends Secretary of State William Jennings Bryan to California in a futile effort to secure less provocative language in the pending legislation.

May 26 At a press conference, Wilson claims (erroneously but effectively) that big business is lobbying heavily in opposition to tariff reduction.

May 31 The 17th Amendment to the Constitution, providing for the direct election of U.S. senators, goes into effect.

June 23 Wilson again addresses a joint session of Congress, this time urging the passage of banking and currency reform legislation that he has been developing in consultation with congressional leaders.

Summer Onset of Ellen's illness (Bright's Disease).

October 3 Wilson signs the Underwood Tariff, including the first federal income tax under the recently ratified Sixteenth Amendment to the Constitution, into law.

October 27 In a speech at Mobile, Alabama, Wilson promises that the United States will never again seek to annex any land in Latin America.

November 25 Jessie Wilson marries Francis Sayre at the White House.

December 23 Wilson signs Federal Reserve Act.

1914

January 20 In a speech to a joint session of Congress, Wilson urges passage of both a new law clarifying and prohibiting anticompetitive business practices and a law creating an Interstate Trade Commission (later renamed Federal Trade Commission) with discretionary power to advise businesses on competitive matters.

February 3 Wilson announces the lifting of an embargo imposed during the Taft administration on arms shipments to Mexico.

Late winter The United States and Japan sign a treaty banning future state restrictions on Asian land ownership, but the treaty is never submitted to the Senate for approval.

April 9–21 Using the arrest of some American sailors in the port of Tampico as a pretext, Wilson orders the occupation of Veracruz, Mexico, in hopes of forcing the resignation of dictator Victoriano Huerta.

May 7 Eleanor Wilson marries William Gibbs McAdoo at the White House.

May 8 Wilson signs the Smith-Lever Act creating an agricultural extension program on the basis of collaboration between the Agriculture Department and state agricultural agencies.

May 18–July 14 A mediation conference sponsored by Argentina, Brazil, and Chile meets at Niagara Falls, Ontario, to seek a resolution of Mexican-American conflicts. On July 14 Huerta resigns and leaves Mexico.

May–June During his first informal mission to Europe on Wilson's behalf, House studies the diminishing possibility of avoiding war and explores the possibility that the Germans and English might accept American assistance in preventing disaster.

June 28 Austrian Archduke Franz Ferdinand is assassinated in Sarajevo.

July–August World War I begins in Europe.

August 6 Ellen Wilson dies.

September 26 Wilson signs Federal Trade Commission Act.

October 15 Wilson signs Clayton Antitrust Act.

November 23 The last American troops leave Veracruz, Mexico.

1915

January–June During his second trip to Europe as Wilson's informal emissary, Edward M. House explores the possibility that the belligerents might accept American mediation and concludes that there is little prospect of success.

January Japan delivers twenty-one demands asking that China grant substantial control over much of its territory and administrative machinery.

February 4 Germany announces the establishment of a war zone around the British Isles in which submarines will attack belligerent-owned vessels and may attack neutral ships.

February 10 Wilson sends to Germany a note stating that the United States will hold Germany to "strict accountability" for injuries to Americans or damage to American property as a result of submarine attacks.

March 4 Wilson signs La Follette Seamen's Act.

March 23 Wilson meets Edith Bolling Galt.

March 28 An American, Leon C. Thrasher, is killed during a submarine attack on a British ship, the *Falaba,* on which he is traveling.

May 1 An American ship, the *Gulflight,* is torpedoed and three Americans are killed.

May 7 The British passenger liner, *Lusitania,* is sunk off the coast of Ireland, with the deaths of 1,198 passengers and crew, including 128 Americans.

May 10 In a speech to newly naturalized citizens, Wilson declares that there is such a thing as a nation being "too proud to fight."

May 13 Wilson drafts and sends a sharp protest to Germany for the *Lusitania* attack.

June 8 Secretary of State Bryan resigns, convinced that Wilson's insistence that German submarines must conform to traditional international law will lead to war. Wilson appoints Robert Lansing as Bryan's successor.

August 4 Wilson orders American military intervention in Haiti.

October 6 Wilson announces his engagement to Edith Bolling Galt.

November 4 Wilson endorses proposals for army and navy expansion.

December 18 Wilson marries Edith Bolling Galt.

1916

January–March During his third trip to Europe for Wilson, Edward M. House again explores the prospects for peace but concludes the United States will eventually have to enter the war on the Allied side.

January 24 Wilson announces his plan to create a nonpartisan Federal Tariff Commission.

January 28 Wilson nominates Louis Brandeis to the Supreme Court.

February 10 Secretary of War Lindley M. Garrison resigns.

February 22 The House-Grey memorandum is signed. It suggests that the United States might enter the war on the Allied side if the Germans spurn a call for a peace conference

February 22 and *25* McLemore and Gore Resolutions requesting that the State Department deny passports to Americans intending to travel through the German war zone around the British Isles are introduced in Congress (tabled on March 3 and 7).

March 9 Pancho Villa raids Columbus, New Mexico.

March 7 Newton D. Baker is appointed secretary of war.

March 16 American troops under the command of General John J. Pershing enter Mexico in pursuit of Pancho Villa.

March 24 The French passenger vessel, *Sussex,* is torpedoed in the English Channel, with injuries to several American passengers.

April 18 An American note to Germany following the sinking of the *Sussex* demands that Germany abandon its present methods of submarine warfare.

May 4 Germany issues the "*Sussex* Pledge" promising to avoid surprise submarine attacks on freight and passenger-carrying vessels.

May 27 In a speech to the League to Enforce Peace, Wilson promises that the United States will join a postwar "association of nations."

June 3 Wilson signs the National Defense Act providing for an expansion of the regular army and the creation of a federally controlled national guard.

June 10 The Republicans nominate Charles Evans Hughes for president; the Progressives nominate Theodore Roosevelt, who refuses the nomination and endorses Hughes.

June 14 The Democratic Convention meets in St. Louis.

June 16 Wilson is renominated by the Democrats for the presidency.

June 21 American soldiers are attacked at Carrizal, Mexico, by Mexican government forces, with twelve Americans killed and twenty-three captured.

July 11 Wilson signs Federal Aid Road Act.

July 17 Wilson signs Federal Farm Loan Act creating a new system of banks to provide credit for farmers.

August 29 Wilson signs Jones Act promising independence to the Philippines.

August 29 Wilson authorizes the establishment of a Council of National Defense made up of six cabinet members and charged with coordinating industry and resources for national defense.

September 2 Wilson signs Adamson Act mandating an eight-hour workday for railroad workers.

September 3 Wilson signs Keating-Owen Child Labor Act.

September 6–January 1917 A Mexican-American commission meeting at New London, Connecticut, fails to resolve outstanding issues between the two countries.

September 7 Wilson signs the Shipping Act creating a U.S. Shipping Board authorized to build, buy, or requisition merchant vessels.

September 16 Wilson's sister, Annie Wilson (Howe) dies.

November 7–9 Wilson is reelected after uncertainty about California's vote.

November 26 Wilson orders military intervention in the Dominican Republic.

December 18 Wilson sends an appeal to the belligerents to state their war aims publicly, in the hope of finding a basis for American mediation.

1917

January 6 An imperial conference in Germany decides to begin unrestricted submarine warfare, in hopes of forcing Britain and France to surrender before the United States can mobilize.

January 22 Wilson proposes terms for ending the European war in his "peace without victory" speech to the Senate.

January 31 Germany announces unrestricted submarine warfare.

February 3 Wilson severs diplomatic relations with Germany.

February 5 American troops are withdrawn from Mexico.

February 24 The Zimmermann telegram proposing a military alliance among Germany, Mexico, and Japan in the event of an American declaration of war on Germany is given to Wilson by the British.

February 26 Wilson requests approval from Congress to arm American merchant ships. The House approves overwhelmingly, but in the Senate the proposal is filibustered to death on March 4 by opponents whom Wilson describes as "a little group of willful men."

March 5 Wilson's second inauguration.

March 9 Wilson announces that a 1797 law authorizes the arming of merchant vessels.

March 12 The Menshevik Revolution in Russia overthrows the tsar and establishes a democratic government.

March 18 Three American ships, the *City of Memphis, Illinois,* and *Vigilancia,* are sunk by German submarines, with fifteen Americans killed.

April 2 Wilson asks Congress for a declaration of war against Germany.

April 6 Congress votes to declare war.

April 13 Wilson creates the Committee on Public Information to manage news from the war and build public support for the war effort.

May 18 Wilson signs the Selective Service Act establishing a draft for the military.

June 15 Wilson signs the Espionage Act providing fines and imprisonment for anyone convicted of assisting the enemy and authorizing the postmaster general to censor the mails.

July 28 Wilson creates the War Industries Board, which replaces the Council of National Defense as the coordinating body for economic mobilization.

August 10 Wilson signs the Lever Food and Fuel Bill placing the production and distribution of food and fuel under the supervision of Food Administrator Herbert Hoover and Fuel Administrator Harry A. Garfield.

October 3 Wilson signs the War Revenue Act making the income tax the principal source of wartime revenue.

November 2 The Lansing-Ishii agreement acknowledges that Japan has "special interests in China."

November The Bolshevik Revolution in Russia brings a communist government to power.

December 7 The United States declares war on Austria-Hungary.

December 26 William Gibbs McAdoo is appointed railroad administrator and the railroads are nationalized for the duration of the war.

1918

January 8 In his "Fourteen Points" speech to a joint session of Congress Wilson defines his vision of the peace that should follow the end of the war.

January 16 Federal Fuel Administrator Harry Garfield issues an emergency order closing most factories east of the Mississippi for five days to resolve massive railroad tie-ups.

March 3 The Treaty of Brest-Litovsk withdraws Russia from the war.

March 20 Wilson creates a war cabinet made up of the heads of mobilization agencies.

March 21 Germany launches a massive offensive on the Western Front.

May 16 Wilson signs a Sedition Act making criticism of the war effort illegal.

May 20 Wilson heads off a congressional effort to wrest control over mobilization away from the administration by signing the Overman Act, which authorizes him to reorganize the government as needed to prosecute the war effort.

June 6–July 1 American soldiers take part in their first major engagement of the war in the Battle of Belleau Wood.

July 17 Wilson reluctantly agrees to contribute a small number of American troops to a joint allied intervention in Siberia; they will remain until April 1920.

September 12–16 American forces launch the first offensive, at the St. Mihiel Salient, in which they take primary responsibility.

September 26–November 11 Most American forces in Europe are engaged in the Meuse-Argonne Offensive.

October 6 In a message from Prince Max of Baden, the new head of the German government, Germany offers to surrender on the basis of the Fourteen Points.

October 25 Wilson issues an appeal to the voters to elect Democrats to Congress.

November 5 In midterm elections the Republicans win majorities of one in the Senate and forty-five in the House.

November 9 The German Kaiser abdicates.

November 11 The war ends with the signing of an armistice.

November 16 Wilson announces he will personally head the American delegation to the Paris Peace Conference.

December 4 Wilson sails for Europe aboard the *George Washington.*

December 13 Wilson lands at Brest, France.

December 14 Massive demonstrations welcome Wilson to Paris.

1919

January 12 The peace conference begins serious work with the first meeting of the Council of Ten.

January 18 The first plenary session of the peace conference meets.

February 14 Wilson presents the text of the League of Nations covenant to a plenary session of the peace conference.

February 24–March 13 Wilson returns to the United States to attend to domestic affairs and build support for his peace efforts.

March 3 Henry Cabot Lodge, incoming chairman of the Senate Foreign Relations Committee, presents to the Senate a "round robin" resolution objecting to the proposed terms of the peace treaty and appending the signatures of enough senators and senators-elect to defeat it.

March 26 Wilson meets with the congressional foreign affairs committees to explain the peace treaty taking shape in Paris.

Spring 1919–1920 Major labor strikes and a series of bombings provoke a "Red Scare," which Attorney General A. Mitchell Palmer exploits to authorize arbitrary arrests and deportations of foreign-born "radicals."

April Wilson suffers an attack of what his physicians believe is influenza but continues to work on the peace treaty from his sickbed.

May 7 A draft of the peace treaty is submitted to the Germans.

June 28 The Treaty of Versailles is signed in an elaborate ceremony in the Hall of Mirrors at the royal palace at Versailles.

July 8 Wilson returns to the United States.

July 10 Wilson presents the Treaty of Versailles to the Senate in an emotional speech.

August 19 Wilson defends the treaty in a tense three-hour meeting with the members of the Senate Foreign Relations Committee.

September 3 Wilson leaves Washington for a speaking trip throughout the West to build popular support for the Treaty of Versailles.

September 25 Wilson collapses after a speech in Pueblo, Colorado, and is rushed back to Washington.

October 2 Wilson suffers a massive and paralytic stroke.

November 6 Lodge proposes fourteen reservations to the Treaty of Versailles.

November 19 In a series of votes, the Senate rejects the treaty, both with and without reservations.

1920

January 8 From his sickroom Wilson issues a call for making the autumn election a "great and solemn referendum" on the Treaty of Versailles.

January 15 National Prohibition becomes effective under the 18th Amendment to the Constitution.

March 19 The Senate rejects the Treaty of Versailles for a second time.

April 13 Wilson meets with his cabinet for the first time since his stroke on October 2.

August 26 Woman suffrage becomes effective under the 19th Amendment to the Constitution.

November 2 Warren G. Harding is elected president.

1921

March 4 Harding and Calvin Coolidge are inaugurated as president and vice president.

March 15 Friends and admirers of Wilson gather at the Biltmore Hotel in New York City to plan an endowment in his name. The conference will eventually result in the establishment of the Woodrow Wilson Foundation.

Summer 1921 Wilson and former secretary of state Bainbridge Colby enter into a law partnership, opening offices in Washington, D.C.; the firm is unsuccessful because Wilson refuses the high-profile cases commanded by his status as a former president.

1922

April The Women's Pan-American Conference meet with Wilson to pay tribute to his peace efforts.

December 31 The Wilson/Colby law partnership is dissolved.

1923

August Wilson's last article, "The Road Away from Revolution," is published in *The Atlantic Monthly.*

November 10 Wilson urges American membership in the League of Nations in a radio address from his home.

1924

January 16 Two hundred men and women from the Democratic National Committee make a pilgrimage to Wilson's home in order to commend him for his service to the nation and the world.

February 3 Wilson dies at his home on S Street in Washington.

February 6 After a funeral service, Wilson is entombed in a chapel of the National Cathedral in Washington.

Appendix C
Wilson's Cabinet, 1913–1921

Title	Officeholder	Dates of service
Vice president	Thomas R. Marshall	1913–1921
Attorney general	James Clark McReynolds	1913–1914
	Thomas Watt Gregory	1914–1919
	A. Mitchell Palmer	1919–1921
Postmaster general	Albert Sidney Burleson	1913–1921
Secretary of the navy	Josephus Daniels	1913–1921
Secretary of the Treasury	William Gibbs McAdoo	1913–1918
	Carter Glass	1918–1920
	David F. Houston	1920–1921
Secretary of state	William Jennings Bryan	1913–1915
	Robert Lansing	1915–1920
	Bainbridge Colby	1920–1921
Secretary of war	Lindley M. Garrison	1913–1916
	Newton D. Baker	1916–1921
Secretary of the interior	Franklin Knight Lane	1913–1920
	John Barton Payne	1920–1921
Secretary of commerce	William C. Redfield	1913–1919
	Joshua Willis Alexander	1919–1921
Secretary of labor	William Beauchop Wilson	1913–1921
Secretary of agriculture	David F. Houston	1913–1920
	Edwin T. Meredith	1920–1921

Works Cited

Axson, Stockton. 1993. *"Brother Woodrow": A Memoir of Woodrow Wilson.* ed. by Arthur S. Link and others. Princeton: Princeton University Press.

Baker, Ray Stannard. 1927–1939. *Woodrow Wilson: Life and Letters,* 8 vols. Garden City, N.Y.: Doubleday, Page & Co.

Blum, John Morton. 1956. *Woodrow Wilson and the Politics of Morality.* Boston: Little, Brown.

Buckingham, Peter H., comp. 1990. *Woodrow Wilson: A Bibliography of His Times and Presidency.* Wilmington, Del.: Scholarly Resources.

Burdick, Frank. 1968. "Woodrow Wilson and the Underwood Tariff." *Mid-America* 50 (October 1968): 272–290.

Burns, James MacGregor. 1966. *Presidential Government: The Crucible of Leadership.* Boston: Houghton Mifflin.

Calhoun, Frederick S. 1986. *Power and Principle: Armed Intervention in Wilsonian Foreign Policy.* Kent, Ohio: Kent State University Press.

Chambers II, John Whiteclay. 1987. *To Raise an Army: The Draft Comes to Modern America.* New York: Free Press.

Clements, Kendrick A. 1992. *The Presidency of Woodrow Wilson.* Lawrence: University Press of Kansas.

———. 1987. *Woodrow Wilson: World Statesman.* Boston: Twayne.

Coffman, Edward. 1968. *The War to End All Wars: The American Military Experience in World War I.* New York: Oxford University Press.

Cooper, John Milton. 1976. "The Command of Gold Reversed: American Loans to Britain, 1915–1917." *Pacific Historical Review* 45 (2): 209–230.

Cronon, E. David, ed. 1963. *The Cabinet Diaries of Josephus Daniels, 1913–1921.* Lincoln: University of Nebraska Press.

Dimock, Marshall E. 1957. "Woodrow Wilson as Legislative Leader." *Journal of Politics* 19 (February): 3–19.

Ferrell, Robert. 1985. *Woodrow Wilson and World War I, 1917–1921.* New York: Harper & Row.

————. 1993. "Woodrow Wilson: A Misfit in Office?" in Joseph G. Dawson, ed., *Commanders in Chief: Presidential Leadership in Modern Wars*. Lawrence: University Press of Kansas.

Floto, Inga. 1973. *Colonel House in Paris: A Study of American Policy at the Paris Peace Conference 1919*. Princeton: Princeton University Press.

Friedman, Leon, and Fred L. Israel, eds. 1969. *The Justices of the United States Supreme Court, 1789–1969, Their Lives and Major Opinions*, 5 vols. New York: Chelsea House.

Grayson, Cary T. 1960. *Woodrow Wilson: An Intimate Memoir*. New York: Holt, Rinehart and Winston.

Grey, Edward. 1925. *Twenty-Five Years*, 2 vols. New York: Frederick A. Stokes.

Hagedorn, Hermann, ed. 1923–1926. *The Works of Theodore Roosevelt*, memorial ed., 24 vols. New York: Scribner's.

Hamm, Richard F. 1995. *Shaping the Eighteenth Amendment: Temperance Reform, Legal Culture, and the Polity, 1880–1920*. Chapel Hill: University of North Carolina Press.

Handberg, Roger Jr. 1976. "Decision-Making in a Natural Court, 1916–1921." *American Politics Quarterly* 4 (July): 357–378.

Heckscher, August. 1991. *Woodrow Wilson*. New York: Scribner's.

Hirst, David W. 1965. *Woodrow Wilson, Reform Governor: A Documentary Narrative*. Princeton: Van Nostrand.

House, Edward Mandell. 1912. *Philip Dru, Administrator: A Story of Tomorrow*. New York: B. W. Huebsch.

Houston, David F. 1926. *Eight Years with Wilson's Cabinet, 1913 to 1920, with a Personal Estimate of the President*, 2 vols. Garden City, N.Y.: Doubleday, Page & Co.

Juergens, George. 1981. *News from the White House: The Presidential-Press Relationship in the Progressive Era*. Chicago: University of Chicago Press.

Kyvig, David E. 1996. *Explicit and Authentic Acts: Amending the U.S. Constitution, 1776–1995*. Lawrence: University Press of Kansas.

Lane, Anne, and Louise Wall, eds. 1922. *The Letters of Franklin K. Lane* (New York: Houghton Mifflin), 131–133.

Link, Arthur S. 1971. *The Higher Realism of Woodrow Wilson and Other Essays*. Nashville, Tenn.: Vanderbilt University Press.

Link, Arthur S. 1947–1965. *Wilson*, 5 vols. Princeton: Princeton University Press.

————. 1947. *Wilson: The Road to the White House*.

———. 1956. *Wilson: The New Freedom.*

———. 1960. *Wilson: The Struggle for Neutrality, 1914–1915.*

———. 1964. *Wilson: Confusions and Crises, 1915–1916.*

———. 1965. *Wilson: Campaigns for Progressivism and Peace, 1916–1917.*

Link, Arthur S. ed. 1982. *Woodrow Wilson and a Revolutionary World, 1913–1921.* Chapel Hill: University of North Carolina Press.

Link, Arthur S., and others, eds. 1966–1994. *The Papers of Woodrow Wilson,* 69 vols. Princeton: Princeton University Press. For a breakdown of the material contained in each volume of the series, see "Note on *The Papers of Woodrow Wilson,*" following the list of references.

Lunardini, Christine A., and Thomas J. Knock. "Woodrow Wilson and Woman Suffrage: A New Look." *Political Science Quarterly* 95 (winter 1980–1981): 655–671.

Martin, Lawrence. 1973. *Peace Without Victory: Woodrow Wilson and the British Liberals.* Port Washington, N.Y.: Kennikat.

May, Ernest R. 1960. "Wilson (1917–1918)," in Ernest R. May, ed., *The Ultimate Decision: The President as Commander in Chief.* New York: George Braziller.

Mulder, John M., Ernest M. White, and Ethel S. White, comps. 1997. *Woodrow Wilson: A Bibliography.* Westport, Conn.: Greenwood.

Pratt, Walter F. Jr. 1999. *The Supreme Court under Edward Douglass White, 1910–1921.* Columbia: University of South Carolina Press.

Reynolds, John F. 1988. *Testing Democracy: Electoral Behavior and Progressive Reform in New Jersey, 1880–1920.* Chapel Hill: University of North Carolina Press, 1988.

Sarasohn, David. 1989. *The Party of Reform: Democrats in the Progressive Era.* Jackson: University of Mississippi Press.

Saunders, Frances Wright. 1985. *Ellen Axson Wilson: First Lady between Two Worlds.* Chapel Hill: University of North Carolina Press.

Schlesinger, Arthur M., and Fred L. Israel, eds. 1971. *History of American Presidential Elections, 1789–1968,* 3 vols. New York: Chelsea House.

Seymour, Charles, ed. 1928. *The Intimate Papers of Colonel House.* 4 vols. New York: Houghton Mifflin.

Smith, Carolyn. 1990. *Presidential Press Conferences: A Critical Approach.* Westport, Conn.: Praeger.

Smith, Gene. 1964. *When the Cheering Stopped: The Last Years of Woodrow Wilson.* New York: William Morrow.

Stein, M. L. 1969. *When Presidents Meet the Press* New York: Julian Messner.

Van Cise, Jerrold G. 1962. *The Federal Antitrust Laws.* Washington, D.C.: American Enterprise Institute.

Walworth, Arthur. 1978. *Woodrow Wilson,* 2 vols. New York: Norton.

Weinstein, Edwin A. 1981. *Woodrow Wilson: A Medical and Psychological Biography.* Princeton: Princeton University Press.

Widenor, William. 1980. *Henry Cabot Lodge and the Search for an American Foreign Policy.* Berkeley: University of California Press.

Wilson, Woodrow. 1885. *Congressional Government: A Study in American Politics.* Boston: Houghton Mifflin.

————. 1889. *The State: Elements of Historical and Practical Politics; A Sketch of Institutional History and Administration.* Boston: D.C. Heath.

————. 1893. *Division and Reunion, 1829–1889.* New York: Longmans, Green.

————. 1902. *A History of the American People,* 5 vols. New York: Harper.

————. 1908. *Constitutional Government in the United States.* New York: Columbia University Press.

NOTE ON *THE PAPERS OF WOODROW WILSON*

The most comprehensive collection of the writings of Woodrow Wilson is contained in the sixty-nine-volume series edited by Arthur S. Link and others, *The Papers of Woodrow Wilson* (for complete bibliographic information, see citation in reference list). The following is a breakdown of the material contained in each volume and the year it was published.

Vol. 1 (1856–1880), 1966.
Vol. 2 (1881–1884), 1967.
Vol. 3 (1884–1885), 1967.
Vol. 4 (1885), 1968.
Vol. 5 (1885–1888), 1968.
Vol. 6 (1888–1890), 1969.
Vol. 7 (1890–1892), 1969.
Vol. 8 (1892–1894), 1970.
Vol. 9 (1894–1896), 1970.
Vol. 10 (1896–1898), 1971.
Vol. 11 (1898–1900), 1971.
Vol. 12 (1900–1902), 1972.

Vol. 13 Contents and Index, vols. 1–12 (1856–1902), 1977.

Vol. 14 (1902–1903), 1972.

Vol. 15 (1903–1905), 1973.

Vol. 16 (1905–1907), 1973.

Vol. 17 (1907–1908), 1974.

Vol. 18 (1908–1909), 1974.

Vol. 19 (1909–1910), 1975.

Vol. 20 (1910), 1975.

Vol. 21 (1910), 1976.

Vol. 22 (1910–1911), 1976.

Vol. 23 (1911–1912), 1977.

Vol. 24 (1912), 1977.

Vol. 25 (1912), 1978.

Vol. 26 Contents and Index, vols. 14–25 (1902–1912), 1980.

Vol. 27 (1913), 1978.

Vol. 28 (1913), 1978.

Vol. 29 (December 2, 1913–May 5, 1914), 1979.

Vol. 30 (May 6–September 5, 1914), 1979.

Vol. 31 (September 6–December 31, 1914), 1979.

Vol. 32 (January 1–April 16, 1915), 1980.

Vol. 33 (April 17–July 21, 1915), 1980.

Vol. 34 (July 21–September 30, 1915), 1980.

Vol. 35 (October 1, 1915–January 27, 1916), 1980.

Vol. 36 (January 27–May 8, 1916), 1981.

Vol. 37 (May 9–August 7, 1916), 1981.

Vol. 38 (August 7–November 19, 1916), 1982.

Vol. 39 Contents and Index, vols. 27–38 (1913–1916), 1985.

Vol. 40 (November 20, 1916–January 23, 1917), 1982.

Vol. 41 (January 24–April 6, 1917), 1983.

Vol. 42 (April 7–June 23, 1917), 1983.

Vol. 43 (June 25–August 20, 1917), 1983.

Vol. 44 (August 21–November 10, 1917), 1983.

Vol. 45 (November 11, 1917–January 15, 1918), 1984.

Vol. 46 (January 16–March 12, 1918), 1984.

Vol. 47 (March 13–May 12, 1918), 1984.

Vol. 48 (May 13–July 17, 1918), 1985.

Vol. 49 (July 18–September 13, 1918), 1985.

Vol. 50 The Complete Press Conferences (1913–1919), 1985.

Vol. 51 (September 14–November 8, 1918), 1985.

Vol. 52 Contents and Index, vols. 40–49, 51 (1916–1918), 1987.

Vol. 53 (November 9, 1918–January 11, 1919), 1986.

Vol. 54 (January 11–February 7, 1919), 1986.

Vol. 55 (February 8–March 16, 1919), 1986.

Vol. 56 (March 17–April 4, 1919), 1987.

Vol. 57 (April 5–22, 1919), 1987.

Vol. 58 (April 23–May 9, 1919), 1988.

Vol. 59 (May 10–31, 1919), 1988.

Vol. 60 (June 1–17, 1919), 1989.

Vol. 61 (June 18–July 25, 1919), 1989.

Vol. 62 (July 26–September 3, 1919), 1990.

Vol. 63 (September 4–November 5, 1919), 1990.

Vol. 64 (November 6, 1919–February 27, 1920), 1991.

Vol. 65 (February 28–July 31, 1920), 1991.

Vol. 66 (August 2–December 23, 1920), 1992.

Vol. 67 (December 24, 1920–April 7, 1922), 1992.

Vol. 68 (April 8, 1922–February 6, 1924), 1993.

Vol. 69 Contents and Index, vols. 53–68 (1918–1924), 1994.

Index